THE
HIDDEN TEACHING BEYOND YOGA

By
PAUL BRUNTON

PILGRIMS PUBLISHING
◆ Varanasi ◆

THE HIDDEN TEACHING BEYOND YOGA
PAUL BRUNTON

Published by:
PILGRIMS PUBLISHING

An imprint of:
PILGRIMS BOOK HOUSE
(Distributors in India)
B 27/98 A-8, Nawabganj Road
Durga Kund, Varanasi-221010, India
Tel: 91-542- 2314060,
Fax: 91-542- 2312456
E-mail: pilgrims@satyam.net.in
Website: www.pilgrimsbooks.com

Copyright © 2008, Pilgrims Publishing
All Rights Reserved

ISBN: 978-81-7769-714-8

The contents of this book may not be reproduced, stored or copied in any form—printed, electronic, photocopied, or otherwise—except for excerpts used in review, without the written permission of the publisher.

Printed in India at Pilgrim Press Pvt. Ltd. Lalpur Varanasi

CONTENTS

CHAPTER		PAGE
I.	BEYOND YOGA	7
II.	THE ULTIMATE PATH	34
III.	THE RELIGIOUS AND MYSTIC GRADES	52
IV.	THE HIDDEN PHILOSOPHY OF INDIA	70
V.	THE PHILOSOPHICAL DISCIPLINE	92
VI.	THE WORSHIP OF WORDS	120
VII.	THE ARBITRAMENT OF THINKING POWER	149
VIII.	THE REVELATION OF RELATIVITY	177
IX.	FROM THING TO THOUGHT	207
X.	THE SECRET OF SPACE AND TIME	230
XI.	THE MAGIC OF THE MIND	263
XII.	THE DOWNFALL OF MATERIALISM	290
	EPILOGUE: THE PHILOSOPHIC LIFE	316
	INDEX	353

PREFACE

That there is a higher philosophy in India may never be discounted, for hidden in its ancient past are many strands of knowledge. So many of the world's intellectual and spiritual themes have originated from the earliest thinking of man on the subcontinent.

It comes as no surprise, then, that such a little-known philosophy has been rediscovered here. It follows ideas that are yet more complex than the long-established traditions of Yoga. The author, perhaps by sheer chance or destiny, stumbles upon these complex ideas on his journey across the land.

One of the leading Oriental philosophers of his time, Paul Brunton has put his controversial findings into words. His narrative certainly caused a stir for, not long after its publication, the book received some frankly hotly expressed derogatory comments and criticism, as he seemingly contradicted some of his earlier works on Yoga.

He suggest that this highest order of philosophy was intended for educated intellectuals, high priests, kings, princes and leading statesmen. Only now has it been exposed to the masses, who over the last century have become a substantially well-educated populace, able to grasp its more esoteric and extremely difficult themes. The world of today is a rapidly developing one and with wars, declining morality across the globe and other misfortunes afflicting the human race, it is timely perhaps that we should have access to new ideas that fully challenge the direction of mankind. There is so much that seeks to disrupt man's constant desire to find a peaceful lifestyle and a meaning for his existence.

The author suggests that there are three levels of Yoga, and that it is the third of these that leads to the highest plateau of attainment. He discusses the great faiths of the world, yoga and other methods of seeking the truth, explaining their limitations and why a higher thought process is required.

"He must strip naked his innermost characteristics, taking and making no excuses, but boldly seek to understand the bitterest truths about himself. He must see himself as he really is, exposing self to self."

The path to such absolute knowledge involves many theses, none easy to master. One must seek the truth above all else, hold on to hope in a positive way, think, be calm, be detached from emotions and stresses, overcome emotion and give up ego. These are but a few of the ideas to be considered.

"The desire for truth really means the desire to get rid of ignorance."
The author does not discard the great wisdom embodied in conventional meditation and yoga. Rather he suggests that these too are useful tools on the way to seeking a higher path through philosophical directions, to find a way free of all definitive definitions that a mind can impose on itself. He further suggests that the limitations of yoga may impede the student seeking a greater knowledge.

We are led to consider the 'higher teachings beyond yoga' to be encapsulated by the themes of 'the yoga of philosophical discernment' and 'the yoga of the uncontradictable.'

These themes and philosophies, which are possibly more than three thousand years old, are known as the 'Ashtavakra Samhita. Whether these ideas constitute a completely new philosophy or are merely extensions of the more-established forms of meditation and seeking of truth, only time may tell. Whatever one's own instincts may be, the ideas set forth in this book will certainly test the boundaries of contemplative thought about the meaning of one's own existence.

Bob Gibbons
Siân Pritchard-Jones
Kathmandu 2006.

CHAPTER I

BEYOND YOGA

THE more I wander around this turning globe the more I realize that it is not only individual men, parties, governments or peoples who are to blame for the distressful condition of the human race—so mesmerized by popular follies and so deluded by traditional fables.!—but also common ignorance concerning three fundamental questions : *What is the meaning of the world and experience ? What am I ? What is the object of existence ?* I perceive with startling precision that the bursting of this integument of ancient ignorance will do more than anything else to make enduring peace descend on our troubled earth.

The pith of the world problem is too plain for our complex age to perceive : all acts are sprayed up by the hidden fountain of mind, and when men learn to think rightly they will act accordingly, not before. Their deeds can never be greater than their ideas, for the unheard declarations of the mind decide the noisy journeys of the feet. The world's bitter sorrows and bestial-sins are but symptoms of a disease whose cause is old ignorance and whose only cure is new knowledge. It is the inescapable duty of every intelligent rational human being, troubled by half-conscious and inchoate yearnings for a better life, not to rest in mental sloth but to persist in searching for the answers to these three questions ; that is, for the scintillating asterism of TRUTH.

It is a commonplace remark that we live today in an unparalleled world situation. We are born at a crucial juncture in recorded history. Certain new currents of thought, feeling and activity have been strongly stirring the whole globe since this century opened, and less so for a few centuries earlier. The war has but brought them to a fuller and dramatic convulsion. The slow chronicle of former epochs fades into petty insignificance when compared with our own. The sightless multitudes stand bewildered before its iconoclastic changes and staggered before its devastating events. Mars has put this planet on the torture rack. Nemesis has moved among the nations like a judge, putting on the grim periwig and sternly holding the forgotten scales. And all peoples wander blindly through one of the most momentous transitions which time has ever imposed on the race.

Seven new transforming features of our time are most remarkable from the standpoint of the philosopher, however, and possess an ultimate bearing on the publication of this book.

The first noteworthy feature is the incredible development of mechanical transport between villages, towns, countries and continents, through the use of steam and electric trains, petrol-driven automobiles, omnibuses, steamships and aeroplanes. Thus the planet has shrunk and mankind has been involuntarily drawn together. *This has definitely widened the space-sense of millions of people.* It has brought them into personal contact with their own neighbours, with strangers and foreigners ; hence we witness a resulting interchange of racial cultures, a multiplication of ideas and an expansion of outlooks. Something has thus happened to the world which has no recorded equivalent. Ideas can no longer be insulated, except under the pressure of brute force, and then only for a limited time. And one underrated consequence has been that the voice of Asiatic wisdom is now being heard by European and American ears.

The second feature is the phenomenal raising of both the political status and the economic standard of living of the working classes, when compared with two or three generations ago. This has unfolded within them a sense of self-respect which they lacked when they were tied with the bonds of inherited serfdom. Aristos has handed his sceptre to Demos, unwillingly no doubt, and Demos is wielding it—considerately but uncertainly or dictatorially and decisively. He worships multitudes and abases himself before magnitude. The crowd carries the day ; its verdict is the last word. But the brighter consequence of this unprecedented emancipation has in turn been the unfoldment of an interest in life beyond the unavoidable grind of earning a livelihood. The masses have begun to "look beyond their noses" and to free themselves from a parochial outlook. The larger questions and arguable issues of religion, politics and culture are no longer entirely outside their range.

The third feature is the elimination of illiteracy and the democratization of education. Knowledge is no longer the monopoly of a fortunate few. Free and compulsory education has worked marvellous changes within a single century in the mind of those who were formerly treated as children by despotic ruling classes. The educational tide has flowed with increasing pressure throughout the world with the consequence that the masses are far less unsophisticated today than they once were. They have outgrown to a marked extent the kindergarten doctrines with which they were fed. The setting-up of the first few letter-types sounded the throwing down of all the old epochs of gross ignorance. Where the European peasant or workman of a thousand years ago was unable to read a letter and could not even sign his name, the European and American peasant or workman of today can not only read all the letters of the alphabet but also write them. Nor is this progress confined to those continents although it has reached its crescendo there. Asia and Africa are on the move, too.

But we must not fall into the superficial assumption that this has greatly helped man's capacity to think rightly. Education is of two kinds: that which merely diffuses facts and helps men to memorize them, and that which helps them to think rightly about those facts. Most education belongs to the first category, which depends on the use of intellect only, but some belongs to the second, which depends on the higher faculty of reason. However, the general increase in the area of knowledge does lead to some increase in the area of enquiry, and this in turn to a consequent if still smaller rational awakening. People are now more ready to apply reason to life than they formerly were, although they are not ready enough to make such an application play a vital part in their existence. Therefore it may reasonably be hoped that many more neophytes will seek for philosophical initiation when its deep and difficult tenets are freed from their opaque veil of forbidding phraseology and put into more lucid words.

The fourth feature is the list of striking inventions to improve communication which have succeeded each other ever since Gutenberg printed the first black-lettered word on white paper in Germany and William Caxton set up a creaking hand-press in London. The printing press, the cheap post, the electric telegraph, the telephone, the cinema and wireless transmission are civilizing instruments which have combined to communalize and popularize knowledge and make it swiftly available to all. The consequence has been that a continuous interchange of facts, thoughts, ideas and views is proceeding everywhere. Time has lapsed into little account when wireless and cable can combine to bring the entire planet's news to one's house in a flash, when newspapers or printed periodicals place a description of today's scientific discovery in England before the eyes of a reader in China the same week. A man broadcasting in London will hear the echo of his voice in one-seventh of a second, during which flash it has travelled the globe and penetrated the ears of innumerable listeners. *Thus these inventions have also succeeded in altering and expanding the time-sense of most people.* Moreover, the opening up for study of immense evolutionary periods in the past history of man and universe has begun to accustom the educated to think in terms of tremendous time-vistas.

The old-fashioned sense of time as being a slow-moving thing has gone with the wind of progress. We live now in a moving world, not a static one. The tempo of American life has altered to a rate undreamt of by Inca or Aztec. The domestic arrangements and mechanisms of European households allow for numerous daily activities never contemplated in the programme of leisurely old Romans. The habits of a hundred generations are disintegrating before our eyes, but those who spend their whole lives in Occidental cities may not note and appreciate this astonishing alteration so much as those who sojourn at times in Oriental villages where days may be passed remote from all signs of our science and our time. The evolution of men's minds is therefore much more rapid than in earlier centuries.

The newspaper, produced at the rate of twenty thousand per hour, has become a great formative force in modern life. Where the medieval man could not procure a single book to read because of its high cost and great rarity, his present-day descendant can now procure a newspaper every day and read a cheap new book every week. The printed sheet has spread knowledge, prepared the way for science, publicly proclaimed it in every modern language, and may now clear a new if narrower path for philosophy in general. The birth of the printing press signalled the death of all the eras of esotericism. The time has come to open more fully for the Western world the little-visited track of a hidden Oriental philosophy.

The fifth feature is the appearance of science on the intellectual horizon of mankind. For good or for worse it has affected the mind of today. Its birth in Europe ushered in the era of fact and compelled the world to begin to bid adieu to the era of fable. Men are rising from the primitive rule of magic to the maturer rule of logic. The growth of human mentality may not be very great, but it is clearly noticeable and it is antagonistic to human superstition. The rise of the one means the fall of the other. Scientific facts were once nervous intruders into the forum where guesswork flourished, but today they dominate the world scene. Bacon was but a precursor of the Darwinian war of reasoned teachings against dogmatic beliefs which left such a deep mark on the thought of the last century. Whatever may have been the place of blind faith during former centuries, it cannot again *for long* assume leadership in a century when reason has so visibly and so tangibly shown its triumphs all around us. We have begun to grow up, and the jejune chatterings of primitive minds will sooner or later annoy our ears.

The achievements of science are the inseparable facts of our day. Its marvels fill our homes, throng our streets, float on the five oceans and move invisibly through space. Thus they have decisively demonstrated to the whole world the superior value of applied reason. The advent of new scientific knowledge published to the whole world has begun to shift the foundations of human life, to affect the spirit of our time and to alter our outlook. Every man who faithfully follows its discoveries has had to make a fresh appraisal of all existence, including his own.

The historic moment of the modern scientific era's arisal really began when Galileo broke away from the stronghold of tradition and performed his famous experiment in the leaning tower of Pisa. It was the beginning of a vast series of world-wide researches which culminated in the scientific picture of the world as a huge, causally governed automatic machine. God as fussy creator, as capricious supervisor and arbitrary judge, was conveniently dropped out of the old medieval picture. This was the first revolution in the Western outlook. The second came when Röntgen discovered the electrical basis of the atom. Research moved still more rapidly; so rapidly, in fact, that the scientists are now again repainting their picture. The universe is no longer a machine. What it has now become nobody knows for certain. The new picture is blurred and vague, even amorphous, but this is because it belongs to the domain of philosophy. For there has been a gradual process of abstraction, a transition from the empiric standpoint to the metaphysical, a growing tendency for science to become part of its own field of investigation and to turn matter and mechanism into concepts. All signs now indicate that science is not merely shaking hands with philosophy but that Mercury is even preparing to marry Minerva! What is of special interest is that science is also unwittingly moving into the camp of the hidden philosophy, for some of its latest tenets as formulated by Einstein, Planck, Heisenberg, Jeans and others were anticipated and affirmed by the Indian sages at a time when Western civilization was babbling in its infancy. For the first time in history it is possible to formulate the products of Eastern thought in Western terms—that is to say, in scientific terms—and to synthesize them with the rich results of Western researches. Europe and America have furnished new and broader foundations for the Asiatic wisdom. The latter can now be expounded with an amplitude which has never before been voiced. Thus ancient sage and modern scientist unconsciously meet and it is now possible to construct a tremendously significant intellectual synthesis, *a universal ideology of truth which could not have been possible before.*

The sixth feature is the comparatively increased leisure which has been made available for people of all classes, but especially of the working classes, through the applications of machinery to every department of human existence, consequent on the industrial revolution.

It is customary for the moderns to complain of lack of leisure, but the truth is that the caveman had far less. He had to fight inclement Nature, uncontrolled man and ravenous beast. He had to fight for his sheer existence, food and satisfaction. It was, therefore, possible for man to turn to think of higher things only *after* he had sufficiently conquered these wants. When in all history has man achieved such an overwhelming conquest as today? He has more time to undermine his own ignorance. Therefore if a few men could study philosophy in ancient times, the extended leisure of today renders the hour ripe for more students who are willing to use their leisure wisely to be attracted to its illustrious tutelage.

The seventh feature is the historical fact that post-war periods generate religious doubts in many minds with the consequent search for a more acceptable explanation of life in some of these minds. But when two wars have been waged within a single generation, when they are the worst which the world has ever seen, and when they have spread on the most gigantic scale history has ever known, it is undoubtedly no error to predict that faith will sink seriously after the shock of the cataclysm. The despairing feeling that life is without a purpose will spread through all classes of people. The power of religion to control men ethically is likely to be much weakened, which will constitute a position of profound social danger. The breaking-down of these old sanctions amid unrest and upheaval demands their reinforcement or replacement by new ones. For most men cannot live in comfort with the thought that there is no fundamental meaning and no great purpose in life. They will soon seek out some faith or theory that will bestow direction to existence. Therefore the present convulsed and collapsed epoch will witness a search for such doctrines as no previous epoch has yet witnessed. And because these changes will always be most marked among the more educated classes the forms which this quest is likely to take will be mainly mystical and occasionally philosophical rather than religious. Mysticism will probably receive a larger number of adherents than it has known for a long time, for it offers an emotional inner peace urgently needed after the maniacal frenzies and horrors of war, but philosophy will also have to welcome within its portals a modest modicum of new enquirers who have changed their intellectual gear.

If these seven factors mean anything at all they mean that history is in the throes of turning its sharpest corner, that the cultural growth of mankind has been notably accelerated, that a new and unique epoch in human knowledge is opening before the educated world, that the potential field of receptivity to the philosophy of truth is wider and deeper than ever before, that secrecy is becoming superfluous, and that for the first time a new world-wide propagation of higher views has been rendered possible. Moreover, the international political and economic conditions today are such as to *force* people everywhere to see events and things in their relation to the whole, i.e. to begin to philosophize ! Nothing like this opportune phenomenon, which requires the utmost emphasis, can be found in centuries other than the twentieth. This astonishing age of social transition, general dissolution, technological revolution and mental illumination is, in short, a continuous acceleration of the process of turning man from a primitive to a scientific animal. But even this is not enough. Man should live in the way that is proper to him, and not after the manner of the beast, the reptile and the parasite. Hence the time is ripe to disclose a doctrine which does not, like most religions, contradict the findings of science, but actually draws support from them. It is really advisable under such conditions to relax the ancient restrictions and release sufficient of the old *genuinely* Aryan knowledge to help the better cultured classes act more wisely that something nobler may emerge and that we may all advance towards the shaping of a finer human world. For it is to them that the sheep-like masses must always look for guidance ; it is their ways of thinking which are set up as criterions to be aimed at ; and it is their ways of living which are held up for ambition or imitation. Progress flows from the top, from the leading circles and higher classes of every community, downwards until it permeates the populace. The ideas and beliefs held by the most educated and enlightened strata slowly come to be received by those below. Their outlook and attitude count most in influencing the world. Therefore it is to them particularly that the hidden philosophy is now addressed.

The enthusiastic activities of European scientists can now be harmonized with the calm contemplations of Oriental sages. The butterfly of true integral wisdom can ere long burst forth from its cocoon, wherein it has matured and sheltered during the past. This union may presage the new East-West civilization which may one day arise when the spindle of time has spun far beyond our counting and the primacy of materialism has been deposed, and when truth may sit enthroned to direct the real renaissance of all human life and labour. The manhood of humanity must eventually arrive, and if this grand conception could spread among the educated classes of a warless world from Siberia to Spain, and from Colombo to California, the consequences would be remarkable. Unfortunately the materialization of such a vision seems quite remote. It is indeed very far off. Nevertheless the immense renovation which must follow the world's gigantic collapse will surely bring more candidates to the portals of philosophy in eager quest of new roads, new knowledge and new axioms. Both the sufferings and knowledge of our times have united to act as a cataclysmic agent which must arouse a new orientation in the world-mind. Not that the new is to be regarded as the better, but rather as having the opportunity to be better. Such are the reasons which render it advisable for this hoary old wisdom to emerge from its hiding-place in the minds of a microscopically small number of Asiatics and become accessible to a wider if still limited circle. Its advent is clearly a product of historical necessity. No other all-comprehensive culture can fit so well into the recently expanded time and space sense of mankind.

Who Am I ? With this treatise, therefore, I rise with my readers part of the way to such a higher view. The ascension will demand much from them, but it will give more, for it will, when completed in a further volume, finally solve all such problems, remove their deepest doubts and furnish them with an impregnable rock-like support throughout life. Moreover, the thoughtful scientist who cares to study these pages with a free mind may find the further clues he needs for progress towards the self-disclosure of reality ; the devotee of religion who wishes to worship the living God rather than dead dogma may discover the secret mainspring of his own faith ; the mystic may learn how to rise from his blissful thought of God, which is but an image, to the thought-less and image-less God as He really is ; whilst the philosopher whose brain is distracted by the diverse opinions which prevail everywhere may here meet with an attitude of mind which is finally infallible and can dispose of all criticism. For its roots stretch far back into primeval Asia, when Napoleons had arisen in the world of thought to unshackle themselves from hieratic tradition and to force their passage through Alpian problems. Paradoxically yet inevitably this archaic culture must soon levy tribute from the adolescent young Western world. Even time itself can never antiquate the antiquity of such a culture. It is time-conquering because it arises out of the ever-enduring reality within which the universe is embraced.

I did not know, when I first landed on India's surf-sprayed shores, that I had embarked on a quest which would ultimately carry me even beyond the doctrines of mysticism and the practice of meditation itself, which for so long I had deemed the highest life open to man. I did not know, as I slowly but steadily penetrated to the inmost secrets of orthodox Indian yoga, that the enterprise of winning the truth about life would not only take me into and through its confines but also set me wandering again far beyond them. I did not know that I had thrown dice with Destiny and that the game was not to be concluded in the manner I had been led to expect—that is, by settling down to an existence which made physical and mental withdrawnness in profound contemplation its highest goal and sublimest fulfilment.

For the benefit of readers to whom the terms are unfamiliar it must here be mentioned that *yoga* is a Sanskrit word which appertains to various techniques of self-discipline involving mental concentration and leading to mystic experiences or intuitions, techniques which will be described in a later chapter, whilst *yogi* is the person who practises such methods.

Like the yellow-robed Indian yogis I sat in trance, but later arose, first to compose a chronicle of their lives and then to tell my Western brethren of the way to find and the worth of finding this mental quiet. Yet, when the intermittent satisfactions of mental peace entered into conflict with an innate, ever-enquiring rationalism, tremendous questions slowly became insistent. I perceived that although the little pool of light in which I walked had indeed grown wider, the area of darkness beyond it was as impenetrable as ever.

Quite naturally, when thought, time and experience raised certain fundamental problems, I turned in the first hope of finding clear guidance to the Maharishee. It will be remembered, by readers of my book *A Search in Secret India*, that this is the name of the renowned South Indian yogi with whom I practised meditation several years ago. But the guidance never came. I waited patiently in the hope that time might draw it out of him, but I waited in vain. Gradually it dawned upon me as this question of obtaining a higher knowledge than hitherto rose uppermost in my mind, that so far he had never instructed any other person in it. The reason slowly emerged as I pondered the matter. From my long friendship with him it was possible to gauge that primarily this was not his path and did not much interest him. His immense attainment lay in the realms of asceticism and meditation. He possessed a tremendous power of concentrating attention inwardly and losing himself in rapt trance, of sitting calm and unmoved like a tree. But with all the deep respect and affection I feel for him, it must be said that in his few attempts to explain philosophy he got out of his depth. The role of a teaching sage was not his forte because he was primarily a self-absorbed mystic. This explained why his open disdain for life's practical fulfilment in disinterested service of others had led to inevitable consequences of a disappointing kind in his immediate external environment. It was doubtless more than enough for himself and certainly for his adoring followers that he had perfected himself in indifference to worldly attractions and in the control of restless mind. He did not ask for more. The question of the significance of the universe in which he lived did not appear to trouble him. The question of the significance of the human being did trouble him and he had found an answer which satisfied him.

But this was the same answer which all mystics, whether in ancient Asia or medieval Christian Europe, had also found. Meditation on oneself was a necessary and admirable pursuit, but it did not constitute the entire activity which life was constantly asking of man. It was good, but it proved to be not enough. For the efflux of time had shown me the limitations of mystics, and more time showed that those limitations were accountable by the one-sidedness of their outlook and the incompleteness of their experience. The more I associated with them in every part of the world the more I began to discern that their defects arose out of sheer shrivelled complacency, the hidden superiority-complex and the holier-than-thou attitude which they had unjustifiably adopted toward the rest of the world and also out of the premature assumption of total knowledge of truth when what they had attained was only partial knowledge. The conclusion was finally forced on me that the perfection of human wisdom would never develop out of any mystical hermitage and that only a synthetic complete culture could offer any hope for its unfoldment.

Thus I gradually travelled a road of reflection which made me see that the Maharishee's classic formula for meditation, *Who Am I ?* which I discovered later was borrowed from certain old Sanskrit authors, was not enough, albeit admirably proper in its own place as a milestone on the way to wise self-mastery. For this reason I deemed it advisable some years ago to alter this formula, which I did when writing my more recent books, where I offered this seed for analytic meditation with the new variation, *What Am I?* The difference between the two short initial words was a difference of only two letters on paper but of a most important divergence of outlook in thought. The word "who" was a personal pronoun and formed fit enquiry for the mystic who was preoccupied with himself as an individual and separate entity, whereas the word "what" was an impersonal interrogative pronoun whose reference rose to a higher level. "Who Am I?" was a question which emotionally presupposed that the ultimate "I" of man would prove to be a personal being, whereas "What Am I?" rationally lifted the issue to scientific impersonal enquiry into the nature of that ultimate "I". Not that the first formula need be abandoned. It was necessary and excellent in its place, but that place was for novices, whilst the further formula was for the use of those on a higher level.

The passage of the last few years, with its widening comprehension consequent on incessant search and its gradual growth of unusual experience, did not permit me to rest satisfied even with this important development. The instructive episodes of daily living confronted me, with deepening disillusionment, with the limitations and deficiencies of mysticism and the intolerances and defects of mystics, from whom I did not even exclude myself, and the efforts to understand the problems that arose eventually brought me to see the insufficiency of even this expanded outlook. I saw that just as resigned religious faith in mere dogma was insufficient for the mystic, so his own intuitional feeling was insufficient for me *now*, and that intuition must be put in its proper place and not be expected to perform miracles. Both had been tested and found wanting.

Yet the other source of knowledge available—intellect—was also realized on all sides as imperfect if better, and unable to stand the test of experience. It could become as deceptive as the other ways. For intellect was logical thinking, and Archbishop Whately had once proved, with perfect irony, that logically we were well entitled to doubt the historic existence of the great Napoleon! Logical induction was quite useful so far as it went, but it was too incomplete to yield finality. Its results were always liable to change with further experience. There was something in all these three ways which man needed for balanced living. I had used this combination for years, taking guidance from the words of men deemed wise, i.e. authority, from my own sensitive feeling in meditation and ecstatic absorption, i.e. mysticism, and from the check of self-doubt and self-criticism, i.e intellect. Indeed I had prided myself on being a rational mystic and on refusing to be cast in the conventional shape. Yet even the totality of this combination did not suffice to unveil a truth that need never be revised. Was a further and finally satisfactory source of obtaining knowledge available? This question also demanded an answer.

None of the Maharishee's devotees had ever posed himself these problems, so far as I knew, and consequently my own inability to obtain any further enlightenment from him would probably have been attributed by them to the insatiable spirit of enquiry engendered by my "poisonous" modern Western education. Nevertheless I respected and revered the Maharishee for his unusual attainment in mental quiet, for few others had so successfully ascended that psychological peak, and that might have sufficed to have kept me at his side until this day, as a friend even where I could not stay as a seeker after truth, bearing in solitary resigned silence the gnawing questions which he could not answer. But during my last two visits to India it had become painfully evident that the institution known as the Ashram which had grown around him during the past few years, and over which his ascetic indifference to the world rendered him temperamentally disinclined to exercise the slightest control, could only greatly hinder and not help my own struggles to attain the highest goal, so I had no alternative but to bid it an abrupt and final farewell.

Fame is the inexorable penalty of success in my profession; jealousy is the unwanted penalty of fame and hatred follows as its ugly fruit. Low manners eventually win the courage of their verbal vituperation and stoop to threats of physical violence. I realized however that I must cling to this precious talisman from the Buddhist *Dhammapada*: "Among men who hate us, let us dwell free from hatred"; and that nobody should be exempt from the wide sweep of compassion. Nevertheless these bitter experiences of life taught me severely the exact price to set upon that fragile thing which is verbal human friendship and outward show of holiness. Those who cannot understand are always prone to misunderstand. But the rare ones who, through fine temperament or altruistic experience, instinctively reach out their hands through the world-darkness quite compensate for the hurts caused by malicious lying ignorance. With them we are members of an unseen church that unites those who were born *dedicated* to leave their corner of the world a little better than they found it.

What is the Meaning of the World? It is time to take up anew the train of thought which I have been recording. Graduation from the formula for analytic contemplation of *Who Am I?* to *What Am I?* did not end there. Both questions still came within the purview of mysticism and the painful logic of certain events had finally and fully clinched what the logic of critical reflection had begun to reveal. I became acutely aware that mysticism was not enough *by itself* to transform or even discipline human character and to exalt its ethical standards towards a satisfactory ideal. It was unable to link itself thoroughly to life in the external world ! This gap was too serious to be ignored. Even the emotional exaltations of mystical ecstasy—wonderfully satisfying though they be—were fleeting both in experience and effect and have proved insufficient to ennoble men permanently. The disdain for practical action and the disinclination to accept personal responsibility which marked the character of real mystics prevented them from testing the truth of their knowledge as well as the worth of their attainments and left them suspended in mid-air, as it were. Without the healthy opposition of active participation in the world's affairs they had no means of knowing whether they were living in a realm of sterilized self-hallucination or not.

Meditation apart from experience was inevitably empty ; experience apart from meditation was mere tumult. A monastic mysticism which scorned the life and responsibilities of the busy world would frequently waste itself in ineffectual beating of the air. The truth obtained by contemplation needed to be tried and tested, not by pious talk but by active expression ; a so-called higher knowledge which failed to appear in homely daily deeds was badly learnt and might be nothing more than vacuous vagary. The true sage could be no anaemic dreamer but would incessantly transform the seeds of his wisdom into visible and tangible plants of acts well done. Emotional exaltations won through religious devotion were indeed personal satisfactions but might become dangerous illusions when they failed to find a proper external balance. Society represented an opportunity for the spiritual dreamer to examine the truth of his dreams and to test the strength of the castles he had built in the air. But to do this he needed to change his attitude towards the despised world of activity, to stand intermittently aside from his dangerous ascetic pride, and to broaden and balance his outlook by intellectual culture.

Time, experience, and thought had thus proved faulty and incomplete the theory which tradition had turned over to me of a short cut to the kingdom of heaven, and in the end silently pointed away and bade me continue my quest elsewhere. Mysticism was an important, necessary and generally neglected factor in human life, but it was only a single and partial factor after all, and could never do duty for the whole of life. A more integral culture was needed, one which could be perfectly rounded by reason and which could survive the test of every experience.

Such a culture could only come from facing the fact that man was here to live actively no less than to meditate passively. The field of his activity was inevitably out there in the external world, not here in the trance-world. Whilst the practice of meditation did lead a man to a certain degree of self-knowledge in so far as it penetrated the strata of his thoughts and feeling to their more peaceful foundation, it did not lead him to self-sufficiency. This was because the external world was always confronting him on his return with the silent demand that it also be thoroughly known and properly understood. Unless therefore he enquired deeply into its real nature and united the resulting knowledge with his mystical perception, he would remain in the twilight and not in the full morning sun, as the entranced mystic thought himself to be. Most mystics in attempting to know themselves metaphorically shut their eyes to the profounder enigma of the surrounding world, but that act did not lead to its dismissal.

The last logical extension of this argument led one to perceive that the significance of self would inevitably become clearer when perceived in its proper place within the organic unity of the whole of existence. For just as a *completely* correct view of any part of a machine was possible only from the standpoint of the whole machine itself, so a perfect view of the individual man was also possible only from that of the universal existence in which he was included. One had to learn to distinguish between the trembling touch of quarter-truths, the hesitant feel of half-truths and the firm grip of the whole truth. The old Asiatic tale about the four blind men was instructive. They wanted to know what an elephant was like, so they asked its driver to let them touch it. The first touched its abdomen and exclaimed: "It is like a round basin." The second touched a leg and retorted, "No—it is like a tall pillar!" The third felt an ear and protested it was like a basket. Finally the fourth man felt its trunk and said that the elephant was like a bent stick. Thus their limited views of the animal led to an inconclusive argument. The driver finally settled their controversy by laughing and saying: "You have all taken a part of the elephant for the whole of it and so you are all wrong."

The mystic worshipped the half-truth of himself whilst the

whole truth which put together both inner self and the external world waited ignored or misunderstood.

Contemporary history plainly foreshadowed that the scientist who was preoccupied with the external world alone and ignored his internal world would, if he were mentally penetrative enough and temperamentally courageous enough, finally have to turn his preoccupation towards himself. Thus the man who started with the formula "What is the Universe?" was forced to finish with its mate "What Am I?" Eddington's latest book *The Philosophy of Physical Science* was nothing less than an open confession of the truth of these statements. But the reverse was equally correct, as experience had proved to me. The mystic who started with wonderment about himself would, if he cared more for truth than for delightful moods, be forced to finish with wonderment at the universe. So long as he avoided or neglected the question "What is the universe?" he himself remained unbalanced and his knowledge incomplete.

If we endeavoured even for a single minute totally to withdraw any creature from his external sense-activity, we would not only withdraw him from the universe but also from his conscious self. For in that condition he would at once be plunged in sound slumber or sudden swoon, when he would know nothing of the I and could never know anything of the I. This indicates that not only is he a constituent part of the world *but the world of sense-impression is a part of him*, because it disappears together with the disappearance of his ego. Hence the right knowledge of self in its fullness must depend on a right knowledge of this time-fronted and space-backed world. Truth might be won only by a comprehensive analysis of the Whole, which necessarily included world-analysis and individual analysis.

It was much to the merit of German Hegel that he had foreseen by pure thinking the same problem which now confronted me on the different road of mystic experience. He pointed out that individual experience was partial and finite and therefore could not embrace the fullness of reality. So long as it remained what it was, isolated from the universal experience, it was filled with the clash of contradictions and anomalies. But the latter disappeared as soon as we merged the individual in the Whole, whose existence was already pre-supposed and always imminent. Hegel perceived, in short, that the individual could be adequately explained only in terms of the whole and that when asked to explain its own significance it pointed beyond itself.

Thus I moved heretically to the climax of this entire thought-process and confronted the final formulae. From "What Am I ?" I had graduated at last to "What is the Meaning of this World-Experience ?" and "What is the Object of All Existence ?" I had come to recognize that the questions involved an ascent from advanced mysticism to pure philosophy itself.

Apprenticeship to Yoga. There is a fit time for all events, says Nature as she ritualistically shows her four diverse faces to us every year. The man who would profit by her silent instruction will follow her ancient and tested method of making all self-revelations only at the appropriate hour. The time has certainly come for me to follow my old revered tutor. Hence the first two chapters of this book are purely autobiographical and may therefore sound egoistic in a work which is frankly of a philosophical character. Nevertheless their patient reading is essential as a preparation for the correct understanding of a seemingly new departure in my published work. Moreover, readers will not have to suffer this note of egoism again, for it has been my endeavour that nothing personal shall be found in the rest of this volume to detract from its objective.

I must now tell in plainer words what I hardly hinted in the first chapter of *A Search in Secret India*, the first book in which I spoke to my contemporaries. Therein I confessed that long before I met the first half-clothed Indian yogi "I had lived an inner life totally detached from my outward circumstance. I spent much of my spare time in the study of recondite books and in little-known by-paths of psychological experiment. I delved into subjects which always have been wrapped in Cimmerian mystery."

Nothing has since been added to those unrevealing words. I have kept silent so long as silence served its purpose, but that purpose has now worn itself threadbare. On the other hand, recent happenings have shown that, in the face of continued misunderstandings by the ignorant and constant misrepresentations emanating from certain so-called spiritual ashrams,[1] no less than from the so-called materialistic world, silence has become injurious.

All this is but a preamble to the necessary confession and defence that when I first came to India I was no novice in the practice of yoga, no gaping "greenhorn" seeking to learn the A B C of a foreign art in its native home. The narrow matrix in which heredity attempted to mould my nature I early broke and discarded, for my whole thought and temperament were of another cast. Boyhood

---

[1] Indian monastic institutions where monks are supposed to spend their lives with their thoughts wrapped up in God.

years had been shadowed by a terrible and tremendous yearning to penetrate the mystery of life's inner meaning. With no maps to make its intricate mazes clear, with no guide to show in which direction to travel and what dangers to avoid, surrounded by a civilization which scorned the very attempt as futile, I yet set forth to explore—or rather stumble through—this twilit land. That which frightens most people away from the investigation of mysticism was exactly what first drew me to it. The very depths of its enigma made me want ardently to explore them. I did not emerge unscathed in nerve and body from these explorations in the labyrinths of my brain and the depths of my heart for "the soul". I made mistakes and had to pay for them. Chance, however, seemed suddenly to provide a better road. Before I crossed the threshold of manhood the power of inward contemplation had been laid up as treasure in heaven, the ineffable ecstasies of mystical trance had become a daily occurrence in the calendar of life, the abnormal mental phenomena which attend the earlier experience of yoga were commonplace and familiar, whilst the dry labours of meditation had disappeared into effortless ease.

This fugitive bliss of the mystic which makes the mundane movement seem so poor and pretentious has not lacked for laureates, as a reference to the world's poetry soon proves. During those spacious reveries when, hitherto immured in red blood and white bone, the mind overstepped its *imagined* limits, the physical world was left as a remote and alien thing, the physical body with its inevitable accompaniment of difficult problems and irritating cares and unsatisfied desires took on a secondary and subordinate aspect, all one's major interest and attention being focused inwardly on this incredible and amazing experience of an enchanting serenity that seemed to lift the mind high above the commonplaceness of earthly existence. In the deepest stage of trance I seemed to become extended in space, an incorporeal being. When, later, I came across translations of Indian books on yoga in addition to the medieval European books on mysticism I found to my astonishment that the archaic accents of their phraseology formed familiar descriptions of my own central and cardinal experiences. Thus I had unconsciously enfranchised myself in the kingdom of yoga and embarked on research activities which were one day to lead me far beyond it.

But in those days it did not occur to me that I was anything but a stumbling beginner. I had begun to understand man through introspection, but I could only begin to understand life through retrospection. I suffered from that defect of inexperienced youth—lack of self-confidence. My imagination painted vivid—nay, even fantastic

—pictures of what might be accomplished given another twenty or thirty years of practice. Consequently I placed all yogis and mystics who had reached middle age on a high pedestal, whilst those who had finished their fourscore years were veritable supermen in my eyes! The fallacy that all progress was in a continuous straight line confused my reasoning, and it was taken for granted that whoever had practised meditation for even a couple of years longer than I had was necessarily to be revered almost to the point of worship.

That my own evolution went off suddenly at a tangent from constant contemplation of external life as a parade of flickering shadows into strenuous external work amid the high pressure of editorial cynicism and journalistic materialism not long after, or that I could never cross the familiar limit of my further occasional contemplations, taught me nothing. This unexpected change and this tantalizing inability were ascribed to my own personal defects, and I never ceased hoping that one day some sudden joyful burst of progress into an unexplored world would enhearten me. Had I but known it, these failures were more silently instructive than successes!

The time came when I could wait no longer. Knowing that India held the tradition of yoga—however attenuated—more livingly today than any other country, I went off finally in its quest and in the hope of finding its chief protagonists and of perfecting my technique. I travelled throughout the heat-soaked plains of India and devoted precious young years to such investigations. That knowledge was eventually found profusely written in many books and actually embodied in a few men. Among the latter I regarded the Maharishee and still regard him as the most eminent South Indian yogi. With him I spontaneously relived afresh my earlier ecstatic moods. The life of rapt inward absorption became again the only life that really mattered. Under his influence and that of the slumberous Indian atmosphere I returned brusquely from my tangential excursion, scorning and despising world-activities and world-service anew as being nothing more than purposeless and perfunctory whippings of a dead horse. Once again thought was redirected in profound concentration upon negating itself. Once again I gave myself up to repeated practise of yoga as being the highest end of man, whilst the old hope that a wonderful spurt of progress into a totally new dimension of consciousness would eventually reward me dwelt perennially in the heart.

The description of my profoundest trance experience whilst with the Maharishee given at the end of *A Search in Secret India* is accurate as a description of what I felt, although I did not then understand the sharp distinction between feeling and knowledge. What I omitted to state and now reveal was that it was no new experience, because many years before I had met the saintly yogi of Arunachala I had enjoyed precisely similar ecstasies, inward repose and luminous intuitions during self-training in meditation. My debt to this truly remarkable mystic was chiefly due for reviving those beautiful experiences within me, a debt which I gratefully acknowledged but which has been amply repaid by the work I have done in making him very widely known to his countrymen, and revered by them in consequence. It will therefore be clear to perspicacious readers that I used his name and attainments as a convenient peg upon which to hang an account of what meditation meant to me. The principal reason for this procedure was that it constituted a convenient literary device to secure the attention and hold the interest of Western readers, who would naturally give more serious consideration to such a report of the "conversion" of a seemingly hard-headed critically minded Western journalist to yoga. For the general motive that governed my researches reflected itself in my main aim in writing the book, which was to draw European and American people to this much-neglected path to inner *peace*, i.e. to *serve* them. And the general Western attitude was that it had no use for the moribund survival of yoga any more than for other superstitions of a senile and sterile India. I had therefore to show that yoga at least possessed some living value, and this could best be certified by using living persons to illustrate this value.

The years passed and my eagerness to unravel the higher mysteries of yoga did not abate, so meanwhile I wrote about the lower ones which were familiar and no longer mysterious. I found in India that the truth about the yoga-system was that, in its twentieth-century practice, it was no system at all, for it had become as mixed as an Irish stew. It was hard to recognize what was mythical and what was mystical. Yoga had been thought largely useless to the modern world because it was held tight by fantastic faqueers in the crippling and unfortunate embrace of superstition. Dogmatic religion had deflected much of it from its psychological goal, whilst primitive magic had distorted another portion of it into a circus performance. I had not come to India to dig up the graves of old errors and rattle the bones of their skeletons. I made herculean efforts to rescue what was workable in yoga and then turn it into a consciously formulated rational praxis, first for my own clarification and then for the world's.

My pilgrimage still went on with its inevitable accompaniment of arduous struggles and unforgettable ecstasies, intermittent disillusionments and glorious revealments. I did not make this pilgrimage alone. An unseen and unknown host increasingly travelled by my side. This crowd of fellow seekers was cosmopolitan and classless. It was scattered all over the planet. Whenever the higher bidding affected my reluctant personal will I communicated my discoveries to them. Thus my books were born. Those who were tied by duty to concentration upon the turning wheel of modern materialistic existence were able to profit by the findings of one who had made good his own escape. It was not easy for me to write words which would appeal to a practical matter-of-fact age. Sometimes I could hardly understand why, when so many more exciting and objective books were on the market, anyone should want to read mine. But yet there were these misguided folk who showed such a perverse inclination! I could but thank them and my stars for the encouragement given me. What this meant my pen could answer better than myself. May Allah grant such good people length of days!

But once again I reached the old position of standing at what seemed an impassable barrier. My connection with the Maharishee did not avail me in crossing this barrier. Many Indians envied me for having plumbed the depths of yoga, for they did not know that I was inwardly dissatisfied with my attainment, but a few friends were perplexed at the knowledge. For puzzling questions punctuated my ecstatic satisfactions. It is true that the ability to throw onself into a mystical trance is no little matter; the capacity to concentrate thought at will for long periods of time is no common one; the power to enjoy ineffable if temporary peace by a mere inward reorientation of attention is no paltry acquirement. All these and other characteristics of yoga were in my possession. What then was the true cause of this dissatisfaction? Unless this is explained to the reader he will be perplexed.

After one emerged from the state of trance or contemplation the exalted feeling slowly and gently subsided, leaving at last only a lingering after-echo. Therefore one had to repeat the experience daily if one wanted to live again in the original condition, just as one had to repeat taking one's dinner daily if one wanted to live without hunger. If one was expert in the matter one could protract the sweet after-effects for a longer period, but one could not engage in any kind of practical activity without eventually losing it again. Thus the illuminations gained by yoga were always temporary ones. They needed to be renewed daily at the cost of temporary renunciation of practical duties and worldly activities.

This transiency of the contemplative state became a serious problem which engaged much of my earnest consideration. That this problem had troubled more experienced yogis than myself became known to me some years ago during one of my visits to the extensive Ashram of Sri Aurobindo Ghose, at Pondichery, French India. There I was once shown a number of letters which he had written to his disciples, and one contained the following paragraph, whose truth struck me so forcibly that I copied it straightway. The authoritative value of this statement will become apparent when it is added that Sri Aurobindo is probably the most famous of living Indian yogis and certainly the best-educated one. He wrote :

"Trance is a way of escape—the body is made quiet, the physical mind is in a state of torpor, the inner consciousness is left free to go on with its experience. *The disadvantage is that trance becomes indispensable and that the problem of the waking consciousness is not solved, it remains imperfect.*"

Moreover, the man who has to live and work in this world, who must share in its activities, caught in its crucible of work, pleasure and pain, must sooner or later turn away from his meditation and resume his activity just as he earlier turned away from the world to resume his meditation. "Take what thou wilt but pay the price," said Emerson somewhere with Greek clarity of statement. The price of yoga was world-renunciation ; the proof that this was so lay in the fact that those Orientals who began to make some progress with meditation and sought further advancement usually ended by listening to the melancholy melody of asceticism and fleeing from wife, family, home, property and work ; they took refuge in ashrams, caves, monasteries, jungles or mountains, so that with the world well left behind their efforts to reach the contemplative mood might be made more uninterrupted and continuous. Seeking the day-long enjoyment of yogic peace, they had perforce to sacrifice the day-long business of worldly living.

Furthermore, this plain fact that the *overmuch* daily practice of meditation inevitably unfitted a man for activity in the practical sphere of existence became increasingly and disturbingly clear to me. Indeed, I had had to give up my own career in editorial and journalistic work for a time partly because of having overdone the practice and partly because of a resultant hyper-sensitivity which made most environments a torture. It was much easier to write books because this was an activity which could be executed on a remote mountain-top, if necessary, far from the busy turmoils of city life. All the same, I perceived that at least ninety-five per cent of Western humanity were caught involuntarily in crowded whirlpools and had no hope of escape from them. A complete system of yoga could not therefore be offered as a practical possibility to the generality of people. Then how could a way of life which offered the world a reward of merely intermittent peace constitute in itself the ideal of a perfect, true and integral way which thoughtful persons had ever been seeking ? The combination of meditation practice and worldly work was valuable ordinarily only to those who were satisfied with the compromise of imperfect attainment in meditation.

There was a single exception, however. The system which formerly prevailed among the Zen Buddhists in old Japan was sensible and practical. Young men who showed a liking and fitness for meditation were brought to the Zen monasteries and trained there for a period of about three years. During this time there were no distractions to hinder them, so that the work of mind-mastery could go on uninterruptedly. The Japanese masters, with a sense of realism and practicality which their Indian confrères often lacked, did not permit their pupils to overdo meditation or trance but insisted on strict moderation. Contrary to common opinion, the Japanese capacities went beyond slavish imitation. The Japs never became blind adherents of the Indian-born and Chinese-transmitted customs. They used what was applicable to their own needs and rejected the rest. The ultimate aim of medieval Zen was to create keen determined men with crisp clear mentalities who would be calmly active and skilfully concentrated in all their undertakings ; who would spontaneously sink self in the service of their country. The dull lethargy, spectral melancholy and anti-worldliness of many Indian monks did not suit such a virile, optimistic and practical race. The students were not allowed to pass the day in lazy, futile or parasitical existence, but were given active duties to keep them busy. The Zen aim being a balanced existence they were made to work hard and to meditate well. But at the end of the disciplinary period, with the exception of those who felt an inborn and overwhelming vocation for monkish retreat, they were sent back to worldly life to marry, take up a career and make good. Equipped with the power of instant and sustained concentration, poised to meet the difficulties and vicissitudes of practical living with undisturbed equanimity, universally respected for their high character, they generally forged ahead of other men and became highly successful in their chosen careers. Many of Japan's most famous soldiers, statesmen, artists and scholars were Zen trained men. Their ideal was a perfect balance of the inner and outer man, with *efficiency* as the keynote of both. The quality of their meditation was so high that a half-hour daily was sufficient after their departure from the monastery to keep them in contact with spiritual peace; thus their worldly life did not suffer but was enriched.

There appeared to be little room for such an arrangement in modern life, so meanwhile we had to look at the facts as they were today.

Waiting for Wisdom. Such were the unpalatable conclusions which I drew after my Western and Indian courses of experience in yoga, *as I then knew it*, both of which brought me to the point of intense inward abstraction but no farther. It will be apparent that my concern was not merely personal alone, but to some extent altruistic. I had devoutly hoped to find in mysticism a system that could completely satisfy the higher aspirations of all those who, like myself, made experience the final test. I had once thought that the contemporary materialism might find its partial cure in mysticism.

Such perceptions came to me only after I had made the initial mistake of believing and occasionally supporting all the traditional claims on behalf of yoga exercises which one had heard. It was only later and with great difficulty that the growing breadth of my approach enabled me to separate what was sound from what was superstitious in these claims.

These words might easily be misunderstood. Mental quiet has been strongly advocated in my books and I do not regret or retract such advocacy for a single moment. The infiltration of a little peace into a busy life is relatively of great value, and even the memory of a morning's half-hour bathed in blessed tranquillity sweetens the harshest labour and disciplines even degraded pleasures. I have frequently stated in my books that it was never my purpose to induce Westerners to flee into ashrams but only to flee for a while into themselves. Those books show such a way, the practice of their exercises offers such an abundant reward, and the latter may well be enough for most people The other benefits of meditation, *if correctly practised*—which is not often—also constitute a valuable asset, possessing a practical bearing on life and conduct. They are chiefly: the ability to concentrate thought at will; greater pacification of emotion and passion; greater power to keep undesirable or troubling factors out of the mind, and finally a better understanding of oneself. Such benefits are obviously not to be despised and are most useful even amid the ordinary avocations of daily living. From my personal knowledge several well-known and active men of affairs—such as Lord Kitchener, the late British Field-Marshal, and Lord Brabourne, the late Governor of Bengal—had been privately interested in these practices.

But for the few, again like myself, who sought to understand the meaning of life and to unravel the imperious problem of truth, peace or self-discipline could not alone still for ever the keen hunger of the mind—however valuable in themselves. In short, I sought the realization of those promises of ultimate knowledge which the old Sanskrit books held out as pertaining to the higher mysteries of yoga.

I ought to pause upon this parenthesis to render clearer what I mean by the words "higher mysteries of yoga". They represent the difference between *knowing* something and *feeling* it. In the depths of meditation one felt, apart from transitory emotional exaltations, the world to be like a passing dream, the body to be but a drag on one's true self, and the only permanent value to lie in the heart's ineffable depth. Through long practical tests I had plumbed the depths of yoga, as the mystics and yogis of my acquaintance seemed to know it, and found the proper limits of its usefulness; it certainly gave much, it gave the misty *feeling* of having reached truth, but it did not give the irrefutable *knowledge* of truth. Yoga gave only these vague feelings but could not turn them into definite formulation; moreover, it could only convert these intermittent experiences into permanent attitudes if one were willing to abide in meditation the day long. This was not only impracticable to most men but also, I know now, impossible to all men.

My bafflement had been intense until the notion slowly dawned on me that such permanence could arise only out of the balance between knowledge and feeling. When intellect had discovered what emotion glimpsed, when it had established that discovery upon an irrefutable basis of fact for ever proved, and when reason and feeling had perfectly fused into spontaneous action, the whole being of a man would be harmonized, his outlook firmly established and his inner peace welded like steel into an unbroken and unbreakable element. It would then no longer matter whether he were active in the noisy world or plunged in silent trance, for his life would be an *integral unit*. There were statements in the old Indian texts which supported these notions. Although such understanding of the inmost nature of the world, such insight into the subtler meanings of life, could come into real rather than theoretical existence *only so far as it was of one's own making*, it was equally true that some ancient finger had to emerge out of the darkness and point out the way which led to it. Thus the knowledge that there were apparently summits still unclimbed, and that no paths leading to them were nowadays discernible, filled me at times with aching discontent.

This need of wider intellectual enlightenment concerning both the nature of the world and its correct relation to the mystical view of man—in short, Truth in all its fullness—caused me to look around and consider where else it might be satisfied. I knew several of the answers of the West, knew too that they were often excellent as far as they went, but they did not go far enough. Science frankly confessed its own insufficiency, and the foremost scientists like Jeans, Eddington and Planck had begun in sheer compulsion to point their venturesome fingers towards philosophy. I knew something of the Western philosophies, admirably reasoned and laboriously worked out as they were, but their tremendous conflict of opinion largely cancelled out each other's value and left the student bewildered. I knew however that the foremost thinkers of Asiatic countries had leisurely pondered this problem long before the first city Greeks had begun to ponder it in Europe. Moreover, there was this vital difference—that whereas the Western thinkers usually claimed that nobody had discovered ultimate truth and that human limitations were so narrow that nobody was likely to discover it, the authors of old Asiatic books claimed that ultimate truth was certainly discoverable and that a few sages had definitely known it.

I remembered the enthusiasm with which, in my younger days, I had hotly advocated this claim to a sceptical French artist as we walked beside the Seine on moonlit nights. But alas in those days I had used the words "sage" and "mystic" as interchangeable; now I knew a little better. I felt therefore that if hope lay anywhere it lay in Asia, the continent where the world's most renowned religious, mystic and philosophic teachers from Jesus to Confucius had been born. It needed but slightly more consideration to narrow the search to India because I knew from wide study and personal travel that all the Asiatic lands, like Tibet, China and Japan, had directly or indirectly derived their philosophic knowledge, yoga systems and religious speculations from this single fountain-head. The stream of philosophic thought was likely to be purer at the source, and so I examined its position in present-day India.

At first sight it was evident to any man whose brains were not closely packed with dusty cobwebs that the medley of contradictory opinion and barrenness of useful result which afflicted Western philosophy was just as prevalent in India, too. There were six classical systems which claimed to explain the universe rationally, but each started from totally different premises and appealed to totally different facts. Consequently they all arrived at irreconcilable notions of what constituted the Truth. There were also innumerable theological and scholastic systems which masqueraded as philosophies, hiding their ultimate appeal to faith by an immediate appeal to reason, or priding themselves on their magnificent structure of reasoning whilst beginning with the biggest of all dogmas, that of the existence of a personal God. There were not a few seers and saints upon whose heads the populace had thrown a nimbus of holiness, who claimed to be on intimate terms with the Supreme Creator and who explained verbosely what the significance of the universe was according to the explanations which the Creator had personally vouchsafed to them. Here again there was so much conflicting doctrine that one could only decide that the divine plan was changed from month to month according to the Creator's momentary mood! There were also numerous would-be authors who offered the maximum of verbiage with the minimum of meaning. Wherever one went in this talkative country agile-minded teachers could be found who performed breath-taking feats of logical legerdemain and who were willing to pour out on the least provocation a profuse spate of lengthy words—often meaningless, sometimes cryptic and generally combining to form unproven or unprovable statements. But what experience in this world meant was finally as elusive as ever. I wanted a philosophy devoid of dogma whose truth could be proved as irrefutably as one could prove an experiment in science—in short, to walk on sure ground.

Most other men in my position would undoubtedly have remained content with their yogic acquirements and enjoyed the daily peace of meditation, retreating to the inner self and leaving intellectual busybodies to worry over the meaning of the universe! Unfortunately my temperament was differently constructed. The stars of cold reason and quixotic strangeness were in conjunction at my birth. I had had sufficiently ripe experience of society and its appalling aridity to know how transitory and how defective were the external satisfactions it offered in comparison with inner achievements. Great poverty had dragged itself on miserable crutches towards me when the fullness of a rich existence was my aim, and I had loathed it. Great wealth came fawning to my feet at a time when the simplest of lives was my ideal, and I had spurned it. Now I disregarded both because my personal life had been committed to higher hands and I could take whatever came to me with contentment.

BEYOND YOGA

I had reached a mature age when the first grey hairs had grown alarmingly and the mind had grown sufficiently to make me feel that any attempt to evade its insistent questions would do violence to the integrity of conscience. I had been thrown by time into an epoch tremulous with fateful consequences, when the whole world was being dazed and stunned by a devastating series of startling experiences and caught in a complicated web of events from which it would emerge either ruined or rejuvenated. It was an epoch which had tried to equip itself as a candidate for death. Because I belonged to the ink-stained fraternity I was naturally interested in the fate of my fellow-dwellers on this sad star. The aspiration to serve the minority of earnest seekers among suffering ignorant humanity with a compassionate offering of Truth—however humble and imperfect—as I had earlier tried to serve them with an offering of Peace, burned like a consuming fire within me. There were not many years left for an overworked body and I could not afford to wait supinely for the grave whilst these questions remained unanswered.

But I was caught in a mental cul-de-sac, from which there seemed no way to emerge until I remembered that if there was no one in India's living present to help me, there might yet have been someone in her dead past. Her most serious reflections on the meaning of existence lay entombed in a multitude of oblong yellowing palm-leaf manuscripts. Perhaps among those muted voices it might be possible to find one or two which could speak sympathetically and understandingly to me across the centuries. So I decided to search for such an author's work.

CHAPTER II

THE ULTIMATE PATH

> "*Trust you will place before the Congress the goal of the truth of Indian philosophy, the attainment of the happiness of all beings, as enshrined in the great Sanskrit sayings: 'Sarve Janah Sukhino Bhavantu' (May all humanity be happy) and 'Sarve Satwa Sukho Hitah' (Which brings about the welfare of all that exists).*"—Telegraphic message from His Highness the late Maharaja of Mysore to the Indian Delegate to the International Philosophical Congress, Paris, 1937.

"SIT not with a disputer about fate nor begin a conversation with him" was the wise admonishment of the practically minded Prophet Muhammed, who thus dismissed the question at a single stroke and doubtless saved much time and endless speech for his trusting followers. Certainly someone like Fate, who had not seldom befriended me in the past when I invited her attention by determined effort, now appeared and took a sudden hand in this celestial game.

I grope on the darkening shelves of memory for the book of this incident. I had gone high up into jungle-covered hills to escape from the society of my kind for a time and to work at shaping a medley of research notes which had accumulated around me. The needs of a hypersensitive temperament rendered imperative such a withdrawal from society at recurring intervals. Formerly I had cherished the hope that in the supposedly spiritual society of a certain ashram, the Indian equivalent of a fraternal hermitage or monastic institution, I might find the harmony of lofty thought and peaceful conduct which would suit those periods of escape from worldly activity. The hope finally turned out to be a laughable illusion, whilst the ashram turned out to be a miniature fragment of the imperfect world I had deserted. To those who feel the same inner need I would therefore strongly recommend through experiment and experience the only perfect environment which will fit their case. It is to return to Mother Earth's friendly scenic solitudes and to make her enchanting beauty their mistress. In shady silent forests or on lofty rugged heights, beside quiet-flowing streams or unpeopled wave-beaten shores, in the earth's stillness, the sky's colour and the mountain's purity, they will always find healing balm for the wounds caused by contacts with a harsh unlovely world.

The new perch which I had established through the generous hospitality of His Late Highness the Maharajah of Mysore was one such blessed spot. As one's eyes travelled the whole circle of this inviting and inspiring south-west Indian horizon no village came into view, no city stretched out its cruel tentacles like a giant octopus to seize the green countryside. Nature was my companion, her wild solitary grandeur was my joy. In her beautiful presence, under expectant peach-bloom dawns and hushed coppery-red sunsets, I knew that I would soon recover what I had lost among petty-minded men as well as accomplish a modicum of pressing work.

Three inspired weeks passed by when there suddenly befell an unlooked-for event. My servant appeared one afternoon and handed me a letter which had been given him by a stranger. It was nothing more than a simple request for a few minutes' chat from an Indian gentleman who wrote that he was familiar with my books, and having come into the neighbourhood on a vacation had discovered that I was there: yet, had I but known it, on this slip of greyish-white paper was inscribed the next phase of my tortuous destiny. I could not help being amused at this unexpected visit, for I thought that I had well and truly secured solitude in this obscure place. I savoured something of the surprise which filled the mind of a famous missionary-explorer long lost in the jungles of Central Africa, who was suddenly confronted by the figure of a white man appearing as if from nowhere. The latter politely raised his hat and said, "Mr. Livingstone, I presume!"

Presently the writer appeared—a white-turbaned, bespectacled old Brahmin gentleman of placid countenance and short stature, with three small books tucked under his arm. It is a fact that within ten minutes I was listening eagerly to him, the while he talked vigorously of the very problem which had so troubled my mind! Thus the serpentine coil of fate began to unfold again in a curious but momentous manner.

Soon he was turning the pages of one of his books, the famous classic *Bhagavad Gita*, and expounding quotation after quotation in ardent advocacy of his unconventional theses, which were: that the orthodox view of yoga was generally inaccurate and certainly insufficient, that the practice of meditation was an excellent mental preparation for the quest of truth but by itself could never yield truth; that ninety-nine per cent of Indian yogis practised preparatory disciplines under the widespread but mistaken notion that all of them led directly to the same highest goal; and that hardly any contemporary yogi knew or followed the only path which could bring a man to the realization of ultimate truth, which was called "the yoga of philosophical discernment"[1] and whose culminating stage was "the yoga of the uncontradictable".[2]

He picked up from the table the second of the volumes which he had brought and said, "Permit me to introduce a book which is scarcely known, much neglected and rarely read because its contents are either beyond the comprehension of ordinary students or obnoxious to the preconceived notions of ordinary pundits. It is called *Ashtavakra Samhita*.[3] It is not less than three thousand years old and may even be many thousand years older, for our remote forefathers did not burden themselves with keeping dates. This is the mysterious book which Bengal's much-revered sage and yogi of more than a half-century ago, Sri Ramakrishna, used to hide under his pillow and produce only when he was alone with his most developed and favourite disciple, the famous Swami Vivekananda. None of his other followers was ever instructed in its lofty doctrines, for it would have upset their most cherished beliefs. From this you will perceive that this is not a book for beginners. It describes the highly advanced teaching given by the sage Ashtavakra, who had personally realized the ultimate goal of Indian wisdom, to King Janaka, who was an ardent seeker after truth, yet remained faithful to his practical duties as the ruler of a nation. Its later chapters emphasized the fact that the true sage does not flee to caves or sit idly in ashrams but is constantly engaged in work for the welfare of others. It points out that he will even outwardly pretend to be just like ordinary people in order not to be put on a pedestal by them. But the tenet to which I particularly wish to draw your attention is condensed in verse fifteen of the first chapter: 'This is your bondage, that you practise meditation!' The meaning here is that meditation constitutes a practice for developing calmness, abstract subtlety and concentrative sharpness of the mind, and that the earnest seeker must not be so captivated by its resultant peace as to tarry at this disciplinary stage, but should complement it by seeking the higher truth. Ashtavakra warns his royal disciple not to rest content with mysticism, ordinary yoga or religion alone, but also to take the further step necessary to acquire a knowledge of the philosophy of truth. That step is con-

---

[1] Gnana-yoga.   [2] Asparsa-yoga.   [3] *The Song of the Sage Ashtavakra.*

THE ULTIMATE PATH

tained in a higher system, called 'philosophical discernment', for which such power to tranquillize and concentrate thought as is given by ordinary yoga is certainly an essential but nevertheless only an attendant move. You will now understand why such revolutionary doctrines are not palatable to popular taste.''

The visitor put the book down, paused in his speech and looked at me through his large round spectacles. I felt a deepening interest in him. Assuring him of my warm interest, I begged him to proceed.

He now tenderly handled the third book in his little collection, the while he produced and praised it so highly and then showed it to me. The volume consisted of a very brief text entitled *Mandukya Upanishad*,[1] containing only twelve terse paragraphs, together with a long supplement entitled *Gaudapada's Karika*,[2] containing two hundred and fifteen short paragraphs, and finally a lengthier commentary written by the renowned Shankara on both text and treatise. "He who intellectually masters both texts and commentary thoroughly has mastered the highest statement of truth of which India has remained the unique custodian through thousands of years and fragments of which have been borrowed by the rest of Asia," remarked my visitor. "This work contains the master-key to those higher mysteries beyond yoga, of which you have heard and which you have sought, known as 'the yoga of philosophical discernment', which in its turn culminates in the ultimate approach called 'the yoga of the uncontradictable'. These methods begin where meditation leaves off, for they are really philosophical disciplines using the intense concentration generated by yoga practice, and they are directed towards freeing the mind of its innate ignorance and habitual error. Hard indeed are they to comprehend for us of the East, but harder still for you of the West. These advanced yogas are ignored by almost all our own Indian yogis and usually misunderstood by almost all our pundits. Yet knowing these neglected systems you will need to know no others. If in India, the land of its birth, this text is so little cared-for and less understood, how hopeless it is to look for correct penetration of its meaning among your Western Orientalists!"

Now among all the mainsprings of my variegated Indian travels that which primarily drew me to visit Mysore in response to its ruler's generous call was the unique reputation enjoyed throughout India by His Highness the late Maharaja. His irreproachable character, sincere devotion to culture, and untiring effort for improving the welfare of his people during a long reign of more than forty

---
[1] *The Secret Doctrine of the Sage Mandukya.*
[2] *The Concise Stanzas of Gaudapada.*

years had made him the most universally respected and widely beloved of all the native rulers. Gandhi had admiringly acclaimed him with the unique title of *Rajarishee*, i.e. king-sage. When I came to know His Highness more intimately I discovered that the secret source of all his greatness lay in the philosophy with which he had identified himself, and which I shall endeavour to explain in this book.

From sea-splashed Cape Comorin to the venerated Himalayas he had travelled to meet the most renowned scholars and holy men of his land ; from Kashmir to Benares he had conversed with the leading pundits and yogis ; and he had even crossed the snowy ranges into cold Tibet on a mystical quest. He sounded the depth of all these men. He was therefore better entitled than most Indians to judge what was of most worth in his country's culture. And this he finally found in the hidden philosophy, whose true interpretation he embodied not only in personal but also in public life.

His Late Highness summed up the practical value of what he had learnt in the message to the International Philosophic Congress quoted at the head of this chapter, the message that all humanity should be treated as one family. No loftier message nor a more valuable one could have been given to the world at such a bewildering time. No institutional religion or exoteric philosophy has yet really given it because all religions and philosophies have by the mere act of labelling themselves hitherto excluded the followers of other faiths or other teachings from their folds. Europe did not heed this warning, not knowing that the concepts of genuine philosophy, far from being futile, contained actual implications for ethical guidance, and the worst war of its history broke out within two years.

The two Sanskrit passages mentioned in this message were chanted daily in the Mysore Palace. His Highness proved in his own State that philosophy could be practically applied with outstanding benefit to the common people. Mysore well earned its familiar description of "a model State" as well as its frequent mention of being the most progressive one in all India. His fame had spread far and wide, and at his death *The Times*, the leading London newspaper, eulogized him as having "set the standard" for the rest of India. Such was the practical fruit of true philosophy.

It might also be permissible to mention here that the late Maharaja took a close personal interest in my philosophical and literary progress, and said to me some years before his death : "You have studied and carried yoga to the Western people ; now study and carry *the*

THE ULTIMATE PATH

best that India has to give—our higher philosophy!" The hour of fulfilling the second part of the duty which was then laid upon me has at least arrived. His Highness was so anxious for the vindication of Truth that he warmly encouraged my labours on the present book, and it is my grief that he did not survive to witness its publication.

The vanished sages declared from their tower of sapience the existence of an ultimate path which alone brought the questioning mind of man to rest in the perfect wisdom and hidden power, the ethical beauty and universal beneficence of ultimate realization. In that sublime consciousness even amid the terrific tempo of modern life everything and everyone was known to be non-different *in essence* from oneself. THAT indeed was to be sought for.

I came to understand yoga better after such a long period of research ; I came to separate the preliminary and intermediate from the advanced and little-known stages for which that research had been really a preparation.

The Three Grades of Yoga. A brief bird's-eye survey may now be made of the relation between this hidden doctrine, which claims to be the crown and fulfilment of yoga, and the more popular inferior yogas. This will necessitate the inclusion of a few anticipatory glimpses of material properly belonging to more advanced studies.

This relation will come out more clearly if we divide the yoga praxis into three progressive degrees through which we rise into wider awareness. The most elementary group is devoted entirely to *physical* exercises in concentration because these appeal more readily to those—always most numerous—whose intellects are uncultivated. The beginner in mathematics is likely to be much bewildered if he is started on his course of study by a presentation of the Binomial Theorem, which is therefore reserved for a later phase of his studies. Similarly the novice in yoga who is temperamentally and educationally fit for nothing better is put on one or other of these physical exercises. But some of them possess a further aim than the cultivation of concentration, being intended to improve the health, increase the strength and help to heal the maladies of the aspirant. It is recognized that a sickly body disturbs the mind and chains thought to the ailment itself. Therefore these exercises are not infrequently prescribed as a preliminary step even to those who are cultured enough to start in a higher degree. The methods employed sound strange to Western ears, but they are not without remarkable efficacy for their special purposes. The first method consists in placing the body in a specific unusual posture and keeping it fixed and unmoving therein for some time. The second method involves various peculiar exercises in rhythmically disciplining for set periods of time the inhalation, retention and expulsion of the breath. The third method is the practice of looking with unwinking eyes at some particular point for the same period of time every day. The fourth method is to mutter a thousand and one times daily a scriptural name of God. The fifth method is to chant specified sacred syllables in rhythmic conjunction with the ingoing and outgoing breaths.

The second or intermediate group of yoga practices rises beyond the gross body to the higher level of educating the *feelings* in devotion and training the thoughts in concentration. It includes various mystical exercises in meditation whose ultimate aim is the attainment of emotional and mental peace ; it may also embrace the inculcation of constant yearning for the presence of God. The generic character of this group will be outlined in the next chapter. His meditative reveries and ecstatic trances give the aspirant glimpses of the world's basis non-materiality and of its underlying harmonious unity, but these glimpses are nothing more *in the end* than transient if exalted feelings. He has next to learn how to convert them into permanent understanding, which can be done only by interpreting them in the higher light of reason, an activity which belongs to another stage. Successful attainment in this second degree is marked by the power to attain and remain in prolonged reverie with perfect concentration, and with attention withdrawn from outward surroundings. With the profits in self-preparation gained from the business of these earlier methods he climbs to the third step, the yoga of philosophical discernment.

This is the highest group of the yoga family ; it is finally supermystical but initially purely intellectual and rational. It is the hidden doctrine. Part of it is outlined in this book, but *before* the threshold of the advanced portion with its final astonishing revelation, the yoga of the uncontradictable, these pages must perforce stop for the present. In this third stage the student strives, along with concentrated and disciplined feeling and thought, to sharpen his reason and to apply that sharpened intelligence to a guided philosophical consideration of the meaning and nature of the whole world and of all life. Hitherto he has been preoccupied entirely with *himself*, with his own little ego ; now he expands the entire horizon of his outlook and makes the world-problem his own problem. He must train himself thoroughly to impress these new ideas upon every atom of his being. He must think deeply and think hard about these subtle

THE ULTIMATE PATH

truths he learns until thought becomes established as *insight*. When these efforts finally and successfully mature he reaches the very summit of the yoga of knowledge and seeks by the sheer power of his now-illumined intelligence to fathom the final mystery of all—the relation between the grand ultimate reality of the world and himself. He has reached the climax of an adventure where his whole mind and body must now travel and strive and toil in unison. This peak-path is the yoga of the uncontradictable. It first proves its own ultimate tenet of the *secret* identity of man with the universal reality, and then shows him how to realize this amid practical life.

Higher than this his mind cannot go; and his remaining years will be engaged in unremittingly establishing the truth in his own consciousness, in living with it every moment and every day, in expressing it practically with sustained and uncompromising thoroughness, in repeatedly dwelling in its spirit and atmosphere until it loses every vestige of unfamiliarity and becomes first-hand, ascertained and verified knowledge. Knowledge must become dynamic by getting itself practised until the practice itself is lost in its complete fulfilment. He has then finished with the formalities of religion, with the visions of meditation, with the reasonings of philosophy. Just as a scaffolding is carefully erected and remains throughout the building of a house, only to be ruthlessly torn down at the end, so first religion, then yoga, and finally philosophy, are now seen to be but scaffoldings which enabled him to build up the structure of truth. In the end and when climbed they too are all rejected. But this rejection applies only to their claims to give *realization* of the truth through their individual channel alone, and not to their lesser uses. Once permanently established the master may dwell in all these different worlds, if he wishes, and be equally at home in each. He may still study philosophy for the sake of guiding the mental currents of his time, he may conform to the rites and requirements of orthodox religion for the sake of encouraging others who cannot rise beyond it, he may even enter into meditative trances for the sake of personal relaxation, but he will never again be deluded into regarding any of them as sole and final avenues to truth. At best they may yield its reflection in *thought*; he himself must become conscious of its *substance*, and no wizardry will do this. The reader will misunderstand these explanations if he does not grasp the important point that those who have not mastered the yoga of the second degree will therefore not be able to master the yoga of the highest degree. For the practice of reverie is needed to render successful the pursuit of philosophy. Enquiry into truth is the content which should fill the meditative trance. Ascetic discipline of the will, the body and the ego must run side by side with their study, and implement in action the theoretical findings of philosophy. Yoga as it is ordinarily understood is therefore not to be given up, albeit it no longer becomes an end in itself but only a means to the end. The capacity to practise yoga is not only essential at the very beginning of the ultimate path but also at its terminus. It is the perfect combination of keen rational enquiry merged into profound meditative reverie and revealing its logical consequences in practical daily living that yields the fruit of ultimate realization in the end. The mere intellectual grasp of the hidden teaching without the parallel yogic capacity to sustain that grasp unbrokenly is as partial, as incomplete and as unsatisfactory as the mere yogic power to withdraw attention from externals and hold it in abstracted moods unfilled by philosophic effort. Neither a dry academic intellectualism nor an unenlightened yoga practice can lead to truth, nor both if unvivified by action.

Thus the novice graduates from one degree to another, from the bodily discipline to emotional discipline and thence to the intellectual. The three groups combine to constitute a progressive unfoldment of his capacities and understanding. It is important to note that they are steps, not stops. The truth that he learns is always proportionately relative to his level of understanding.

The confusion between the second and third yogas is somewhat general throughout the religious and learned world of India today. Patanjali is often quoted, but he speaks only of the goal of controlling the mind and the senses, not of union of the soul with the Ultimate. It is true that he makes a reference to Ishwara (God), but this is done only to indicate a method of practice. Those who would make the yoga of mental concentration a final path are utterly mistaken. *The Bhagavad Gita* plainly declares in the fifteenth chapter that there is nothing equal to the yoga of knowledge, and in the thirteenth chapter that it is the highest means of realization. Therefore we must not confuse matters. We must keep religion clear from mysticism in our minds, and mysticism clear from philosophy. If through sentiment, habit or error we mistake one for the other, we shall lose our path and end in bewilderment. It will be seen that the various yoga methods successively lead from one to another and are emphatically *not* paths leading to a common central goal, as is popularly but erroneously taught nowadays in India. Did not Atmarama Swami himself, the author of the standard classic manual on the yoga of body-control entitled *Hatha Yoga Pradipika* confess that he had composed it to help those people who found it impossible to practise the yoga of mental concentration ? "It is only for the attainment of concentration-yoga that body-control yoga has been prescribed," he wrote. The popular yogas are quite inadequate to the high purpose of supreme realization ; at best they yield mediate or indirect knowledge of truth, but never truth itself. They are but units in a progressive series, preliminary rungs in a ladder, and we must step from one to the other in order to rise higher ; no single round will bring us to the top except the culminating one. Similarly, no single yoga is self-sufficient and none will bring final realization except the culminating yoga of the uncontradictable. The term yoga is a wide umbrella which shelters many diverse ideas and practices. It covers the ascetic squatting in self-torture on a bed of spikes as well as the thoughtful philosopher who applies his wisdom to practical life. That is why those who would limit yoga to meditation practice whilst excluding philosophical enquiry adopt an unwarranted attitude.

The *practical* value of each step nevertheless remains in its own place as much as ever. But to the few who originally take up yoga in the hope that it will lead them to truth above all else, who practise the elementary and intermediate methods with some degree of satisfying result, there is always the unspoken invitation to explore the higher method. If they entertain this invitation to supplement the yoga of experience with the yoga of knowledge they will not be deserting the yoga-scheme but will rather be fulfilling it. For the work of complete yoga does not end with meditation nor does devotion exhaust its possibilities. The change can be made by the wise without any damage to their intellectual integrity, whereas the foolish will see only danger and disruption in the higher method. The danger is illusory and consists only in giving second place to the blissful experience of meditation which old habit has made them regard as primary, whilst the disruption they fear is only the yielding of intuitive feeling to the higher check of rational insight. They may keep their meditations and intuitions, nothing need be lost or given up, but the excessive claims of meditation and the stubborn extravagances of intuition to sole supremacy must be given up whenever they collide with philosophically trained reason. Indeed, the inability to practise meditation successfully, and incapacity to enter at will into sustained reverie, would render quite impossible the grand ultimate realization. They are asked to choose, therefore, between the winning of momentary peace and the winning of durable peace. The work of yoga does not end with meditation, does not end with devotion, does not end with postures or breathings ; it ends only with established realization which alone yields a peace that is ever-present whether the man practises his meditation or not.

Thus reality may be conceived from four different standpoints, which are set along a path to be travelled by progressive stages. It may be first worshipped religiously as apart and separate from oneself. It may next be meditated on mystically as being within oneself. It may thirdly be studied philosophically by dropping all false conceptions of it. It may finally be realized consciously as what it is *in itself* and by ultra-mystical processes.

Where I now stand. Without the power to enter the mystical trance and without the emotional re-orientation it brings about, philosophy can only end in sterile disappointing intellectualism. Life is a product of the whole man, and when philosophical thought has run its full course and yielded the truth which comes from making thought go as far as it can reach, yoga must again step in to implement the philosophical conclusions by its own unique power to absorb the world-idea into the self. It is not through any arrogant estimation of my own insight that this book is offered to others, but rather through a desire to pass on to them an attitude of mind which has been of immense help in answering clamant questions. This is the best service I can render them.

Let there be no misunderstanding about my present position in relation to these matters. I now follow a lone path. It is quite true to say that I have ceased to search for yogis and teachers in the conventional sense, and do not identify myself with their ashrams any longer. This is partly because I have personally exhausted the serviceableness of such a search, and partly because long experience of certain ashrams and ascetics has fatally disenchanted me. Formerly I confused yogis and others with sages—as most of us do—but I know better now. I still regard my past mystic experiences as having been quite indispensable in their own place, and similar experiences will always be so to others. The change which has come over me lies in the direction not of denial but of interpretation of those experiences. Profounder research and better guidance have helped me to estimate their precise value and put them in their proper place. Nevertheless they are essential phases of mystic experience which must be passed through by all seekers. Moreover, I would not dream of passing a single day without some interlude, however brief, of mental withdrawal from personal affairs and worldly activity into that serene beatific tranquillity of profound meditation which long habit and constant practice have enabled me to attain at will at any moment and in any place. I have not given up

THE ULTIMATE PATH

meditation, but still keep it as a brief attractive and essential part of the daily programme. However, I refuse to confuse the issues any longer. Visions, ecstasies and intuitions are now the mere accidents of meditation and constitute its non-essential by-product. There is no universal standard by which their validity may be gauged, consequently I know that it is better to keep the essential purpose of meditation solely in view.

In two earlier books I promised to give eventually the complete intellectual statement of those ultimate truths which both fulfil and lie beyond yoga as it is ordinarily known. The work of formulating it in the present volume, which has long been awaited by an international audience, is not complete even now, and does not exhaust the full stock of what has yet to be given to the world. That task demands a second volume. What is here presented constitutes *part* but not all of the yoga of philosophical discernment alone. The remainder, together with the crowning keystone of the arch of truth which I am endeavouring to construct, has perforce been left untouched. If these pages kindle enough interest, then both the missing doctrines and the yoga ôf the contradictable, which is the last stone, will be built in and the task completed. The undertaking of the final volume will be extremely difficult and its separation from the present one is essential. For the latter not only acts as a bridge thrown across the chasm between my earlier work in mysticism and this newer work in pure philosophy, but it also re-orientates the reader's mind and should effectually prepare him for the highly advanced study with which his rational quest may come to a close.

Common language is defectively constructed as a medium for conveying abstract concepts ; hence the need usually felt for inventing a special philosophical terminology. I have tried, however, to remember for whom I am writing—and it is certainly not for cloistered pedants or academic metaphysics, but for men in the street who yet take some thought for the meaning of life—and hence have reluctantly refused to make use of this remote and unfamiliar terminology except where it is necessarily unavoidable or easily understandable. So far as could be, my researches into these complex abstractions have been brought down into the realm of non-technical language comprehensible to ordinarily intelligent people, without sacrificing their accuracy or depth. The brain-racking truths they contain were once confined to the closed circle of an intellectual *élite*, yet, although I have not written for morons, they have here been put into words so plain as to be understandable by most who can understand the words of a good-class newspaper. Nevertheless those who have never practised meditation or concentration nor pursued philosophy may find no taste for such thoughts, while those who walk the narrow path of rigid religious orthodoxy will be scared by them. And every reader will find that although these pages are open and accessible to anyone who cares to pick them up, the penetration to their true meaning is closed to all who are unwilling to make a little mental effort. He would therefore do well to read but little at a time and then pause to reflect over the philosophical fruit he has thus plucked.

It might be as well to anticipate in print some criticisms which I have already heard in private and even read in an Indian newspaper of the lowest class, which acts as the mouthpiece of certain pitiful creatures who have taken up the vain labours of personal enmity. These criticisms will certainly be more widely crystallized with the appearance of the present book. First, the charge of serious inconsistency will be laid against me. It will be said that I have iconoclastically shattered previous definitions and doctrines, changed an established viewpoint, altered earlier estimates of men and experience, and thus proved unstable in character and unreliable in judgment. Personal friends will doubtless be highly amused at the injustice of the last ten words, whilst the general charge betrays a definite misunderstanding of my present outlook. I have not recanted old views but simply enlarged them. Anyway, the integrity of my purpose compels me to confess frankly that consistency is not my hobgoblin. I have concerned myself with it only so far as keeping up the quest of truth was concerned ; if the results of that quest alter and differ as I advance, then let them ! I shall not flinch from acknowledging the fact. The honesty of my past purpose gives me present courage to do so. For a writer who has established his fame on the basis of his researches into an advocacy of yoga, the open confession of its limitations is no easy matter. It should be obvious that only the weightiest reasons and the lengthiest experience led me to this responsible step. I am constantly engaged in learning and verifying new facts and in maturing my judgment. When this happens it is inevitable that a man may have to modify his earlier conclusions and the earlier interpretations of his experiences—unless he is nothing more than a blind believer in what others tell him or a blind accepter of whatever happens to him.

This quest is like climbing an unfamiliar mountain, a journey which entails successive changes of landscape. You see what appears to be the summit high above. After much arduous effort and many arduous years you reach the top of the ridge. Alas ! at the fateful moment of success you discover that the real summit lies still higher

THE ULTIMATE PATH

and that you will have to struggle upward again for more arduous years before it greets your gaze. Mystical visions, yogic experiences, religious beliefs and scientific theories are ridges which you pass on the way up its steep sides and mistake time and again for the final peak. You get different and hitherto unsuspected views of the truth as the old landmarks disappear behind and you succeed in struggling higher. The ultimate exists, let us not doubt that, but if historic records read aright it can be found only by those who have the courage to be inconsistent! Even the Buddha, when he glimpsed a loftier path, did not hesitate to reject elementary forms of yoga which he had practised for six years.

The second charge which has issued from ignorant lips is that I am a renegade. This is absurd nonsense, because I have never espoused any other cause than that of truth, to which I am still wedded. If unenquiring superficial minds have hitherto regarded me, as I am well aware they have, as a convert to Hinduism, or as a propagandist for some particular Indian ashram, that is their vain self-created presumption and was never my personal attitude. But if, however, a sincere passage from a lower to a higher point of view makes me a renegade, then I gladly plead guilty.

The third charge, that I have disavowed yoga, is equally nonsensical. I have not lapsed from my own formulary. I do not oppose but continue to esteem it highly in its own place, as before, but I refuse any longer to concentrate my whole gaze upon it; rather do I try to appreciate, criticize and understand it more fairly against the larger background of ultimate truth. Moreover, I no longer accept every grossly exaggerated claim on behalf of the *inferior* yoga-paths which uncritical irresponsible yogis care to make, and I now regard these paths as directing us eventually to a region beyond themselves. I do not disown yoga, but develop it. As a partner of philosophy, yoga will admittedly yield truth; standing alone it can only yield peace. The other charges, instigated by interested parties, are too petty and too ridiculous with which to spoil good paper, and shall receive the silent contempt of a clear conscience.

Every truth-seeker, every man who has dared to think honestly and to accept the results of his thought—whether they be as bitter as wormwood or as sweet as honey—has been a wanderer. His views have never been cast in iron finality. He knows that wisdom is the last residue left over from life's agitating process of distillation, and not the first. The quest on which he is engaged is a dynamic and not a static one. He cannot lower himself into an intellectual grave and put up the tombstone of a stubborn viewpoint to tell of his death.

Therefore I want as readers only those who are ready to go into the forbidding wilderness with me. The effort to discover truth is a grand adventure, an age-long move forward into increasing experience of the unknown and not a petty stay-at-home rut. The pioneer must labour and suffer to learn as a new truth that which his successors will enjoy as an old one. Consistency is to be worn like a welcome new suit of clothes when it helps the pursuit of truth, but it is to be discarded like a shrivelled old one when it hinders it. Most questions are expansive; they have more sides than one. If the sails of a man's ship have veered in the past to this side and now veer to another—well, so much the better for a truer view!

Time has certainly made me a little wiser in these matters, a little more critical of myself and my experiences, as well as of the renowned ashrams and belauded mystics personally known to me. I have dug more deeply into their foundations to get clearer understanding of them. In this effort I have drawn on the findings of the most competent modern Western and ancient Indian psychologists. It would have been more flattering to my vanity to have followed the long company of fellow mystics—whether of dim antiquity or bright modernity, whether of the young West or the old East—in unquestioning acceptance of these extraordinary visions and ineffable experiences which I had previously viewed in the rosiest light and let the matter rest there. But Fate was kinder and by hurting my self-esteem led me into a higher atmosphere of truth. Both delightful successes and dreadful disappointments were minor teachers which prepared the way. Most invaluable was philosophy's favour in showing me how to evaluate mystic visions by the light of that Supreme Truth which few care to seek because it crushes egoistic desire and shames every personal motive.

Those, therefore, who will view this book as a symbol of the defect of inconsistency will view it wrongly. I have no need to apologize weakly before the bar of reason. Some of the new teachings here presented are not altogether inconsistent with my earlier statements. They were already known to me as long ago as the time of writing *The Quest of the Overself*, where it was plainly stated as follows in the first chapter that the last word was still unwritten:

> "Every writer or teacher must perforce take up a different position according to the grade of development of the mind with which he is dealing. . . . The purpose of these pages should not be misconstrued. They are designed to show a yoga-path suited to

Western people. . . . they show how to achieve certain satisfactions, but they do not attempt at this stage to solve the mystery of the universe. . . . When peace of mind and concentration of thought have been gained, then only will one be fit and ready to embark on the quest of Ultimate Truth. We are still in the process of unveiling a subtle and startling wisdom which not one person in a million has yet grasped."

And in the same chapter it was stated that in the Maharishee I had found the highest embodiment of Indian *mysticism*. The last word was deliberately used, though with all fitting respect. I had begun to perceive that truth lay as far beyond mysticism as the latter lay beyond religion. In the succeeding book[1] I boldly and frequently admitted that mysticism was not enough and that there was an ultimate path beyond it. But only with the present work has the time arrived for a clear explication of the reasons for my change from a fragmentary to a fuller view.

Every book that I have gathered out of the fluid gloom of ink represents, therefore, a milestone which has been passed, an oasis where I camped for a while on my journey through the desert of this world in search of a valid explanation of life and reality. I may never live to write a last philosophical will and testament or a final credo, but in the present volume readers will assuredly find the Quest carried closer to its final terminus. Let them not think that the former volumes can now be ignored. Such a mistake would be fatal to their growth. The earlier teachings remain, but they are supplemented. Those writings will live and be needed so long as men have to struggle upward from stage to stage for truth, so long as human minds must ripen like the fruit on a tree; that is to say, they picture gates which cannot be avoided and must be entered and passed. There is no sudden miraculous transition into ultimate truth overnight for those who are in a breathless hurry. Therefore those earlier books, in representing as faithfully and as lucidly as my pen could do so what I indubitably thought, felt and experienced at the time they were written, are factual records which represent also what many others will perforce think and experience as they follow and progress along the same path.

Einstein found that a ray of light curved its way through space. All earlier scientists took it for granted that it proceeded in a straight direction. Were they mistaken or were they liars? The Theory of Relativity dispels both criticisms. It demonstrates that the earlier

---
[1] *Inner Reality*.

explanations were quite accurate when regarded from the standpoint where the observer had established himself. I was like a restless scientist working his way through one experiment after another in the laboratory towards a fuller understanding of them all. Even the accepted principles of mathematics have to be taken as possessing a relative character only. The thirst for absolute knowledge kept me from the lethargy of satisfaction with existing discoveries. It is true that I have written with strong conviction and with apparent dogmatism. The justification is that I have been practising meditation for a quarter of a century and having found its benefits naturally sought to pass them on to others. I felt it necessary to play an advocate's part and forcefully to draw the attention of my fellow human beings in the West to the fact that such a line of experience was also open to them if they would but interest themselves in it.

The present effort is more than a mere excursion into book-making. It is a structure of welded East-West thought built for our own age. It is a twentieth-century interpretation of a mellow old wisdom that captured the loyalty of grave aged sages who lived long before Christ. It is a contribution towards the understanding of life's most obscure and paradoxically most important theme, written in response to the further pressure of fate and inclination. I shall frankly regard its present achievement and future completion as the highest and holiest task of my career so far. In an age which venerates the authority of science and which rejects anything incapable of intellectual demonstration, it is no small task to attempt to organize thought on behalf of the wordless transcendental reality, and make it march by its own inherent and inexorable logic. We can prove that two and two make four, that the earth is round, and that water is merely a combination of two gases; but how shall we prove the reality of that which is above formulated thought, which is wholly inaudible and for ever invisible, and which cannot be known until all argument disappears? There indeed is a provoking paradox, when that which is appears as that which is not! We can arrive at the ineffable dimension of the ultimate by travelling through a series of thoughts and experiences, but the ultimate itself is neither a thought nor an experience. Truth in its absolute nature can never be enfleshed by words nor conveyed by anything else. Hence the mysterious silence of Christ, of Buddha and of the Sphinx.

But the lonely way towards august truth can be chalked out by human words, the flinty path to its realization can be delineated by them, and men can be led by a process of close reasoning to a position which will indicate how they can make it real to themselves. Once the secret thread of Ariadne is put into their hands, analytic reasoning yoked to yoga can take them to the very gate of reality. It can never enter that gate, however, for then the reasoner himself drops the instrument of thought to the ground as he perceives at long last what he really is. He who stood in his own light by deceiving himself with the notion that he was only a finite person, tied to a few inches of poor earth, is awakened by the inherent force of his own yoga-held reasoning when it is sufficiently strong to affect and fuse his will and feelings, and lets the ancient illusion lapse for evermore. In that moment he disappears within the gate and his journey is at an end. I would not waste my own and my reader's time in asking him to strain after unattainable altitudes, but I do ask him to seek out the meaning of all earthly existence on the one hand and to find out the purpose of his fleshly embodiment on the other, until he can live thereafter in harmony with both.

CHAPTER III

THE RELIGIOUS AND MYSTIC GRADES

SOME age-old queries have persistently confronted mankind. Is life simply a tremendous yet pathetically tragic joke played on mankind by its Creator? Has this vast panorama of glowing stars set in tremendous space a meaning or not? Are we but biological accidents parading uselessly through time? Is man but a guttering candle that throws its little pool of light amid the shadows for a few minutes and then vanishes for evermore?

The primitive answers to these questions were formed by men into the first religions, now lost in the gloomy abyss of pre-history, whose echoes have travelled down to our own time through their successors. A little research soon shows that no faith is entirely new, that few dogmas are peculiar to any one religion, but all have a mingled ancestry. Just as in linguistics the Sanskrit word *bhrater*, the Latin *frater*, the French *frère*, the German *bruder* and the English *brother* indicate a common Aryan stock, so too does the similarity of several religious doctrines indicate the influence of older contacts. The recorded researches of comparative religion and the revelations of comparative mythology have already put a sorry face upon the narrow notion that any one creed contains the only revelation of whatever Gods there be. In each religion we hear more or less of the same sounds: fear of the shadowy other-world, wonder at the pageantry of Nature, praise of a marvellous superior Being who made both the known and the unknown, supplicatory petitions for personal or national favours, consolations for those in personal distress, muffled murmurs of deeply philosophical tenets and faint adumbrations of high truth—all curiously mixed and all ending in beneficent moral injunctions.

Religion may briefly be defined as belief in a supernatural Being or Beings. Each religion in its origin was certainly entitled to be called a revelation, for it was an appeal to the faith and fancy rather than to the critical reason of man.

Most important and most significant of all religions was the consequence of an attempt by a truly wise man, later turned by

THE RELIGIOUS AND MYSTIC GRADES 53

history into its titular leader, to share his knowledge with illiterate masses in the only way that they could grasp his instruction—by feeding them with symbolic beliefs and simple fables rather than with straightforwardly expressed truths. Such men have crossed the orbit of our world-fate but rarely. We need not turn them in imagination into superhuman beings, as their followers generally do, yet we have to recognize that a deep destiny has allotted an unusual importance to their personal lives and spoken words. Even Macaulay, broadly sceptical as he was, could not resist writing that "To give the human mind a direction which it shall retain for ages is the rare prerogative of a few imperial spirits. It is such spirits who move the men who move the world."

Such a sponsor of a genuinely inspired new faith came with lighted torch in hand to dispel some of the ethical darkness of his time and environment, to decipher the first meaning of life for the slumbering many and to open the first gate to ultimate salvation for the seeking few. Out of wide compassion and noble sympathy he wished to make a little part of his wisdom available to those who were mentally unfit to comprehend its dazzling whole. He did not want to screen his knowledge from the toiling masses, but he dare not ignore the psychological fact that it could only be imparted in its unabridged plenitude to those who had attained a stage which rendered them fully qualified to grasp it. To all others it would be tiresomely unintelligible.

For the final truths of life were remote and abstract. They belonged to the region of philosophy, which term is not here to be confused with metaphysics. The latter has come to mean *speculation* about truth, whereas philosophy is here meant as the *verification* of truth. Such views could not be brought within the reach of immature minds without first throwing them into solid and concrete form. This could be done only by converting them into popular symbols and a system of such collated symbols would constitute a historic religion. The symbolism would have to appear in the forms of ritual, legend, myth, pseudo-history, simple dogma and so on, but whatever shape it took it would necessarily represent a disappearance of profoundly abstract conceptions and a substitution of crudely concrete ones. Thus philosophy would apparently die only to be reborn in the dwarfed guise of religion. The metaphysician might lament this transformation but the true sage would not. He would know that the masses who found philosophy unpalatable and unlearnable would thereby be helped in their own way and not left in utter darkness. He would know too that the populace would very slowly but very certainly rise from these faint emotional adumbrations to the intellectual apprehensions of their origin in the fullness of time.

A God who was not partial and personal, who was not warmly interested in the individual lives of his faithful devotees, would have appeared coldly bleak to them. Their minds were too uneducated and too undeveloped to grapple successfully with abstract notions, their intelligence was too dull to visualize an impersonal Mind remote from their petty interests. As an expert psychologist the wise religious leader perceived this. He did not wish to bewilder but to help them. Consequently he considered it a mistake to give to the gross many that which was fit only for the refined few. He fully understood that the presentation of philosophic truth must necessarily be determined by the limits of his followers' understanding, and that a long time must elapse before it could become accessible in its purity to the crowd.

He had no alternative therefore but to make this presentation in a somewhat crude manner, using the vesture of mythological anecdote in which to dress his subtle truths, offering the ultimate reality under the heavy veil of a personal Deity as the object of the people's prayers or as the focus of their concentration in worship, and lifting them to a nobler code of ethical precepts than the one already current amongst them. He was compelled to put knowledge into symbolic terms, to take that which was most immediate and present to his people—the phenomena of Nature—and to invest them with easily imagined invisible beings whose power was more extraordinary than the power of human beings; to embed his wisdom in interesting half-historic tales, to appeal to the picturesque sense of immature minds and capture their imagination by dramatizing some of its facts in ritualistic ceremonial forms; to hint at a higher reality by expressing it in the form of an immensely exaggerated man, i.e. a personal God, and to harness the whole to its immediate practical object by delineating the pleasant rewards of virtue as against the unpleasant punishments of wrongdoing. What else could he do when he was dealing with intellectual children? Do not children everywhere love fairy tales and revel in fables? A religion created by a genuinely wise man was therefore always a significant fable, a tremendous metaphor, whose ultimate purpose was to direct the thought of the masses towards higher ideas and nobler ideals, and whose immediate purpose was to inculcate through the appeal to fear and hope some degree of moral responsibility in their personal lives.

What was its practical significance? It provided a credo to satisfy the curiosity of the minds of ignorant labouring masses, who had no leisure and no capacity to cast far-reaching plummets of enquiry into the stream of life. It offered a faith to satisfy their strong need of consolation amidst distress and to bring comfort amidst hardship. It set up a salutary ethical code to guide their footsteps amid the perplexities of human behaviour, to guard them against their own worst natures, and to erect an elevating ideal for their aspirations. It was an authority to give practical guidance in the shaping of social forms and the binding of individuals into entire nations. It was an aesthetic force to inspire and foster the fine arts. It was a first hint that a grander existence than being tossed and buffeted by circumstance, than this endless harassment of unsought sorrows and short-lived joys, this constant struggle against outer misfortune and inner weakness, this long catalogue of material agitations that end in dust and disappearance, for ever awaited man in all its beneficence and serenity.

Thus the entire structure of religious dogma and formulated doctrine, ornate ceremonial and legendary miracle, was originally but an *emblem* of loftier matters. Those who went into church or temple and worshipped God were not wholly wasting their time nor indulging in the luxury of empty soliloquy. They had taken a definite step on the road to recognition of the fact that the material world did not exhaust reality, albeit it was only a first faltering step. The hushed awe which they felt in what they believed to be the sacred home of divinity was a faint recognition of the truth that man might know the presence of this ultimate reality. The comfort they derived from the scriptural teachings and graven images which postulated the eternal existence of a Deity was their elementary introduction to the philosophical value of the concept of an everlasting existence which subsisted beneath the ever-changing world. The conceptual symbolism of religion was usually anthropomorphic, a fact which made it intelligible to the herd's mind. Their worship was therefore really directed towards an imaginary Being, but it was the only way in which they could worship what they believed to be truth at all. When in the long course of evolution their intellectual capacities would develop sufficiently, doubts would infallibly arise and thus drive them to seek a more satisfactory concept. This would lead them eventually to penetrate the surface of the symbol and approach nearer to its true meaning. They would try to unveil God as He really was and not as He had been imagined to be. The primitive instinct of worship was therefore a sound one, but the way in which men yielded to that instinct had necessarily to differ in accordance with their different grades of culture.

From this we may draw the right inference that the mass of humanity always need a worthy religion as a primitive far-off glance at philosophy, but that its scriptural symbols and historical emblems, its pontifical dogmas and traditional doctrines, are not eternal but only tentative, and may be altered or improved without harming the real aims of religion.

Such are the nature, values, operations and services of a *worthy* religion. But we hear much from scornful rationalists of terror-stricken savages who carve a grotesquely ugly wooden fetish to represent their God, of primitive folk who personify the impersonal forces of Nature as Spirits on whose right side it is desirable to get through ceremonial sacrifice and propitiatory worship, and of sacred rituals that are undisguised phallic worship. The sceptical notion that every faith drew its first breath out of the timid fears of ghostly ancestors or the animistic superstitions of untutored early man alone is opposed by the pious notion that an anthropomorphic God sent a special emissary equipped with a sacred book to an arbitrarily chosen group of fortunate persons and made them His chosen race. Both are too biased to perceive correctly why it is that religions arise and what is their rightful place in society.

Every religion provides a different case for examination. If one has arisen through the desire of an ambitious, aggressive and unscrupulous character to wield influence over weaker minds, another has arisen through the honest if mistaken belief of a well-meaning and highly imaginative man that he was the recipient of a sacred mission to "save" other men. If one faith was an attempt to propitiate powerful natural forces a second was really an effort on the part of a profoundly benevolent man to elevate his less ethically disciplined fellows by inculcating higher ideas of good and evil and by enforcing social restraints through a fixed code.

That even a worthy religion may degenerate in the course of time and bring misery to mankind is sadly admitted; that sincere earnest believers have persecuted and even murdered each other is the testimony of all history; that charlatans, scoundrels and brutes have used religion to satisfy their selfish motives and personal lusts is equally true, and that the world's progress has periodically been hampered by ignorant and fanatical religionists must be granted. Colossal sins stain the pages of religious history. In a complete treatment of the subject such criticisms must be dealt with frankly yet constructively by the light of philosophy. Here it is only desired to point out the position occupied by religion in relation to the hidden Indian teaching. It is but the primal attempt to understand life, and appeals to men who are in the first degree of mental evolution. The time will come when doubts about the truth and value of religion will insistently enter the mind of the more thoughtful man who may want neither the salvation offered by popular religion nor the annihilation offered by orthodox atheism, for he may find the first tawdry and the second terrible. Where then is he to seek ? The hidden philosophy is usually beyond his ken and capacity, besides being very hard to find anywhere. And no man may jump the high hurdle between simple religion and subtle philosophy. The feat is beyond his powers. Life is a growth, not a leap. He has to find an intermediate stage which will be more accessible to him. And this he can find in mysticism, which constitutes the second step upwards.

What Meditation Is. Mysticism is a phenomenon which has appeared in all parts of the world and among all religious communities. There is no space here to deal with its historical derivation ; many competent pens have already traced out its earlier lines. Stripping off the mere externals arising out of dogmatic ignorance, geographical difference, religious environment and racial outlook, it may fairly be said that the mysticism of the West can be equated with the middle degree of Asiatic yoga in its two branches : the yoga of Devotion[1] and the yoga of mind control.[2] The reader is therefore asked to assume that the word "mysticism" in these pages and indeed throughout this book covers both these yogas, and that the word "mystic" is intended to include the yogi also. The literary convenience of such a practice far outweighs the trouble of acknowledging in this condensed examination the minor differences which exist. Moreover, the word "yoga" has now become as ambiguous in the land of its birth as the word "mysticism" is in Europe or America.

We may rightly regard mysticism, with its attempt to penetrate beneath the commonplace surface of religion and its search for internally born satisfactions rather than those derived from external rites, as an inevitable phase of the development of the human mind when it becomes dissatisfied with the narrowness of orthodox faith. This change-over proceeds by slow but sometimes by sudden development from ordinary theistic worship. It can come in three ways. In the first case the seeker becomes disappointed with the actual results of religion or disgusted with the ancient hypocrisies

---

[1] Bhakti-yoga.   [2] Raja-yoga.

which are practised in its name, or dissatisfied with theological contradictions and conflicts, or disillusioned by the seeming impotence of God to help a war-stricken world. The once-honoured symbols lose their historic glamour and are no longer sacrosanct.; he passes through a period of chilling doubt and bleak agnosticism, possibly even militant atheism, where he remains anchorless for a time. It is succeeded, however, if he keeps to his further quest, by the interesting discovery that a small minority of men have found it possible to hold a large view of religion—a view which enables them to stand aside from unsatisfying orthodoxy and its sacerdotal organizations and to come closer to the original atmosphere of a religion. He becomes as interested in studying the literature of such a broad view as he was formerly interested in clinging to the narrower one. Then he hears further that a practical method—mystical contemplation—exists whereby he may experience for himself the beauty and peace of an ever-present divine spirit in which formerly he could believe but never know. All that is asked of him by those who testify to such experience is that he should experiment with the prerequisite exercises Such promises are attractive to not a few persons in an age which wants definite results.

Or his change-over may come without any earlier phase of disbelief at all but through the intensity, ardour and sincerity of his religious aspiration, leading him by degrees from the formal repetition and materialistic petition of conventional verbal prayer to the spontaneous silent aspiration which matures gently and of its own accord into inward concentration and quietening of the mind, i.e. meditation. His prayers are then no longer personal requests but sacrificial self-offerings. The religious devotee who finds satisfaction in ordinary prayer must necessarily visit some temple or church either to praise and propitiate or to obtain assistance from its Deity, or to seek consolation from some holy figure contained within its holy precincts, whereas the devotee who achieves satisfaction through meditation has no need to do this. He finds it sufficient to retire within himself and discovers his heart is already a holy place inhabited by the Deity. He replaces the material image he once worshipped in a temple by the mental image which he now worships within his mind. He substitutes his own heart for the stone, his own spirit for the scripture and his own thought for the priest. Meditation is, therefore, superior to prayer in the sense that the man who is able to practise it necessarily possesses a higher mental capacity because he does not depend on material things or places. He can carry his object or place of concentration as a mental image or concept wherever he goes. He finds that spoken prayer is but a parable, and that in the holy silence of humble contemplation there arises a wordless orison which needs no uttered speech. The ethical results of *successful* attainment are also important. The man ceases to sacrifice his sheep and cattle or their equivalent on priestly altars and begins to sacrifice a greater or lesser part of his excessive materialism, his unbalanced activities, and his short-sighted pursuit of physical pleasures on the altar of his own heart.

The third way in which this change may arise is through the coloured gate of appreciative receptivity to beauty, whether man-made as in good music or Nature-made as in green landscapes. From a practical standpoint the physical forms in which beauty is pressed or found possess their own intrinsic value, but from a higher standpoint its enjoyment is an activity which exists not merely for its own sake but still more as a means to a higher end. A man who is fond of yielding himself to the impressions received through such channels as fine Art and grand Nature will one day spontaneously experience a sensation of being lost to himself, as when listening to beautiful bars of sound or contemplating the superb prospect of snowy peaks mounting to the sky or yielding to the sublime sunsets which come trembling with the close of day. This gentle feeling bubbles softly like a brook from he knows not where and carries his self-centred thoughts along with it. All argument by care and all resistance by self are washed clean away. The feeling may grow imperceptibly into an unforgettable ecstasy. His mind has slipped away from the fetters of time, as it were. A supreme quiescence enthralls his heart and enfolds his emotions. Such a state is difficult to describe adequately. Nietzsche momentarily felt it in his elevated mountain home and wrote: "The greatest Events—these are not our loudest, on the contrary, the quietest hours. The world turns itself not around the discoverer of new noises, but around the discoverer of new values; unheard it itself revolves." The German writer's reference to the change of values indicates the new view of life which is induced by the intense stillness of thought, a view which makes material existence seem ephemeral, transient and unreal, but alas! the glimpse is only momentary. Nevertheless this exquisite feeling has revealed higher possibilities. Thereafter the man will be haunted by its shoreline memory until he learns that through the mystic discipline, pure aesthetic joy may be deliberately recovered without external aids and intermittently repeated. Thus he begins to understand how subjective is its basis when pure contemplation can evoke, as with a magic wand, every variation of such inspirations from faint pleasure to wild ecstasy. Such effects are by no means an exclusive characteristic of either the pure mystic or the pure aesthete, but belong to both. These statements are equally true of the man who produces artistic forms as of the one who enjoys them. The creative mood carries him through similar impressions, rhythms, reveries, silences, stillnesses, ecstasies and other emotional deepenings of being.

The basic principle of all mystical practice is mental abstraction, which may be illustrated in two ways. Whoever is "lost" in following intently a train of thought or in full surrender to the fancies of reverie becomes less aware of physical conditions and eventually hardly notices them. Thus the cripple nearly forgets his deformity, the pedestrian hardly observes the crowds swirling past him on the sidewalk, the author is almost oblivious of his domestic surroundings, and so on. Such instances show that consciousness may temporarily free itself from its habitual assumption that it is confined to the immediate limits of the physical brain and body. They are signs indicative of the larger possibilities of the mind, when released from its universal and overwhelming gravitation towards the physical senses, a gravitation which prevents it from becoming aware of its own non-material nature and which unconsciously converts physical existence into its life-long prison-house.

In the other illustration we may picture the surface of a lake, when it is agitated by frequent waves and repeated storms, as being like the habitually restless condition of the average human mind. The waves of this lake may drag an uncontrolled (i.e. rudderless and oarless) boat hither and thither regardless of the welfare of the boatman, so that his mind will constantly be anxious about his life. Similarly our thoughts incessantly drag our attention hither and thither in purely mechanical response to physical existence and regardless of the true welfare and peace of the mind, which is the only "soul" of whose existence man *knows*.

The methods used by yogis and mystics vary greatly, but they generally consist of following a prescribed course of rigid physical asceticism or worldly renunciation, together with attempts to induce a certain contemplative mood by disciplining during fixed periods the confused drift of thoughts and impressions which make up man's inner existence. This mood arises when all irrelevancies are shut out of the mind and only the chosen line of concentration persistently adhered to. The key to success is twofold: constant practice and expert help. This effort is to be repeated every day and the will must exercise itself to gain control over the external wanderings of the mind, over the restless workings of ideas. It is not easy to do this, and many novices become disheartened, for the tide of thought surges and subsides in a rebellious manner. The faculty of attention must be so controlled and so made to recede from externals that a state of complete undisturbed abstraction arises. It must then be held as fixedly as a lizard waiting for its prey. This effort may be linked in imagination with the purely religious notion of finding the presence of God, or it may be linked with the purely psychological notion of finding one's real self, or even with the purely magical one of entering an invisible world. Success reveals itself by slow degrees when the meditator is able to relax all effort, and when the tempo of his thinking slackens till it lies quiescent and he enters imperceptibly into a state of intense inward absorption, undistracted and undisturbed by the spectacle of worldly existence. The fully advanced mystic need make no conscious effort to destroy intruding thoughts, for the firmness of his intention keeps them away. By regularly forgetting the external world and its affairs for a brief while and turning thoughts inward upon themselves with sharply concentrated attention he may enter a hinterland of mental peace and get into an emotional stillness which is profoundly satisfying. Sometimes the bodily senses may even fall into a temporary coma. Ecstatic trance, in various degrees of depth, may also supervene. Both states are usually harmless, but sometimes terrifying to those unfamiliar with them.

There are certain fugitive and subjective accompaniments of the mystic experience. The religious devotee may see visions of environing light, or of the beloved "Spiritual Guide"—whether living or long dead—to whom he has looked for help in his endeavour. Other practitioners may fancy themselves floating outside the body or conversing with spirits or receiving commands from some angelic being. Although such mental phenomena differ so greatly there are certain factors common to most advanced mystic experiences, such as (a) feelings of serene delight, of blessed calm; (b) sensations of the remoteness of physical surroundings ; and at rarer intervals (c) ecstatic exaltation above bodily and personal existence. These arise after the conscious and voluntary struggles with the waves of thought have achieved a measure of success.

The mystic usually derives extreme satisfaction from such experiences and when he attains the ecstatic state considers that his quest is at an end, that he has entered into union with God or found his own immortal soul. The subtle exquisiteness of this state can only be appreciated by those who have actualized it in their own being. Nevertheless the vital sap which feeds the tree of mysticism is drawn up from its roots in feeling alone.

The essential benefits of successful yoga practice indubitably exist, whatever critics may legitimately say in criticism of its incidental visions and religious intuitions. It would appear that the curse of Babel came upon men when they first began to think. Their minds are now normally in a state of such continuous motion that the power to rest them adequately has been lost. When the brain is weary of its never-ending thoughts and the heart is tired of its ever-changing moods, when the world tires both and nerves are frayed, our great need of mental rest and inward peace is manifest, and this can be partly satisfied through the habit of calm meditation. A certain system of memory-training found a host of purchasers throughout the world in the years during and after the 1914-18 war. Nowadays many distressed people who are overwhelmed by troubles would like to buy a system on the art of forgetting! Count Keyserling has ventured the prediction that the very materialism of Western civilization will drive it at least into the reaction of mysticism, and few competent observers will disagree with him.

We are caught like squirrels in the revolving cage of this world. We climb the steps of that turning cage thrilled with the illusion of incessant activity. The wiser ones cease their climbing now and again, rest interiorly and save their strength. They go farther than we do, for they at least reach a measure of peace, and we . . . ?

The discipline of mental quiet was discovered thousands of years ago, yet holds just as true today in this era of mechanical marvels and auto-filled streets. It still shows man how to let his faculty of attention work for him, and not against him.

These psychological advantages have nothing to do with the religious side of meditation, although most mystics would deny such a statement. They cannot but do otherwise because their approach is prejudged, biased and unscientific. Nevertheless the impartial investigator may find for himself that meditation may be practised even by an atheist, let alone an agnostic, and yet the same benefits may be obtained!

Undoubtedly the introduction of a carefully considered, simplified, non-religious and impeccable technique of meditation as an adjunct to right living should prove highly advantageous to the modern world and especially to the modern Western world. Such a system ought to be purely rational and purged of all the absurd superstitions often attached to yoga in India. The deep need for it becomes more urgent every year. In the feverish strain and harsh struggle of

European and American life, meditation, as a method of developing the ability to keep out disturbing thoughts, securing better emotional balance, calming fretting fears and attaining pleasurable inner peace, would seem to be a paramount necessity. Its introduction as a part of daily living deserves strong advocacy. Its exercises could and should be introduced at a suitable age into the educational curricula of high schools and colleges to discipline the students' minds and concentrate their thoughts. But the ignorant prejudices of parents, the suspicious attitude of ecclesiastics and the complete unfamiliarity of pupils themselves erect high barriers to the consummation of this important project.

A Summary of Mysticism. Such is the second degree in man's ascension to truth. Mysticism might be cryptically described as a mode of life which claims, without long and laudatory praises of God, to bring us nearer to Him than do ordinary religious methods; as a view of life which rejects the all-too-human God made by man in his own image and out of his own imagination, replacing it by a formless infinite divinity; and as a psychological technique which seeks to establish direct communication with this spirit, through the channel of interior contemplation.

Certain collective tenets of mysticism are not confined to any one faith, to any one country or to any one people, and are roughly universal. These cardinal positions of the mystic's thought are five in number and may be briefly picked out and exhibited as follows. Mystics hold first that God is not to be located in any particular place, church or temple, but that His spirit is everywhere present in Nature and that Nature everywhere abides in it. The orthodox notion that God is a particular Person among many other persons, only much more powerful, yet still saddled with likes and dislikes, anger and jealousy, is rejected as childish. Pantheism is therefore the initial note to be sounded. Right thought hallows a place or makes it profane, and real sacredness dwells within the mind alone. Next they hold that as a corollary from the first tenet God abides inside the heart of every man as the sun abides in all its myriad rays. He is not merely a physical body alone, as materialists believe, nor a body plus a ghost-like soul which emanates from it after death, as religionists believe, but He is here and now divine in the very flesh. The heavenly kingdom must be found whilst we are yet alive, or not at all. It is not a prize which is bestowed on us in the nebulous courts of death. The practical consequence of this doctrine is embodied in the third tenet of the mystics, which asserts that it is perfectly possible for any man, who will submit to the prerequisite ascetic discipline, to enter into direct communion by contemplation and meditation with the spirit of God without the use of any priest or prelate as an intermediary and without the formal utterance of verbal prayer. This renders it quite unnecessary to lift upturned palms in suppliant adjuration of a higher Being. Silent aspiration thus replaces mechanical recitation. The fourth tenet is as obnoxious to official religion as the last, for it declares that the stories, events, incidents and sayings, which in their totality constitute a holy scripture, are merely a mixture of imagined allegories and actual happenings, a literary concoction whereby mystical truths are cleverly conveyed through the medium of symbolic myth, legendary personification and true historic fact; that the twentieth century indeed could quite justifiably write its new Bibles, its new Qurans, its new Vedas afresh if it wished, for the divine afflatus may descend again at any hour. Mystics hold, fifthly, that their practices ultimately lead to the development of supernormal faculties and extraordinary mental powers or even strange physical ones, either as the gift of God's grace or as the consequence of their own efforts.

It will be plain that when mystical ecstasy is strong it must logically lead a man to regard himself as a bearer of divinity and in extreme cases as Deity itself. Thus a renowned Muhammedan Sufi mystic exclaimed to the astonished people of Baghdad, a thousand years ago, "I am God!" Unfortunately the Caliph thought otherwise, and punished his impiety with Neronian tortures, finally throwing his body into the Tigris. Such was the fate of the celebrated Hallaj.

The broadening effect of mysticism upon man's religious outlook is an incentive to tolerance and therefore a definite asset in this intolerant world. To take the Bible, for instance, as the sole authentic basis of religious truth, completely ignoring the possibility that other races, such as the Hindus or the Chinese, have produced scriptures which deserve at least an equal claim to consideration, is a narrow view. This religious bigotry which can see no other faith than its own is out of place in our broader time, when the study of comparative religion can demonstrate amply the family ties between the world's faiths. Religious loftiness is not the exclusive possession of any single man, movement or race. The fully developed mystic understands that God's sun shines on all alike, and that he is free to follow any particular creed or none. That which he seeks he must discover for himself and from himself by meditative introversion.

The inspirer or founder of a religious cult who is really advanced would know how to grade his hearers and devotees, when to give the populace entry to the first degree but no farther, and when to give the more mystically minded entry to the second degree. We may take the words of Jesus as an example of this knowledge, when he said to his closest disciples: "To you it is given to know the Mysteries of the Kingdom of God, but to them it is not given ... therefore I speak to them in allegories ; because ... hearing, they hear not, neither do they understand." The word "Mysteries" in the original has the meaning of "formerly hidden but now revealed", whilst Moffat has not hesitated to render it as "secret truth" in his translation of the New Testament. But such mysteries have no reference to philosophy. That Jesus instructed some of his personal followers, and through them the later apostles, in the tenets and practices of the second degree, i.e. yoga and mysticism, there is ample evidence in the words and lives of his early followers, such as in the mystic trances of John and the mystical sentences of Paul.

This merely mystical understanding of truth on their part brought certain defects into their own teachings later, as well as certain misapprehensions of the real nature of Jesus' personality, defects and errors which the later Gnostic philosophers saw up to a degree and tried to remedy. But if the history and mystery of Jesus baffled his own people we need not be surprised that they have baffled the whole world since.

A careful perusal of the New Testament sections will show that although most of them may conveniently be classified as first degree, i.e. purely religious matter, there is also a thin vein of mysticism of the second degree running right through them. For instance, the sentence "The kingdom of heaven is within you" has absolutely no connection whatever with official religion and entirely refers to the experiences of yogis and mystics. The explanation why such a mixture of concepts exists is twofold. Firstly, the compilation of these records in a single volume did not occur until a few hundred years after Jesus is believed to have passed away. The obscure Council of Nicea found numerous gospels extant when it sat to make the compilation, consisting of a mixed collection of religious books intended for the masses and mystical ones intended for the elect few. The immense number of bishops who constituted this council had quite a fight over the nature of Christ ; they naturally made their selections and rejections according to their personal temperaments and outlook.[1] Hence the somewhat uneven selection of authentic

---

[1] The official account of the miraculous self-movement and self-classification of the books during the darkness of night may be dismissed for what it was—a childish tale intended to impress the ignorant.

gospels and unjustifiable rejection of certain apocrypha. Secondly, Jesus was in revolt against the stiff orthodoxy of the Jewish priests, most of whom were not only ignorant of the higher degree themselves but deliberately persecuted those who were mystically inclined. His indignation expressed itself in the words, "Woe unto you! Ye entered not in yourselves, and them that were entering ye prevented." It is evident that his sympathy with the ignorant helpless masses was so large and overwhelming that he deliberately opened the doors of the higher mystical teaching to a little extent for them, although only his close disciples were fully initiated. Buddha was undoubtedly actuated by precisely the same feelings and opened the same doors even wider than did Jesus.

Hardly an ancient people existed but cherished its mystical tenets. When we search their more recondite records we find that nearly all exclaim with Epicurus: "Gods exist but they are not what the common people suppose them to be." Similar notions are known in certain high quarters of some world-religions even today, but closed lips are usually maintained about them. The Vatican knows how to keep its historical secrets and to guard its store of rare mystical manuscripts and books. Some were not a little surprised at the frankness of the significant confession recently made by a former Dean of St. Paul's Cathedral, London, when he publicly said: "As for repudiating obsolete dogmas, it is very difficult. We have no right to offend these little ones that believe. . . . It is perfectly hopeless to try to compose a creed which will satisfy both a learned scholar and his kitchenmaid."

Mysticism is not enough. But the law of life is movement. Man cannot remain immobile like a hibernating toad in prolonged trance. He has to get out of it at some time or other. He has to associate with his fellow mystics or with his family or with the world at large. Or he has to attend to one physical need or another. Moreover, he will sooner or later be brought up against the various limitations of mysticism and the characteristic defects of mystics. Some of them are serious and important. The seeker who has never met with them, or having met them has never had the courage to face them adequately, can never rise beyond the second grade, but will put a premature end to his quest and remain a smug and self-satisfied undergraduate. As this chapter deals only with the practical value of mysticism and not its philosophical or truth-value, consideration of problems involving the latter must be deferred to a later one.

Thus will the seeker one day arrive at the wall which limits the range of mysticism. He will see that, whatever good it can do, there is much that it cannot do yet wrongly claims to do. He will see, further, that the social value of historic mysticism is as little as its individual value is great, and therefore it cannot constitute a complete solution of the problem of human existence, or offer a complete panacea for the malady of human suffering. He will turn in disgust or disillusionment from the veiled exploitation of their followers' ignorance, credulity, financial resources, diseases, anxieties or desires by most of those who profess to teach this subject or who proclaim their competency to guide its aspirants. He will ask why it is that such harmful charlatanries and gross superstitions have clouded the sky of mysticism's history. The final view can only be that the very possibility of these defects reveals the insufficiency and limitations of mysticism. On its meritorious side it is admirable, yet it is not perfect. There is something lacking in it. That missing element is precisely the same as the missing element in religion. The one makes its direct appeal to emotional faith; the other to emotional experience. *Neither makes an appeal to the criterion of highest truth.* Both lack a rational foundation and even glory in their lack. For him who breathes the rarefied atmosphere of truth no charlatanry, no superstition and no exploitation can ever be possible. He will not permit self-deception to touch him and will certainly never knowingly deceive others. The variations and contradictions of mystical experience necessarily indicate that *ultimate* truth must lie beyond its province. For there must be one such truth of life, not two or more. The ethical failures of mystics and occultists must be attributed to their personal failures to discover and realize this supreme truth, and to their dependence on an unstable and uncertain source of inspiration, viz. feeling, which is notoriously changeable no matter how exalted it becomes temporarily by contemplation. Their intellectual difficulties are the logical result of their disdain of logic and of their inner opposition to tested rational processes in preference to debatable intuitive ones. It is clear that he who seeks the highest must one day make up his mind to travel farther than mysticism, however useful and necessary a stage of his onward journey it has been, and must always remain.

The inability to obtain satisfactory and convincing answers to such questions as fullness of experience and love of knowledge will eventually arouse must lead the thoughtful enquiring mystic who has not settled down into smug self-laudation or conservative quiescence to a wilderness where he will walk in lonely bafflement for a time, just as once he may have walked into the wilderness of doubt, despair and scepticism when he emerged from the self-contradictions of dogmatic religion. The operation of reversing gear, from surrender to mystical feeling to sharp self-criticism by reason, for a man who has driven for years in the former is neither easy nor quick to make. Some time-lag will be needed for its accomplishment, and the principle of gradualness will hold good here. Could he but know it, the very discontent which has crept into his mind is a harbinger of his close approach to the invisible frontier of a higher region of thought. Yet the frontier will remain closed to him unless he persevere with his solitary journey and refuse to be held back by old habits or other opinion. The courage which is required from him now is not less than that which he needed in that earlier momentous escape from religion or agnosticism to mysticism. Few were ready to accompany him then, but he must expect infinitely fewer still to accompany him now into this howling wilderness. But if he keeps in view the gravity of his undertaking he will not flinch from acceding to these requirements. He will come to perceive, if dimly, that the inner urge which imperiously drives him out must be respected beyond all else, for its ineffable holiness is something far beyond the imputed holiness of religious faith or mystic intuition.

The elementary position of all religious and mystical systems becomes clear, therefore, when they are co-ordinated in the larger conceptions of philosophy. Whatever of truth they contain is but the symbolic translation of subtle philosophical tenets. The pious confections of a humanized God afford useful pabulum for common folk; the peaceful reveries of meditation are benedictions to more evolved minds: but to both of these classes the caviare-like food of a moral, emotional or intellectual *élite* is inevitably cold and unattractive.

So the mystic whose motto is "Excelsior!" must suffer and struggle, even amidst the frequent if fitful interludes of contemplative peace which he has now attained. The moment will arrive when he will stand at the very gate of the frontier itself. A few more paces and he may stride across it. Beyond lies a new land, vastly mysterious and hardly trodden. It is the region of the third degree, the empire of the supreme wisdom open to man. Yet he will not know how close he is to it unless a guide now appears to make the revelation and to escort him farther. The guide may be an ancient one and speak to him across the generations through the inscribed pages of a manuscript or the printed pages of a book. Or he may be a living one and speak to him face to face. The first is a chart which may take him slowly some of the way, while the second will take him quicker and farther. But once the new journey has begun and the frontier lies behind him, he will never again know the meaning of complacent rest or selfish ease. For the new acolyte of the Absolute must now struggle incessantly, first towards his own final position and then for the beneficent liberation of *others*, under the authoritative command of a superior power—TRUTH!

CHAPTER IV

THE HIDDEN PHILOSOPHY OF INDIA

THE readers who come with a kindly attitude to these chapters do not come with a prepared one. It is to be feared that some propositions must have startled them and others must have alarmed them. But the teachings which are yet to be set down will come as a surprise to those who have relished the writer's narratives of yogic adventure or accounts of mystic experience. Let them bear patiently, however, for in the end they will find that all the real gold in religion and mysticism will not be lost and that full assay value will be returned for their patience. All that is admirable in religion and well serves toiling mankind shall here be well respected too; all that makes mysticism a boon to struggling individuals shall receive the favourable evaluation it merits. Our scales are just. Nevertheless they cannot be deceived. They will not accept the spurious along with the genuine or the fictitious with the factual. Nor will they permit the detrimental to crowd into their pans under the shelter of the beneficial.

Although the appeal of these pages shall be made only to rational understanding and not to sentimental faith and credulity, nor even to easily stirred imagination, such is the distinctive amplitude of truth that it covers all things with its comprehensiveness. An undreamed-of unity, a sublime synthesis bringing together the Real, the True, the Good and the Beautiful, awaits them at the end. The endless wars of doctrine and the bestial hatreds of men here find their last grave.

The relation of philosophy to religion has been considered and its relation to mysticism has been freely hinted at. The interrelations of all three are such that if religion be regarded as the vestibule of mysticism, the latter will occupy the same position with reference to philosophy. However, it is here necessary to bring out more clearly the relationship of the hidden philosophy towards what is frequently but often erroneously termed philosophy in both the West and the East. This demands some preliminary reflection upon the general meaning of the term.

No tortured animal has ever asked with benignant Buddha why universal suffering existed, or has ever gone behind momentary appearances and asked what larger meaning underlay the enigma of life. Man alone of all living species has done this.

The monkey is the animal most nearly like man, yet the ethical conflicts of religion, the aesthetic appreciation of art and the tormenting questions of philosophy have never entered its head. What then is the most marked difference between the mind of a man and the mind of a monkey? Most animals certainly have thoughts and retain memories, whilst many undoubtedly possess intelligence. Some, like the Indian elephant, possess an extremely high degree of intelligence. But there is one thing which no animal can ever do, and that is to use its intelligence in the abstract. It cannot reason theoretically nor bring reflection to transcend its physical environment. Its actions are invariably determined by the concrete conditions which surround it.

A further mental activity which lies beyond the intelligence of the most intelligent animal in the world is to think impersonally. No animal has ever been known to attempt to communicate with another animal dwelling on a different and remote continent, because none feels the need of troubling about those who do not touch its immediate environment or are unlikely to touch it at some time. This implies that it cannot rise beyond individuality into impersonality, the cause being its inability to bring an isolated item of its experience into proper relation with the universe. It cannot stand away from its own body and contemplate with complete selfless detachment the character, nature and life of another beast moving a hundred yards away, let alone the stars overhead when they appear at night. For every beast the primordial needs of the body are its chief concern. The hub of its universe around which everything revolves is and for ever remains itself, and all other creatures are reacted to according to their relation to its own fears, desires, etc. Life is a simple fact for such a creature, whereas the intellect of man is fated to create problems and then torture itself trying to solve them.

Man alone has deemed it worth while to agitate his mind and do all these things. He alone is provoked by the universe into posing questions and seeking their answers, which proves that he possesses distinctive mental faculties which are denied to animals. And the sum of those faculties is nothing more than the thinking-power developed not only to a higher degree but also to an abstract impersonal level. Man's intellect may rise into purely theoretical activity; it may engage itself in the most impersonal studies like astronomy and trace the movements of remote planets; it may disdain the exigencies of cramping material surroundings and soar aloft into questions concerning the cause and course of the entire structure of the universe; whilst it can take the facts and items of experience and by constant reflection relate them into rational connections, finally weaving them into a comprehensive and systematic pattern of explanation. When we seek the significance of all this we have to conclude that an opportunity has been vouchsafed to man alone to possess the capacity of arousing interest in, enquiring into, reflecting upon and perhaps eventually understanding the truth about his own life, as well as the surrounding universe. No insect, no plant, no animal possesses this unique and lofty privilege of seeking truth and reflecting upon it. Vasishta, an ancient Indian sage, exclaimed: "Better the rock-bound toad, better the crawling earthworm, better the blind cave-serpent, than the man without enquiry." Such enquiry is called philosophy.

But let nobody think that philosophy is something to be chosen by a man when it so pleases him; on the contrary, *it chooses him*! The very fact that he is a human and not an animal being has perforce made him a philosopher, albeit an unconscious one. True he did not ask for this distinction, but he cannot escape it! The first few crude disjointed thoughts about his environment which floated through the mind of the earliest savage, the primitive odd pieces of knowledge about himself and other men which he picked up during brief hazy reflections, the wonderment and adoration which the advent of the morning sun always stirred in him—these were the beginnings of a mental life which distinguished man from beast and marked his early unwitting steps in that quest of wisdom to whose last and final stage he one day awakens and affixes the name of philosophy. Then his attitude becomes a conscious and reasoned one; then it attains high rank. Henceforth his movements are no longer slow, groping and blundering, but quick and direct. By asking abstract questions, by enquiring deeply into universal existence, he shows how far he has travelled beyond the brutes. But the quest is really a unity, even though it may be divided into these two clearly defined stages.

Everybody therefore is something of an actual philosopher even if he be an imperfect, inarticulate and inchoate one. It has already been explained why religion is an elementary initiation into an inferior form of philosophy, and hence every religious person likewise comes under this category. Only he prefers parables where the intelligentzia demand reasoned explanations. The business man who is too busy to trouble his head with such barren and worthless intellectual fabrication as he deems philosophy to be nevertheless possesses his own outlook on life, his own views as to what he is here for and how far matter is real. He may believe that there is no meaning in the cosmic masquerade, that the essential purpose of his incarnation is solely an economic one. He may regard the chair in which he sits as being possessed of a materiality which is so obvious as to be beyond a single moment's consideration or question. Whether these views are correct or not is beside the point, for the mere act of holding them proves that he too, like the academic metaphysician whom he contemptuously despises or ignores, has a philosophy. Moreover, it influences his conduct and possesses a practical bearing on his life just as much as the other man's.

Thus we arrive at the little-known truth that the ordinary man's criticism that philosophical reflection is utterly useless and that the points at issue with which philosophers struggle are meaningless and trivial *is itself the outcome of philosophical reflection*! He is using the same method which the philosophers use, albeit crudely. The barrenness of practical results and the lack of settled conclusions of which he complains in philosophy are partly due to the fact that philosophers are much more cautious in approach, much less hasty in procedure, much more clear-seeing in mentality to be willing to arrive at the premature judgments which please him. Even the very wording of his own criticism itself constitutes a conclusion reached by generalized logical thinking upon given facts—which is precisely the method used by philosophy. Therefore his judgment against philosophy is itself invalidated by the way in which it is obtained! Moreover, he has to think about life whether he likes to or not and whether he wants to or not, because the most commonplace facts and circumstances of his personal existence demand some thought, however little, about them and their meaning. The difference between him and the philosopher is that he reflects casually and superficially, whereas the latter reflects deliberately and deeply, never ceasing to ask questions until all is quite clear to him.

It is an oft-heard plaint that philosophy will not fill the kitchen larder. People nowadays say, "Let us put our economic house in order, or our political house in order, and then we shall have time to philosophize." The old Romans said very much the same thing in their proverb: "First one must live, then one may philosophize." People were making the same plaint when Nebuchadnezzar ruled in sultry Babylon, and they will go on making it when the architectural colossi of New York City are but thin phantoms of the past.

Every man is perfectly free, therefore, to ignore the stupendous problem which life silently sets him and nobody will care to reproach him for neglecting it. Twentieth-century existence is difficult enough with its stress, strain and struggle to justify a man looking only to his immediate wants and deferring all consideration of such *apparently* remote questions as philosophy raises. This he usually does. He relegates the whole subject to a few academic hermits who have no better business to attend to than to indulge in such abstruse speculations on an abstract Ultimate. Such is his first and superficial glimpse of the place of philosophy. But like many first glimpses it is quite a questionable one and open to revision with time.

The general objection carries the implication that the world can get on quite well without philosophy. It does not occur to the world that those who first decide whither they may best journey before mounting their horses may arrive at a better place than the others who leap on their steeds and rush off they know not where. According to all reports the world is still trying to extricate itself from the widespread difficulties into which such a "practical" but unreflective policy has brought it. Its distresses are melancholy attestation to the absence of philosophy from its midst.

The particular plaint that it is easier for a rich man to indulge in this study than a poor man, and for a free man than an enslaved one, is certainly true. But the law of compensation starts working here and renders it easier for a poor man to *practise* philosophy than for a rich one! This truth will become more apparent later.

It is also justifiable to say that some amount of free leisure is needed to carry on this study as well as to reflect upon its points, and some amount of educational background is demanded for its understanding. So far as the latter point is concerned biography is full of instances where men without means have practically educated themselves rather than submit to cultural defeat, and so far as the former is concerned those who complain that time for study cannot be found have only to steal it from their sleep. In this way they can get at least one hour daily. This will not cause them any suffering, for it is little and given in a good cause. But there are others who could make the time more easily. They have too many irons in the fire and should take a few out. They need not neglect essential duties nor cancel existing relationships in order to accomplish this adjustment. But when they have found a way to fit in the study-period they will find their reward with it. Thus the final truth is that the aspiring and the ambitious will always bestir themselves whilst others moan.

If none of us then can escape being a philosopher, why should it seem a puerile request to ask that we learn to philosophize correctly, consciously, systematically and with open eyes instead of faultily, sleepily and blindly ; in short, to be a real philosopher and not a drifting fool ? Our endeavour to deny the supremacy of such generalized directed thought by ignoring it will always be in vain. It cannot be a stupid nor a useless pursuit, but rather an indispensable one which would have us lift the whole of our life-activity from the level of groping effort to that of a deliberate one. Life presents us with its own educational curriculum in the shape of painful and pleasurable experiences, but the *conscious* quest of truth is an item which we must ourselves insert.

The thoughts that are habitual lead to their consequences in action. The ordinary man's general outlook will always determine the course of his actions just as much as will the philosopher's. But whereas he is usually blown by the wind of circumstance, and hence afflicted by uncertainty, the philosopher has the advantage that he has long reflected and brought to light certain *principles* of sound action. A man who has never asked fundamental questions, who has never worked out a reasoned attitude of his own, will find himself gripped by doubt or darkness when the first big crisis of his life occurs. On the other hand, he who has mastered true philosophy will be quietly ready in all situations, all eventualities. The lack of predetermined principles leads unwary man to acts detrimental not only to his own well-being but also to that of others. And yet the man of the world is impatient with philosophers !

People are even frightened away by the mere sound of the name philosophy. Even Plutarch could glorify only public men, warriors and politicians in his *Parallel Lives*. Thus he praised Lycurgus and sneered at Plato for being a philosopher, for "while the first stabilized and left behind him a constitution the other left behind him only words and written books". Nevertheless philosophy played a leading part in the old Corinthian culture. The Greeks had some regard for right thinking. But the attitude of a jazz-minded age is, "Why should we fret our foreheads with such problems ?" Most of the men and women of our time prefer the crude chatter which passes for conversation and they are satisfied to slip from cradle to grave with both eyes closed. These intellectual incapables have little use for a climb to the mountain-tops of thought and a soliloquy in that rarer atmosphere. In the average person's imagination the subject is a dry, dead and barren tree, a monotonous and colourless weaving of thoughts. There is some good ground for his mental image because much dubious matter passes for philosophy which is nothing of the kind, but when we enquire a little more deeply into the basis of his fear and dislike we are likely to discover that they arise out of his ignorance rather than out of his acquaintance with the subject. He rightly thinks, however, that it is going to lift his mind from the familiar ground of concrete reality into unfamiliar altitudes of life, and so, like many elderly persons prior to their first flight in an aeroplane, he fears it. And when he happens to meet a desiccated human being who calls himself a philosopher he adds irritation to his fear because the man seems to be wandering about in a deserted wilderness where nothing that is fruitful and nothing that is edible can be found.

Our scientific friends add to this dismal chorus of complaint. They sneer in disdain at the barren results of the world's three thousand years of recorded philosophizing; they point with pride to the immense encyclopaedia of ascertained and agreed facts which science has attained in less than three hundred years. They utter the ancient joke about the philosopher being like a blind man searching in a dark room for a black cat which is not there, although the twentieth century has brought the joke up to date by adding a theologian to the philosopher and announcing that he succeeds in finding the cat! He who is so bold as to talk of a philosophy of truth must surely be an ignoramus, unacquainted with philosophical history and raising hopes in himself and others which are foredoomed to vanish dismally.

These plaints are just ones. The story of philosophical exploration is a fascinating account of inconclusive adventures in futility. All history shows that the philosophers have no settled platform of knowledge upon which they can stand in agreement, and that they are still in the realm of conjecture when they attempt to interpret the meaning of the world.

What one philosopher built up so convincingly was torn down so cogently by the next; what the eighteenth century thought to be a fine discovery was disproved and rejected with contempt by the nineteenth; the venerated systems of one people were thrown into the lumber-room by another. Countless pages of innocent paper have been deluged with black ink by eager thinkers, but still the shape of truth remains unseen. Certainly those grave discussions whether life has a graveyard goal or not are as tormentingly unsettled as they ever were. The answers of philosophers to the questions they posed themselves have been as different and opposite to each other as are the North and South Poles. The importance of being frivolous is impressed upon readers every time they take up many of these stilted ponderous pages. They may indeed finally be reduced to exclaim, in Anatole France's flippant and ironic words: "Things have diverse appearances and we know not even what they are . . . my opinion is to have no opinion!"

It has already been observed that this same demon of self-contradiction haunts the houses of mysticism and religion too. Is no escape possible from it then? Is Herbert Spencer right in declaring that absolute truth is to be relegated to the domain of the unreachable? Do the religious, the mystical and the philosophical seekers journey along a path which is but a blind endless maze without discernible starting-point and without attainable goal?

The wonder is that men have not ceased to philosophize altogether. What is it that urges them to construct and reconstruct, to criticize and to destroy, the theories of their predecessors and the speculations of their contemporaries? Why do they not abandon in irritation this vain pursuit and thus follow the example of gifted Persian Omar Khayyám, who

> When young did eagerly frequent
> Doctor and saint, and heard great argument
> About it and about, yet evermore
> Came out by that same door wherin I went.

The fact is that they *are* ceasing, and with increasing tempo, to philosophize. She who once sat in regal enthronement over the empirical sciences is today a neglected Cinderella. Those who care for the study of philosophy as the pursuit of Truth are rapidly diminishing in number. The process of decline in prestige and disappearance in interest is going on all over the world. Germany, which a single century ago could claim to be the home of European philosophy, now scorns that subject as useless and derides it as a mere game of intellectual marbles. India, which, a thousand years ago, maintained universities like that of Nalanda, where none could obtain admittance save those who could answer the most abstruse metaphysical questions, and where ten thousand students were once to be found despite this difficult initial bar—India, which has fed all the other Asiatic lands with her thoughts, cannot today find sufficient college students to form more than ridiculously small classes in the same subject. Indeed, it is a well-known fact that several colleges have now abolished the chair in philosophy. It has in fact suffered a severe downfall and its systems have become everywhere in the world a collection of desolate antiques, with its professors busy as melancholy curators of this metaphysical museum!

The modern mood is usually irritated by any attempt to entice it into the cobwebbed parlours of metaphysical speculation.

The Philosophy of Truth. Such criticism is justifiable only where so-called philosophy leads away from action and not to it, where it runs around in a vicious circle and remains for ever inconclusive, and where it starts its movement of thought with mere fancies instead of with ascertained facts, although even in these cases it may be useful to those who want to enjoy the intellectual stimulus of mental gymnastics. But all this has nothing to do with the hidden philosophy.

The world-wide error which has jumbled personal fancy with philosophy or opinionative theology with metaphysics makes it necessary to utter the warning that the philosophy of truth *as revealed in India* must not be confused with such philosophical *speculation* on truth. If half-philosophy and pseudo-philosophy have now run their course and been dismissed, then the way is left open for true philosophy. The former soars into realms of fancy like a free bird, whereas the latter is strictly chained to facts. It begins with them so far as they are available and refuses to outrun them. It takes nothing for granted, starts with no assumptions, no dogmas, no beliefs *of any kind*. It proceeds solely by the use of strict reasoning upon these facts, the acutest and sharpest reasoning ever practised by the human mind, and it concludes by applying the test of *all* human experience. Many famous metaphysicians have exhausted their ingenuity in *imagining*, for instance, a hypothetical Noumenon, Substance, Spirit, Absolute, etc., underlying the world-appearance, but the philosophy of truth does not permit either its exponents or its students to seek a single fancy nor accept it without enquiry as true. Spirit may indeed exist, but it has to find out its existence by investigation and not start by assuming it. Fact is its sole foundation and actuality its superstructure.

Academic philosophy presents a picture of conflicting opinion chiefly because of the diverse standpoints taken up by philosophers. Only one standpoint is possible to the true philosopher, and that the highest. Such a standpoint must be based on the facts of all experience. Therefore all assumptions, all dogmas, all blind faith, all surrender to sentiment, all dreams of the unseen and unknown, are immediately ruled out of court. Wherever philosophy has failed its failure has partly been due to violation of this factor. Life can never be satisfactorily interpreted by studying our fancies in place of its facts.

To this extent, therefore, genuine philosophy must embrace science, must start with it, must walk by its side, even though it will later outstrip it because it is more venturesome. Science is indeed a part, albeit the preliminary part, of the philosophy of truth. And by science is meant principally the scientific method, the scientific approach, the vast collection of verified facts, but not the fluctuating guesses and opinions of individual scientists.

To many a Western person metaphysical speculation is a hobby or game for dilettantes, or at best an exercise in intellectual ghost-hunting. Genuine philosophy is an infinitely more serious and fruitful occupation than that. It regards this life of ours as a precious opportunity to gain eternal profit out of its seeming transiency. Consequently it cannot afford to waste time on vain or useless efforts which are foredoomed to end disappointingly in emptiness. It uses the method of philosophical enquiry not to find excuses for living less fully but to find guidance for living more so, not to attenuate human interests but to expand them, and not to pursue fleeting spectres but to seek the enduring Real.

We shall consider in a later chapter a further special characteristic of the higher philosophy which is its actual justification (where all other philosophies fail to do so) of the claim to provide an all-comprehensive world examination and connected synoptic view of Life. Its success in proving its claim explains why Indian minds should have succeeded in fully penetrating the world-darkness where Western minds still regard the task either as impossible or as set for possible completion in a remote future.

We have already seen that the explanations of religion are excellent for simple or timid folk but too elementary and too adverse to the conscience and common sense of cultured ones. We have also learnt that the tenets and practices of mysticism are ampler and better, but they too are insufficient because they yield only a partial view of life. It is the claim of the hidden philosophy of truth—which will henceforward be named by the single word "philosophy" in this book, partly as a verbal convenience and partly because the derivation of the word points to *truth* and not to the mere speculation into which it has frequently degenerated—that it alone seeks to enquire into every phase of total universal existence, leaving nothing out, and it alone strives to get the fullest explanation and the final one; moreover, it not only starts to enquire but pushes on with iron determination until it successfully reaches the goal.

From this statement it may be gathered that true philosophy is no monochrome but is so rich that it must not only embrace the methods used by religion, mysticism, science and art, for instance, as well as all the results achieved by them; it must not only take within its scope of examination such diverse matters as business, industry, warfare, marriage and maternity, bright dreams and base drudgery, because they form a part of human life; it must not only include the vast array of animals and plants and rivers and mountains within its examination because they belong to universal existence; but it must even turn back critically upon itself, for, after all, every enquiry—whether it be religious, mystic, scientific or philosophic—is made with the mind. Hence philosophy seeks also to discover why the mind wants to know all these things, why it takes up the quest of truth, and what is its own nature, what are the limits of its capacity to know truth, how it comes to know the world, and what in short is the ultimate truth of all the truths that we already know. It demands truth in its entirety, not half- or quarter-truths.

Philosophy values the contributions of the departments of fact or faith already named, and indeed of all others, whilst escaping from their restricted specialism because it refuses either to pause at any single one of them or to limit its enquiry to it. Science, however valuable it be in providing us with a reasonable approach to life and in organizing our knowledge of the world, is obviously limited. It deals in fragments. The average scientist cannot be expected to understand the significance of music, for example. He works, like all specialists, with blinkers, for he keeps within a certain department and has to accept both the limitations and the constricted views of that department. Every specialist is unconsciously influenced by the emphasis placed upon the particular aspect of life with which he concerns himself. The consequence is that he forces his notion of truth within the confining walls of a compartmental outlook and ignores the goal of truth as it is when freed of such limitation. However workable this be for practical purposes, it becomes a hindrance when the wider objective of ultimate, universal and uncontradictable truth is set up.

It is hard to know how to place so remarkable a mental attitude, for it is too up-to-date to be antique, too rational to be medieval and too historic to be modern. Such is the paradox of the world's most archaic wisdom, which is still so far in advance of contemporary knowledge that we are only now beginning to catch up with it! Such is the uniqueness of a philosophy which is a courageous endeavour to get at the meaning of existence, to use man's loftiest faculty of intelligence for the loftiest imaginable aim, and to discover an adequate criterion for ethics, an unassailable canon of truth and wisdom for the sustenance of social action. Only the superficial dare doubt its practical utility and marked advantage, but admittedly such an endeavour does not belong to the everyday life of the crowded plains. It must necessarily belong to distant mountain trails. The plain-dweller is entitled to refuse to forgo his comforts and travel to this unfamiliar region, but let him not despise those who put fear aside and essay the climb. They will find no dullness there, but on the contrary a fascinating and stimulating adventure. It is really engrossing and, when its full practical bearing appears on the horizon of study, will be found to hold vital human interest. Henceforth the episodes of their everyday personal lives will be seen against a perspective of growing grandeur.

We have seen how the approach to truth arranges itself in a graded series, and have followed it to the end of its second phase. This is in accord with the ancient Indian teaching, which postulates three stages of evolution through which the mind of man must pass, three progressive attitudes towards life. The first is religion and is based on faith; the second, mysticism, is controlled by feeling; and the third, philosophy (which is inclusive of science), is disciplined by reason. Nor can it be otherwise, for man's understanding of the world must necessarily grow parallel to his mental capacity. His outlook is invariably and inevitably limited by the degree of his intelligence. Hence it is impossible for all men to answer life's queries in the same way.

We must stand now at the door of the third degree in the archaic temple of wisdom and knock hopefully. If we are to reach our optimum development we must cross this threshold and learn what lies beyond it. Over the lintel we may behold deeply carved in dignified lettering four words, *The Philosophy of Truth*; whilst above them the figure of Minerva's owl is solemnly staring at us. For this peculiar bird becomes active when the shades of night are falling, and it clearly sees varied objects where man sees only sable darkness.

But who has ever heard of such an unlabelled philosophy? We have heard of German philosophy, Greek philosophy, Indian philosophy; we remember as from a remote past some of the world's most unintelligible volumes, written by the world's most intelligent men, marring our student days with tormenting emotions of confusion, despair and final bafflement; we recollect having fuddled our brains by reading a spate of tedious books on the subject, but instead of advancing us into clearer light the contradictory theories and speculations carried us back into greater darkness; we believed ironically what seemed to be a general rule in philosophical discussion, that the more trivial the point at issue the graver became the argument; we have picked up a little of the lingo of the system of Spinoza, the system of Anaxagoras, the system of Immanuel Kant, but we have never found, nor do we know of anyone who has ever found, a philosophy which represented more than the views of one man or one school.

There exist a few, however, who have *thoroughly* explored the twilit lands of religion, mysticism and metaphysics and not merely coasted along their shores, who know also what science can say about the world, and who possess no such pessimism. Their initial wonder has waxed into the desire to know, and this again into the passion to understand, and that finally into the search after reality. They feel that this all-engrossing search which has driven them onward and upward reacts in response to something that *is*. An inextinguishable hope lures them. For what they had half believed with religion, fully felt with mysticism, rationally suspected with science and speculatively argued with metaphysics is that some ultimate essence exists as the true nature of things and men, that this essence, being ever and everywhere present, bestows the highest possible significance on the universe, and consequently the first and highest human duty is personally to *know* it. But they perceive that before it can be finally and certainly known in any way it must first be intellectually and speculatively known for what it is and certainly for what it is not. Hence they realize the need of a fitting philosophy—not the philosophy of this or that school, person or country, but solely the philosophy of *truth*. Such a philosophy, if discovered, would act as an indispensable map with which the explorer could then set out to discover the truth for himself.

But why should not the hope of these unconventional few be nothing more than self-deception, an illusion created by personal desire masquerading as profound intuition? Only one answer is possible to this just complaint, but it is an answer which will raise surprised eyebrows and curl sneering lips in Western circles suffering from superiority-complexes justifiable perhaps by sheer ignorance of what men have been doing and thinking in the other hemisphere for the past few thousand years. However, it possesses as much right to our ear as any other, as will be amply demonstrated during the course of this book. It is the bold declaration that the hope of a few has been converted, at infrequent intervals however, into the tested realization of uncommon individuals, and that whatever the public archives of world-thought may say, both the unwritten and written records of India indicate that the truth which the West deems unattainable has already been attained by such individuals in the past and may even now be attained by those who prize it enough to pay its high cost.

When we have witnessed the wonders which the human mind has achieved in changing the earth's face, are we to be so hopeless as to believe that the whole of Nature fears the unveiling of truth and has cunningly plotted to prohibit man from ever understanding the ultimate significance of his life on this planet ? And if anyone asserts that this significance is quite unknowable, then he is unconsciously affirming that he is already aware of what future generations may or may not succeed in knowing—an entirely unjustifiable and unprovable assumption. But why can we not condescend to learn from the ancients what we cannot learn from the moderns ?

The Secret Doctrine of India. An Indian recondite doctrine, which constitutes this philosophy of truth and is placed on a level higher than those of religion and mysticism, has existed during a period which scholars admit cannot be less than five thousand years in extent, but is in fact very much older, for its origin disappears into historically untraceable epochs. It was the traditional possession of a few initiates who formed a closed exclusive circle and who guarded it with great care as being the acme of all their country's wisdom, permitting none save qualified aspirants to have access to it. (Indeed, until the dawn of the modern era a Brahmin who dared reveal that the truth which lies latent in religion becomes actual only in philosophy was liable to be punished.) They transmitted it from generation to generation, but kept it so firmly secret in the process that the stray echoes which floated accidentally or surreptitiously into the larger world quickly became queerly distorted ones. Self-styled and self-deceived representatives appeared in public later and turned the few echoes of pure philosophy which they had heard into religious scholasticism in some cases or into theological mysticism in others. Miscomprehension led to mutilation, and thus converted a grandly universal into a shrunken tribal truth. Nevertheless, even when its true and faithful living representatives all but died out or disappeared from this earth, it maintained an immortal existence in a few rare neglected writings and fragmentarily in several more popular ones. However, erroneous interpretations invariably result from their being read without the proper personal elucidation by a competent teacher, which is indispensable.

It is therefore to be expected that several of the explanations which are being given in these chapters may be denied as unauthentic by most of the learned scholars of present-day India or abused as perversions by the generality of her conventional mystics and yogis or denounced as atheistic by the majority of her religious authorities. Let it be so. We do not address ourselves to them or their numerous followers but to strictly truth-seeking minds. The truth may be hidden from view for countless ages, for it depends on the secret suffrages of a rare few, but it is unkillable; it will outlive like the vast ocean the froth of mortal *opinion* and the foam of prejudiced interests. Although our unconventional presentation of this knowledge is a modern and Western one, its original source is an ancient and Indian one. Both silent texts and living voices which have informed our writing are mostly Indian, supplemented by some Tibetan documents and a personal Mongolian esoteric instruction. A million men may gainsay the tenability of the tenets unfolded here, but none can gainsay the fact that they are Indian tenets, albeit little known, without twisting the most authoritative ancient documents to suit their mediocre minds. If we do not quote those texts here it is because our readers are primarily Western and we do not wish to burden them with the troublesome necessity of exploring exhaustive glossaries for unfamiliar Sanskrit names. Indeed, the very failure to use more than two Sanskrit philosophical terms in this book will be an added charge against it, because it is claimed that certain Indian philosophical ideas are not only incomprehensible to the West but also inexpressible in any traditional Western language. It is quite correct that we have here to deal with ideas that are expressed in Sanskrit by a single word, whereas a string of English words is often required to equate their meaning. But truth existed before the mesmerism of Sanskrit was born; it will surely endure long after that language has vanished. Men must have found or invented expressive terms before it appeared, and as the need presses them perhaps they may do so again.

There will also be vociferous denial and personal opposition from those narrow circles in both the West and East which assume the title of "esoteric" and claim the possession of "occult" wisdom. The confusion and misunderstanding among these half-informed people is pardonable. They believe, and believe rightly, that some of the renowned world-teachers taught a secret doctrine to their closest disciples. They also believe, but believe wrongly, that this doctrine consisted largely of magic and marvel, thaumaturgy and theology. These great masters had better work to do than that. The ultimate purpose of the Indian esotericism was to lead men to detect the essential meaning of human life, to help them gain insight into the real structure of the universe and to point out the grand sun of absolute truth shining on the horizon of all existence.

Even before the victorious wanderings of Alexander brought Oriental and Hellenistic thought into fertilizing contact, fragments of this doctrine had been brought back to Europe by enterprising travellers like Appolonius of Tyana and Pythagoras. In our own epoch fragmentary proofs of the existence of this hidden teaching have crept into the outer world as the growing band of Western Orientalists have given to the world the harvest of their century-long search through India's cultural treasure. They have broken down the walls of secrecy and exclusiveness which have kept the most important books in the possession of a small number of Brahmins. Whoever cares to rummage through them may find for himself numerous indications of a guarded teaching which was hidden from all save those who could fulfil certain difficult conditions and who possessed certain rare qualifications of character and capacity, as well as constant references to the fact that full knowledge could only be obtained *personally* from a competent teacher. Such verification may be found not only in the ancient rule that initiated Brahmins who revealed their knowledge to unqualified outsiders were liable to be punished, but in the English translations now available of Sanskrit texts like the *Upanishads, Bhagavad Gita*, the *Commentaries of Shankara thereon, Vivekachudamani, Brahma Sutras, Panchadasi*, etc.

With these statements we may match the following words of the Buddha, taken from *The Saddharma Pundarika* :

"Superior men of wise understanding guard the doctrine, guard the mystery, and do not reveal it. . . . That knowledge is difficult to understand; the simple, if hearing it suddenly, would be perplexed. . . . I speak according to their reach and capacity; by means of different significances I accommodate my doctrine (to them").

We have already seen how, according to this hidden teaching, there are progressive stages of development through which the seeker after reality must pass. This is plainly stated by the sage Gaudapada in his very ancient book already mentioned in the following words :

"There are three stages of life corresponding to three powers of comprehension—the lower, the middle and the high. . . . It (the yoga of the uncontradictable) is hard to be attained by the yogis who are devoid of the knowledge prescribed in the higher philosophy . . . those other yogis who are also traversing the path but who possess inferior or middling understanding."

Commenting on these sentences the great teacher Shankara observes: "The orders of mankind are also three in number. How? It is because they are endowed with three grades of understanding, i.e. low, middle and high."

Pythagoras, who travelled all the way to India and succeeded in obtaining initiation into the secret wisdom of the Brahmins, divided men into three classes, placing those who loved philosophy in the highest class. It was indeed in this connection that he coined and used the word *philosophy*, and was thus the first European to do so. Ammonius, who founded an important mystical and philosophical school at Alexandria, also divided his disciples into three grades, placing them under oath not to reveal his higher philosophical teachings. His rules were copied from the more ancient Grecian Mysteries of Orpheus, who, according to the historian Herodotus, brought them from India.

It should not be thought that the strong secrecy with which this teaching was once enveloped was entirely wilful. It developed out of four prime factors. The first was a clear perception that if the real truth of religion was made commonly known the whole fabric of public morality would be seriously endangered. The indiscriminate publication of a teaching which described God as He really is and repudiated God as He is commonly imagined to be, and which revealed all rites and sacrifices and priesthoods as unnecessary supernumeraries, would soon destroy the influence of institutional religion amongst the others who need it, and with this destruction would vanish its dependent ethical restraints and moral disciplines. The confused masses of uneducated people would then turn against their accepted idols, but could not grasp the undoubted benefits of higher philosophy in exchange, for the latter would be rejected by them as being too remote. They would be left with a mental vacuum, or at best with a bewildering misconstruction, with the consequence that society would be thrown into bewilderment and social life might revert to the ruthless law of the jungle. It would be harmful to unsettle the minds of the mentally adolescent masses by removing their faith in traditional religion when nothing which they could assimilate could be offered to replace it. Hence the sages therefore carefully and wisely kept their knowledge and confined to the select few who were ready for it, who had become dissatisfied with orthodox religion and wanted something more rational. In addition to the mentally ripe, initiation was also given to kings, statesmen, generals, Brahmin High Priests and others charged with the responsibility of guiding a people's life; thus they were better equipped to carry out their tasks wisely and effectively.

The second factor rested in the aristocratic nature of this philosophy. It was not fit for the sheep equally as for the lions. It could not be carried into the caves and huts of unlettered men and there hope for an understanding welcome. It was so mentally abstruse and so ethically advanced that it lay far beyond popular reach. If it could have found easy acceptance it would have achieved that soon after it was first formulated. It was also self-condemned to obscurity by the law which renders it useless to impose upon the many ideals which only the few can obey. Its tenets could only be mastered by persons with well-developed intellects and noble characters; they were too subtle and therefore too incomprehensible to unripe minds, to the dull and stupid, the petty and the selfish. The early populations chiefly consisted of peasants who laboriously toiled in the fields from dawn till dusk or herdsmen who mechanically followed their flocks. Both classes could not easily develop minds able and willing to consider for long periods the most impersonal abstract topics which were seemingly quite remote from field and home, but they could give credence to simple tales. Therefore they were quite content to take the easy path of believing in whatever their parents had believed. The masses generally were illiterate and uneducated whilst they lived in a world where they had perforce to be quite busy for their livelihood, in order to attend to their immediate physical wants, where the giant octopus of personal activity and family responsibility held them tightly in its tentacles, so tightly that they had neither the will nor the leisure left to explore the subtler significance of their own existence, let alone ultimate knowledge of the more remote universal one. To work, to suffer, to propagate their species and to die made up their limited horizon. They hardly suspected and hardly cared what they were here for in the higher sense. How then could it be rightly hoped that they should understand tenets and appreciate values which were as beyond their orbit as post-graduate university lectures are beyond that of elementary school pupils? The young popular mind must be given time to grow, and it could not be expected in those early times to judge matters which were often beyond the capacity of the cleverest.

Moreover, "Many are called but few are chosen" of the New Testament text has its Hindu equivalent in the sentence "Out of the thousands one man, perchance, struggles to realize truth", of the *Bhagavad Gita*. There is no arbitrary exclusiveness here, but one based on human limitations, for the latter book also says, "I do not reveal myself to all and sundry, most people having their vision clouded by illusion."

The third factor of such secrecy was that the few sages who had mastered this doctrine usually dwelt in small forest hermitages or obscure mountain retreats. This mode of living away from the multitude was not chosen for their own personal need, for they had attained a rock-like impregnability of mind and character which could pass unaffected through the mingled activities of crowded cities, as in the case of Shankara,[1] or could remain unchanged amid the gilded grandeur of royal courts, as in that of Janaka.[2] Such seclusion was chosen for the benefit of those who needed it, i.e. for the restricted handful of pupils who were ripe for such special tuition. The sustained concentration and profound reflection demanded by the goddess of hidden wisdom from her votaries for several years found the least opposition and the least interruption in her last outposts amid the wild solitudes of beautiful forests or the immense grandeur of lonely mountains. So much was this tendency to resort to such places for study recognized that the old texts used by these teachers in their expositions were and are still called *The Forest Doctrines*. It would be a profound error, however, to confuse such deliberate withdrawal by a few from the world for the sake of becoming better equipped through severe study to understand and afterwards usefully serve mankind, with the cheap asceticism which prevails in most of the large, present-day populous caricatures of these tiny vanished hermitages. Sterile lethargy and superstitious speculation now take the place of mental effort and disciplined study. The ancient students in the third degree were men who realized that too long had they been busy like ants without understanding what they were busy about, and that too long had they danced in mad haste like puppets upon the world stage to the tune of someone else's making. They had come to the point when they wanted to know what it all meant, why they were here on this earth

---

[1] Shankara was an ancient philosopher who reached the highest illumination at an extraordinarily early age and then travelled throughout the length and breadth of India to help the ignorant masses and enlighten the cultured few, each class in its own way.

[2] A king who ruled a large State in North-east India and simultaneously studied the hidden doctrine under the Sage Ashtavakra to such good purpose that he personally realized the ultimate essence of things. He was equally at home with the calm sage sitting in a forest or the worried subject petitioning for help in an audience-chamber of the palace or with an army ready for action in the field.

THE HIDDEN PHILOSOPHY OF INDIA

at all, and whither was the fated compulsion of life leading them and others. They felt that they must find some place in their programme for the study of philosophy. Life totally devoid of deeper thought was reckoned unworthy of a man, since it brought him to resemble an animal. In short, they wanted to know truth. Hence they withdrew from the busy world for a time and played the runaways, not in emotional disappointment but in consecration to a serious intellectual task. Such prolonged absence from society, although intended to be a temporary means and not a permanent end, inevitably if gradually withdrew the knowledge gained from the common cultural tradition of society until the very word in Sanskrit which means "The Forest Doctrine" came also to mean "The Hidden Doctrine". Not that the sages always kept themselves hidden, but when they did venture into public notice they taught people only what suited them, i.e. pure religion in most cases and pure mysticism in others.

The fourth factor has already been mentioned. It was the danger that the traditional texts would be misinterpreted and misunderstood, so that gradually falsity would pass as truth and actually be labelled as such by later generations. Those who were ethically and mentally unprepared and undisciplined would assign their own meanings to the texts, would imagine interpretations to suit their personal tastes or temperaments. And this danger was very real, for the texts were highly condensed and needed discursive explanation.

Thus esotericism first arose as a natural phenomenon, although, with the deteriorating effect of time, it was later pushed to extreme limits by human selfishness on the part of the few, and by human indifference on the part of the many. The materials for a history of this slow declension would be not a little instructive concerning departments quite other than that of philosophy, could they only be secured.

Two questions will now come naturally to the lips of the Western critic. Firstly, if such a philosophy has existed in India for so long a time, why has it failed to lift Indian culture to the pinnacle of world-esteem? The reply is that, as already explained, those Indians who possessed this knowledge were too few at all times and well-nigh non-existent in recent times to make much mark on the culture of a vast sub-continent. Yet although their immediate influence was limited to a select and influential circle, *their ultimate and indirect influence has nevertheless been immense.*

The material and linguistic difficulties of cultural communication between India and Europe until the last century or two, together with the esoteric character of this philosophy, accounted for its lack of world-influence, as is proved by the fact that in the rest of Asia with which communication was much more constant and frequent Indian wisdom was always held in the highest esteem. Nevertheless it is a significant thing that the man who introduced the word "philosophy" into European usage was the first noted Greek to adventure forth as far as India in quest of wisdom. Pythagoras was well repaid for the hazards of his long journey. He brought back new and higher conceptions of truth to the West.

The second question which might reasonably be asked is why, if this doctrine was kept scrupulously hidden from the masses for so many centuries, it should now be brought forward so openly and made plain to the populace. This may be met with a threefold answer. The revelation is not a new one at all, because it has been going on ever since the force of British arms prepared the way for British, French and German scholars as long ago as the eighteenth century. Text after text has been taken by them, in the early days as part of military loot, but since then by orderly purchase from the exclusive Brahminical circles which had hitherto jealously guarded the books. These have now been made available for the benefit of a wider world. Numerous villages have been combed by purchasing agents and numerous manuscripts hidden away for centuries through fear of destructive Muhammedan conquerors or neglected through sheer inability to understand them have been brought to light from their boxes or burrows of concealment. Some of these texts have been translated into European languages and can be studied by anyone, whilst most have been carefully gathered and preserved in their original condition in excellent libraries like those of the Secretary of State for India, the Mysore, Baroda and Travancore State Oriental Collections, the Royal Asiatic Society and so on, where they are now accessible to scholars. Two hundred years ago few of these works could be got at by anyone who did not belong to a small *élite* of Indian intelligentzia. Today several hundred different ancient philosophical works can be got at quite freely by European or American students. No new revelation is here being made, therefore, but a revelation which began one and three-quarter centuries ago is being continued. The presentation which is being offered here will, however, probably be regarded by most readers as a new and essentially modern restatement and certainly as an unconventional one. Nevertheless what is a novel element in these pages is that its principles are partly based on a few books which the floodtide of Western Oriental scholarship has flowed past and ignored, because, their especial importance and difficult meaning were not grasped

THE HIDDEN PHILOSOPHY OF INDIA

and partly on a personal instruction which is perhaps unique in the whole of present-day India.

The further reply to the critic's question is that the chief prohibition of the unveiling of the hidden philosophy in former times was accounted for by its danger to the authority of orthodox religion, and consequently of morality. Since those days so many agencies have been at work undermining this authority that it fulfils its functions of protecting morality somewhat feebly. Conditions are different from the days when Socrates could be put to death for weakening religious faith. The minds of the people are now unsettled and their religious supports damaged. The position today is so altered as to be somewhat paradoxical, for the hidden philosophy, instead of destroying what is left of religion, could save it through its symbolical exegesis and through its justification to educated minds of the place and purpose of institutional religion. Its revealment now would hardly affect the masses because they would ignore it as they ignore all abstract philosophy, or where they did not ignore it they would fail to understand its subtleties.

The third factor which has provided the occasion for a franker, bolder, fuller and freer explication of the higher philosophy than ever before is quite exceptional and the most important of all. Since the days when its teachings were first formulated and concealed the world has greatly changed and mankind with it. The details of such changes as affect the position of this philosophy have been fully given in the opening pages of this book.

CHAPTER V

THE PHILOSOPHICAL DISCIPLINE

THE simple fact that the average person permits whatever desire for knowledge he may possess to be overborne by dislike arising from his superficial impression of philosophy or by a feeling of fear of the abstract itself unfits him to pursue such study. For there are certain cardinal characteristics required of every man before he can even be permitted to cross its very threshold. Nobody can hope to philosophize with profit who lacks seven psychological qualities. They are necessary because they represent the means whereby he may hope successfully to reach his end. An explorer who wishes to penetrate into difficult new territories, who will have to cross mountains, rivers and deserts on his journey, should, if he knows his business at all, first prepare for the expedition by obtaining a proper equipment. He who seeks to explore the hidden philosophy and penetrate into the new territory of truth must likewise look to the nature and quality of his own personal equipment before his mind may venture forth into an activity which is likely to try and test his capacity to the uttermost.

It is not anybody and everybody who can undertake such an expedition. Those who will fulfil the preliminary conditions can alone hope for final success. These conditions are not externally imposed but are inherent in the very nature of the apprehension of truth, and therefore their fulfilment is inexorable. Nor are they manufactured arbitrarily by any exacting teacher. They are imposed by Nature herself and accepted by long tradition. However, nobody need trouble himself with them unless he or she belongs to the earnest few who seek to know the ultimate secret of life at any cost. All other persons can comfortably ignore them and take their own time and ease in life. Emerson has well said: "Take what thou wilt, but pay the price." These words fit quite squarely at this point of our quest.

In the Western countries it has always been open for anyone to enter upon a philosophical study, but in Asia the aspirant was first required to show or acquire a modicum of suitable capacity for the task. Until both aptitude and attitude were acceptable he was

THE PHILOSOPHICAL DISCIPLINE

regretfully refused instruction. It did not matter to the custodians of wisdom whether he held any religious faith or none, whether he was an atheist or a Christian or a Muslim, but it did matter that he should get psychologically fit. This difference is an important one and helps to account for the superior result and notable success obtained by the Asiatics. Fichte, however, must have caught a glimpse of the need for this disciplinary preparation, because he once said: "What kind of philosophy a man chooses depends ultimately upon the kind of man he is." The successful assimilation of the higher truth will be in exact proportion to one's personal qualification.

After the reading of the present chapter has been completed the student should earnestly examine himself at leisure in a strictly objective manner to ascertain how far the desirable characteristics are present within his mental make-up. The examination must be conducted on a basis of the strictest honesty. The results of this leisurely survey may startle him if he is earnest, shame him if he is sensitive, or enlighten him if he is eager for self-knowledge. One of the first things it will show him is the extent to which he is swayed by harmful instincts, well-known prejudices, unknown bias, hidden fears, foolish hopes, unjust attitudes, moods of the moment, powerful hallucinations or deep-seated illusions; and how he gropes in a fog of conflicting motives and powerful subconscious influence. Thus he discovers what he really is! Such a revelation will not be pleasant. If he is really unfitted for philosophy this moment will become the crucial one, when he will irritably cast the book aside and drop the subject altogether. But if he is made of the right stuff he will take to the needed discipline and gradually bring about the desired change.

The first concern of a philosophical tutor is to knock down the student's idols made with feet of clay, or to tell him plainly what he is really doing when he worships them. For the tutor is in the unpleasant position of an asylum doctor who has sometimes humoured the lunatics who regard themselves as being what they are not, such as Napoleon, by agreeing with them, but who eventually deems the time ripe to tell them brusquely they are not what they imagine themselves to be! At such an unpleasant moment it is invariably the experience of the doctor to become the most hated man in the institution!

The knowledge that they find themselves in a similar position—for few persons like to be told that they are not competent to receive truth—is an additional reason why the tutors of the hidden philosophy kept it secret for so many centuries. In fact, from the standpoint of philosophy few people are properly balanced and really normal, and hence it takes it as axiomatic that the aspirant has to be treated and cured of this unbalanced condition which he shares in common with millions. For philosophy seeks to put its students at the correct angle whence to view the pageant of cosmic existence *as it really is*, bereft of glamour and deception. This cannot be done until the intellect is well clarified and the strength of its hidden complexes vanishes. The task of re-ordering one's mind is likely to be a painful process. The work of clearing away the falsities and foolishnesses which beset it is likely to leave some emptiness behind.

It is essential to find out what forces are acting in the mind and affect its reasoning and its outlook. Once the student unearths the real bases of his actions and attitudes he can philosophize freely and fearlessly, but not before. He must ruthlessly unmask by searching criticism his hidden motives, his unconscious desires, his darkly covered bias. The complexes which fill the subconscious layer of the human mind and which he neither recognizes nor names are partly responsible for his inability to apprehend truth. A most important department of preliminary activity is therefore to dig out these mental weeds and present them to the clear light of consciousness.

Once he becomes aware of the secret processes of his mind and the secret workings of his wishes he will discover that many false beliefs, many emotional distortions, cling to it out of its long past, acting as powerful detriments of right conduct and preventing the clear insight into truth. He will find that he carries a heavy burden of illusions and rationalizations which resist the entry of real knowledge. Only through such a thorough psychological understanding into what is going on behind the scenes of his conscious personal life can liberation come and prepare the way for further steps on the ultimate path. He must strip naked his innermost characteristics, taking and making no excuses, but boldly seeking to understand the bitterest truths about himself. He must see himself as he really is, exposing self to self. Such is the delicate psychological operation needed to detect for removal from the process of thought and action all those tendencies, complexes, hallucinations and rationalizations which prevent the entry of truth into the mind or drive it along wrong roads. Until these influences are detected by analysis and exposed by interrogation they will not cease their maleficent operation. These complexes come to dominate the man and retard his free use of reason. He has to humble himself from the beginning by not hesitating to admit that his character, both in its open and concealed phases, is a deformed, crippled and unbalanced thing. In

THE PHILOSOPHICAL DISCIPLINE

short, he has to study a little psychology before he can profitably study philosophy. He has to analyse his emotions, examine the interaction of feeling and reason, perceive how he forms conceptions of ideas and things, and tackle the problem of unconscious motivation.

When a particular idea, for instance, recurs constantly and irresistibly to the mind and finally becomes a deep-seated obsession it interferes with the free play of thinking and thus renders accurate philosophical reflection impossible. Or when a man makes a mental reservation in favour of certain beliefs in a particular subject or field of interest and will not allow his faculties to work fully therein his mind is then divided into two or more insulated departments which are never permitted to interact logically on each other. We may then have the spectacle of complete credulity in one department and critical reasoning in the other. He is really unbalanced in one department and yet quite balanced in the other. The excellence of the latter hides the defect of the former. The fault does not lie in inability to think properly but in a particular complex which interferes at a certain point. Again, when a concession must be made to reason for the sake of self-respect or for the respect of others we witness the peculiar process of the person finding a conscious basis for his conclusions which is quite other than the real one. Thus he deceives himself and perhaps others by such rationalizations of egoistic wishes and unjustifiable prejudices. Other difficulties are delusions which assume such a fixed character as to afford an impregnable front to reason. Their persistence usually appears in the domain of political, religious, social or economic belief.

All these may be classed as diseases of the mind and until they are cured they prevent a healthy working of those faculties which are called into play when we seek truth. For they determine the processes of thinking and action.

Such is the self-revelation which awaits the student. It will not be pleasant, but if he will have the courage to accept it like a medicine it will be purifying. There can be no cure as long as he is not aware that he is diseased.

It is difficult to arrive at an accurate analysis by oneself, and here the aid of an expert philosopher, i.e. a sage, is always useful when obtainable, but such men are exceedingly rare. The competent philosopher sees what complexes are operative in a man after a little conversation and without the need of going through the lengthy and sometimes fantastic processes of psycho-analysis. Moreover, he will see them much more clearly than the psycho-analyst because they will themselves suffer from a different set of complexes so long as they have not undergone the philosophic discipline! Such an examination can be most effectively carried out only by one who is himself mentally "free".

However, these pages should assist every earnest reader in self-examination to some degree, whilst the constant pursuit of the lofty ideal of truth will generally do much to cure complexes. No genuine teacher can effect the final self-overcoming for the student; he must bring it about by his own free choice and by his own firm effort; but the constructive criticism of such a teacher is usually illuminating, whilst his personal presence is always inspiring.

This introspective dive into the depths of the aspirant's character and capacity is a venture which must be coolly and boldly made. It will inevitably meet with innate resistances, instinctive oppositions and emotional impediments which seek to check his descent. These arise naturally out of inborn tendencies as well as environment, education or circumstances. They are mostly masked weaknesses or psychological repressions. Nevertheless, as he becomes aware of them by calm self-criticism he should find in their very presence—if he is philosophically minded—a special incentive to correct them and secure right adjustment to life. This demands great intellectual honesty in refusing to evade realities and greater intellectual courage in overcoming obscurantism; it is therefore a task for a mental hero who is not ashamed to learn that he needs altering and not afraid to contribute voluntarily to such a reform. It is an inner metabolistic process which gives temporary pain but leads to permanent health. And this is the only way in which he can fit himself for the mastery of the hidden philosophy.

To persuade people to challenge or change their old habits of thinking is immensely hard, for human nature is conservative at heart. And these old habits stubbornly re-assert themselves at every opportunity. Yet if a man finds that these psychological qualifications seem far beyond his reach, and this standard of intellectual conduct far too exalted, he need not be mortified. The remarkable clinical results achieved by psycho-therapeutic treatment point the way to undreamed-of powers of self-improvement which lie latent in the human mind. None of us has reached the limit of his capacity. Insight always accumulates when we search for new horizons. Many a man might become a philosopher if he would but bestir himself, if he would pay the price in persistent unrelenting effort to break the spell of old fallacies, and if he would take firm hold of a living transforming faith in his own progressive possibilities.

Years ago we used to think that every man was born with a set character, a fixed degree of ability, and a limited amount of mental power and that he could never exceed these limits. Today the penetrating analysis of psychology has banished the myth of the last phrase into the limbo where it deserves to remain. Just as the power of physical culture is nowadays universally acknowledged to be a definite one, just as we know that our muscles can be made stronger and the blood circulation quickened by daily exercise, so we know now that our mental ability and natural characteristics can be developed along precise lines, if we set about the task in the right way.

"A ten-thousand-mile journey starts with the first step," says a Chinese proverb.

No wise man will despair, therefore, over the perplexities and difficulties of studying this philosophy. Nobody has really failed until he has given up. Why should we not today do what other men intend to do tomorrow? Or—to alter Milton's line: they are not served who only stand and wait. We may remake our mentality if we will. For the theories of psychology and the actualities of experience clearly exhibit the fact that the capacity of the mind is extraordinarily flexible and expansive; it can grow beyond recognition when patient effort to understand the apparently incomprehensible is conjoined with hope, which is the last of human possessions, as wisdom is the best. Therefore we must ungrudgingly discipline ourselves mentally and mould ourselves ethically to arouse the right attitude for the arduous journey which lies before us. This is our preliminary step.

If this book presents the world with a doctrine which demands an unusual amount of sustained attention merely to follow it, which requires an intensity of concentrated thought on the part of its students such as few seem to possess, and which holds up an ideal of selflessness that will seem to most men as quite unattainable, the reply in defence may be taken from Thoreau that "we are not the less to aim at the summits, though the multitude does not ascend them".

Nor does this mean that we are required to possess the required characteristics to perfection; it means that we are to make an inner exertion to develop them to an extent sufficient to enable us to grasp the elementary and earlier principles of philosophy at least, and to keep the seven qualifications ever before us as personal ideals. Thus the narrow chink of intellectual light may grow and grow until it becomes a broad beam, illuminating much that was formerly indistinct. A humble beginning may suffice to start with, for by the time we have mastered more of these principles we will have experienced

G

the subtle charm and extraordinary fascination which lie in the soul, deeply hidden behind philosophy's forbidding face. We shall then yield willingly to its demand upon us for further self-improvement in such qualifications, even though we may realize that their fuller acquisition will not be a swift matter nor a simple one. We shall thus unfold the characteristics stage by stage, not all at once.

Most of us begin as sinners; we may only hope to end one day as sages. But there is an immense difference between the man who wallows contentedly in his sins and the man who lifts himself up dissatisfied and discontented after every occasion of sinning. The first is bogged and aimless, whereas the second is not only moving but possesses right direction. For the pure joy of ennobling character, sharpening intelligence and gaining strength as we proceed is one of the uncounted profits of philosophy. A mere glimpse at the qualities needed for such a chastening study will prove that they can be no mere polish to show off a man's intellect nor even a cultural ornament; they demand much from a man but in the end they give more, for they possess plenty of bearing on this business of making both material livelihood and eternal life. They lead to a balanced understanding of the whole of life, not for theoretical display but for effective and sensible action. It has already been shown that the practical justification of religion is its advocacy of the good life; it shall later be shown that the practical justification of philosophy is its advocacy of the best life. Even if this study does nothing more, the practical and psychological aims it sets before us will have laid the firm mental and moral foundation for an exceptional personality, who is sure sooner or later to be marked out for superiority in one sphere or another. It will become a safe guide to proper action and a satisfaction of the purest and most exalted feelings. We shall undergo a profound transformation for the better of attitude, outlook and habits. Thus those sacrificial hours which are given to philosophic discipline or study are not given in vain. The deity whom we thus worship well rewards its faithful devotees.

It would be easy for the inexperienced to undervalue the necessity of these seven psychological qualifications, but the striving philosopher knows that they are his most precious attributes. With them he is rendered ready for enlightenment and may hope to realize life's supreme goal, but without them—never!

The Truth Above All. The first characteristic is none other than a strong yearning to find truth. The aspirant must learn how to go down on his knees for freedom from ignorance. No Asiatic sage of olden days would even touch on the alphabet of philosophy to any enquirer if he noticed that this yearning was absent or extremely feeble. One cannot set a water-sodden wood pile ablaze until it is somewhat dry; neither can any honest teacher take a satisfied worldling, to whom the world needs no questioning and looks good enough as it is, and take his mind to the higher regions of being. This yearning is a higher octave of the same deep-felt longing to get at the hidden heart of life which mystics call "the manifestation of Grace", only here it rises from compelling emotion to calm thought as it takes a more advanced form and demands ultimate truth rather than temporary satisfaction. Not many are born with such an attribute of loving truth for its own sake, for ordinarily the mind does not want to exert itself to find it. Those others who acquire it later in life usually do so out of the depths of agonized suffering, tragic loss or disappointment with religion or mysticism. It may also arise from personal contact with a genuine sage, when the outward demonstration of its *benefits*, especially in critical times, may become both plainly apparent and mentally attractive.

The desire for truth really means the desire to get rid of ignorance. No truly thoughtful man can rest satisfied like a merely sensual animal, but after initial wonder or doubt about the cosmic spectacle must at some time or other strive to tear aside the veil that hides life's meaning. He must be bent on the removal of this ignorance; if he dogmatizes that truth is unattainable he thereby becomes unqualified. Let him strive first, and never desist from such striving, if he wishes to dogmatize correctly on this point.

And whoever is merely or momentarily curious likewise renders himself unfit, for he too will soon fall by the wayside. Wisdom must win a man as her ardent disciple or not at all. He is best fitted for philosophy who is attracted to it by a burning passion for truth rather than by an ascetic repugnance to the world. Truth demands a deep devotion before revealment. Very few want it so strongly. Most men and women may be interested in it as a hobby or for polite intellectual discussion, but stop short at permitting it to tincture their lives. Therefore they are hoodwinked and given shoddy substitutes, because just as in everyday transactions for material things they get only what they pay for. They are soon tested on this quest, anyhow. Those who are unconsciously insincere or whose motives are quite mediocre or whose aims are limited will let their love of lesser but more tangible things outweigh their love of intangible truth. For they will be brought to consider deeply and deliberately whether by time or by teacher not only if they want the highest truth but also if they want it irrespective of its unpleasantness or pleasantness. The right kind of seeker will pursue it to the end and then accept it whatever its taste, be it like poison or like nectar, for he has understood the implication and felt the force of Bacon's saying that "No pleasure is comparable to the standing upon the vantage-ground of truth." Whoever yearns to hear the veiled goddess's call and to follow her wherever she be found, whether in unfamiliar lands or in unfamiliar thoughts, becomes her beloved votary.

Hold On and Hope On. But the goddess will not walk in like an apparition to visit him; he must go in restless search of her. It will be quite natural therefore for anyone who feels such a strong truthward yearning to strive in consequence to possess the second qualification, which is an enduring determination to take up the quest of truth and persevere, come what may, until the goal is reached. The quest is inevitably a long and steep hill which must be climbed with struggle and effort, rather than a flat road where progress is easy and predictable. This single factor of unabated endurance amid all the perplexity and darkness which envelop the aspirant is most essential if he is not to tire in discouragement and forgo the quest. It is essential because it gives him the propulsive force which he needs to drive him onwards through all difficulties, across all disadvantages and against all obstacles, rendering him strong enough indeed to carry through to the bitter end. Even he who does feel the truth-yearning must guard it well, for he is swimming against the stream of superficial present-day environments—a hard task but a manageable one, because whoever is really in earnest receives an undaunted courage born of despair.

Defeatist moods of mind and heart will inevitably blow over him and go, but the determination to carry on with the quest must remain. Mental chameleons who change the colour of their goal with every year cannot suit this path. The seeker must be patient enough to endure steadfastly both trials and temptations, troubles and joys, and yet remain as patiently determined as before. Tests and ordeals will beset his whole worldly path and constantly assail his mind.

Let us return to our analogy of an explorer and say that he has set out to cross Northern Africa from coast to coast. If he were to stop short at any point of his journey and turn back because of lack of water or hostile environment or attacks by sand-flies, snakes and mosquitoes he would never reach the other coast. The seeker after truth must be no less keen within his own sphere of intellectual exploration and refuse to turn aside from pressing onward in his settled direction. He must know how to continue with studies that yield no immediate fruit and how to wait for the favoured moment of illumination. None of us is entirely our own master and all must await the proper time, the destined hour of higher comprehension, and yet we must not slack in our work whilst waiting. Time is thus a factor which must be allowed for. Colonel Lindbergh's leap across the Atlantic was in its day a feat which was sung to the skies in which he flew. But it came only after he had already practised seven thousand lesser trips. The glamour of philosophic achievement gives vivid colour to a historic name, but beneath the story of success runs an unseen river of persistent and patient day-by-day toil. The revelation of truth must grow little by little within oneself as it draws the mind to a gradual transfiguration; albeit its final realization may occur with startling suddenness.

We must fight our own weakness of purpose. The real struggle in life is the struggle of man against himself. It is the one which fewest enter because it asks so much from him. Yet it is the only one which is really worth while. Nothing great or grand can be obtained by mere wanting. To get one must be prepared to give—oneself! There was once a wandering teacher in Galilee who noticed the common inclination to feebleness in his own followers. He had to tell them: "Those that *do* my words shall know my doctrine."

The determined mind achieves most. When the pressure-valve on a steam boiler begins to rise a greater volume of energy begins to come out of the engine. When the same wires which carried a feeble current of electricity suddenly begin to carry a high voltage, results improve as quickly. These things are parables which man should heed.

Finally, philosophic determination to ascertain what is truth refuses to confuse defeat with failure. From the first it draws the dividends of warning or wisdom, but the second it never acknowledges.

Think! The third required characteristic is thinking-power, an intelligence sufficiently vigorous to weigh the relative importance of things or validity of statements correctly and not merely conventionally. Philosophy demands perspective It seeks to see things as they really are. This implies a certain mental alertness which is awake to the trite but true saying that things are not always what they appear to be. The false often appears or is made to appear as the true. Reasoning should be so independent that it produces a stubborn refusal to accept any opinion merely because everyone else holds it. The herd sinks in the flood of the opinions and theories of others because it is held mentally by erroneous beliefs, seeming realities and misleading appearances, but the Thinker stands firm. The way out from this bondage is right reflection, deep analysis and constant enquiry—all combined in quest of truth. This study involves much new and not at all easy thinking; our generation may not assimilate much of it but the pioneer minds certainly can. An intense intelligence is required. We must think, we must act, not for ourselves but for truth. Such cultivation of rational insight will facilitate the understanding of the philosophy.

Nor is this all the implication. Equally important is the keen capacity to distinguish what is ephemeral from what is eternal, the things of a day from the things of a lifetime, the passing show of material existence from the relatively more permanent mental factors. It might be called the sixth sense, which knows what is genuinely fundamental in the game of living. It should so act that it leads to a constant exercise of discernment between those values which are enduring and those which are merely temporary. And it should so love strict fact rather than pleasant fancy that the determination to discriminate the real from the illusory, which is most essential throughout the study and practice of philosophy, gradually becomes uppermost.

Philosophy cannot become intelligible without much mental effort; it is hard to follow—so hard that the effort is often like trying to walk on a logical tight-rope without losing balance—and those who are unable or unwilling to put the effort forth will necessarily find parts of this book a puzzle no matter how plain its language. The intellectually timid and the mentally weak often excuse themselves by saying that such enquiries are unnecessary. This is because they do not know the place of truthful thought in life; consequently they do not understand that to stimulate thought is no less needed than to inform it.

To play with a few problems in order to be able to air some witty remarks to admiring society does not make anyone a philosopher. He alone who will think matters out to their final end, who will hunt every question down to its central issue and not hesitate at any point because he comes counter to a notion held by all other men, who will ruthlessly apply the conclusion he makes to the life he leads, is worthy of the name of truth-seeker. Whoever is unwilling to examine a tenet in order to find out whether it be true or not, merely because its alien face is completely unfamiliar, has no right to receive truth. And whoever is deterred from enquiring into a doctrine because it is not held within his own country or among his own people, but hails from another land and from people of another complexion, is equally unworthy of this priceless gift. Reason knows no geographical frontiers. In this sphere of philosophical research the introduction of political bias or racial prejudice against tenet or teacher is utterly fatal to success.

The ordinary man is impatient of sustained reflection and is governed by immediate impressions; he jumps too quickly to conclusions, often basing them on superficial and misleading appearances. Thus he remains bound by ignorance. This weakness is a defect which can be overcome by discipline. Such a mind needs to deepen and sharpen its own character, and train itself into habits of travel beneath surfaces. No mind which refuses to undergo such strengthening and training is capable of the undertaking involved in philosophy, the quest of what *is*. Sharpness of understanding is needed to take away all those things which are not true, all illusions, and to clear away confusions. Moreover, its need will also become apparent when in the further volume we shall study the significance of sleep and dream.

The ultimate ideal is a mind as keen as a Toledo sword-blade that the steely thrust of its thought may effectively pierce delusions and fancies, sentiments and superstitions. The most cherished and cheerful notions may have to vanish when dissected by such a keen blade, for it will be discovered as this study unfolds that nearly all men harbour plenty of illusions merely because the movement of their mind is faulty and tardy, and because its edge is blunt.

Inner Detachment. When the mind has thus been sharpened it will be better predisposed to unfold the fourth characteristic. This is a settled attitude of inner detachment from both the unpleasant episodes and pleasant attractions which constitute the nadir and zenith of mundane living. Whatever misfortune the turning wheel of destiny may bring to the forefront of the student's life, he must cultivate a hidden indifference, and whatever enjoyment or desires rule the hour he should not be so strongly attached to them that he cannot let them quickly go if need be. If he wants to secure a philosophic perspective he must stand on the ground of such indifference, because his attachments create mental favouritism and thus prevent his reaching a fair impartial attitude when weighing evidence, pursuing enquiries or delivering judgment. Moreover, such a qualification is needed so that the seeker may not be drawn aside from his quest by temporary allurements. For were he so attached to the ordinary experience of the world that it meant everything to him, there would not exist any cause for embarking on this philosophic quest.

An intelligence which is not stupefied by social convention, personal status, inordinate ambition, hilarious hedonism or unsatisfied desires cannot help discerning that life upon this rotating globe is a changing flux of both favourable and unfavourable events *from which none are exempt.* And if this same intelligence is sufficiently sharp it will also perceive that everything, including itself, is perishable, everything is evanescent. All worldly attractions, all earthly possessions, all human relationships, all sensual pleasures as well as their objects may die or disappear tomorrow. Therefore the philosophic student is required to cultivate a correct attitude towards their seductive glamour, which is to be neither one of blind infatuation nor of total repulsion. He must assign an accurate value to this fitful panorama of the passing days if he is not to deceive himself. When he sees that everything is relative and everyone is transient he will understand that they can yield only a relative and transient happiness to him at the best. He must understand that he is not safe if he regards what is fleeting as the end-all and be-all of his incarnation. He must therefore become serious enough to use his intelligence in the uncommon direction of seeking for something that does not die and does not pass away. Whether such a thing can be found or not is a different matter, but the quest of philosophy is for a reality which is enduring and an absolute truth which lies beyond mere human opinion. But not only does he need his intelligence to see all this but he also needs his courage to admit it. If he can travel so far—and few can—he is then prepared to take up the attitude advocated here—a certain stoic detachment from the fluctuations of individual fate and an ascetic equanimity towards pleasure.

There are other minds, however, which may not be so sharp as to see the need of such an attitude and yet they will arrive at it all the same, as the outcome of certain experiences through which they have passed. In them it arises out of great suffering, bitter loss, sudden shock, unsuccessful striving or profound danger. Such persons are often quite rich in earthly experience. When they are bored with paying court to the casual and leaving the fundamental far behind; when they are tired of fretting through the dark years and philandering through the bright ones, they unconsciously form this philosophic characteristic for themselves. The abrasions to women's hearts caused by unkind or unfaithful men, no less than the shadowed emptiness which fickle women bring into the hearts of infatuated men, may eventually cause this qualification to appear. Thus intense suffering injects some indifference towards life into human blood.

The world-wide sorrows and sufferings which have bitterly wounded our century have provided some lesser initiation into such an attitude. When people observe that the existence of their possessions, properties and persons is no longer secure, but may disappear on the morrow; when they have passed through the anguish of losing the substance of their wealth or the presence of beloved relatives, they tend to lose something of their attachment to worldly life. They realize how transient and unstable it is, and the days of dreadful chaos and continued insecurity become less attractive in their eyes. Thus sorrow leads to understanding. Every tear becomes a tutor.

It would be easy for the nature of such a quality to be misunderstood by those who have never felt it or have never seen it in action or having seen it manifested theoretically taken it to be what it is not. It does not imply ascetic running away from human life nor turning away from personal activity nor even estrangement from common enjoyments, but something quite different. A mere temporary disgust due to passing affliction will not suffice. Something profounder is needed—a veritable casting-off of invisible chains. Indeed, he who possesses it may outwardly partake of all the same routine existence of family obligations, work and pleasure as others, but deep down in his heart he will evaluate it at its true worth as being transitory and unabiding.

This characteristic need not divorce him from practical and personal life—he will carry out all their requirements to the letter and his external relationships may even exist as before—but he will form a different estimate of them from the common one. He may act in the same way as others, but will not get lost in his action. He may appreciate the delight of comfortable environments and other attractions and he may know how to enjoy them no less than others. Nevertheless, he does not pin his hopes for happiness entirely to such a basis, for he has a clear sense of the transitory nature of all things. In this sense only may it be said that he abstains mentally.

Nor does this characteristic mean a weakening of worldly capacities. It is to be interpreted correctly only when its emphasis is placed in the background of the mind rather than the forefront. The man will be as firm and matter-of-fact in his practical dealings as any business executive, but duty will motivate him more than desire.

If there is no room here for a facile optimism about life, neither is there place for gloomy pessimism. The goal is too grand for that. The ordinary person may mask his bitter disappointment or secret suffering behind a polite smile or a pungent cynicism, but the philosopher needs no such mask, and even if he has a deeply serious purpose in life he knows that he can be serious without being solemn. He may still like to laugh. He will always hope that the time will never come when he shall be unable to laugh at himself. But should such an unfortunate mishap befall him, if he is a true philosopher he will ask his friends but one favour: to wrap him up neatly in a winding shroud and bear him away quickly to the nearest crematorium! For he would rather not afflict the world with one who thinks so highly of self that he has forgotten that his present birth is but one out of millions, and who thinks so meanly of reality that he cannot play with his surface life as cheerfully as a child plays with hoop and stick. And if in his search after truth by the power of strict reasoning he slay all the poetry of his soul, neglect and lose all the fine nuances of feeling which come to him through the arts and Nature, he is undone. If it brings him to the point where a forest becomes a collection of so many thousand trees and nothing more, nothing of mellow peace and classic beauty, he is undone. If he cannot linger for a few minutes every evening to pause amid his business and watch the play of lovely colours as the sun dies, he is also undone. The zest for accurate measurement by the logical mind need not displace the appreciation of charm and atmosphere by the sensitive heart; there is plenty of room in life for both.

Thus it is both possible and preferable that the philosophic insight which produces detachment should rest alongside the full growth of human culture and human activity. Not the loss of passion or a maimed zest for life is desirable so much as the cultivation of profound detachment deep within those moments of passion or zest.

Concentration, Calmness and Reverie. The need of gaining the fifth characteristic has already been mentioned in an earlier chapter. This consists of ability to practise the technique of meditation. The general aspects of this technique have been fully dealt with in the writer's other books, and here it will suffice to note only three points which the practitioner needs to emphasize specially if he is also pursuing the philosophic quest. He has here no concern with the other consequences of yoga. Indeed, occult experiences, extraordinary visions and similar abnormal happenings will only hinder his progress in philosophy if he pays them undue attention. They have no

THE PHILOSOPHICAL DISCIPLINE

importance here, however encouraging they often are on the mystic path. The first of these points is the power to regulate the thoughts and master attention, and then to concentrate fully in any required direction. The mind possesses a natural tendency to run in various directions and to flit from one subject to another, on account of the pressure of emotional attachments, physical environment or imperfect education. This tendency can be stopped and corrected by the psychological discipline of meditation. The power to become completely absorbed in the subject in hand can then be unfolded. The meaning of such concentration is extreme attentiveness to the topic under consideration, never permitting it to lapse through laziness or fatigue. The mind must move only where the will directs it. Much may be accomplished through this single power of concentration. It is a steady force which, when directed towards any purpose or obstacle, overcomes such resistance. The acetylene welding-ray—which melts the hardest steel—is a fit example of physical concentration. Similarly the faculty of fixing attention at will and retaining it ultimately helps to burn a way through the hardest intellectual problems.

The second factor of philosophic importance to be sought after in the mystic discipline is equipoise—a calm, steady and even disposition of mind which will withstand shocks. When passions rage strongly within a man, when anger flares up too frequently or when desires threaten to submerge him, he becomes unbalanced. And when powerful emotional complexes are opposed by adequate reasons, when domestic troubles or business anxieties unremittingly distract his attention, or when the temperament is unstable and vacillating, flitting from one thing to another, mental conflicts must inevitably arise and harass a man. In all these conditions steadying of the mind may be effected by meditation practice. Through its aid a better equilibrium between feelings and thoughts, between thoughts and thoughts, between passion and reason; may be tentatively evolved and fitfully maintained. Permanent equilibrium, however, can be established only by completing a course in philosophic discipline. Nevertheless, meditation in the hands of a moderately advanced practitioner can quickly remove violence and agitation of the mind, as well as pacify its conflicts. Excited feelings can be subdued, the strength of wrath reduced, and hot desires that distort life put aside by resort to the discipline of meditation. This settles the mind down again and restores its evenness and balance, at any rate for the time being. The Indian yogis call such a condition of resistance to momentary passions and of general self-control "level-headedness". We may prefer to call it "inner peace".

The third point to be noted is the unfoldment of reverie. This is of profound importance and the highest value when, in the more advanced stages, the student attempts to gain the final fruits of his philosophic effort, the realization of ultimate truth. It is that which appears in the constant endeavour of the mystic to cease external activity, to shut out the distractions of his material environment, to stop the operation of his five senses, and to develop a condition of complete introversion. The latter is akin to the profound abstractiveness and creative moods noted in the lives of famous geniuses. This sustained inwardness may consummate itself even in trance, but the essential factor is the capacity to re-orientate the attention at will from the world of concrete things to the world of abstract thoughts. Many a practical man of business or industrial affairs possesses a keen sharp mind but is yet unable to move amid abstract ideas because he can apply his attention only to concrete objects. This capacity for subtle introspection is an unusual one.

It is now convenient to explain a matter in connection with mysticism and yoga which was out of place in the earlier treatment devoted to it, and which will throw some light upon the formula-problem raised in the first chapter. Every philosopher must possess these three qualities of concentrativeness, calmness, and reverie. In these respects he will be a mystic, but most mystics are not philosophers. Mysticism may now be viewed as a disciplinary stage through which the would-be philosopher must pass if he finds, as most do, that he lacks such qualifications. The difficulty of completely concentrating the thoughts in ordinary life, which is so familiar and so personal, is well known ; how much greater must it be in philosophic research, which is so remote and impersonal? The difficulty of such research soon tires the unwilling mind unless it has previously developed the strength which comes through such discipline. And without the complete concentration which mobilizes the mind to a single-pointed end, and which keeps out extraneous thoughts, resistance will beset the effort to grasp either the meanings of philosophic problems or to move onward to their proper solutions. The lengthy trains of thought in which the philosophical student is forced to indulge absolutely demand the presence of this quality. His mind must be competent to take them up without being shaken from its purpose by extraneous ideas or disturbing environments.

Furthermore, the composure of mental peace is an essential prelude to the undisturbed investigation of truth. The man who

THE PHILOSOPHICAL DISCIPLINE

cannot keep conflicts and anxieties out of his mind will not be able to keep his attention uninterruptedly fixed on philosophic matters. The poise needed for such reflection can be got from meditation and will help to prevent emotional interferences, remove ideological obstructions and permit the student to approach his study with a clearer mind. It is a commonplace fact that excitement darkens intelligence, that sound well-balanced judgment cannot be delivered when the mind is full of wrath ; but both are dismissed or disappear under the calming influence of yoga. Even if a man possess sharp understanding he may injure its philosophic value if he uses it when he is angry. The mind must be emotionally free for study. When hostility to another man or an injury done to oneself rankles within it, or when it is excessively discontented, it becomes distracted and to that extent unfit for profound reflection.

It will later become necessary in the course of this quest to defeat the naïve reports of the bodily senses and penetrate to a region they know not of. This task is difficult because the average man more or less believes his mind is imprisoned in the body and unconsciously handicaps himself by this belief, which will be proved erroneous. If this task is to be achieved it can be done only by first detaching the mind from its self-imprisonment and thus rendering it flexible enough to find that region. The habits of introspection and abstraction engendered by meditation prove indispensable pre-essentials here. And in the investigation of the significance of sleep the value of such extreme fineness or subtlety of mind will also be realized. Moreover, all metaphysical thinking is made much easier by an earlier experience of meditation. And when the mind must move quickly from the practical world into the consideration of ultimate principles and abstract themes the intensely sharp attentiveness of the yogi can enable him to grasp them more effortlessly.

From these observations it will be seen that philosophy regards the yoga of concentration as an invaluable psychological training which it prescribes to qualify a man for its pursuit. Such yoga assists the understanding of the world to the extent that it helps to shape the instrument of mind with which we must get such understanding. The mystic who unfolds reverie and calmness through meditation and *stops* there intent upon enjoying the peace or ecstasy he may feel, will remain in ignorance of the supreme truth about life although he will have gone farther than others in self-knowledge. He may feel happy, but he will not be wise. To put the matter in a nutshell, the yoga of philosophical discernment is the necessary sequel to the yoga of mental concentration. The one is required to prepare the mental instrument which must be used in the operation of the other.

It must also be repeated that only when meditation is *correctly* practised is it likely to be useful for this quest or indeed any other. When wrongly done or when carried to excess it becomes a hindrance to philosophic activity, breeding fresh evils, whims and fancies which will need to be overcome and which were not formerly present. It should be practised within suitable limits. When people lose sight of these disciplinary and purificatory purposes of mysticism and magnify it to the exclusion of all else they not only fail to remove their complexes but may even increase them!

It will be noticed that the philosophical aim is definitely different from that of mysticism. In the latter the neophyte rises in the scale by repressing thought; here he rises by exerting thought. The one teaches inertia, the emptying of mind, whilst the other teaches activity, the expansion of mind. Both are correct in their own places, and do not conflict. *The mystic stills the mind in order to get thought-control, but once the control is attained he should begin to think vigorously.* Thus he should kill thoughts only to use them better later! Meditation practice must in this more advanced stage be set *behind* the study of philosophy; the correct order now is to begin with the one and finish with the other. But the seeker who is satisfied with nothing short of ultimate realization may not stop even here. For when his philosophical course is run he will once again drop the labours of thinking and his mystical practice. This time, however, thinking will now come to its deserved rest spontaneously, of its own accord, its purpose fulfilled, whilst his absorption in yoga will now be a natural day-long process, secret, unmanifest, and not interfering with his practical everyday activities. It is not possible to achieve this final stage of ultimate realization unless he has perfected himself not only in both formal yoga and formal philosophy, but also in the art of immediately expressing their logical consequences in vigorous action.

In earlier books, it may be remembered, the writer made a most elementary fragment of the higher analytic philosophy the basis of certain meditation exercises, thus attempting what was rarely done among mystics—to render even the meditation exercises fruitful for later philosophic purposes. This was an original contribution introduced because he did not want his readers to become fools, which so many mystics appear ardently to desire, and also to prepare the way for the work of the present volume. Indeed, it was written in *The Quest of the Overself*: "This is the true fulfilment of yoga—to wield thought as a master and then discard it." Such a statement was quite correct and perfectly justifiable when considered in relation to the level of those for whom it was written, i.e. for those striving to succeed in the yoga of mental concentration. The highest ideal of this level is to still the mind, reduce thoughts and bask in the sunshine of mental peace. But now the student who has made some progress in meditation and seeks to rise to a higher level ought to reverse the statement quoted. There will be no contradiction here ; only a continuation and further fulfilment of the quest into higher strata. In his exercises he should practise stilling the mind first and immediately after that awaken it into fullest vigour for the pursuit of philosophical enquiry. Whereas before he suppressed thought, now he should seek to examine and direct it. Henceforth he will be alert to Nature and note her workings where before he dismissed her and cared only to turn inwards. He may keep his inner peace and stillness —philosophy will not rob him of that—but he should not imagine it to be the ultimate goal. It is a stage closer to the apprehension of reality, but it is not reality itself. If he works in the way recommended here he will approach still closer to the final apprehension of ultimate reality. Only near the end of this quest can formal yoga and philosophy again become co-equals, for then both will have to be fused and then transcended.

Reason Must Master Emotion. The sixth of this group of psychological attributes which marks the competent student is not likely to be palatable to most people. At every stage of philosophical research the student must suppress his emotions and sentiments whenever they come into sharp conflict with reason. Whenever the psychological process has been illuminated it has been found that, especially in the examination of complex problems, as well as in the evaluation of rival ideas, the tendency of undisciplined persons to cloud clear thinking by a confused emotional haze is inveterate. They usually see the world and interpret the experiences of life through this haze. It is the business of the student to clear it away.

The human personality holds within itself congeries of conflicting desires and contradictory impulses. It provides refuge for instinctive passions and ancient urges whose deep-seated character is not always suspected until critical moments bring them fully to the surface. All these forces are so powerful that it is true to say that most men live more by feeling than by thinking. The consequence is that they colour most of their thinking with conscious or subconscious wishes and desires, with irrational neurotic fears and other emotional complexes. They have not seldom been known to put chains on their feet in the form of disreputable personal cravings which are essentially harmful to their own interests. The ebb and flow of these feelings and impulses drives them involuntarily and renders it difficult for them to base their general attitude towards life on solid facts or right reasoning.

We may see the meaning of these statements more clearly by watching unchecked emotion at work in larger fields than that of the individual. During the tense days of war passion sweeps through people and often reaches crescendo point. A nation may then be led like a sheep to slaughter into decisions fatal to its true interest. During political elections whole crowds fall into emotional excitement and are then easily swayed by demagogues; at such times it is obvious that their minds are obfuscated and rigorous reasoning is out of the question. And doctors attached to asylums know that when the emotional excitement of mobs becomes so intense as to be uncontrollable it is recognizably similar to one of the symptoms of insanity with which they are quite familiar. Strong gusts of emotionalism therefore provide a barricade against which the attacks of reason are futile. Emotion unchecked by reason is one of the great betrayers of mankind. Two powerful emotions—hate and greed—are together responsible for many of the crimes in world history. The passions engendered by sex are responsible for terrible troubles. Herein lies one of the causes of the traditional privations and vetoes which society has imposed on the free and full manifestation of emotion in decent social intercourse.

Now the philosophical student especially cannot afford such emotional luxuries. He knows that when feeling inundates the whole life of a man it does so to the detriment of his intellectual nature. And because his chief instrument of penetration into the domain of truth is nothing but the mind itself, sharpened to a delicate edge, he must sooner or later come to a definite choice between the constant exercise of reason and restraint or the constant indulgence of emotion and passion. He more than others must beware of delusions bred by personal sentiment, of letting sober judgment give way to infectious enthusiasm, of sacrificing cold fact to heated imagination, and of swinging through the alluring arc of delusions bred by personal sentiment or sexual desire. He cannot possibly discover truth if he is not willing to depart from an unreliable standpoint at its behest. It is not the pleasure or the pain which any idea or event yields him which is entitled to determine either its truth or its value,

THE PHILOSOPHICAL DISCIPLINE

for these emotions merely reveal something about his own character, but nothing about the true nature of the idea or event itself.

Feelings easily entangle the thinking faculty and prevent its clear operation. The irrational element in the human soul is for ever seeking the feeling of satisfaction and for ever avoiding that of frustration, merely because the one produces pleasure and the other pain. Primitive people who have not evolved their reasoning powers provide a clearer illustration of this principle than civilized men. And who does not know that the verdicts of anger are mostly ephemeral, whereas those of reason always endure?

The questions which come for consideration in philosophy are often so finely balanced that emotion may quite easily obtrude its arbitrary judgment against the cooler voice of reason and thus prevent the student from perceiving the real truth. And his difficulties are enhanced because human feelings know how to camouflage themselves cleverly. Human desires in particular are extremely competent to seduce reason. Few people recognize the real motives for some of their most important actions. There are many internal barriers to such recognition that are of their own building or that are purely inborn. They have wrapped the bandage of many an emotional complex around themselves which must be painfully unwound again before truth can be seen. They twist knowledge not seldom to suit their complexes. A student may in a hypothetical case even have a sharply developed mind and yet his attachment through desire may make him favour his belief in the ultimate materiality of the physical world when all proof might point to its ultimate nature being essentially mind-stuff.

He may also not like this and that person, yet, for the purpose of understanding them, he ought to be prepared to refrain from allowing such a sentiment to sway his examination. Otherwise he will blunt his power of judgment and blind his faculty of insight.

The learner's liking or disliking of certain facts or certain experiences has nothing to do with their truth or with their reality. If he insists on making such attractions or repulsions his guide—as do most people—then he will never succeed in finding either truth or reality. The surface of a lake can reflect an image without distortion only when it is free from disturbance by the wind, and the mind can properly enquire into truth only when it is free from disturbance by strong feelings. Wishful thinking is always pleasant but often unprofitable.

The hope of philosophy lies in following reason, and not in thwarting it by following inordinate desires and emotional vagaries.

H

Even unbalanced ambition and undue vanity will distort thinking and prevent the acquisition of accurate knowledge. Anger and hatred however are notorious misguiders. When unrestrained all these emotions are lying invaders who nevertheless claim to speak truth. Hence those who persist in denying reason in the interests of their feelings thereby render themselves unsuited to this quest, just as those who prefer to keep their mentalities warped, their passions untamed and their instinctive repulsions uncontrolled can never attain a true understanding of the significance of life. For they will engage themselves in the futile and even impossible endeavour of fitting truth to a procrustean bed of involuntary and internal compulsions.

A scientific fidelity to fact irrespective of personal feeling will alone carry the student to a successful issue of his researches. When the reasoning faculty is loaded with thick sentiments and narrow preferences it is soon unconsciously perverted. Every emotion becomes potentially dangerous when it takes upon itself the task of guiding reason instead of letting reason guide it. To think truthfully, therefore, the neophyte must courageously enforce a strict self-discipline. This is the awful sacrifice which he is called to commit, this holy offering of what he desires upon the lofty altar of what *is*.

A manifestation of feeling which is peculiarly prone to bring the unwary student into danger is *undue* unjustified enthusiasm. It is a star which often blazes brightly for a time, only to sink down on the horizon of disappointment. Quite notoriously enthusiasts sail freely over established facts into an empyrean of mere theory ; not seldom they lack discrimination and certainly detachment. Therefore their judgments are often distorted. The seeker must take care therefore not to be carried away by any kind of enthusiasm *when considering evidence or forming judgment*. He should always be on his guard when in the literary or personal presence of the overheated doctrinaire, as well as of the hard bigot who has closed his mind. He should refuse to pronounce upon any subject which he has not investigated upon sounder evidence than the misrepresentations of his personal preferences. If he shirks this caution he is likely to open the gate for phantasies to come into his being or for specious and delusive reasoning to mislead him. The novice in philosophy must seriously set out to train himself to disregard both emotional aversions and emotional attractions during the hours of his study. He has to free his mind from its inherited inborn and acquired distortions. He must not let impossible fancies and wildly visionary excitements sweep him off his feet. All such imaginations must be brought analytically into the foreground of the mind and there submitted to the closest impartial scrutiny. If he resists this process and fails to insulate himself against them—as he is likely to do in the earlier stages—he merely delays the time when his feet can be led to truth.

Thus we arrive at the hoary wisdom that if in the kingdom of men emotion rules for the moment, reason should rule in the end.

These have been hard sayings. They are likely to be much misunderstood. Hence a warning must be uttered for the second time within this chapter that the student is not asked to kill intimate emotion and destroy warm feeling; that indeed is quite impossible; he is asked only to keep them subordinate to reason and not let them when contrary to it rise to the top of his being. He may rightly *and usefully* appeal to emotion when it is supported by reason. Not the destructions of sentiment and feeling should be his aim, but their proper guidance and control. Emotion is a part of man's nature and is therefore incapable of elimination; it must be given its fit place in his life, but reason must direct its course whenever the two come into collision. Nothing worth keeping is to be stifled, but everything is to be brought into right relation.

Nor is the worth of properly directed reasonable enthusiasm to be undervalued. It gives precious driving-force to the novice and insulates him against biased critics and baseless opposition. Indeed, all feeling is the propulsive element in human personality and leads more to action than anything else; hence the melancholy spectacle of unfeeling philosophical bookworms who are unable to live up to their noble reasonings.

However, the aspirant will certainly have to curb the disabling passions of anger and obliterate the abysmal sin of hatred, because only such a self-critical habit fits him to find truth. He must make this resolve plain in every conflict.

He must demand complete candour from himself. Not wanting to face a problem must not be the excuse for shirking it. He may not and will not always be able to control the rising surge of feelings or to check the irrational compulsions from within, but at such times he ought at least to seek to understand them and weigh them for what they are. Thus even when he surrenders himself to them he will no longer do so blindly. It is a considerable gain for the earnest novice to arrive at such a step.

His desires will surely diminish under the probe of keen analysis and thus render his mind more peaceful. And out of such governance of feelings there will inevitably follow a more organized and disciplined governance of conduct. He will begin to live as a better and wiser man.

It should not be surprising after such reflections to learn that philosophy is more the business of the masculine sex than its counterpart, and more of maturity rather than of adolescence. It is generally easier for men to follow this path than for women, although Nature compensates by rendering the mystic path easier for women. Women are naturally more prone than men to permit reason to stoop to the baits of sentimental emotion and to permit them to cloud the sky of thought. Due to social causes Western women are more intellectual than their Eastern sisters, but they cling more strongly to egoism. Hence in the matter of this truth-quest they are no better off. However, it will always remain axiomatic that an exceptional woman will forge her way out of these weaknesses, face the unconscious motives which beset her, and claim her higher heritage from Nature. Finally we find that philosophy is better suited to those who are nearing middle age than to the youthful. The young are more quickly moved by emotion and passion than their elders, who, possessing riper experience in the unwritten discipline of life, are more level-headed. But here again the beautiful law of compensation is also at work. For it is the privilege of youth to tread new paths of thought with a magnificent daring that others lack.

Give up the Ego! From all these struggles there will slowly appear of itself the seventh and final characteristic, but the aspirant must now take up its cultivation in full awareness of what he is doing and after full deliberation. This is the willingness to look directly at life through a clear lens and not through one tinted by the predilections and preconceptions of his ego. It is perhaps the most difficult of all his preparatory tasks consciously to unfold this impersonality. However, its importance can hardly be overrated. Every man who has not undergone the philosophic discipline is inclined to rate his own judgments far more highly than they merit. He usually seeks to arrive at conclusions which gratify his implanted prejudices and satisfy his inherited bias. It is quite customary for him to accept no facts in an argument save those that dovetail into his existing outlook. In this way and not infrequently he comes to reject what he urgently needs, as an invalid may refuse to swallow a bitter-tasting medicine which he needs far more than the sweet confection for which he asks.

Every time a man thrusts his ego into a train of thought its balance is disturbed and its truth-value distorted. If he is to judge every fact by the standards of his earlier experience alone he will thereby prevent new knowledge from arising. When we examine the manifestations of his mentality in speech and act his general if unconscious attitude appears to be : "This fits in with what *I* believe, therefore it must be true ; this agrees with *my* views, therefore it must be true ; this fact does not conflict with the facts of which *I* am aware, therefore I shall accept it ; that belief is quite contrary to what I believe, therefore it must be wrong ; that fact does not interest *me*, therefore it has no value in discussion ; that explanation is hard for *me* to understand, therefore I dismiss it in favour of one which I can understand and which must consequently be true !"

Whoever wishes to be initiated into genuine philosophy must begin by casting aside such merely egoistic standpoints. They show forth his conceit and vanity ; his quest of corroboration of his own preconceptions and prejudices, and not the quest of truth ; his study of the printed page only to confirm his foregone conclusions ; his resort to a teacher not to gain new knowledge but for endorsement of his old beliefs. By keeping the "I" foremost in his thinking he is unconsciously drawn into various and vicious fallacies. The sympathies and antipathies generated by such personal views constitute hindrances to the discovery of what an idea or object really is in itself. They often cause a man to see things which do not exist at all, but which through association of ideas he imagines to exist. It is a pathological fact that the various forms of insanity and mental disorder are rooted in the ego and all the obsessions and complexes are likewise connected with the *I*.

He who has not undergone the philosophic discipline is frequently infatuated with himself and his state of mind is bounded on all sides by the pronoun "I". This "I" cheats him out of truth, for it blocks his path to correct perception. It unconsciously prejudges arguments or decides upon beliefs in advance, and thus he never has any guarantee of reaching right conclusions, but only of returning by the discovery of justifications and rationalizations to the mental standpoint where he started. He is like a spider caught in a web of its own weaving. When such egoism dictates the trend of thought reason must stand aside as impotent. It locks the mind in a cupboard and thus loses the benefit of new ideas which would fain become entrants therein. When ego becomes the centre of obsessive states we meet with minds narrowed by religious bigotry or clouded by metaphysical meandering or hardened by unreflective materialism or disequilibrated by traditional beliefs and overweighted by acquired ones—all blindly refusing to examine the unfamiliar, the unpalatable or the unknown and rejecting them off-hand. They willingly believe what appeals to them and willingly disbelieve what does not, afterwards inventing rationalizations of their own preferences, but in neither case is the question "Is this true?" investigated independently of their predilections, and the result accepted whether it turns out to their liking or not.

All this means that those who have the strongest personal views are the most difficult to lead to truth. Such persons need to absorb the lesson inculcated by Jesus: "Except ye become as little children ye shall in no wise enter the kingdom of heaven." The humility implied in this phrase has often been misunderstood. It means the childlike mind and not the childish mind. It does not mean a flabby surrender to wicked persons or a weak yielding to foolish ones. It means putting aside all prejudices born from experience and all preconceptions born from earlier thought until one is undetained and unperturbed by them when facing the problem of truth. It means being alienated from personal bias and uninfluenced by thoughts of "me" and "mine". It means ceasing to use as an argument the words "I think so" or "I stick to my belief", and ceasing to believe that what *you* know must therefore be true. Such an argument leads only to mere opinion, not to truth. Personal beliefs may be false, asserted knowledge fictitious. We must walk humbly in these philosophical precincts. Teachers of the right kind are admittedly rare, but so are students!

Now philosophy is a purely disinterested study and demands that it be approached without previous mental reservations. But bias is often so deeply rooted and therefore so hidden that students do not always suspect, let alone detect, its presence. Even many so-called philosophers of repute have a subconscious determination to accept nothing that is different from what they expect to learn, and under such self-suggestion they allow bias to overcome judgment and prepossession to enslave reason. Therefore the student who is earnest must deliberately weed out those comfortable subterfuges behind which he hides his insincerities and hypocrisies of thinking, his personal weaknesses and selfishnesses. During the course of his study and whenever he brings his mind to bear on any problem he must endeavour to free himself from the pressure of all individual predilections. Such mental selflessness is uncommon and will come only through deliberate development. The student should always remember that he should first fairly state and then cautiously examine a case from all sides before delivering judgment. Truth has

THE PHILOSOPHICAL DISCIPLINE

nothing to fear from fullness of investigation but is really strengthened thereby. If then he discovers that he is in error he should welcome the discovery and not flee from it because he smarts under the wounds of hurt vanity and unexpected humiliation. He has need of complete elasticity of mind in order to rid himself of slavery to prejudice and to attain an inner integrity and genuine mental health.

Bertrand Russell has somewhere pointed out that "the kernel of the scientific outlook is the refusal to regard our own desires, tastes and interests as affording a key to the understanding of the world." This is an excellent statement of the qualification here demanded, the de-personalization of all enquiry into knowledge, the mental recording of things as they are and not as we wish them to be, the setting of every problem in a detached mental background.

The student may not dodge an issue. He ought not to shrink from wrestling with his own complexes. He has no option but to face them staunchly. He must be truthful to himself at least, trying to rise above private preconception, for in this way alone can he view things in their right perspective. His adherence to truth must be as incorruptible and as admirable as was that of Socrates. A firm intellectual objectivity rather than a weak wish-fulfilment will emancipate his mind from bondage to the ego and enable it to take truth in without offering resistance. Thus it will be raised to an atmosphere of impartiality and impersonality and trained in untainted self-denying thinking which alone can advance him to correct insight. And even those who declare this task too difficult in everyday life can at least endeavour to aim temporarily at its ideal during the minutes or hours devoted to these studies.

Wherever truth leads, there the aspirant must follow. If he betrays his rational insight and proves traitor to his highest ideal at the clamorous bidding of preconceptions which demand a low conformity he condemns himself to the penalty of being perpetually captive to common ignorance.

CHAPTER VI

THE WORSHIP OF WORDS

HITHERTO this study has proceeded on the common assumption that the words used, being in everyday general circulation, were well understood by both writer and reader. But the hidden philosophy, true to its determination to take no assumption for granted, now rises in revolt against such universal complacency and demands that we learn to know more precisely what we are talking about. In fact it stresses immense importance upon the analysis of language and the uncovering of meaning as an essential foundation of the rigorous thinking which enters into its construction.

Nor is the feeling of this need of verbal clarification a peculiarly Asiatic one, although Asia alone has carried its satisfaction not only farther but to the inexorable and logical end. A distinguished Professor of the University of London not long ago made the amazing confession that:

> "When I undertook the task of expressing my own philosophy in non-philosophic language, I found, with considerable astonishment, how vague was my own apprehension of the real meaning of technical terms which I habitually used with considerable precision. The attempt to discover their meaning proved to be the first philosophical discipline to which I have ever submitted, and of more value for the understanding of philosophy than any scholarly study of classical texts." [1]

When a famous philosopher makes such a disconcerting discovery—which is tantamount to admitting that he only half-knew what he had been talking about—we should be prepared for even greater shocks when we come to examine the way in which ordinary people habitually use language. Such an examination forms an essential part of this course, because we cannot get away from words;

---

[1] Professor John Macmurray in *Freedom in the Modern World*.

THE WORSHIP OF WORDS

they constitute the medium of communication, thought, study and understanding. They are the tools with which we work. What will be revealed in this chapter may well make timid people start with surprise or draw back in fear. The student who has survived the humiliations inflicted by the preceding chapter and is yet willing to proceed further may now prepare to have more of his personal idols thrown down. But here the missiles shall be aimed at words!

Thus we are warned to heed the grave importance of verbal expression. It behoves us to be careful indeed in this realm of written or spoken language. For the whole mind writes itself down in the word. Our thinking processes are to a large extent the pensioners of language. We cannot carry on conceptual thought without the help of words. Most of man's *thinking*, as distinct from perceiving, is done in words rather than in pictures. They give form to thought and provide the tools which must be used by reason. In the last analysis words are but servants of thought, and like all servants should be kept in their proper places. We may have therefore to become more cautious and hesitant in our free use of words, but we shall be the gainers even though our neighbours may be the losers.

There was once a British Labour Party politician who could get up on a platform and speak fluently and easily on any subject. He went away for a two-year course of study at Ruskin College, where men of his party and class were given the equivalent of part of a university education. After that time he came back a changed man. He now spoke slowly and hesitatingly. Why? The increase of intellectual capital had made him lose his former cocksureness and conviction: hence he became more wary of words.

The next point to note is to avoid the temptation of seemingly saying too much whilst actually saying too little. Men often disguise the emptiness of their heads in the glamorous profuseness of their flourishing verbiage. Sankara Acharya, an Indian sage of the ninth century, compared the effusive learned among his contemporaries to men who get lost in a forest of long words. Hamlet waxed eloquent in his three-word answer to Polonius' question as to what he was reading: "Words, words, words." The parrot-like abuse of language either ties thought and entangles it in thick knots, which must first be unravelled to think rightly, or it produces a treacherous facility of reading which conveys the illusion of progress in knowledge. Those who mistake verbosity for wisdom and volume for truth like to revel in a pretentious maze of words, but those who know how elusive both wisdom and truth are treat words gingerly. They speak before they think, tracing and retracing their steps in constant confusion, whereas the others think before they speak.

On the other hand, it is equally dangerous to accurate comprehension to say too little. Two schoolboys read the word *pencil*. The first is poor and immediately thinks of a broken wooden stub of lead pencil. The other is rich and at once connotes the word with a gold propelling pencil. The writer of the word was thinking of neither, for he meant a full-length wooden pencil. Thus fragmentary and inconsequential statements cannot lead to correct understanding of communicated experience. Language should be adequate to meaning; when it is not, then we are either left to grope in mental twilight or apt to supply meanings of our own manufacture which may turn out to be false assumptions.

It is a common mistake to assume that the meanings of most words are self-evident. The fact is that many have different nuances of significance. The language of incompleteness is an obstruction to adequate comprehension. It is often said, for instance, that a particular public measure, if passed into law, will be a great *boon*. But what is a boon to one man may be the reverse to another. If it is a question of driving a railroad through a farmer's land the proposal might be a boon to the public but an injury to the farmer. Similarly it is quite useless for anyone to say that the world is progressing and to leave it at that. The horrors which have been let loose on humanity during the two major wars of this century indicate technical progress, but they do not indicate any moral progress on the part of those who have perpetrated these horrors, but rather the reverse. It is therefore necessary to particularize the application of such indefinite terms. Unless this is made explicit by extending a statement such terms are useless from the point of view of the enquirer into the truth of a matter, however useful for oratorically impressing and mentally dazzling a thoughtless public.

A word that is read but not thoroughly understood is a word that is dead. Unless completely intelligible meaning flies from the spoken or written word to the mind we are left unprofited. How much more then should we learn to give careful attention to the words we use in important study and serious discussion?

This uncertainty is the real source from which many an unnecessary controversy flows and the real cause of many a useless dispute. Much intellectual disputation about "facts" is really about the actual meaning of words without reference to things, and thus becomes as meaningless as the dispute whether it is the convex or concave side of a circumference that forms a circle. When we move amid ambiguous language we move amid treacherous people of whom we should beware. Century-old bickerings still drag on because of this defect. Nebulous words have been responsible for giving a three-thousand-year-long headache to bewildered metaphysicians. How can two people hope to attain perfect mutual understanding when they use two different thoughts for the same word or two different words for the same thing? How many avoidable disputes, how many unnecessary arguments, have arisen from such a hidden cause?

Suppose someone utters the word *man* during a discussion in which five other persons are taking part. And suppose that he is thinking of an Indian monk with slim figure, brown skin and shaven head. What happens in the minds of those who hear him? The first forms a mental picture of an extremely tall man with powerful figure and ruddy complexion. The second sees with his mental eye an extremely short man with stout figure and sallow complexion. The third thinks of a man with middle stature, medium build and fair complexion. The fourth pictures to himself an old grey-haired man, whilst the fifth frames in his mind the idea of a young brown-haired man. Which of these five definitions corresponds to the idea held by the speaker himself? None of the six people therefore could give a settled significance to this simple and common word *man*. This seemingly easy word can give rise to a plethora of different definitions. When hearers react variously to the utterance of such a common word, when they fail to exhibit uniform agreement in such a simple case, it becomes clear that many conflicting meanings are created or found by those who receive words which are never intended by those who utter them. Nor is escape from such ambiguities wholly avoidable. Those who would make *man* stand everywhere for the same idea must immediately limit it to the single instance of a particular man out of the millions who dwell on this teeming earth and thus leave all the rest unnamed! Such a procedure is quite impracticable. For the everyday affairs of life it usually suffices to use any workable definition of this word, but for the higher affairs of accurate reflection this is a dangerous habit. The only satisfactory method of treating it, then, is to demand or supply a more extended description of the kind of man about whom we are talking.

But this is only an instance of unintelligibility arising out of the incomplete use of a single word. When the same word brings different images to the minds of different persons, what is likely to happen when several words of such ambiguous significance are combined into a number of sentences?

Satisfactory communication is achieved only when a content is communicated and understood by the reader precisely as the writer himself understood it.

The service which a word renders will depend on the significance it is given by those who use it. A word which does not possess a common meaning for all ceases to possess a common value for all. When it is used so indefinitely that it can be used to refer to several mental concepts it becomes dangerous ground on which to tread. How many people talk at cross-purposes, indulge in bitter controversies or argue in vain, merely because the same words mean different things to the minds of different persons! If, therefore, to free language from its interpretational pitfalls and to translate perfectly meaning from one mind to another is infinitely harder than the multitude supposes, how much more difficult must it be when making philosophical enquiries? Socrates was probably the first semantic enquirer outside Asia. We may now understand why he went about questioning teachers and troubling talkers for definitions.

It is therefore not always enough to define the meaning of a word: we must often define the precise application of a word. Otherwise in speaking or reading a word may be given one meaning in the mind of one party but something different may be the thought of another. What seems wealth to a destitute person will seem poverty to one with a large bank balance. In a case like this it is necessary to relate the word "wealth" to a particular sphere in order to bring out its full significance. Although it is more befitting children than grown men to talk without having clear and distinct ideas of what they are talking about, a little enquiry will reveal that people habitually move in a haze of vague thought and unclear notions, merely because they never trouble to go deeply into what their terms signify.

Then, again, meaning fluctuates with every man that uses a word. He can perceive in it only what his past experience and present capacity permit him to perceive. Consequently the same word may mean much to one man and little to another. Let us not be blind to such limitations of language. To the poor peasant in Italy the word *America* once conjured up a vision of a land where wealth abounded and where he hoped to emigrate in order to get rich quickly. The same word in the mind of an unemployed Italian workman living in Chicago now evokes quite a different meaning. He pictures a land where reigns a merciless struggle for the survival of the fittest and where poverty grinds more harshly than in his native country.

THE WORSHIP OF WORDS

The derivative meaning of a word is nothing. Whatever society or the individual chooses to affix to it becomes its acquired interpretation. Usage alone counts. A meaning may even vary from one century to another and from one author to another. A modern English Lexicon may hardly approve of the meaning given by an obsolete one. Thought must inevitably fall into fallacy when it is inconsistent in the use of terms and assigns now one meaning and now a different one to the same word. Not that it is suggested that words shall be fixed in meaning unto all eternity and that they shall never be used except in a single sense. Such a desire would be impossible of fulfilment. Even today with all our dictionaries it has proved impossible. Language is a flux and for ever on the move. It adapts and re-adapts itself as it tries laggardly to catch up with the times. It is not, never has been, and never can be static. It has grown simply because it possesses the characteristic of change, expansion and loss. It is as subject to the processes of birth and decay as any other form of human activity. But what is desirable is that significance must first be clearly settled by mutual definition and then consistently adhered to whenever such a word is used, if it plays an important part in instruction or discussion. To take for granted that we know what it means is to put on mental blinkers.

No words are really wrong ones and none right. A word becomes so only by the wrong or right use we make of it. It becomes defective only when we understand it defectively. And for everyday use no word is quite meaningless because every word is given a significance by the mind of its user or hearer. Therefore we must separate the intended meaning of a word from the accepted meaning if we would achieve accurate transmission. But it is when we turn to philosophical usage that grave problems arise and we find baffling obscurity and sable darkness where the outside world finds complete clarity and sun-like brilliance.

The Psycho-Pathology of Words. An act which is beyond question *never* permissible to any mathematician is the introduction of personal favouritism, emotional bias or subjective self-interest in either his use or understanding of an algebraic sign or geometric symbol. The student must take a valuable lesson from such a specialist and apply it to his own handling of linguistic signs and symbols, i.e. words. Thus many persons pronounce such a judgment as "This is excellent tea!" when they would be more correct if they confessed, "*I regard* this as excellent tea." The difference between these two linguistic forms may be unimportant when mere tea is at stake, but it is vital when philosophic truth is at stake, because it is the wide difference between objective fact and unconscious personal projection upon fact. Indeed, many erroneous popular assumptions are the consequence of such structurally defective language.

Psycho-pathological factors peep through every phrase used by the undisciplined mind when its speech comes forth. When an object or an event is distasteful to a man he uses quite a different term of reference than he would use were it to his liking. But because in both cases his individual feelings—and not the object or event itself—have dictated the adoption of the particular term, the terms used cannot constitute accurate indicators of the referent. It is dangerous in fact to assume that we know what a word means merely because it stirs strong feelings in us. How careful therefore must the seeker after truth be when he enters this realm of language!

People suit meanings to their personal wishes. When somebody succeeds in overturning a government by violent means he refers to himself as the *head* of the new government, but to his rivals as *traitors*. During the struggle for power, however, he was himself referred to by the then existing government as guilty of committing treason and therefore branded as a traitor. If he were then a traitor he could not have ceased to be one afterwards, and if he were not, then the former government was using the word in a wholly incorrect sense, or, in plainer language, telling lies. Hence a traitor never succeeds, because when he does he ceases to be one in both law and fact. It is only the unsuccessful who are dubbed traitors! In both cases the word represents a confusion of thought with desire, and has taken on a purely private value.

We colour interpretations of words with personal emotions of like or dislike and thus play false to accuracy. Labour leaders are not infrequently referred to as "agitators" by unsympathetic employers but as "bourgeois conservatives" by workmen who hold extreme views. Thus if we listen to both sides and are too lazy to make a critical analysis for ourselves we shall learn that the definition of *labour leader* is someone who is simultaneously a revolutionary and a reactionary! From such instances the immense value of verbal analysis becomes clearly apparent, for it assists us to separate stark fact from prejudiced opinion.

When the religious propagandist or the political controversialist uses a name like *atheist* or *radical* with such heated scorn as to make the name itself deliver judgment before any rational discussion is possible, it is evident that he is uninterested in reaching the truth about these terms but merely wishes to sway emotion and mesmerize his audience into acceptance. When an innocent term is uttered in tones of contempt or disgust as though it were an abusive epithet the mentally unguarded masses rarely pause to examine fairly the idea which underlies it but fall victim to the subtle psychological suggestion.

Catchwords and slogan-phrases are favourite methods of unprincipled politicians, cheap demagogues, unethical advertisers and all who care more for gain than for truth. They use such phrases to let loose in large numbers of people's minds over-emphasized emotions, concealed misstatements, deliberate half-truths, or distorted images that obstruct sound judgment. People repeat such slogans under the delusion that they are thinking. However handy these catch-phrases are to such propagandists, it is advisable to enquire more closely into their meaning before we may accept them, just as we must look beneath the embellishments of oratory to find its substance.

Superficial conceptions have become so strongly ingrained in our language that truer ones can dislodge them only after meeting with and vanquishing the utmost resistance. The ordinary unthinking loose-lipped man is unwilling to trouble himself with this clash and conflict of significances, so the philosopher must bear the struggle alone. Language—the choice of words and the structure of sentences—may markedly help or hinder the philosophic quest, and that is why the philosopher must be tremendously more careful about its use than others. The irresponsible carelessness of ordinary men becomes utterly unpardonable in him.

The successes of modern science have been chiefly achieved because it deals essentially with facts. The failure of medieval logic or scholasticism arose because it dealt essentially with words. The success of the hidden philosophy in solving the problem of truth has been largely attained because it deals with both facts and words. Medieval theology or scholasticism is filled with numerous pseudo-questions, such as how many angels can rest on the point of a needle, merely because it never took the trouble to find out what it really knew. "Better be ignorant than be a theologian and know so much that is untrue" said an American business man who worshipped in his own mystical way and knew how to die nobly and high-faithed when the *Lusitania* was sunk.

The dangers of metaphorical phrases are far better known than the dangers of literal ones. When we shall come to the study of mind we shall discover how the conjunction of a tiny preposition of two letters with an anatomical figure of speech is accountable for much that is wrong in our outlook. For when we speak of a thought being "in my head" we unconsciously force the mind into the bony box of the skull. Thus we give it certain limited dimensions in space without ever having enquired whether it be so located or not. We shall discover at the end of our enquiry that this is not a fact and that the use of this dangerous spatial metaphor misleads us into confusion and error.

Ordinary language is careless language. It tolerates illogicalities, ambiguities, unrealities, illusions and deceptions. Words, statements and definitions possess an important bearing on the solution of philosophical problems. Thus the ordinary man is quite rightly content to say "I see a tree." This kind of statement is perfectly in order for everyday practical use, but it is insufficient for philosophy. The student has to learn to ask: "What is the correct significance of the statement that I see a tree?" Through this dissection of word and sentence he gains the inestimable benefit of separating fact from assertion and truth from assumption. It is the bringing into the full glare of light the everlasting struggle between what is certain and what is uncertain. It is indeed a solid achievement to find out what he really knows and what he does not know but wrongly thinks he does! Thus he can move forward, but otherwise he is either brought to a standstill or wastes years in pursuing phantoms. Thus he pares away smug notions of assumed knowledge, cuts them to pieces as it were.

Men may unconsciously enshrine their whole attitude towards life in two or three words which they carelessly utter. The individual process of mentation reveals itself in the shortest phrase and the longest sentence. What is our reaction to the word *supernatural*? It will be piously defined in one way by a clergyman but in quite a different and scornful way by a sceptic. Thus the same word will certainly yield conflicting definitions. Whatever meaning both individuals may arbitrarily associate with this word, they believe that they are getting a definition, but what they really get is a thought that answers to their *personal* idea of the definition. Hence they will mistakenly suppose that they are interpreting facts when they are only interpreting their own or other people's *imaginations* concerning these facts.

In the end the definition which a man gives depends on his individual theory of the universe. Meaning becomes a *creation* of the mind! Thus the element of personal preconception, against which the philosophical student has already been so strongly warned, will tend to creep again into the most unsuspected places, into his use or understanding of these counters of thought which totalize into language.

Every word has therefore two meanings: the external meaning, which is the objective *fact* or event in external experience, and the internal meaning, which is the *idea* of that fact or event which is formed in the mind. The fact itself and the statement of it will always differ and never meet, do what we like. Whatever meaning we may assign to a term, it can never wholly correspond to the thing which it labels. For it is only a preferred abstraction—using the latter term in its technical sense. We all know what Napoleon said to his troops before the Battle of the Pyramids, but nobody knows the precise shade of tone in which his words were spoken and the precise feeling they aroused in each soldier. Therefore we would be more accurate in confessing that we know something about his famous exhortation but we do not and can never know all about the event.

Words tell us what is in our imagination, not what is in the thing itself. They speak about our own imagined definition rather than about what really *is*. In consequence there is a further snare which lies waiting for the heedless against which we must also be on guard. It is impossible to verify *directly* any statement made by another concerning his personal experience. We can only accept the truth of his statement on an analogical or inferential basis, i.e. indirectly. Whatever he tells us, all we can do is to *imagine* the idea that is held by his mind. Therefore where we dupe ourselves into the belief that direct understanding has been reached and duplicate verification achieved, we really get an individual imagination. When we use the same name as others for an object, we are often deceived into thinking that all are concerned with the same object. But no object can possibly be alike in all respects to all observers. The mountain which I see is not the same as that seen by another observer who is standing in a different position, for instance. Yet we both call it by the same designation! Let us be frank with ourselves in such cases and realize that we often entertain mental images different from those of other persons, whilst both of us apply the same label to these dissimilar entities.

The man who has received news of the death of a most beloved friend may, in response to a question, explain how sad he feels about the event. But his hearer can only get a rough grasp of what he *hears*, never of what the other man *feels*. And because powers of verbal expression may be feeble in the other man's case, even this approximate understanding may be still more imperfect than it would have been in another case. Anyway, the essential point is that

I

there is and must be a gap between what the bereaved man says and what he actually feels. Therefore this gap is a pointer to the fact that verbal meaning is necessarily both incomplete and imperfect meaning, i.e. not strictly accurate!

Hence the word does not and cannot represent all the idea. It tells us something *about* the idea, it is no more than an excerpt of the total meaning, that is all. The smug satisfaction which we often feel when we speak to express ourselves is a fallacious one. It is and shall ever be only partially supported and supportable by successful communication. Is the meaning of the word *table*, for instance, the mental image which rises in someone's mind with its utterance or is it the thought of the particular object at which his hearer sits down to dine? If it is the latter we are then faced with the problem that the particular image which rises in the hearer's mind may differ largely from the table which was being thought of by the speaker of the word. His may be a three-legged one, whereas the other is four-legged.

Linguistic conventions cannot be trusted. We must evidently go beyond the mere word or its sound if we would get precision. We ought to keep clearly before us the actual relationship between the term and the thing itself. The educated man will irritably assert that he knows what words mean, but really he frequently mistakes his mastery of grammatical correctness and his width of vocabulary for the actual knowledge which this language-structure represents. For words are not things. It is easy to confuse the written word with the actual thing or to forget that the spoken word is only an *abstraction* made from the thing it signifies. At the best a word will convey only a selective approximation of the thought or emotion, the event or the fact, which is in its speaker's *mind*. Such an error may turn the word into a stumbling-block which prevents a proper knowledge of the object itself.

The student of philosophy must therefore take care to separate the word from the thought it stands for and the thought again from the thing it stands for. Then only may he perceive accurately what worth the word has for him. He must analyse individual words and sentence-structures by retranslating them into factual rather than imagined referents. This demands probing beneath surfaces as a surgeon probes with his lancet. He must be quite clear on this point: that the meaning of a word may itself be purely verbal, i.e. nothing more than a number of other words, or it may be utterly non-verbal, i.e. an actual thing; and if it is the latter there is the further question of how much of that thing is symbolized by the word. Descriptive sentences tell us something about a part of an object, but they fail to tell us about the whole of it because they are necessarily always abstractions. For this they are not to be blamed as they possess, like all things, their limitations and we ought not to expect them to perform miracles. But, this said, we need not make matters worse by being loose, slipshod, vague and careless when pouring thought-stuff into the linguistic matrix.

It is customary for most of the untechnical laity, when first presented with these problems of meaning, to brush them aside as being too obvious for special attention or too trivial for prolonged consideration. And even professed students of philosophy are not infrequently highly impatient when subjected to this novel cross-examination of what seems plain and familiar everyday language. They regard it as a waste of time at best and a positive nuisance at worst. They can see neither tangible profit nor particular interest in such a task. Nor can they see its connection with the quest of truth. They ask what has all this preoccupation with mere words to do with philosophy. Is it not the proper concern of the philologist only?

The answer is that the full implication of such semantic study can come only with the fuller unfoldment of this course. Only when this research is well advanced will the student come adequately to realize *for himself* why the importance of this investigation has been insisted on, in face of the fact that most educated people assume that they understand quite well the words which they habitually use. Nevertheless, even within the limit of the present chapter something of its usefulness will be shown.

The would-be philosopher who has equipped himself psychologically for his expedition will see the whole expanse of existence as his province. He has to set out to explore sub-surfaces for the truth of what he hears or reads, as well as what he says or writes, for the truth of the world around him, for the truth of what he thinks and what others think, and for the truth of the world within, i.e. the mind. But he has to start somewhere and it will be most convenient to start at the nearest point, which means that he should begin with words, because all his other knowledge will have to be formulated in words.

His enquiry starts then by making himself as mentally uneasy and as linguistically uncomfortable as possible! He has to go out to do some ghost-laying! For most men, perhaps all men, have been conversing with thin phantoms and dealing with transparent wraiths under the delusive impression that they were solid figures of flesh. In short, he has to find out how much of his word-formulated thought and speech is sheer nonsense and how much is verifiable and veritable fact, how much is mere misunderstanding and how much is authentic interpretation. The more he makes his meanings clear to himself and to others, the nearer he gets to truth. Non-ambiguity is therefore an essential ingredient of the efficient philosophic vocabulary. The arbitrary use of words may often be unimportant in the world of mundane matters, but where the reception or communication of truth is in question he must be extremely careful to fix their precise significance, so as to render them immune to misunderstanding.

With a well-defined set of terms constituting a common language between writer and reader, both may hope to make some progress. Without it both may fall into the old trap of building up an entire philosophical structure out of nothing more substantial than mere ambiguity.

To consider such verbal dissection as pure pedantry is therefore quite wrong. *It is part of the essential equipment for ascertaining truth.* Whoever will not give time to this preparatory effort is doomed to remain outside the porch of philosophy. Many hope to evade this fatiguing labour and yet gain the slow-growing fruits of philosophy! How little do they know that an appreciative mastery of verbal analysis will later enable them to turn the flanks of specious arguments and false assumptions, thus clearing the ground for their onward progress towards truth! For words grow into sentences, which in their turn develop into entire systems of statements that embody whole trains of thinking. If the words themselves presuppose what is actually false, who can get at truth by mingling them with other words?

If men persist in maintaining an attitude of indifference towards the problems of meaning they render themselves unfit to proceed with further philosophical study. For the psychological effect of their obstinacy is nothing less than the desertion of the labour of thinking and nothing more than an unspoken claim to knowledge, which, in fact, does not really exist inside their heads. It is equivalent to a sudden paralysis of the reasoning faculty. It leads to acceptance of specious arguments. They ignorantly imagine that such problems are purely fanciful and academic and belong to the region of worthless medieval discussions, such as the one already mentioned of how many angels could dance on the point of a needle! In this they are wholly mistaken. The solution of these problems has both a practical and philosophical application, a value quite unsuspected by those who have not deeply delved into them.

This demand for philosophic precision in the handling of terms is not an arbitrary one. It is really a demand for clearing the ground, because progress is impeded by false and misleading notions. It is a demand that we examine words in order to draw a clear line between fact and falsity, detect the fallacies which underlie their use, and lay bare unwarranted or unconscious assumptions. We are thus to watch for unguarded expressions which give a status to meaningless nonsense.

Strange Discoveries about Truth, God and Spirit. Philosophy is the comprehensive quest of impregnable truth, the underlying significance of all existence. Most men who subscribe to the doctrine of a particular religion, cult, or school of thought lazily adopt an attitude which regards those doctrines as constituting the last word in wisdom, an attitude which is often most impatient of contradiction. The unconscious implication of such an attitude is therefore, "*I know that this is true.*" But how is it possible for them to be certain that what they know *is* true if they have not previously examined its very foundations analytically and critically, if they have not made a similar study of all comparative and conflicting doctrines, and above all if they have not still earlier endeavoured to ascertain the proper meaning of truth? We cannot do better, in order to provide a glimpse into one philosophical application of the principles just laid down, than to start examining into the meanings given to this word *truth* by some contemporaries.

Let us take pains to discover what the learned can inform us about truth. We find it defined in a standard dictionary as "being true or truthful; a true statement; accuracy of representation; the real explanation". When we turn to the writings of philosophers to ascertain their definition, an interesting variety of *theories* of truth or *opinions* of truth is put before us! The Pragmatic school says, with William James, that "the true is the name of whatever proves itself to be good in the way of belief". Those who hold to the Correspondence theory say that "truth is that which conforms to fact and corresponds to the actual situation". The protagonists of the Coherence theory say that truth is consistency. Others say that the word *truth* is liable to four further interpretations: it may firstly be taken as something that is unopposed. It may secondly be taken as indicating a factual reality; it may thirdly be taken as merely a statement about that factual reality; lastly it may indicate a correct relation existing between two things, two persons or two units as $3 + 2 = 5$.

From this medley of mutually conflicting definitions we perceive that the term is so protean that it is strictly no better than a strange jargon, and that the common belief that everyone knows its meaning is merely an erroneous assumption. The differences in connotation are too wide to make clear-cut sense. Yet the world uses this word "truth" glibly and pretends to possess an adequate understanding of its meaning. This is where the world obviously deceives itself. The ordinary man soon falls a victim to the seductive simplicity of this short word and never dreams that it is nothing more than a starting-post in the race for philosophic understanding. Yet to him it is the finishing-post!

The hardest thing in the world is to reach truth, the easiest to reach its simulacrum. That is why every man *fancies* he knows the truth. In the philosophical dictionary this word should be assigned the most important place of all, as it is in the best texts of India, but the West has been unable to find a fixed definition to which its thinkers can agree. Generally they have not occupied themselves with the question of defining truth although they are familiar with the importance of the general principle of defining their terms. But it is their common belief that the nature of the ultimate truth cannot be determined and that therefore it is useless to attempt to define the unknowable. But if philosophy is to live up to its professed purpose of ascertaining the meaning of the Whole, i.e. the truth of the Whole, what other fate awaits its writers and readers than a fall into obscurity when this most important word evades uncontradictable definition? Those few, however, who have attempted the task offer such unashamedly different denotations that it is quite clear they are offering mere opinions under elaborate linguistic guise. All the current definitions have their weaknesses and can be overthrown by a keen mentality.

We thus arrive at the appalling position that the meaning of some of the most important words used in the quest of truth is not fixed but is purely relative to their interpretation. Such a discovery helps to explain, however, why Buddha maintained a calm silence when a hearer questioned him as to the nature of Nirvana and why Jesus maintained a similar silence when Pontius Pilate questioned him as to the nature of Truth. Whatever answer either of these two would have given would inevitably have meant something imagined, hence something different, in the mind of the questioner from what it meant in the speaker's own mind. But the complete explanation of these mysterious silences belongs to the most advanced part of this course.

It will perhaps be asked where is the grave importance of arriving at a universally acceptable and completely uncontradictable definition of the nature of truth before actually arriving at truth itself? The answer must be that we are like explorers in an unknown continent who must have a guide to direct their movements, whether that guide be a living man or a mechanical compass. A trustworthy definition of truth would provide right direction for the efforts of thinkers by showing them the path to be followed for its attainment. It would warn them like the moving needle of a compass whenever they were headed for delusion, error and deception, and it would encouragingly reassure them whenever they were going forward to the right goal. It would blaze perpetually in the mental sky like the pole-star so that they need not lose themselves in useless speculation or grope vainly among fanciful theories. Nor is this all. It would prevent them deceiving themselves into the acceptance of a "truth" merely because it be pleasant to their taste. It would enable them to avoid acceptance of their own or someone else's imagination about truth as being truth itself. It would give a final certitude of outlook unpossessed by those who do not *know* whether what they believe is truth or not and who are therefore always liable to change their mind.

A further glimpse of the philosophical value of vigorous verbal analysis may now be given. How many men are wholly drugged or half-awed by the mere sound of an impressive word like *God* and thus deflected from calm verification and impartial analysis of all its implication? This word gives great comfort and magical solace to millions of people, but the truth-seeker, alas! can derive no comfort from it in advance before he has considered the thought itself rather than the word. Because society has used this word continuously throughout several centuries superficial minds come to assume that the word must therefore represent a "something" which exists within human experience, which *is*. The student, however, must first analyse psychologically what they have done. For he must start with a basis of enquiry which shall be dogma-free and yet fruitful for the growth of understanding, otherwise it is mere verbiage. Specific and accurate definition must be this starting-point in study. He has not the good fortune of those glib clergymen and wise theologians who speak of God with such familiarity and such certitude as to give the impression that they were doubtless present when He created the world, or at least as if, in the words of Matthew Arnold, "he were a person in the next street".

The first thing which he then discovers is that this brief three-letter word can be understood in many different senses. As he rummages through the cluster of pious associations which it possesses he soon perceives that ten men may utter the word *"God"* but important differences of view may lie concealed beneath each utterance, although it is heard as one and the same sound. The word may mean a personal or an impersonal being, it may mean the abstract totality of the laws of Nature or a particular individual existence, a piece of carven wood or a moulded metal image. In the mind of a primitive man it is a purely animistic term, whereas in the mind of the late Lord Haldane it was an abstract and absolute one. The student should not limit his enquiry to the conception held in his immediate locality or in his country or among his race ; he is a seeker after the truth of *all* life and therefore he must collect and compare conceptions from every quarter of the globe. He will then discover that there are racial gods like Jehovah, tribal gods galore, personal rulers of the universe like Vishnu, and impersonal and universal spirits without any form at all, and that the human mind, in its primitivity, worships a Deity totally unlike that which it worships in its maturity.

His attempt to get under the skin of this term and fix its full significance thus carries him into a weary task which is as interminable as it is inconsequential. For do what he may he is wholly unable to discover what exactly is meant by this disarmingly short word. It is susceptible of a diversity of strange interpretations. It may furnish fifteen meanings to as many persons. It has probably given rise to more nebulous vapourizing than any other word in the dictionary. All that he can discover is what a multitude of persons, ranging from simple Fiji Islanders to finished university graduates, imagine, believe, hope, suppose, trust or visualize the meaning may be, but none—not a single person—really *knows* what it is. The bewildering consequence is that all their definitions contradict each other. The diversity of definitions given to "God", not merely by uncouth barbarians but by educated people, is really scandalous. Few mental Gods are alike. Because they are forced to use words as prime elements of their thinking, because meaning must first flow into word-shapes before it can be properly appropriated by the mind, this motley multitude of talkers about God do not really know what they are talking about when they do not know the precise meaning of the word. And not only do they not know themselves what they are talking about but those who listen to them do not really understand them either. For the notions that are received and formed in their minds are likely to be quite other than those formed by the minds of the talkers. All, in fact, have objectified their personal assumptions into the word and through the latter into the world that environs them.

The student of philosophy should not submit unresistingly to such an extraordinary situation. He must put himself on guard and take antiseptic precautions against these serious dangers to mental health. He has to apply the test of disinterested thinking to the confident talk about God which constantly pours into his ears or passes in print before his eyes. He cannot do this merely by consulting a printed dictionary for an answer to the question, "What is the significance of God?" He should know that all dictionaries are merely attempts to stabilize meanings and that they have never fully succeeded in their aim because different dictionaries offer different meanings, and that after all they are but indicators of interpretational opinion existing at the time of compilation: their authority is not absolute. He can do it only by reframing his question thus: "What is felt in my mind when I use this word? What is there in experience of the world or life which corresponds to the term *God*?"

Thus when we deeply consider "the meaning of meaning" we find that it is, after all, only an idea in the mind, a thought which we hold, or even an imagination which we construct. And because it possesses a purely mental existence it is never possible to compare the idea held in one man's mind with that held in another's. Two external objects such as pencils can easily be placed side by side and compared, but not two internal ideas. Consequently each hearer or reader of a word may and will imagine only what *he* prefers as the meaning. Accurate communication and perfect reception are thereby defeated. Such a defeat can only be averted by entering more carefully into cautious examination and prior definition. When the student has not only understood how to assess the worth of words, but also how to assess the meaning of meaning, then the time has come when he may hope to discover what God truly is, in contrast to what some people merely imagine Him to be, but before then—never! His discovery will not come at once, it will not be made indeed until the end of his philosophic quest, but if he perseveres it will come, and thereafter he will no more be deceived by the graven images of false Gods.

A word which has also played much part in entrapping men in false conceptions or bewildering them with vague ones is *spiritual*. It has been used by totalitarian dictators to label their outlook on life, but it has also been used by their opponents! There is something ironic in the way in which dictators and democrats have mutually accused each other of being materialistic and unspiritual. There is obviously much confusion here in the notions possessed by politicians about this attractive word. But when we enter into the spheres of religion and mysticism the confusion increases greatly. We hear of "spiritual" experiences which, on analytical examination, turn out to be magnificent emotional titillations, or extremely imaginative flights, or beautiful moods of intense peace, or crudely sentimental conversions, or visions of immaterial beings, and so on. The possible interpretations are therefore many. Finally, if we say that a certain man is very spiritual one hearer thinks it means that he is noble in character, another believes that it indicates he is possessed of a tranquil temperament, a third imagines that he lives a life of ascetic simplicity and solitude, a fourth pictures him as being ultra-religious, whilst a fifth regards him as living in a mysterious state of consciousness unknown to ordinary mortals and so forth. Thus each definition differs from all the others.

Let us now analyse more deeply the implication of the word *spiritual*. Whatever be the nature of anyone's spiritual experience or consciousness, trace it to an analytical terminus and it will be discovered that it is his mind that tells him of it and it is his mind that enables him to know it as existent in his life. Now the mind can only make us aware of anything—whether it be a tiny fly or a great God—by entertaining the thought of it. Therefore whatever is known in any way is known ultimately as a thought. Spiritual experiences and spiritual consciousness are no exception to this universal rule. They too are really nothing more than thoughts, however unusual in character they might otherwise be. Hence there is no difference between the word *spiritual* and the word *mental*. All conscious life is thought-life. The most "spiritual" man lives in thoughts as much as the most materialistic man. He cannot do otherwise and remain awake.

It is now possible to understand not only why people form no clear and consistent notion of the meaning of *spiritual*, but also why they never can form one. All that they can do is unconsciously to construct imaginatively a meaning which pleases their personal taste or temperament. The philosopher must refuse to be captivated by the charm of this word and by deeper thinking discipline his own use of the term so that he achieves clarification of what he is talking about.

What is a Fact? A fourth linguistic enemy, against whose superficial acceptance the philosopher must war lest it deceive and entrap him in illusion, is *fact*. For the philosophy of truth prides itself in being based on facts rather than on beliefs. But what is a fact? Here is a word whose meaning in everyday usage is commonly taken for granted, but even a slight analytical enquiry will show that it treacherously shades off into quite a number of other nuances. If anyone arbitrarily accepts the first or third of all these interpretations because the effort of further enquiry is too troublesome, how can he assure himself that his knowledge is really based on facts?

Suppose a boy is walking home in the dim twilight and notices that a coiled snake is lying beside the road. He hurries on and later meets another traveller, who, however, is proceeding in the opposite direction. The former deems it his duty to inform him of the *fact* that a snake is resting further along the road and to warn him against accidentally treading on it and being bitten in consequence. The next day the boy meets the same man, who informs him that he shot at the snake and then approached it. To his astonishment he found it to be no reptile at all but merely a coil of thick rope. The dimness of the light had deceived them both! The reptile was but a creature of their unverified imagination, an unconscious self-deception.

Was it a fact that the boy saw a snake? The answer must be yes. Was it a fact that the object seen was really a rope? The answer must again be in the affirmative. But suppose he had never met the other man again. Would he not have stoutly asserted it was a fact that he had seen a snake just as the man would now stoutly assert the "fact" that the boy had not seen any snake at all?

It will be clear to the thoughtful mind that we must be more wary when using this term. If a fact is something reported by the five senses, then it is possible for the senses to deceive us and to provide us with a misrepresentation of it. In that case the student must add the word *fact* to the list whose uncritical use he ought to regard with suspicion. If, instead of thinking, "I have seen a snake," he had thought, "I have seen something which appears to have the characteristics of a snake," he would not have misled himself and others so easily.

This, however, is the simplest of his difficulties in accepting the term. Words which belong to the pre-scientific age and to conceptions far off in time and space still permeate our language and may actually mislead him now that their referent is something about which contemporary knowledge shows an enormous extension. The results which have been achieved in our generation could not have been achieved in any earlier age, for they have largely been made possible by the marvellous new instruments and delicate apparatus which have been devised and invented to help the five senses function where they could not function so finely before. Thus the microscope, the telescope and the spectroscope, the sensitive photographic surface and the photo-electric cell have made visual reports possible which the unaided human eye could not have got otherwise.

The microscope, for instance, reveals a new world to our eyes, a wonderful world which shows that the corpse we thought statically dead is in truth dynamically alive with active parasites, that the water we thought uninhabited simply teems with minute living creatures, that the razor-edge we thought perfectly straight is saw-like and crooked, and that what is perceptible to the gross senses is only a pitifully slight abstraction of what is still imperceptible. A few centuries ago everybody glibly said that the unaided first impressions referred to facts, whereas modern science now declares that the later ones alone refer to facts. Both groups of observations seem to contradict each other, or appear to falsify each other. Yet millions of people have been thinking and many still think of the simpler observations as being *facts*.

We still go on applying the old primitive terms to such phenomena, although every student of science now knows them to be technically inaccurate and misleading. Our minds still use concepts of the world as it is signalled by the naked senses. Our talk still embraces verbal expressions based on those delusive concepts. Language trails like a laggard far in rear of our knowledge. How can those who unguardedly use such a deceptive medium of thought, understanding and communication ever hope to bring the ultimate truth of life within their reach?

For what in the last analysis is the significance of these statements? It is that men may easily read their own *beliefs* into the word *fact*. When we consider matter scientifically we learn that every material object is constituted of whirling electrons. Your typewriter may report itself to the senses as continuously existent and constant, but it reports itself to modern laboratory enquiry as an energy whose waves undulate away in a moment. Still more, science, having failed to find an ultimate substance, has dropped the word "object" for the word "event", so that your machine is a complex of events in "space-time" which can never identically recur twice. The typewriter, as a space-time fact, can never be identical at successive moments of time. So long as your concern with the machine is merely a practical one, these considerations may not interest you, for they have no value when you want to write on a sheet. But when your concern is a scientific one, because you seek to learn more truth about the typewriter as a material object among many others, these considerations become vitally important. It would then be erroneous and misleading if you thought of the word *typewriter*, i.e. defined it, in the same way that you would think of it from the practical standpoint. Should you stick stubbornly and slavishly to the old pre-scientific definition it is quite obvious that you would never get at the scientific truth, but be tricked by the five senses and corrupted by the word itself. If you insist on regarding the term "fact" as holding only the superficial content which the ordinary man usually assigns it, i.e. referring to matter in its crudest sense, to whatever is tangible to the unaided five senses, you remain in an atmosphere of thought which prevents the acquisition of truth.

Nor is this all. If you could wait for thousands of years and watch the process of gradual rust and eventual decay through which the typewriter would pass, it would eventually crumble away into dust and vanish from sight altogether. It would thus be transformed into some other "stuff". In an altogether new form it would somehow continue existence. Enquiry into the nature of that ultimate existence is a work that rises beyond science into philosophy, which then reveals a previously unsuspected version of the meaning of "fact" to which the student will come in due course, and which is at present beyond the horizon of the specialized scientist.

Philosophy is thus not satisfied with knowing the fact of a moment : it wants also to know the permanent fact, if there be one. Hence it is of little use to the philosopher to be told that something is a fact when the statement is made by someone who has never sought to know the characteristics and tests of a fact. If he wants to get effectively at *ultimate* truth he has indeed to retranslate some part of the terminology of everyday life. He cannot use even such a pre-scientific term as "fact" *indiscriminately* without mutilating modern knowledge, for it is but one of a number of major words borrowed from the realm of everyday experience which carelessly used may hinder him from attaining right thinking because their meanings are too blurred by popular misusage. How much more will this be the case when he ascends beyond the scientific level into the still more rarefied atmosphere of their philosophic interpretation ! Such correction of his vocabulary will lead to the correction of his thinking, because both are inseparable. Unconsidered words of this character carry a heavy burden of ancient half-understandings, primitive miscomprehensions and erroneous modes of early thought from which they ought to be purified whenever they are utilized for anything higher than rudimentary practical purposes. Release from these defects should be sought. Language is linked with knowledge and should logically evolve with it, not drag painfully behind it.

Our examination of these four terms, *truth, God, spiritual, fact*, has revealed the contradictory definitions which each one may yield to different users. They are glibly uttered by everybody, by men in the street who have never given a day's thought to them, by many who are even incapable of giving them such thought, and—let it be said!—by every mystic who presumes his ecstatic experiences entitle him to speak the last word concerning them. How can any of these people rightly possess certitude when he has not taken the trouble previously to ascertain what it is that corresponds to his words? But the haziness of his thoughts provides him with convenient shelter under which to take cover against troublesome questions or sudden doubts. The student cannot afford to tolerate such weakness.

This examination has also shown the vital importance of obtaining a definite understanding of word-thoughts which can act as a working compass to lead him out of all this confusion and give him right direction in the quest. This effort to reach semantic *understanding* is what the student must seek to achieve from now onwards, and he must also bring within its scope certain other important terms of a similar nature as they arise. He must guard against using words which bring emotional satisfaction but lack intellectual enlightenment; he must beware of terms that cater to ancient prejudice and ingrained habit but define nothing factual. He must recognize that to release himself from the tyranny of superficially used language is to release his mind from the burden of ignorance and misunderstanding. He must protect himself against false theories which rest not on verified fact but on fictions of purely verbal construction.

It is not the purpose of the present chapter to take up all the chief ideas expressed in religious, mystic, philosophic or everyday terms and analyse them. Words like *intellect, reason, reality, exist, mind* and so on will appear and be defined in the course of this book, and a re-education of thinking may be effected when their meaning is properly attended to. The precise purpose here is to prepare the reader's mind by broadly showing the way to deal accurately with the verbal problems that arise, by explaining the general *principle* which must be followed from now on. The first difficulty of the problems of philosophy is that their real nature is usually hidden from those that seek to solve them because the language terms in which these problems are stated stand at the end

THE WORSHIP OF WORDS

of a long series of known and unknown processes. Analysis helps to unearth what is implicit in them.

The seeker will therefore have to apply the method of verbal discipline not only now but at every further step of his study. Hence he must here learn to pick up a special intellectual characteristic. He was told in the previous chapter to pick up certain other characteristics essential to philosophical enquiry. These two chapters are therefore quite complementary. A consequence of this effort will be that he will gradually escape from the delusion which often haunts so many religious, mystical and metaphysical people among others, that they have learnt something veridically new whereas they have actually learnt nothing but sounding words. He will discover that people explore words for ideas which they do not contain, never have contained, and never can contain, words that are often mere hollow sounds. He will come specially to beware of those indefinite meanings, those emotional words which sound so full of sense but are actually full of non-sense. Politicians, orators and demagogues particularly are fond of using grandiloquent words, slogans and phrases which either reek with gross overstatement or mean absolutely nothing relevant at all, or which are intended to arouse strong blind feelings, or which seek to cover uncomfortable facts—and do!

They possess a glamorous spell, a mesmeric effect which gives a semblance of significance to them but which hides their emptiness. When he resolutely analyses such sentences he can destroy their false pretensions to knowledge.

The use of meaningless words may lead even a reputedly intelligent man to believe that he is investigating given data and objective facts, when in reality he is merely investigating his own hallucinations in which he may be thoroughly entangled like a fly caught in a spider's web. Most people are under the delusion that every word must necessarily represent a non-verbal thing. But there may actually be nothing at all behind its surface. The falsity of this belief that every word must needs possess a meaning is demonstrated by the possibility of using such phrases as "the son of a sterile woman" and "flowers in the sky", which are clearly ridiculous even to a schoolboy, but are no more ridiculous to a philosopher than numerous expressions which are thoughtlessly used by people in the highest to the lowest circles.

The basis of this criticism is that one ought to be silent about the *truth* of those things whose existence one has never verified and can never verify. To speak in such a case is to imagine, and therefore to depart from the straight road of strict fact. We ought not to permit a word to deceive us into believing that we are dealing with objects, experiences and existences when in actuality we are doing nothing of the sort.

"Does this word designate something real or something fictitious?" should become a constant query when faced with assertions made by many advocates and most propagandists. When a word does duty for the inconceivable it may soon blind the judgment of a man and lead him to accept the non-existent. This is pseudo-interpretation, this shooting one meaningless term after another and moving in a circle which returns to the original word without having provided any real explanation of meaning during its journey. Magnificent verbal worlds are thus constructed in which their creators live happily ever after! Men everywhere entertain false opinions through their incorrigible habit of inferring that something named is something that exists, through their traditional tendency to mistake empty words for substantial realities. Hence the need to examine statements to ascertain whether they are really thinkable or whether they are merely pseudo-meanings—sets of symbols with nothing substantial in human experience that actually corresponds to them. In short, it is the need to get at what is truly known, to unveil hidden assumptions, and to elucidate what is being done when a thing is said to be true.

The student of philosophy has no option but to *begin* by distrusting every word which does not represent a particular thing within definite and universal personal experience. He must doubt the verbal idols which former men or present tradition have set up for his worship. He must put aside the simple faith that the existence of a word necessarily signifies the existence of a thing or of an idea denominated by that word. He may then discover, to his astonishment, that its supposed existence is no existence at all! Of course, although such a word does not represent any existent object, as is supposed, it may represent a feeling of the one who utters it and in its turn it may stimulate another feeling of the same class in the hearer.

Thus he has to seek for the solid substance behind the show of language, to get at the "meaning of meanings". Before he can rightly start with a sentence like "What is the nature of the world around me?" he should ask, "What is the character of this expression 'nature of the world'?" He has to learn how to frame questions rightly if he is to secure correct answers. Eighteenth-century chemists lost themselves in the falsity of the phlogiston theory because they asked "What special substance is involved in the process of burning?" instead of asking, "What kind of process is burning?"

Language must be adjusted to fit the pursuit of philosophy, and not *vice versa*. Words which carry no meaning must be ruthlessly abandoned. Words which carry false meaning must be rigorously corrected. Words which carry ambiguous meaning must be sharply clarified. Words which pretend to represent fact but really represent imagination must be revealed for what they are. All such words hold the budding philosopher in fetters and limit the field of his enquiry until he sunders the conceptual reality of their meanings from the actual reality, the fictitious significance from the real significance. The elucidation of their ultimate meanings is a necessary stage in the elucidation of ultimate truth, because it involves the wholesale reconstruction of thought.

The re-orientation involved in this revision of verbal evaluations to bring them into conformity with the philosophical outlook is admittedly painful at first. It may be troublesome to become meticulously linguistically self-conscious, but the arduous effort passes into easy habit with time. Nevertheless the half-educated frankly find it a bore, whilst the feminine sex usually find it a bother! Hence we observe few women take to philosophy and few men care for it also, unless either their mental background or yearning for truth is of the right quality.

It is true to add that the general effect of this verbal self-training will certainly appear within the field of everyday living. As the mind becomes more exacting in its demands on thoughts and words during philosophical enquiry, so will it slowly and automatically extend the habit to include ordinary practical affairs. The universally careless condition which characterizes most thinking, permeates much writing and distorts daily conversation will give way gradually to significant, purposeful and realistic certitude. These consequences are likely to be far-reaching indeed. Not merely the labels but the very stuff of thought will be altered and improved. When we pay attention to meaning we are paying attention to something whose range extends far beyond the sphere of communication or learning; it is carried over by its own impetus of habit into other environments and other fields of activity where we reap the consequent benefits. It is not too much to say that it leads to a mental re-education. We thus unfold a capacity for independent thinking. "Words plainly force and overrule the understanding," confessed that master of words, Francis Bacon. He was shrewd enough to point out that of all the obstacles to right reasoning those imposed by words were "the most troublesome of all", and his warning to all would-be-philosophers is to be ever remembered · "Words, like a Tartar's bow, do shoot back upon the understanding and mightily entangle and pervert the judgment." If the structure of language is after all but a system of implication, the possibilities of error and uncertainty are very real. Statements which imperfectly represent a thing may always lead to incorrect thought upon it.

As before in this book it is necessary to utter another warning. There should be no misunderstanding of the function of linguistic analysis. It is not meant that speech should exist *only* for the purpose of conveying facts. It is not meant that all metaphorical language, all the beauties of poetry, all the pleasures of fiction, all the relaxations of humour and all imaginative work should be neither expressed nor appreciated. The light and often grossly exaggerated touches which humour gives to conversation, the colourful patches which the reading of novels gives to leisure, are not to be rejected in disdain. There is nothing said here against such reasonable enjoyments of life. "Be a philosopher," counselled Scotch Hume, "but amidst all your philosophy be still a man."

What is really meant is that, whether talking or appreciating humorous nonsense, one ought not to be oblivious of the fact that it is nonsense; that when writing or reading fanciful unrealities one ought to know just what one is doing and not fall into the belief that there is any substance to these fancies; and that amid all the petty talk inseparable from social life one is not carried away into unconsciousness of its pettiness or into confusion of the practical with the philosophical necessities. What we require for everyday life is not necessarily to be judged by the standards of what we require for philosophical research. We may indulge in as much nonsense as we please in connection with the former within the limits of personal taste, but we may not indulge in the slightest nonsense in connection with the latter. We may utter a million meaningless words during the gossip of a lifetime without doing much or any harm to ourselves, but we may not utter or think a single meaningless word during the philosophical quest without losing our right direction. We may load our sentences with as much artistic imaginativeness or emotional colour as we wish, so long as we do not deceive ourselves thereby and can acknowledge what has been done. We may peruse page after page of fiction so long as we understand the unphilosophical nature of the language we are dealing with. We may even harangue a political audience with misleading metaphors and figurative innuendoes if that be our lot, but we ought not to fall into the errors which we prepare for others.

Language need not be drained of colouring and fancy, provided we retain the consciousness that it *is* colouring and fancy. Art is as admissible into the philosopher's life as into the empiricist's. We may enjoy all these to the full, only let us not set them up as the standards whereby truth also is to be judged and let us keep them in consciousness outside the purlieus of our keen quest for what is ultimately real. We must renounce them to ascend the altitudes like a cold ascetic renouncing the world, but we may pick them up again calmly the moment the mind turns from this study. Thus a twofold viewpoint will gradually develop, the practical and the philosophic. Such a duality will last as long as man is a seeker, but to the sage who has attained the hidden goal all life becomes a sublime unity and there is nothing for him to guard against.

What is it that the mind does when it searches for a meaning? This question provides a philosophic task of the first magnitude and its answer is itself a mental triumph.

This chapter may be summed up by the statement that when a man speaks or writes he reveals not only what he does know but also and unconsciously what he does not know. His ignorance, no less than his knowledge, lies naked in his sentences to the philosophic insight. They constitute a document of self-revelation, a manifestation of his subconscious no less than of his conscious mind. Only the sage can ever achieve an exact formulation of his knowledge, where others reveal the poverty of their thinking by their use of ambiguous, biased, inexact or empty linguistic constructions, for he alone has burrowed to the roots of his own ideas. Thus too only the sage can detect from the style of man's speech, the character of his linguistic structures, the precise stage on the road to truth to which his intelligence and his knowledge have advanced.

Philosophical analysis in linguistic matters along the lines indicated here will help the student to see whether any statement which he or others may make conveys genuine information or mere misinformation. For the philosophy of truth is taught in a particular and peculiar way. It begins to lead men to truth by pointing out their error, by showing where they think or talk nonsense, by causing them to unlearn illusory knowledge and then by reminding them that penetration to a deeper level of enquiry is possible and desirable. It is established in the mind of its students not so much by the affirmation of what *is* as by the elimination of what is *not*. It displays the leading principles of all other known views of existence and then proceeds to show their falsity and mistakes. When these false views are once thrown out of the mind they carry away with them numerous problems, pseudo-problems and tormenting questions which have troubled the thoughts of all ages but which have never been brought to an issue because they never can, for they need never have arisen. And it says finally: "God exists, but He could not be revealed to you *as He really is* before you had rid your mind of the erroneous ideas concerning Him which filled it. Now only is the way prepared for you to find Him, to find Truth and to find Reality, the holy trinity which are really One." Hence the high importance of this method of critical analysis.

Thus the subtleties of language may be shaped into a master-key which unlocks many gates of the mysteries of thought and being.

CHAPTER VII

THE ARBITRAMENT OF THINKING POWER

"WAS a further and finally satisfactory source of obtaining knowledge available?" Such was the question asked in the first chapter of this book after a brief reference to religious faith, logical thought and mystic experience characterized them all as partial, insufficient and devoid of absolute certainty. The subsequent chapters have supplied further facts for this conclusion. An analysis must now be conducted and an answer found, if possible, to the question which heads this paragraph. It should not be thought, however, that faith, intuition, logical thinking and mystic trance are valueless. On the contrary, they have their proper places and particular uses, but they should be regarded only as steps. They are not and can never be perfect instruments for the service of a man who is seeking nothing less than complete certitude. Had they really been such, then the world would have answered its age-old queries long ago and its long-drawn quest would today be unnecessary. The mere presence of many conflicting views which still puzzle mankind alone proves the insufficiency and indecisiveness of such sources, upon which mankind has chiefly relied in the past.

The weary enquirer may well be provoked into asking whether the human mind is at all capable of solving ultimate problems. This is an important question. It is indeed the same as our preliminary one, but in another form. Its answer involves the answer to other questions, such as "How do I get knowledge? What is meant by knowledge? Which kind of knowledge is true?"—all of which must be dealt with by the philosopher if he is to walk warily in the light and not dubiously in darkness.

All enquiry into the final meaning of experience and the mystery of the world would be a waste of time if the very limits of such enquiry were set for us beforehand by hard impassable barriers that encircled the available means of knowledge. It is therefore better to know the worst, if worst there be, than to indulge in the folly of pursuing an unattainable quest. It is to the honour of Immanuel Kant that he was the first Western thinker to raise the question whether man possessed a mental instrument fit for knowing truth. He came to a negative conclusion. Fortunately we need not be so pessimistic, for we shall find, as the ancient Indian sages found, that only the best awaits us in the end and that the riddle of life *can* be solved with man's present resources.

An infant is too helpless to find its way about life alone. It has perforce to rely on others, i.e. its parents. So too grown men who feel more or less ignorant and uncertain about the interpretation of existence in general have to seek the help of others. Thus to satisfy such a need arises the earliest guidance offered to man, which is that of authority, whether religious, political, cultural or otherwise, and whether traditional or not. It says: "Believe and you will be safe!"

We must therefore begin an examination of such authoritarianism with the startling postulate of universal ignorance. And this means that the teeming masses are still infantile in some ways. Millions and millions of grown-up men and adult women living in the world today are still intellectual children who fully accept and completely believe much that is nonsensical and more that is false. We ought not to be afraid of such a statement. In the operations of arithmetic we find that the figure of one million multiplied by nought still remains equal to zero. In human life the same calculation evaluates the *knowledge* of most people. But society being what it is, the masses of mankind, busy with toil or suffering in trouble, must trust in authoritarianism and in normal times can usually find no better guides through the maze of life-problems than their traditional ones, provided the trust is not abused.

Take the instance of religion. A religion has to establish its authority by congealing its views into formal assertions and fixed dogmas. It has to announce these doctrines as supernaturally revealed "sacred" truths, not as arguable human ones. The moment it is willing to discuss its tenets on any other basis than that of given and infallible revelation it has opened a door to numerous schisms and to slow but sure weakening of its entire position. Continuance of such weakening will one day lead to its collapse. Therefore religion prudently offers its knowledge to man as something received from a higher source, from a higher being or a higher world, which he must piously accept on unquestioning faith and reverently maintain as an unquestioned tradition.

Let us examine this position. It is historically satisfactory to the masses, who naturally set out in life with the simplest possible conceptions and who are willing to accept the universe in which they find themselves without troubling their heads overmuch about it.

THE ARBITRAMENT OF THINKING POWER 151

Its value is little, however, to the few who are engaged in the quest of ultimate certitude and who are therefore counselled to begin with the exercise of agnostic enquiry.

Why have the sages enjoined such a cautious attitude? Because, after all, every famous scripture is nothing more than a book which some man or men once wrote or else it could not have come into being, and because religious beliefs flourish in such an immense variety of bewildering contradictions. Whoever ventures to enquire impartially into all of them will arrive at the end in inescapable confusion. He will be totally unable to resolve the mass of conflicting claims into any kind of unity. He can never *know* for certain which of the worshipped Gods really exist, or which of the cosmological stories are correct, or how to harmonize either irreconcilable dogmas or the different accounts of heaven and hell. He cannot even peer into the mind of another man who is standing before him because mind is the sole characteristic which is never normally open to public inspection. How then can he peer into the mind of a totally invisible being—God—and assert that the latter is all-merciful? For aught he can tell God might be all-merciless. Knowledge of what is going on in God's mind must necessarily be confined to God Himself. If he attempts to read the mind of God he can only succeed in reading the mind of his own *idea* of God, i.e. his own imagination! His belief concerning God is in the end his imagination about God; it is certainly not verified knowledge. And when he perceives the hand of divine intervention in his own or others' lives his perception is really but an imaginative effort on his part; such an effort may fully satisfy his personal feelings and bring him much solace, but will not be better than any other imagination as a criterion of what is true.

In short, his mind can come to complete rest in any religion only because it is incapable of investigating deeply or tired of acute thinking, not because it has found truth! Faith has often been shown in this world by the record of national history and the test of individual experience to be unreliable; hence it cannot lead to uniformly certain knowledge.

It will be asked, perhaps in horror, then do the sages teach atheism? The charge can neither be admitted nor denied. They teach it where dubious Gods are concerned, i.e. imagined Gods. They deny it where the true God is concerned, i.e. God as He really is. But they do not dogmatize about the latter. What God is must constitute part of the object of our search and can only be ascertained *after* such search. It is a riddle to be solved, not a dogma to be set up. If in the beginning we have to doubt the ready-made Gods and reject them and their legacies of revelation as sources of sure knowledge, this is only to clear the ground for a thorough investigation into what is the irrefutable truth about the whole matter. And if later conclusions may here be hopefully anticipated, we shall happily succeed through philosophy in rediscovering the true God, not in losing Him.

A famous contemporary scientist, after admirable support of the value of philosophy to science and of the truth of metaphysical idealism, proceeded thereafter to cut himself adrift from both philosophy and science and floated away into mere speculation. He wrote reverently of the "divine architect" who is responsible for this world. He fell into the easy fallacy of thinking that because the best classes of human beings plan their houses architecturally before building them, therefore God must also plan His universe in the same way. He thus reduced his almighty God to the level of a mere human being. Where is the justification for lowering the stature of Deity in this way? The scientist did not see, unfortunately, that all these anthropomorphic speculations were but refined blasphemy ! Such a God existed in his personal imagination and could not be proved to the satisfaction of everybody else to exist in fact.

The student of philosophy should not make an offering of faith before such an altar, because he above all others seeks truth ; i.e. he must confine his quest to facts and not to speculative imaginations.

These words will not be palatable to sincerely pious persons. But whatever critics may make of such statements there is always one inconvenient fact from which religionists usually turn their faces. God has endowed us all—in however feeble a degree—with thinking-power, with the potential capacity to discriminate and reason for ourselves. Should we not therefore use His gift and not scorn it ?

However, our concern at this point is less with the existence and nature of God than with the help to be derived by the truth-seeker from the revelations of religion in their popular form. The question lies enfolded in a larger one, that of the validity of belief in any authority at all whether it be religious or otherwise. Here the reader must again be warned not to make the error of confusing different systems of dimension in the world of thought. The same rule should not be used to measure both utility and truth. We are not at the moment concerned with the practical value of authoritarianism ; this has its undeniable place and is indeed absolutely indispensable for regulating the affairs of society. We are studying the question from a higher dimension altogether, that of philosophy, the search

THE ARBITRAMENT OF THINKING POWER

for ultimate truth, and *for the time being* the reader must drop the lower dimension of thought completely; otherwise he will mix the issues and bewilder his mind. And it is now that the essential qualifications which have already been described in a previous chapter will prove their worth. Indeed, without their passport he cannot even pass the very threshold of this dimension.

There must be adamant refusal to be overawed by authority. There must be an attitude which keenly probes and dissects every dogma which is set up for consumption; there must be a freedom from the ancient prejudices and irrational predilections implanted by heredity, environment and experience; there must be the courage to resist the emotional pressure generated by conventional social forces, a pressure which carries most people along the stream of untruth, dissimulation and selfish interest.

What shall we find when the authority of a book, bible, man or institution is offered as sole sanction of the philosophical truth of any statement? We shall find that it is always possible to discover elsewhere another book, bible, man or institution that may also be offered as the sanction for a directly contrary statement! Whatever can be put forward on one side can always be opposed, whether justifiably or not, on the other. There is hardly a religious, sociological, economic, political, literary, artistic, metaphysical or mystical tenet in the history of ancient, medieval and modern culture which does not have or has not at some time had its contradiction equally existent. There is hardly an assertion which has not been vigorously assailed by opponents who make counter-assertions.

He who declares that "the Hindu religion promises many lives on earth to man" will be met by another who objects: "The Christian religion promises only one life on earth to man." He who quotes a passage from Buckle to show that history is but the outworking of man's individual and national effort will be opposed by another who quotes a passage from Bunsen to demonstrate that history is the outworking of God's will in the world. Such a setting-up of authorities against each other can go on endlessly and has done so during the past ages. Religions will boldly contradict each other, writers will gravely oppose one thesis to another, two historians will unashamedly find the same event as a proof and as a denial of purpose in the world drama!

Whence have all these conflicting tenets and discordant assertions been derived? They have invariably been proffered on some dead or living authority. They cannot all be true; many even cancel each other out! The timid enquirer usually ignores this awkward position, but the more courageous one will face it fully, for it indicates that somewhere among the statements there is a logical fallacy. He will then be compelled to confess what the sages have long taught, that the mere say-so of any man, be he as world-revered as Muhammed or as world-reviled as Nero, possesses no value at all to the philosophic student but must be thoroughly enquired into if it be true, no less than the statement of the most obscure and the least esteemed of men. Nor can any authority permanently prevent people from enquiring into dogmas forced on them. Even the ant runs hither and thither examining various substances to enquire if they be edible! Credulity arises out of mental weakness: it is to be overcome by strengthening the mental fibre.

If the seeker may not make any individual authority final, that is because such a source has often proved fallible in the past and may again fall into error. Its only use for him is as a possible indicator of truth but never as its arbiter. He has no right to accept beliefs solely because somebody else accepts them or because most people accept them. For if the others hold their beliefs on the same basis, then all may have accepted complete falsehoods as being completely true. Hence philosophy is unable to bend the knee before fallible persons but only before hard facts. It applies this formula to all men without exception, whether they be enthroned and crowned as kings, barefooted and yellow-robed as yogis, mitred and cloaked as cardinals or writers mantled with a fame that makes millions follow their every word. Quotation of a thousand sentences is quite valueless as philosophical proof, although quite valuable in empirical existence in many cases where the authorities quoted are experts in specialized knowledge.

The method of disagreement can be applied to all those who quote some authority as final. If they say as proof that A asserts one thing, that does not settle the matter. It is always possible to take up an opposite position and quote B as asserting something else that disagrees with A's statement. This is enough to show that no man can be taken as a final authority. The student on the philosophic quest must therefore entirely discard blind faith, unquestioning acceptance, easy following of tradition and submission to the tyranny of large numbers, for all these are to be reckoned as fallacies of thinking! Though useful to the majority of men for the practical purposes of everyday living as they are, they are useless to him for the ascertainment of a truth which cannot be belied.

This is not to say that all such authorities are always wrong; on

THE ARBITRAMENT OF THINKING POWER

the contrary, they are sometimes right; it is to say that they *might* be wrong, that we have no guarantee ensuring their perpetual infallibility.

The very occurrence in man of the desire to know, the need to understand, whether it take the form of belief or not, indicates that ignorance is likewise there. Hence it is better to recognize that he must take to a different path if he would gain knowledge, and this he can do only by beginning with doubt. Unless he introduces the element of courageous questioning into his everyday conceptions he cannot hope to learn more about their validity.

It is not possible to reach the summit of knowing the truth of everything unless we start at the bottom with the first step of doubting the truth of everything! This is the only way in which to obtain a guarantee that every further step taken will be a safe one and that we shall not afterwards have to retrace our path in disappointment. It is important to realize that the term "doubt" is used here in no sceptical sense but in an agnostic one. It is not a correct attitude to deny intolerantly what we do not even understand, but it is perfectly correct to observe: "I do not know. I have not seen. Therefore I cannot start with any dogmatic assumptions, whether they be in affirmation or in denial." Such a position will not be taken up by those who are naturally impatient, who are ready to believe anything at once because it pleases them, who are not willing to suspend premature judgment and to pose pertinent questions before advancing forward into acceptance of any claim. Those who jump to the first and easiest conclusion free themselves from the trouble of internal conflict but they unconsciously commit the fallacy of primitivity. In the end, therefore, their defective attitude must one day yield its fruit in disappointment. An unhurried spirit is therefore an advantage here.

This is not to say that we are to rest satisfied with our doubts and be content with the gloomy confinement of agnosticism. It means that we shall make our doubt act as a constantly pressing spur to deeper investigation, and not as a cold clammy hand to dishearten us. The sages say that doubts are extremely valuable provided we are induced to overcome and solve them by persevering search which carries us eventually to a higher level of understanding. They are not to be forcibly expelled or feebly smothered. And if we foolishly let doubts paralyse all further search, then we have no right to dogmatize pessimistically about the unattainability of truth in general, as so many in the West do.

The hidden philosophy says, in a manner contrary to authority:

"Welcome doubt fearlessly as being the first step to certainty. Doubt and you will be saved!" But it says this only to the seeker after the *highest* truth. To all others, to all those who have no time to take thought for such a long quest or no will and no capacity for it either, it unhesitatingly endorses the injunctions of authority. It is well aware of the practical value to such men of ready-made institutions, which, through sacred books and appointed priests, enthroned rulers and office-holding leaders, shall dictate their customary forms of thought, their regular habits of conduct and their basic outlook.

It will now be clearer why, when describing the qualifications needed by the philosophic enquirer, great emphasis was laid upon the elimination of the ingrained human tendency to view things from an egoistic platform. For we may now observe that the authoritarians of every kind are so imbued with the colours of their personal predilections and emotional pre-suppositions that they unconsciously set limits to their possibilities of getting at the truth of things. The hidden root of their assertions is—the ego! I am right, says one; no, I am right, retorts another.

The *I* lurks beneath the gregarious ignorance, the fatuous mistakes and the primitive misunderstandings of men.

Of all the false beliefs and deceptive illusions which darken the mind, the strongest is that whatever one knows, believes, sees or mentally holds is necessarily true. "I know!" is the statement which any fool can make, as the sages say, but whether what he knows is correct he seldom stops to enquire. This is why doubt is needed. It is a characteristic of such people—and it should be remembered that this means almost the whole of mankind—to believe that they plainly understand when they really do not. Hence the sage who is initiating the candidate into the ultimate path takes as his first task the unveiling of this universal defect. He explains that "I know!" is the conscious or unconscious presumption of mankind and that humility in its truest sense must be sought and found by the aspirant before he can take a single step forward. And this sense is not only moral but psychological. "I know!" usually means "I feel" or "I experience" or "I prefer"—none of which is a fit criterion of truth. Hence the need of rigorously doubting what we think we know, of sternly putting aside our imaginations, of verifying the ideas and testing the concepts we hold so fervently and of raising questions in points where we are confessedly ignorant. We should not believe in belief. For belief steps in where reason fears to tread.

THE ARBITRAMENT OF THINKING POWER

From Intuition to Logic. The student must put on his shoes and depart from the hall of authoritarianism. He has tried faith but it has failed him. Whither shall he go ? The first reaction from depending on others is to depend on oneself. Thus arises reference to personal feelings underived from reference to external experience, as a better guide than authority, i.e. to intuition. So he passes upwards to the second degree of human intelligence, where the knowledge which is offered him seems superior to blind faith. Those who are weary of the contradictions of credulously depending on others sometimes turn away to these personal sources and find therein a fresh certainty, as it appears, and a satisfaction that seems to set them free from such doubtful dependence. We have examples of this in Immanuel Kant, with his interior "categorical imperative" in the matter of morals ; in George Fox and his Quakers, humbly waiting in the silence for words from God, and lastly in our own times in Dr. Frank Buchman, whose Oxford Groups listen-in during the "quiet time" for intuitive messages of guidance concerning their personal activities in the world.

An intuition is a thought or idea which springs up spontaneously and unsought, to be asserted to by the ego without demur. It arises in a flash of its own accord, remains independently of our volition, and departs without even asking permission. It may profess to tell us at a moment's glance something of the real nature of a thing or it may be prediction of future happenings or it may be description of events which happened in remote antiquity or it may—as is most common—proffer immediate guidance for a course of action when faced by a certain set of circumstances.

Is it possible to fix here a source that will yield by itself sure knowledge about the object of existence and the meaning of the universe ? Alas ! a little historical enquiry will soon yield the disconcerting information that the intuitionists of all ages have differed from one another in their final conclusions, have had absurdly contradictory spontaneous guidance and have ventured into bold statements that time has mockingly falsified. Not all their predictions have failed of fulfilment nor all their intuitions been in vain ; there have indeed been striking instances where words have amply justified themselves and have been verified as correct. The discovery of outstanding technological inventions and useful scientific laws has sometimes come to birth intuitively and of its own accord during moments of relaxation or reverie. But these instances have been so relatively few in number that nobody could in advance guarantee the infallibility of any such statement. On the other hand the instances of disagreement, unfulfilment, emotional bias and obvious departure from known facts have been so numerous that we must regretfully confess that the ground upon which the intuitionist walks is unsure and unsafe. If his inner guide has served him unerringly sometimes, there is no guarantee that it will continue to do so. If it remains faultless he will be unique among men, for experience shows that intuition does not hesitate to mislead the same man whom it has earlier led aright. The best that can be said of an intuition is that it may or may not be true. Most of us find in everyday life that intuitive thoughts strike us from time to time and often prove incorrect even though they have sometimes been correct. In any case, intuition is not forthcoming at will and therefore is not to be unfailingly relied on. Moreover, those who have not undergone the philosophic discipline are easily apt to mistake sudden impulse or overpowering emotion for intuition.

Once again the student must take his regretful leave.

He may ascend to a higher level and knock at another door—that of logic. Everybody uses it to some extent. The bird, the beaver and the fish are guided by a natural instinct, but man must find his way by using some thinking-power. Logic possesses immense worth in the realms of day-to-day living; it can arrange our thinking in coherent and orderly fashion; it can detect gross errors and various fallacies in our journey from premise to conclusion; it can usefully show us how not to think; but we must humbly confess that the theoretical knowledge of logical rules has never prevented men from making numerous and absurd mistakes.

Lawyers use logic in presenting their case to a court. But as their conscious or unconscious purpose is to win the case it is not infrequent that truth is mauled in the process by every overweighting of lesser issues, by every suppression of awkward or inconvenient facts, and by every appeal to the emotional bias of a jury. Moreover, when we examine the stock syllogism of logic from a philosophical viewpoint we find it to be quite fallacious. "All men are mortal. Socrates is a man. Therefore Socrates is mortal." Beneath the plausible syllables of this classic syllogism hides the gigantic *assumption* that we have known all men who ever lived in the past, all men who are living today and all those who shall live in the future. This is entirely impossible. Therefore the syllogism starts with asserted knowledge which, in fact, is no knowledge at all. Logically it is perfect, but philosophically it is defective. It will suffice for the limited conditions of practical everyday purposes, but for the higher purpose of final truth it is completely unacceptable. Expert logicians themselves

THE ARBITRAMENT OF THINKING POWER 159

admit now that it cannot yield *new* truth but only draw out what is already contained in the given facts. Logic is an imperfect instrument and as such cannot yield absolute certainty. It operates within a limited range of usefulness and validity. And therefore it cannot reveal the ultimate meaning of existence; the walls which surround it are too steep.

It occasionally happens that those who become aware of these incurable defects of logic take a short cut to intellectual relief by turning backwards in their despair or darkness and descending to the vacated level of intuitional feeling—a course which appears to be the only one open to them. Here the intellect may voluntarily abdicate and find repose for a while; but severe disappointments and blatant contradictions are likely to occur sooner or later, thus indicating that no real relief can be got in this easy manner. Others who are unwilling to retrace their steps have begun to desert the old formal methods and to construct non-Aristotelian systems of logic. But these are still in the stage of experiment.

The seeker who wishes to leave logic for a higher method will ultimately proceed to the next step, which is that of mystical experience. This is illustrated historically by Ralph Waldo Emerson, with his symbolical "influx of the divine mind into our mind", by Jacob Boehme with his sudden "illuminations" gained from the three trances that marked his life, and by Emmanuel Swedenborg with his strange visions of the spirits of dead men and women amidst their heavenly or purgatorial habitats. A mystic experience is sometimes spontaneous but usually self-induced. In the latter case it arises out of the practice of mental concentration or intense emotional aspiration or attention inwardly turned, self-absorbed and prolonged into a condition of reverie or even trance. During these states visions of men, events or places may appear before the mind's eye with extraordinary vividness; voices may be audible to the mystic although to none else, and these may convey to him either a message, a warning, a series of instructions or a religious revelation; God Himself may even be felt as an environing and exalting presence; the mystic may fancy himself being wafted into space, as sometimes happens in dream to the non-mystical also, so that he is able mentally to visit distant scenes, persons and spheres. Or he may reach the final consummation in joyous ecstasy which may be violent and erotic or serene and settled, but which he will take as the sign of entry into a higher realm of being, which he usually calls "spiritual", "the soul", "divine reality" and so on.

Mysticism Under the Microscope. We have now to consider such experiences from a higher standpoint. First, applying a tenable criterion, let us see how far are the mystics from contradicting each other. Without making a long excursus into a debatable land, it may briefly be said that it must not be thought that mysticism is so unique an experience that all mystics thereafter find themselves in harmony. Far from it. Just as we find that men of religion, from the crudest peasant to the most cultured preacher, vary greatly in personal calibre and mental outlook, so shall we find that similar individual differences exist among mystics, and that once we put aside their five common tenets mentioned in an earlier chapter even the mystics betray by word and deed that they have achieved not much more unanimity themselves. Although there are several similarities in their doctrines and practices, there are also many unbridgeable differences. Whereas most spend much time ploughing up problematic esoteric meanings buried in scriptures, a few disdain scriptures and regard this practice as imaginative acrobatics and not as spiritual discovery, holding that the time would be better spent in meditating on themselves. Whereas most still cling more or less loosely to the name of some sacred personage like Jesus or Krishna, a few declare that it does not matter much whom one follows provided the presence of divinity is felt. The doctrines about which they disagree are replete with prolific fancies and are much more numerous than the five specified essentials about which they are all likely to agree.

Those who dispute this fact—and they are mainly well-meaning but uncritical people—should endeavour to imagine a solemn conclave of the following famous historic mystics imprisoned in a room until they could emerge declaring their complete unity of outlook (would they ever emerge at all?): Cornelius Agrippa, who mingled mystical piety with strange magic; Emmanuel Swedenborg, who chatted familiarly with angels and spirits; Simon Stylites, who sat in lonely self-mortification for many years on the top of a stone pillar; Anna Kingsford, who openly claimed she had killed vivisectors by thought-power in order to save the lives of animals; Miguel Molinos, who brought Spanish emotional intensity into his union with God; Eliphas Levi, who applied queer Cabbalistic interpretations to Catholic theology; Jacob Boehme, who was ecstasy-rapt amid the old shoes of his cobbler's shop; Hui Ko, who taught his mysticism to the Chinese peasants and was cruelly martyred for his pains; and Wang Yang Ming, who discovered a divine world in his own heart!

For this is the hidden limitation and undetected weakness of mysticism, that it is not a quest of conclusive truth so much as a yearning for emotional experience. Therefore the mystic is more concerned to get his feelings temporarily held by a great peace or temporarily thrilled by a great vision or temporarily flattered by a personal oracular message. Hence philosophy accosts or startles him with the question, "How do you know that the source of your communion really is God or Reality or Jesus or Krishna?"

But he will listen to no criticism, however impressive it be, of the possible irrelevancy of his conclusions. He will insist on making the undeniable fact of his own experience the deniable criterion of its validity. It is quite inevitable and perfectly human that under such circumstances he should be so irresistibly carried away by the feeling of extraordinary immediacy in the event and by the strength of his uncommon exaltations that he lays stress upon the less essential and that it suffices to satisfy him without his making any further enquiry into its hidden nature and truth.

The *value* of meditation for inner peace, sublime ecstasy and world-free self-absorption is immense. But its value for the quest of *truth* and *reality* unaided by philosophy is quite a different matter and demands searching investigation by sympathetic yet impartially critical minds possessed of a sense of proportion and philosophic acumen—qualities usually absent from the mystic's make-up. Ecstasy is indeed a form of personal satisfaction, but it is not either a complete criterion of reality or an adequate evidence of truth. For satisfaction *of any kind whatever*, however noble it be, is no evidence of truth. Indeed, the warmer a man's feelings and the more propulsive his enthusiasm, the more he should cool and calm them in order to examine experience impartially and impersonally. If it be true, it will lose nothing by such examination, but if it be false his calmness will greatly help him to detect its falsity.

Furthermore, we are faced with the insuperable difficulty that it is impossible to verify the inner experience of another man because ordinarily it is impossible to enter directly into his mind. Even thought-transference and thought-reading, although genuine possibilities, are still uncommon and still imperfect. We may draw inferences, creatively imagine or make conjectures, but this is not at all the same as actually and perfectly participating in the knowledge or inner experience of another man. The latter must needs be beyond normal human range. So even if a mystic tells us that he has seen God we have no undeniable means of either confirming or refuting his vision. It is not transmissible. Even if we succeed in reproducing it mentally, it will then be our *own* production and we can never place both visions side by side and compare their likeness. And granting the occasional accuracy of particular knowledge gained in meditation, it is unfortunately not possible for most other men in other parts of the world to be sure of duplicating the same discovery in the same manner for themselves: they must either resort to mere faith or forgo this method entirely. Hence mystical experience is utterly individual and possesses only a personal certainty. Thus the lack of universal certitude which was found among men of faith is now found among men of vision. Where is the guarantee that what they now feel to be the highest state, what they now take to be the loftiest consciousness, the final reality, will not later be replaced by a different one? Goethe correctly pointed out that mysticism was the "scholastic of the heart and the dialectic of the feelings". The whole level with which it deals is that of unchecked feeling. But how does the mystic or yogi know that what he has come in contact with during meditation or ecstasy *is* the ultimate reality? "I felt it, therefore it must be real," is the general attitude of most mystics who never pause to enquire. They assume the reality of their feelings because they are so much attached to them as to be blind to the important difference between the seeming existence of a thing and its proven reality, or between what appears to be and what is. How do they know that they have reached the highest state of knowledge? Why should extraordinary peace constitute a sufficient title to the estate of truth? Why should it become a synonym for omniscience? We are quite justified in posing such crucial questions, for in doing so we render a double service—to ourselves and to truth. The votaries of meditation who have found the final truth within its quietude should pause to enquire if it be truth, even if that pause takes a few months or a whole lifetime.

Inasmuch as mystics have not penetrated beyond their feelings, however exalted these be, we have to conclude that whatever knowledge they purport to bring us from meditation might not be ultimately true. Why? Because feeling is liable to change; what is felt now as true may be discarded tomorrow as untrue. Even Plotinus, who is hailed by ancient mystics and modern theosophists alike as being one of the most illustrious of their band, has confessed that the highest mystical realization yields no emotion, no vision and no concern with the beautiful. Had he not been a disciple of Ammonius he might never have reached this understanding. For Ammonius' school at Alexandria taught *both* mysticism and philosophy, the latter, however, being reserved for the highest class, and was based, as previously explained, on a tradition of initiation which drew ultimately from India.

"What do you want?" asked Ramakrishna, the illustrious sage who lit up the nineteenth-century darkness of India. Replied his famous disciple Swami Vivekananda: "I wish to remain immersed in mystic trance for three or four days at a stretch, breaking it just to take food." Said Ramakrishna: "You are a fool! *There is a state which is even higher than that."*

Our quest of a valid source of knowledge can come to an end only when it will yield one that is universally and for ever unalterable, which will be the same and hold to the same laws of verification at all times and in all conditions, not during meditation alone.

However, a further means of assaying the work of mystic guidance is at hand. Let us consider how many mystical statements pass unchallenged, how many are without counter-assertions, how many are absolutely beyond all doubts. Let the annals of sceptical science and orthodox religion provide an answer!

It is clear therefore that as a sole source of *certain* knowledge, mystical or yogic experience cannot be relied on. Its chief value exists for the particular individual who experiences it, but not for society in general. Hence only when a disciple has passed through all the preliminaries of personal self-discipline and has completed a long course of meditation practice is he regarded as being ripe for initiation into the higher mysteries of knowledge beyond ordinary yoga. Then the student on the ultimate path who is fortunate enough to secure a personal teacher will notice that the latter begins to suggest certain doubts to his mind. This is done so cleverly and so carefully that the pupil is insensibly led by slow degrees from his present position to a higher one. It is not done suddenly and violently, or he will only lose faith in his present standby without being able to find support in a new and stronger one. This change is achieved by the teacher making certain indirect observations and asking certain cryptic questions of the pupil in such a way that his mind begins to acquire more strength and to grow in clearness until certain doubts arise of their own accord. The more he submits to this discipline of doubt, the more is he likely to relinquish long-held attitudes of mind. He gets the courage to question his *own* experiences and to re-estimate them anew after a critical examination from a fresh standpoint. Only so can he read their meaning aright. He will then begin to see the insufficiency of his attainments, the invalidity of his beliefs and the limitations of his practices. Whatever illusions have held him will begin to loosen their grip. But his master warns him not to rest until all these doubts are fully cleared.

This analysis does not mean we are to despise meditation exercises as futile or dismiss the mystic's experience as worthless. Peace, tranquillity and ecstasy are not worthless things. And no scornful sceptic can rightly deny that the successful mystic gets them, albeit intermittently. Neither the sage nor the novice need discard these or other satisfactions, only the former will never permit them to deflect his mind from truth. Meditation becomes a hindrance only when it consists in hugging imagination as though it were reality or clinging to vision as though it were truth, whereas it is indeed a partner to philosophic technique when it consists in one-pointed surrender to utter tranquillity.

We who seek truth may reject the mystic's uncriticized visions and his narrow view of the world, but we would be foolish indeed if we rejected the valuable gifts of concentration and peace which mysticism offers us. The novice who has practised meditation faithfully for some period may unfold a fair degree of concentrativeness and subtlety which will be most valuable when he passes to a higher degree, for he will be expected to keep his mind thoroughly one-pointed during his development in the yoga of philosophic discernment.

Through Reason to Insight. Thus we arrive again at the question with which this chapter was begun. Is there a further and fully satisfactory source which we can tap for truly uncontradictable knowledge? The ancient sages declared there is, that, to put it shortly, the method of reasoning upon *all* available facts raised by the utmost concentration to the high stature of immediate insight is precautionary and preliminary to such a source which is in sight and transcends reasoning.

Before we proceed further it is essential to rid the term *reason* of the widespread ambiguity and confusion with which it is frequently associated. It is the faculty which apprehends and judges *truth*, distinguishing it from falsehood, opinion, imagination or illusion. And here it will be fitting to introduce the sages' definition of the term "truth". It has been earlier demonstrated that without such a definition men wander in a dry wilderness of hollow fancies, unfounded opinions, worthless theories and hypostatized words. This definition may sound quite simple, but its implications are most profound. It should be graven deeply on the heart. Here it is :

TRUTH is that which is beyond all contradiction and free from all doubt; which is indeed beyond the very possibility of both contradiction and doubt; beyond the changes and alternation of time and vicissitude; for ever one and the same, unalterable and unaltering; universal and therefore independent of all human ideation.

The quest of this philosophy is knowledge which is independent of the endless vicissitudes of human opinion. Applying the criterion of this definition, we discover that all reliance on changeable human authorities, all belief in written or spoken words, all acceptance of anything short of adequate reason as the final court of appeal or guidance, immediately brings us within the region of contradictions, counter-statements and possible doubts and therefore rules out these dubious sources of knowledge from our operations. There is no *certitude* in them. The word "reason" is therefore not used here as a mere synonym for dry logic-chopping. The Scholastics of an earlier day used the word in this sense and showed how even astute men could find many reasons for supporting hollow assumptions. *Logic* is the art which seeks to ensure correct sequential thinking, but unfortunately it does not seek to ensure that it starts with correct data; it may and often does start with assumptions that may be mere fancies or wrong data. *Reason* is the faculty of correct thinking, which seeks truth and which ensures that its activity shall start with all the observed facts of actual experience. The logician whose premises are faulty may nevertheless think correctly and yet arrive at wrong conclusions. Reason avoids this mistake.

Nor is the term used as a synonym for mere speculation. The annals of metaphysics are replete with numerous flights of sheer fancy which have been given a seemingly rational direction. Such thinking as ignores the facts of experience is not reasoning in our sense. And such reasoning as is restricted to the facts of personal experience alone is likewise not reasoning in the full sense. Although both logic and reason set up the same criterion that thinking shall not fall into self-contradiction, and that it shall not be loose and crooked, the former is satisfied with partial facts whereas the latter demands nothing less than totality of facts. Again, *intellect*, which may be defined as the activity of logical thinking, is swayed by personal desires and individual bias to choose its data preferentially, whereas *reasoning*, which may be defined as the activity of truthful thinking, is rigorously impersonal and ascetically detaches its feelings from the handling of facts.

Only when thinking is not only rigidly logical but also rigidly impersonal; only when it is pushed to its farthest extreme and throughout its course based on facts which are universally valid, which can be tested and verified in the deserts of North Africa equally as in the streets of New York and which will still hold good in ten centuries' time as in ours, only then does it deserve the lofty name of reason.

Such competent reasoning, such intellectual integrity is rare. We shall find that it possesses a twofold self-expression. The first dwells in science, but this is only a limited and imperfect one. The second exists in philosophy, and here it finds the best and fullest play. Therefore it may be noted that science is the porch of philosophy. The vanguard of modern scientists are themselves beginning to make this discovery, for, do what they will to escape, the pressure of their own results and the force of their own reasoning lead them pace by pace into the quest of the ultimate meaning of all experience, which is philosophy.

It may be objected that the ancient Indians never knew science as we understand it today. That is correct if reference is made to the method of experiment inaugurated by Bacon, but the sages among them knew the scientific principle of verification and the philosophic value of observation which are essential elements of their doctrines.

Both the scientist and the mystic share this common factor, that they are tired of blind beliefs and seek the satisfying verification of experience. This is why mysticism is placed so high in the scale of mental evolution as to be beyond faith, intuition and logic. Certain differences of much importance must, however, be noted. The mystic seeks and finds satisfactory his own experience, whereas the scientist is not satisfied with the validity of personal experience but seeks also the experience of a larger number of individuals, i.e. a group. Hence his verification is wider. Science is a collaboration; its results are the results of the efforts of groups such as biologists, chemists or physicists. It is the irremediable weakness of mysticism that it rests its validity on what one man feels and finds *within himself*, a region which is inaccessible to others and therefore most of his findings cannot be verified. It is the admirable strength of science that it rests its validity on what can be found quite accessible in Nature or in laboratories and hence can be verified by any other member of the scientific group, who are thus able to agree among themselves. It is the impregnability of genuine philosophy that it alone appeals to *universal* experience, to what any man at any time in any place may verify if he has the requisite mental capacity.

It is a fashion among mystics, intuitionists and some religionists to speak caustically of the shifting hypotheses of science, and to pour the acid of scorn upon its most modern achievements and technological applications. Moreover, when war breaks out nowadays part of its horror is blamed on science too. All this shows confused thought and emotional bias. If the changes of theory reveal the imperfections of science, as they admittedly do, we ought to recognize that they also reveal a twofold inner aim which philosophy would gladly encourage and value as possessing extreme significance. Firstly, a search after truth which generates a readiness to drop faulty views for better ones when their faultiness has been conclusively demonstrated by additional facts. Secondly, an effort to generalize data, to formulate universally comprehensive laws. This is in reality an attempt to enclose the many within the one, to receive the differentiated multitude of things into a grand unity. These are characteristics which, pushed to their terminal point, will unfailingly bring the marching army of scientists into the ever-waiting camp of true philosophers.

So far as the censuring of science for the worsening of war is concerned, it may be said that like everything else it has its bright and dark sides, its attractive advantages and repulsive disadvantages. If it has given us high-powered explosives and low-diving aeroplanes, it has also given the great convenience of electric light, power and heat.

Science is not to be blamed because some men are too foolish or too unethical to use it rightly. It is utterly neutral. The same explosive chemicals which can blow a platoon of living men to the sky can refertilize exhausted soil and cause new crops to spring into life. The same internal combustion engine which propels the death-dealing armoured tank can propel the utilitarian omnibus. The same broadcasting station which fills the minds of a million listeners with lies, hate and distorted propaganda can also fill them with grand, noble and instructive truths. Scientific discoveries have poured into the twentieth century like an advancing flood. Scientific knowledge may be well used or badly abused by man, as he wishes, but its remarkable advances cannot stop. It has come stubbornly to stay. It is the outstanding phenomenon of our age. We have to accept it. The mystic may try to ignore it, but he cannot succeed. No modern man can carry on for a week without availing himself a hundred times of the fruits of scientific research. And is it not better that we enslave steel machines rather than groaning men?

It is a further fashion among Oriental mystics, of whom Gandhi is a conveniently illustrative type, to denounce everything modern in favour of everything medieval and consequently to ascribe a satanic origin to science but a heavenly one to primitive forms of culture and civilization. No other reply is needed than that which is afforded by their own lives, for even Gandhi himself did not disdain to utilize the latest methods of scientific surgery to secure the removal of his pain-bringing appendix ; yogis do not hesitate for a moment to take advantage of steam-drawn railway trains to carry them nearer their retreats in the foot of the Himalaya ; pilgrims enthusiastically crowd the motor-lorries which ply in stages across the plains to the holy cities ; and even those critics who send forth such denunciations write them with fountain-pens on paper which is mill-manufactured often with a view to having them printed on machine-presses for wider circulation ! Science thus occupies its inescapable place in their lives, however ungrateful be those whom it serves. Its capacity for harming mankind through war and violence, however regrettable it be, can be entirely removed in one way alone, and that is through bringing philosophic truth into mankind's purview.

It is now necessary to utter a warning based on facts known to practising psychiatrists and professional psychologists. The reasoning faculty may be highly developed so far as its application to a special sphere of interest is concerned, and yet in the same man it may be almost entirely unapplied or at best working weakly when a different sphere comes into question. This is the singular phenomenon called schizophrenia, or mind-splitting. For example, a man may have risen rapidly to the forefront of his profession through the effective use of reason, and yet as soon as his attention is turned to other matters no belief may be too silly to engage his wholehearted assent !

It is quite feasible that one and the same man may be a child in religious matters and an adult in business affairs ; consequently he may be mentally apart, yet bodily together !

The mind may be divided into idea-tight compartments, one of which is reasonable and efficient but the other, being dull or even deranged, is totally insulated against it. Certain famous judges and statesmen of proved shrewdness have historically exhibited this peculiar mental infirmity, as when their reason recoiled from questioning the bases of traditional religion. This defeat of intellectual "compartmentalism" arises out of a conscious or unconscious refusal to use reason when thinking about certain reserved subjects. In consequence we see the pitiable spectacle of an otherwise sensible man indulging in special pleading to support ridiculous beliefs. People are duped into believing that because a man is famous for his keen capacity in one field, or is doing his public work in an efficient manner, his opinions about matters outside the sphere of his professional work have the same value. They do not know that insanity can be localized in particular parts of the mind, as it were.

Mind-splitting is frequently found among the insane. But there are various grades of insanity. It is only when an insane person becomes dangerous to others or harmful to himself that he is labelled as such and confined in a lunatic asylum. Large numbers of people do not come within this category but are still sufficiently unbalanced to be partly insane, although neither they themselves nor society at large can realize this. It is not too much to say that the wars, crimes, hatreds, conflicts and social struggles which afflict the world exist because most of mankind are more or less insane. And according to the hidden teaching, only the sages have achieved full sanity and complete balance !

Insanity tends to grow gradually. What begins as a mild and harmless form of superstitious belief may develop into outright inability to manage the ordinary concerns of life.

The attempt to justify mere baseless fancies or wild inherited superstitions by a plausible show of logic is rationalization. The effort to think strictly and impersonally upon facts is reasoning. The distinction between both can be observed in the cases of many public men by the curious.

The word *reason* has such a familiar sound, it is so often upon the lips of orators and the pens of writers, that the reader who has waited expectantly for some kind of novel revelation is now likely to recoil in disappointment. He has hoped, perhaps, to learn that the sages of the Far East, as the crest-wave of human mental and ethical evolution, had evolved in their own persons a new organ of knowledge, something that the rest of the laggard mankind would themselves evolve during the course of future ages. And now he is told that they had nothing newer to offer the modern world than its own trite, commonplace and much-talked-of faculty of reason, married, it is true, to a yoga technique and thereby converted into a higher octave of itself dignified with the bold title of insight. He is likely to feel that this chapter has led to an anticlimax.

Let us see. Were the sages so foolish and so unaware of the history of world culture as to proffer an instrument of knowledge which was apparently tried extensively by the Greeks and is still being tried extensively by Eur-American scientists and philosophers, but which has led in neither case to a single solution of the world-problem that is likely to remain *for ever* uncontrovertible ; were they so ridiculous as to designate such an instrument as perfect ?

The answer is that both ancient Greek and modern thinker have three principal charges laid to their door to account for this failure: (*a*) neglect to gather *complete* data, (*b*) ignorance of the applicability of the law of relativity not merely to observed physical phenomena but also to observed psychological phenomena and finally to the mind of the observer himself, (*c*) neglect to push their line of reasoning to its last possible terminal-point, and thus to exhaust all its still unknown possibilities. These charges are weighty, but they shall be made good. Nevertheless, even if the three defects were rectified, still the truth would be beyond the grasp of the average scientific investigator unless he were willing to discipline himself in a certain way. With all this done, however, then the human mind, purified of its native egoism, concentrated to a perfect degree, sharpened to the most metaphysical subtlety of reasoning upon adequate data and abstracted into intense reverie of deliberate self-watchfulness, can hope at last to gain a unique insight into the real nature of things, into the ultimate meaning of universal existence and into the hidden truth of its own mysterious being.

The first charge may now be justified. Western philosophy has not lived up to its own credo. That which has most attracted thoughtful men and generous minds to the study of philosophy through the centuries has perhaps been its claim to seek—alone among all the branches of human culture—a comprehensive view of life *as a whole*. Yet it is singular enough that the whole historic tradition of Greek, European and American philosophy completely ignored and omitted from its enquiry an aspect of life which is of such importance that it occupies no less than one-third of the duration of human existence.

We refer to the condition of sleep. Those few who studied this subject were psychologists or medical men, not philosophers, and consequently interested only in some of its limited physical meaning.

It is not to be wondered at that the Western thinkers failed to arrive at any agreed solution of the problem of existence when they all failed to investigate the problem of sleep and thus took only a fragmentary and incomplete view of life, although their claim as philosophers was to investigate the whole panorama in its entirety! It need not surprise us that they wandered around so inconclusively, for without the facts to be elucidated by such investigation they were insufficiently equipped for their ambitious task and were foredoomed to return baffled and undecided to their starting-point, much as a mutilated tiger wanders vainly in circles through the jungle on its three sound legs. How could they have covered in thought the whole of our complex human life when that wide section which is spent in peaceful slumber or troubled dream was regarded as too insignificant to be worth studying, when all their emphasis was unfairly thrown on the waking state alone? Such an outlook was totally inadequate to the aim they set before themselves and their defeat was thereby rendered certain at the very start of their battle for truth. There can be no finality about any system of thought which excludes the study of sleep, but only liability to erroneous, faulty or imperfect conclusions.

If science is to evolve into philosophy, and if logic is to evolve into reasoning, they must take all three states of existence into their orbit. It is to the little-known credit of the Indian sages that even when the civilization of Europe was still in its infancy they had seized on this special aspect of life and were proclaiming to listening pupils that it offered a key to the profounder mysteries of being and they early included it as an object of their philosophical studies. Indeed, they declared that an investigation of the nature and implications of dream and sleep was most essential, because these phenomena of life were as fully important to its understanding as the waking state.

There is a common but pardonable notion in the West that only primitive people need pay attention to dreams and that scientific minds have nothing to learn from deep sleep. The superficiality of this view will be amply demonstrated when the subject comes to be dealt with in detail.

A further handicap for the Western philosophers as well as for the scientists lay not only in their insufficient data but also in their imperfect instrument. The tool with which a philosopher must needs work is his mind. The ancient sages did not permit a man to begin philosophic studies until he had put his mind into proper shape so that it could function efficiently. This preliminary phase consisted in a practical course in the yoga of mental concentration often coupled with a parallel course in ascetic self-abnegation. Both courses, however, were usually temporary and continued only so long as they were necessary to bring the mental faculties to a reasonable degree of concentrative competency, and the pupils' character to a reasonable degree of self-detachment, sufficient to undertake the difficult task of philosophical reflection.

Western thinkers have made admirable attempts, but they have failed to win success partly because they lacked this tool of a yoga-equipped, ego-purified and body-subdued mentality with which to force open the shut gate of truth.

The lack of a course in yoga-training likewise accounts for the inability of certain distinguished Western scientists to proceed to the fullest implications of their own discoveries. Therefore, those scientists and philosophers who have not acquired the enduring mental benefits of mystic practice (as opposed to the fugitive visions and feelings) will have to retrace their steps and do so.

This lack is partly responsible for the second charge against them, for amid all their investigations they have been unable to detect, as will be demonstrated in the second volume, that their own ego has entered into and interfered with their work, although it is as relative, as transient and as objective as all the other phenomena they have observed; and furthermore, it has prevented most of them from seeing the subtle truth of the mental nature of all phenomena, whether of the world outside or of the ego within.

The justification of the third charge will likewise be fully given in the further volume, but it will suffice for the moment to point out that despite the discoveries of Heisenberg, author of the *Law of Indeterminacy*, and of Max Planck, formulator of Quantum Mechanics, not a single Eur-American leader of thought has yet dared to take a bold and decisive stand on the question of Non-Causality, but all sit on the fence which separates the old familiar law of causation from the strange new and revolutionary tenet whose full acceptance would involuntarily convert scientists into full-fledged philosophers! However, physics, as the most virile of present-day sciences, has made a noticeable beginning and cast several hesitant glances in the direction of philosophy, which lies immediately beyond its present position and to which it will be eventually forced to travel.

The successful termination of the quest of the ancient sages did not come from blindly believing the words of some personage; it did not come from yielding to the consolations of some religious book; it did not come from mystic intuition, that appeared suddenly and involuntarily; it did not come from the satisfactions of mystic practices or empty meditation; it came only at the end and as a consequence of long-laboured arduous yoga-gripped *thinking*, more rational than any ever known to our modern so-called Rationalists!

Nevertheless it should also be noted that the sources of knowledge which have been found fallible are not thereby excluded from the rational life. Some beliefs are quite reasonable even if many are quite ridiculous. Where authorities and scriptures, intuitions and illuminations, arguments and conclusions agree with universal experience and genuine reason they should be most acceptable.

They may be useful as helps, even though they may not be relied on alone. The philosopher is not unwilling to listen to what these have to say to him, for he knows that knowledge can often be got through such sources, but unlike others he will be determined to judge them ultimately by higher canons for himself, so that he may find out how far they may be relied on. For he seeks a rock-like impregnable position. He rejects nothing in advance but he questions everything in the end to enquire if it be true, whereas unenlightened men deliberately divorce intuition from any contact with reason whilst unenlightened mystics deliberately refuse to submit their "truth" to any test. He will not be so foolish as to repel an intuition, for instance, but he will be ready to accept it only *after* he has controlled, examined and confirmed it. Thus mentally fortified he will so use his own intuitions or expert authorities that they may become a most useful help.

Fidelity to reason does not debar but admits faith, therefore, only it demands that we should test our beliefs and discover if they be true. It likewise accepts the existence of spontaneous intuition, but asks that we check our intuitions and ascertain whether they be correct, not hesitating to reject them where found unsatisfactory. It unhesitatingly admires the unusual tranquillity to be found in mystic meditations, but counsels that we enquire rigorously whether the feeling of reality which it gives us *be* reality. It always approves of the exercise of logic in the organization of thinking, but it points out that the operations of logic are strictly limited by the amount of available data and that at best logic can only rearrange in an orderly manner what we already explicitly or implicitly know. In short, it seeks firm verification.

If, for instance, those who are having mystic experiences will, without necessarily giving them up, subject them to the tests here described, the profit will be much and the progress more. It is one of the functions of philosophic discipline to act as a corrective to mystic experience.

Now how can we test our beliefs, check our intuitions, enquire into the reality of meditation experience, know whether our logic is dealing with all possible facts or not and eliminate the errors of every one of these methods? There is but a single answer to all these queries, a single means of satisfying our doubts concerning them, and that is—we must begin and end with the canons of reason as the sole criterion of judgment. For it is only by critically reasoning upon them that such examinations can be fruitfully carried out.

What is it that even theologians attempt to use when they wish to discriminate between authentic scriptures and spurious ones? They seek to use reason. What is it that tells us of the insufficiency of logic and the fallibility of intuition? It is not intuition itself, not revelation and not vision; it is *reason*. And when it is claimed that both intuition and mystic feeling are above reason, then why do those who make the claim venture to discuss, to argue and to prove by reasoning that what they have felt or seen is correct? Is this not an unconscious reference to reason as the final court of appeal, to the verdict of thinking power as the supreme arbitrament? Is it not a tacit admission that reason alone has the right to sit in silent judgment on the ultimate value of all other faculties? Thoughts cannot cease save in sleep or trance, and every form of thinking—whether used by hard-headed realist or other-worldly mystic—involves some reasoning, however imperfect and however crude the latter be. Why should we then not go the full length, when we have gone so far along this road, and unreservedly accept the supremacy of reason?

A thorough conviction and an unassailable grasp of true principles can only be reached through the adequate exercise of thinking-power intently concentrated and raised to its highest degree. No other method of approach can yield such an enduring correctness in every instance. And it will eventually be the sole means of obtaining world-wide agreement among all peoples and in all places on this globe, because reason cannot vary in its conclusions about truth; it is universally verifiable and will remain so a hundred thousand years hence. Such variations will, however, belong to what pretends to be reason. And they will also exist whenever reason is unjustifiably limited to the experience of waking state alone.

Thus is it possible to arrive at a knowledge of the meaning of world-existence which shall be valid at all times, which some bearded Indian sage dwelling in his Himalayan school forty centuries ago once gladly recognized and fully acknowledged but which shall yet not be antiquated or found false by some keen American scientist forty centuries hence, despite the fact that he shall then be heir to all the knowledge of the vanished generations which preceded him. Such a series of unvarying final conclusions can never be dispossessed by the activities of new thinkers nor displaced by the novel wizardry of modern science.

The ancient Indian sages once stood in certain respects where the scientists stand today, but they did not hesitate to push their enquiry into a wilderness where all familiar landmarks were lost.

They devaluated the personal factor and thus began as heroes sworn never to stop until the last letter of the last word of human thought about truth had been completely spelt out. They firmly pushed their reasoning to its ultimate possibility, to a point where, in fact, it could go no farther for the reasoning faculty ceased to work at the mysterious moment when it detected the hidden truth, itself coming to rest in the same instant. They discovered, moreover, that there are really two different kinds of thinking which might be termed the lower and higher stages of reasoning. In the first the power of analytic judgment is applied to the external world in an effort to distinguish what is substantially real from what is merely apparent. When this has been carried as far as possible—and not until then—thought must critically return to itself *and unhesitatingly examine its own nature*, which final step can only be successfully achieved if success in yoga has previously been achieved.

This is a task of immense difficulty because it requires the utmost concentration of the subtlest kind. Nor can a feeble and fragile intelligence make the needed effort. When this concentration has finally fulfilled its object the knowledge of reality dawns immediately, and in that moment reason ceases to work for its services in judging and discriminating within itself are no longer needed. This spontaneous cessation of thinking is not to be confused as is so often done with the mystic's "direct intuition of reality". It marks the successful conclusion of thinking, not the successful abolition of thinking. Reflection must not renounce itself before it has done its fullest work. Nor does the mystic ever achieve abolition of thought simultaneously with the retention of waking consciousness, the feat being impossible; he only changes one set of ideas for another. Thus what the mystic regards as the final achievement of his task is regarded by the sage as only the half-completion of his own. And where the mystic merely feels, he thoroughly understands.

The sages who have gone looked within self in the quest of abiding reality rather than fitful experience, of final truth rather than emotional satisfaction, and above all in completion rather than in commencement of their examination of the world—hence they alone found the genuine goal. And because they did not flee as did mystics from the vexing problem of the world, they solved that too at the same startling moment that the self was understood. That rare instant of all-embracing comprehension in the depth of thought-filled mystic trance was the culminating point in the pyramid of their philosophical endeavour. It was called by the sages "the lightning-flash", for it moved across the field of consciousness with the tremendous speed of a stroke of lightning. This having been achieved, their further work was to recover and stabilize the gratifying glimpse thus gained. With that their quest came to a perfect end. For the new sun did not rise in the reddening East for them alone. Thenceforth they made the age-old cause of all mankind their own.

What they knew, that they were!

CHAPTER VIII

THE REVELATION OF RELATIVITY

THE student who has determinedly and understandingly followed this thread of thought thus far will have raised himself above the primitive consolations of religion and the unsubstantial conjectures of imagination; he will have awakened from the blissful dreams of mysticism, the systematic self-deceptions of logic and the profound slumber of verbalism; he will have sharpened his understanding and shaped his feelings to engage in the loftiest adventure to which any man can be called—the quest of final truth. He will be well prepared for the first trial of strength which must now be undergone. The problem of the world confronts him first because it is the problem of that which is most familiar and most visible. Whereas the problem of self seems nearer it is actually more remote, and although it seems simple it is really harder to solve than the riddle of this inescapable universe that surrounds him. Therefore it is right to start with an enquiry into the nature of this curious world into which we humans are suddenly thrust and from which we are slowly removed without anyone consulting us in the matter!

It has already been explained why the initial attitude of a philosopher is one of doubt. He must carry this attitude with him not only when seeking a satisfactory source of knowing truth but also to mental distances which may well stagger the complacency of the ordinary man. He must be bold enough to begin his enquiry by seeking to go behind his conventional knowledge of the universe itself!

The alarmed reader may, however, be immediately reassured. He is not asked to doubt the *existence* of this world which is the first fact that confronts his eyes every morning and the last one that he shuts his eyes on every night. He is asked to question the truth of the sights, sounds and feels of which he is aware and the reality of the objects thus seen, heard or felt, all of which nobody but a lunatic would think of dismissing as non-existent. These are two separate and distinct questions which demand different treatment; it will suffice therefore to consider in this chapter how far our knowledge is basically true and to reserve for the following chapter how far what is known is also basically real.

The student, like everybody else, experiences the "given" world all right, but has he ever paused to question the validity of this experience? If not, it is his business to do so now. For if he pushes such enquiry to its deepest point he will make the queerest and most startling of intellectual discoveries.

What was one of the few supreme events in the scientific world during our generation? What revolutionary principle was then established which threw sensational new light on old problems? Without a doubt Albert Einstein's formulation of the Theory of Relativity not only summed up two thousand years of mathematical research and passed in review three hundred years of physical research, but it opened new pathways and expanded enormous vistas for pioneer thinkers. The reasoned proof of this complicated conclusion is filled with formulae which are beyond the brain of the average layman, nor can the doctrine itself be fully explained except in abstruse mathematical equations. Einstein himself confessed once, when asked to put it in a few understandable words, that it would take him three days to give a short definition! However, without losing ourselves in a difficult tangle of complex technical symbols and such indigestible intellectual foods as the calculus of variations and the theory of invariants, we may and must simplify and illustrate certain aspects of Einstein's hypothesis of special interest to philosophers. That he himself looks somewhat askance at philosophy is a natural if regrettable consequence of the prejudice born of his scientific specialism; but it also arises because he confounds mere speculation with verified philosophy, a misconception for which some so-called philosophers and many half-philosophers are themselves responsible. In his abhorrence of metaphysics he has sought to confine his thought upon his work within well-defined limits, but he could never have evolved his hypothesis by mere experiment alone, and to the extent that he indulged in rigorous reflection he was willy-nilly an unconscious philosopher. It is impossible for the physicist to contemplate the question of relativity with the thoroughness such an important principle deserves without rising into ultimate questions and hence without turning himself for the time into a member of the philosophic fraternity. But Einstein is a mathematician and a physicist and wishes to keep strictly to his trade. Hence he refuses to consider the further implications of his work, i.e. he refuses to philosophize.

THE REVELATION OF RELATIVITY

But all his disciples are not so limited. Eddington and Whitehead have ventured to follow up the consequences of carrying his doctrine to realms where thought runs deeper, the first in philosophical psychology and the second in philosophical logic, both regions where the master will not venture. But only in the ancient Asiatic thought is the path of analysis which both have begun to travel been followed to its fullest extent.

We need not let the highly mathematic character of Einstein's calculations depress us or frighten us away from the hypothesis itself. For mathematics is only a kind of logical shorthand whose symbols yield conclusions from given data with a quickness unknown to logic. It abbreviates syllogistic procedure by the substitution of formulae and equations. The conceptual essence of Einstein's discovery was known to the vanished sages of Hindustan, who were not, however, like Einstein, trained mathematicians, whilst Greek philosophers like Plato and Aristotle realized its profound importance. The Jaina thinkers of India formulated a similar philosophic doctrine, Syadvada, which resembles Relativism, more than two thousand years before Einstein formulated his scientific doctrine. Thus the Indian and Greek thinkers anticipated a principle which was not to be experimentally tested and finally proved till many centuries had passed away. What Einstein really did was to corroborate it scientifically, to place it on a foundation of original mathematical observation and experimental proof by illustrating its practical application to a special sphere. He formulated relativity in order to fit the hypotheses of physics to observed data. He made science responsible for the testing and verification of a principle which had hitherto lived precariously either among the arguable speculations of ignored metaphysicians or amidst the antique doctrines of unknown aliens. And it was the growth of such technological sciences as optics and electro-dynamics that made his experimental work, in the investigation of the sun's gravitational influence on light-rays, for instance, at all possible. *Hence this proof could not have been arrived at earlier in history than it was!*[1]

---

[1] Light plays a unique role among the elements. A light-ray is the quickest travelling thing known to science and it is the most important means of human communication with the world outside. The introduction of the theory of relativity into scientific thinking owes its origin to a famous experiment on the speed of light performed by the Americans Michelson and Morley towards the end of last century. Their work determined that the speed with which light travelled remained the same no matter in what direction it did travel or to what body in space it was moving to meet. The experiment showed that light moved at the same rate relative to the earth whether the latter was approaching it or receding from it. It was difficult to reconcile this discovery with the fact that the earth is moving through space. We should expect the rate of movement of light to be greater when light is approaching the

Relativity has taken the unalterable fixity out of time and turned it into a variable dimension. Put in plainer language, time has no particular meaning that is always fixed and the same for all human beings. Those who would limit it to *their* measurement of clocks or of the revolutions of starry bodies are merely airing a prejudice. For the sense of time is not an absolute actuality but an interpretation of both clock and star made by a conscious being. It is the way sensations arrange themselves in the mind. There is no such thing as an absolute measure of time. Close analysis will reveal that all our measurements based on planetary revolutions are *ultimately* nothing else than our relative impressions. Einstein began to point this out, but he did so without realizing its fullest consequences.

The doctrine teaches that movement merely means the positional change of relation between one thing and another, and therefore physical change, as movement, is never absolute but always relative. Once we admit that *standards* of time and space measurement may vary, then we have to abandon our conventional ideas of the sciences of physics, geometry and astronomy. Astronomy talks glibly of the

---

earth. This is on the same principle that the combined speeds of two trains approaching each other from opposite directions is greater than the speed of a single train. Therefore an observer situated on a planet which was advancing rapidly towards an approaching ray of light ought to discover that its rate of movement was higher than when he was receding before it. But the experiment ascertained that the speed of light remained unaltered, being exactly the same, 186,000 miles a second, as before the mutual motion was taken into account. This fantastic result was therefore arithmetically equal to $2 + 1 = 2$!

Why did not the rays of light increase their rate of travel as according to known laws they should have done? No explanation of this peculiarity that was really adequate was forthcoming until Einstein gave it. He pointed out in mathematical language that all previous reflection on the matter was evidently based on principles which themselves wrongly interpreted the experiment, and that it would be wiser to modify those principles until they fitted the facts it revealed. But this put on trial the whole question of the way in which the speed of light was measured, and the way in which every instrument and every observer using the instrument arrived at the time and space dimensions which resulted. If this were done it would then be found necessary to alter inherited and prevalent notions of time and space themselves. They had previously been regarded as something fixed for all time and in all places and under all conditions, but the old standards with respect to them had been proved fallible by this experiment made on the behaviour of light in a rapidly moving system. By making a change in the character of these standards, by depriving them of their assumed fixity and putting them in fundamental dependence on the situation of the observer, by recognizing that all spatial measurement is the comparison of the relative positions of two things in space, and by accepting that there is nothing ultimately constant about time or movement or measures of length, a new world-view would come into being which would not only satisfactorily explain the problem of light's uniform speed but would also explain other physical problems which recent advances in science had brought up. Such were the beginnings of the principle of relativity. Einstein then applied the principle to the influence of solar gravitation on passing rays of light and by its aid made a precise calculation of the deflection they would undergo. When in 1919 astronomical observations during an eclipse confirmed his prediction the principle of relativity was magnificently vindicated before the world of scientists. They could no longer continue to ignore it. The basis of all conventional scientific thought about its own position had to undergo a vital change.

constellations of "fixed" stars. Yet this is a relative term only, for without doubt they too are hurrying through space when seen by somebody who is situated on what is to him a point of comparative rest. We treat the Pole Star as if it were always at rest, yet the phenomenon of the precession of the equinoxes proves that it too is a moving body. Therefore our use of the word "fixed" is quite arbitrary. The fixed stars are thus named not because we really know that they remain stationary in space but because astronomy has not yet been able to devise instruments which will bring them close enough to our perception conclusively to detect any movement in them. When Einstein said that there was no position in the universe which was absolutely at rest, and therefore no position from which the shape and measurement of an object could be ascertained and hold good under all other conditions of observation, he said in effect that science was impotent to come to a final calculation about the world.

We make our space-time measurements of position and motion in relation to some standard which we assume is permanent, unalterable and immutable; in short, ever at rest. But Einstein has convincingly demonstrated that there is nothing in the universe to which we can finally apply the description of "rest". For aught we know it may be moving around a second thing also supposed to be at rest. How can we know that anything is perpetually at rest and never moving when our range of perception is so limited? We habitually judge by plausible outer appearances, by what the limited five senses tell us, and commonly but ignorantly take solid stones for matter at rest. Yet the truth is plainly revealed by modern physical investigation into the wonderful world of atoms and molecules. For the whole of stationary matter is built up out of electrons and protons and neutrons which are incessantly moving like swarms of restless bees. We must revise our simple notion of the world.

If we sit for some time in a running train watching the green landscape slide past the glazed windows our eyes become accustomed to the motion and take it to be a normal condition. If the train stops there is a temporary illusion that the landscape is moving forward or that the train is moving backward. In certain relations to the universe all mankind is like the passenger in the train.

A man who is walking along a bend in the railroad will not notice, if he continually keeps his eyes directed towards his feet, that the very track he is passing over is curved. It will appear quite straight to him. It is only when he lifts his eyes, looks a little distance ahead, and thus alters his perspective that he will see that the rails are really curved. The same object therefore looks different from a different perspective. How much of our world-view would be altered if we could alter our perspective?

A caravan of five hundred camels resting in a valley appears to an observer who is standing on a precipice overhead to be wholly at rest. But this holds good only of the customary ideas of space belonging to pre-relativity physics, and hence ignores the fact that the earth is travelling around the sun and carrying the caravan on its movement too. The observer, being quite unable to detect this motion, *unconsciously* deceives himself into the belief that what is true from his standpoint is also true from every other standpoint within the universe. This is obviously incorrect, for a second observer would certainly witness the caravan's passage through space were it possible to overcome the practical difficulties of placing him on the sun, and were he to survive the ordeal, devise and be provided with an optical instrument adequate to the purpose. All that the first observer is entitled to say is that the camels are at rest relative to the earth; more he may not say with *truth* unless he is able to shift his point of vantage. Yet neither observer is wholly right nor wholly wrong. The fact is, as Einstein points out, each moving body possesses its own standard of time and its own system of space with which an observer will always be in relation. He will not know ordinarily that the other standards and systems may differ from his and that if he persists in sticking to the latter he will be unable to explain the presence of utterly incomprehensible and completely irrational factors in the universe.

These statements are the logical consequence of our knowledge that the earth revolves round the sun. But the movement of any planet can only be measured and described by mutual comparison with something else that is quite still, say with the totality of fixed stars. Hence relativity teaches that we can know only the relations between bodies in space and that the description of them is only comparative. We can only compare one thing with another. We are compelled to deal in dualities. For our conception of space is meaningless without a given standard of reference.[1]

---

[1] A man who listens regularly for the clock of a city hall to chime the hour of noon will assert that he hears the sound proceed from the same spot every day. If, however, it were possible for another man placed on the sun to listen for the event he would have to assert that the sounds proceeded from spots which were successively 300,000 miles distant from each other every day. For the earth and the clock would have regularly moved to a different daily position relative to the sun. Thus the change of standpoint produces an immense change in the results obtained.

If somehow we were so closed in that it was impossible to see the other stars and planets in the sky we could not know that our earth was moving forwards through space. We would feel sure that it was fixed immovably in the firmament. For we would possess no standard of reference. Thus motion is quite relational.

The earth is dynamically working its way through space around the sun at the enormous velocity of nearly 70,000 miles an hour, yet nobody feels the slightest pulse of this movement; everybody upon it, on the contrary, feels that the earth is standing perfectly still!

We glibly use the word "here". Yet even whilst we point out the spot so designated the earth has whirled at a gigantic speed through space, taking the spot with it, so that in a few minutes the latter is many miles distant from where it was before. The "here" becomes therefore a relative term, relational to some point or person on the earth but meaningless when applied to space. Moreover, the earth turns on itself and then revolves around the sun. But the latter is itself moving relative to the Milky Way, and although it is a matter at present beyond our measurement the Milky Way may most probably be speeding through space too. When all these movements are taken into account we must realize that we can form no probable estimate of how far the same spot has *really* shifted in the course of these few minutes. Nor could any experiment ever detect the speed with which it is really moving through space, for there is no body that is *absolutely* at rest with which its movement could be compared. We can only determine its relative place and relative rate of movement. And this will be the result wherever we station ourselves.

Thus we arrive again at the basis of Einstein's doctrine, which is that space has no ultimate standard of measurement in itself and that it is not the same under all circumstances. Space in the ultimate analysis does not possess the properties implied by Euclid in his postulates and axioms. Such is the conclusion of relativity. But long before Einstein both Zeno and Pythagoras in Greece and several sages in India had found the contradictions which inhere in the idea that space has a characteristic existence, an unalterable fixity of its own. They saw that from one point of view it is measurable, purely relational and finite, but from another it is quite immeasurable and infinite in every direction. From the first we may limit it to its parts, which can easily be marked out from the other parts in the extension occupied by physical objects, but which from the second viewpoint have no independent existence separated from the whole, and we can impose no limits on its indefinite continuance. For when we try to put all its parts together we can never arrive at an aggregate which is the whole of space; whatever we think of as being the whole will always have some more space extending beyond it, and so on in an endless regress. Thus if you think of space as a lesser part you deny its existence as a whole. If both views cancel each other out in this way, then we must conclude that space is more a subjective idea than an objective element.

Moreover, if we apply some of the valuable lessons learnt in the sixth chapter to certain words which are used whenever the absolute existence of space is taken for granted, the words *here* and *there*, a curious situation has to be faced. For space is supposed to be that in which something exists or that in which the world-order differentiates itself.

Now think of a point here upon this white sheet of paper. Geometry defines a point as being a position without magnitude. It has no dimension at all. This means that a point has nothing inside it and has no place for anything to be put inside it. Carry this analysis still further and you will see that the point is not spatial at all and therefore space, as represented by its "here", both is and is not, contradictions which thus again cancel themselves out.

Think again of something that is out "there" in space, say the distant continent of Australia. That means it is "not here". But by "here" you may imply here in this city, or here in this country, or here in this continent; or you may widen its embrace to the whole of this world. You can go no farther, because you can no longer have a special standpoint whereby one place can be distinguished from another. The narrowness of attention which restricts your definition of "here" will then be abolished. But in going so far you have included Australia in your "here". Thus "here" and "there" contradict each other, and with that the very notion of space as a separate reality which rests upon them collapses altogether.

What becomes of our ordinary notion of space when radioactive investigation tells us that the sharp point of the sharpest needle made is a minute world where millions of moving bodies incessantly circulate without ever touching each other?

Those who object to the analysis of such paradoxes as mere word-quibbling do not understand the important role played by words in secretly constructing our thought, nor do they comprehend that semantic problems are really logical ones, and quite often they are even epistemological ones. And they do not understand that the meaning of a thing is inseparable from what we ourselves *think* it to be; it is not only what some dictionary prints concerning it.

And they do not understand that the hidden working of the mind in the viewing of the world is something quite other than they usually suppose it to be.

Relativity shows at least that we have got to alter our inherited habits of thinking about the world. Space and time demand examination because they enter into every conception of the external world. They are the forms in which our experience is given us. A complete understanding of this world completely involves them too. Our objective life on earth obviously moves within the conditions imposed upon it by space and time; all our experience is indeed inseparable from them. All measurable bodies and all living creatures are presented to our senses as existing spatially or temporally and we cannot help representing the entire universe to ourselves within a specific frame of space and time. We cannot think of the myriad facts and manifold events of Nature without thinking of them as filling a position somewhere in space and somewhen in time. But the meaning of the latter is always relative and changes with changing circumstances. Therefore these phenomena of Nature can themselves only be thought of relatively. If we change our frame we shall change familiar characteristics of our universe too. It will lose its fundamental fixity, its unalterable absoluteness. There can be no such thing as unique spatial relation or unchangeable time observation. When we look more deeply into space it tends to change its character from what appears to be an outward fact to what is really an inward mental factor. We must, in short, begin to mentalize space and spatialize mind. So far from being a property of the external world, space begins to appear as a mysterious subjective element which conditions our perception of the entire external world.

But this view abandons the old conceptions of physics. It is in line with Einstein's mathematical deductions which have made the mass of a body variable. The old idea of matter was that its most prominent and most tangible characteristic—technically termed mass—was also its most enduring one. This is true of the low rates of movement of everyday objects, but it is no longer true of those beyond ordinary experience where extremely high rates of movement prevail, for Einstein has forced science to discard the old belief inasmuch as he has proved that the mass of matter may vary. Thus physical objects become transformed into fields of electrical force, of pure energy assuming forms dictated by velocity. The belief in a separate something, a solid material substance, has been seriously affected. Hitherto we could not speak of matter apart from the space it occupied, whereas we can speak of energy with far less need to put it into space.

This new notion that energy has mass and that the mass of a material body can change proportionately above certain rates of movement renders the material character of a thing no longer its cardinal one. The imagination cannot here easily catch up with reason, but that must not be taken as an excuse for allowing the former to obstruct the latter. The new scientific view must necessarily offend common sense in thus destroying the static nature of an object. It is impossible for the mind to present to itself in any adequate imagery the idea of how relativity strangely affects the mass of our material universe. We must be content to know, without knowing how.

The Tricks of Time. The strange light which relativity has thrown on our beliefs about space is quite similar to that which it has cast on our beliefs about time. Our confidence in dating a single event is shattered when we learn that it will be seen at different times by two observers who are placed on bodies with different rates of movement; we start in surprise on hearing that two occurrences which are simultaneous in occurrence for one witness will appear to have a lapse of duration between them for the other.

The earth does not spin so fast through space as it did during the earlier days of its hot youth and consequently the length of our day is more than double what it then was!

Such is the relativity of time that the slow turtle which lives for a century may not feel that it has endured more than the swift insect which appears, grows, mates and dies in a single week, for it determines its experience from a different standpoint. The point is how many sensations pass through the mind; if the number is equal in both cases then years do not count. Whoever has experimented with certain drugs knows that one consequence will be the unfoldment of an abnormal sense of time so that a simple act like lifting a hand will vividly take a half-hour to perform in consciousness, yet to a watching person it is but the deed of a moment. Some who have escaped death from drowning by a hair's-breadth report that during the brief period preceding unconsciousness the history of their life flashed like lightning before their mind's eye.

We fall asleep only apparently to awake again soon after in dream, but we know later that we actually awoke only next morning. We feel as much awake during dream as during the day. Yet in five minutes of dream-time we complete a journey that takes three weeks of waking time. We live in dream through a long sequence of dramatic events, often highly detailed, and hours or days seem to have passed in the experience, but enquiry reveals that the whole series of events has occupied only a fraction of a minute! Thus experience reveals the strange fluctuations of our sense of time when we approach the same fact from different points of view.

A man differently situated, say on the planet of Venus, would necessarily have a different time-sense from ours. The notion that twenty-four hours will be twenty-four hours always under all conditions and in all places is not correct. Such a disclaimer may give a deep shock to our most familiar habits of thought. Yet consider the case of a young man who has spent three or four hours with an ardently loved sweetheart. The period will seem to him to be shortened to less than a single hour. Consider as contrast the case of an invalid who has accidentally fallen on a hot stove, and is unable to lift himself up quickly! To him each intensified second will seem as long as an hour! Each man has his individual time perception, as such abnormal instances make clear, and it is illusory to believe that it is any other than his own unique experience. He sees events in the perspective of his own special standpoint, because time itself is only a relation. We never really measure time itself. Even clock-time is only a measurement of a motion in space, i.e. a relation between two things.

We are compelled by Nature to see everything as existent in space and time. Time is immutably presupposed in the thinking process. Space is a necessary condition of the perceiving process. We can never separate a single thing from them. Yet we never see space and time themselves! We get no direct sense-impression of pure space or pure time. We cannot clothe the bare idea of space in any mental image; we can only think of a thing occupying distance, extension; hence we know space only as a property of things and time as a property of movement.

The ordinary way is to regard time as being like a flowing stream or like a constant succession of ticked-off moments. This is perfectly natural, for the human mind cannot even imagine a time which is devoid of the passage of happenings or in which no "before, now and after" of events exist. It is in time that one thought follows another as it is in time that events occur. Can you form any idea of time at all unless you conceive it in beginnings and endings or with breaks and changes? But unfortunately this leads us into an illusion. For we suppose time to be divided into moments, but try to get precise hold of them and they vanish.

Analysis discovers no separate parts, no independent moments; there is no interval between present and past. How can anyone distinguish when the present moment begins or when it ends? Try to find the recognizable point of separation between the past and the future, between "before" and "after". Whatever you take as such a point will no longer remain such the moment you have distinguished it. Yet what is the present moment except such a hypothetical point? It is one of the illusions of time that we perpetually believe ourselves to be living in the events of the present time when no such division really exists. Whether it be a single second or one-thousandth of a second or one millionth of a second later, the so-called present moment will already have lapsed into the so-called past. Our glib talk of the present, past and future phases of time is talk of something which nobody can determine and of which nobody can form an appreciable idea that will be correct enough to defy all analysis. What then becomes of our whole notion of time when no notion can be formed of its separate constituents? Thus what seemed to be a reality seems more likely to be to some extent at least an idea harboured by our minds, i.e. the movement of time is largely within ourselves.

Observe anything that grows, a grass seed for example. Can you state at what precise moment the seed becomes a plant? This is quite impossible. Then where is that moment when the seed was no longer a seed but a plant? If it exists anywhere, it must be in your mind or imagination. Thus the time-changes are really your own experiences. Moments do not really exist. Time is not an addition of non-existences. Add nought to nought and the total sum is still nought; therefore time is not an independent reality but an abstraction which is made from reality. Time, like space, is an abstraction. But when an abstraction is taken to be something real it contradicts itself.

When we push our reasoning still farther we have to admit that our sense of time may contract just as our sense of space may enlarge, and that when we measure the flight of time the mind somehow and to some degree creates it. Relativity teaches that the forms which times takes in experience are never final. They are aspects which may alter in the wildest manner. Yet there is one inseparable element which persists through all their alterations and which unifies and holds them all. And that is the factor of mind.

All this shows that time is not the simple thing we take it to be but is actually pregnant with mystery. "Mankind perishes speedily by thinking time real. The little time I spend in asking, 'Is there time at all ?' has revealed to me the perfect Peace, the very Deity Himself," was the observation of Tirumoolai, a medieval writer in the Tamil language. And still more sagely he asked the question : "Do you not know that time vanishes when its origin is sought for ? What then is the use of limiting yourself to it ?"

It would be a great error to imagine that any attempt is being made to deny that man has any sense of time. Nothing of the kind need be denied. He certainly feels the passage of time and feels its reality strongly. The attempt made here is to cast a little light upon its nature. The hidden source of this feeling of its reality will become apparent as this course unfolds.

The Doctrine of Standpoints. The value of Einstein's work in proving the truth of relativity by physical facts instead of metaphysical fancies is immense. What he has unconsciously achieved has been a critique of knowledge albeit he has limited his enquiry to scientific methods of measurement. The entire principle of relativity raises a gigantic question-mark against all our experience of the universe and hence against all our definitions of knowledge. What do we really know ? The world is no longer a hard fact but a harder problem.

Relativity is a fundamental law which underlies all physical events, all objects in Nature. Nothing is known that is not known in relation to other things. Hence the saying of Lotze, that to exist is to stand in relation. The idea that there are any closed systems in the universe disappears under the searching light of relativity. Each is only a tentative stage in the approach to truth and never the final step. The universe requires constant re-interpretation.

There may be as many relative truths in the physical world as there are possible positions or ways of looking at a thing. This is the anthropocentric flaw which vitiates ordinary knowledge. There may be as many views of truth in the world of thought as there are human beings. Such pluralistic and protean views are dependent on human limitations and are therefore always conditional and often liable to alter. Each is but an aspect, none is the entire truth. The mid-Victorian materialism, for instance, is now refuted by several leading scientists as vigorously as their predecessors had maintained it.

Here is our red signal of warning. An observation may be quite true when it is the consequence of fixing our attention on any particular point of view in the realm where relativity reigns and yet it may not be the truth *in itself*. The two are different.

All these factors are to be looked upon as men's individual and incomplete views because they are dependent on the flexibility of human taste, the kinds of human temperament, the grades of human knowledge or the degrees of its capacity. This is why we see such wide differences of opinion, such strange conflict of experience, and so many varieties of belief, outlook, custom and conclusion. Therefore these departments are called "relative truths". So wide is the possible range of the individual views arising out of such dependence on relative truth that there can be no limit to their number. Each department, like biology or pharmacology, for instance, possesses its own particular view of life or deals with some fragment of it, but none possesses a view which is common to all, just as none deals with the totality of existence.

When the apparition of relativity appeared on the threshold of science it frightened the timid. Well might they fear to push its logical consequence to its farthest end. This they still hesitate to do, so philosophy must take up the task for them. From its lofty standpoint, which, it must be pointed out, is that of ultimate truth and not of practical value, all non-philosophic knowledge, whether scientific or otherwise, stands on treacherous territory. None of its conclusions are or can ever be final. All depend on the parochial standpoint of observers on our insignificant planet, a mere speck among millions of other stars in space. All its results may be modified when with additional knowledge further standpoints become available. It may hope to discover distortions of the final reality by its present methods, but never reality itself. It moves ever from one provisional tenet to another like a restless ever-wandering Jew.

We may therefore well become bewildered as to the nature of the perplexing world in which we live. It is as paradoxical as any that could be conceived. It is a world where reason does violence to experience and where fact offers denial to thought. All human intellectual knowledge suffers from being entirely relative and in the end is chasing its own tail. It travels in a circle from which escape seems impossible. It would seem that we can never get at the final truth of the universe, and that we are captives perpetually doomed to receive only the illusion of fresh knowledge but never the knowledge itself.

Truth has become a myth. Finality is a fiction. It merely means one out of countless possible views. Every outlook may thus receive its justification. No scientific observation may now be declared correct for all time and for all observation. No scientific theory exists but is incurably tainted with this all-pervasive relativism. These different and divergent appearances of one and the same thing when the observers or standpoints are themselves different may well make us despair at ever knowing what is the truth about the world. For men will constantly change their intellectual position and shift to newer notions, only to lose them again next time. Everything thus becomes in the last analysis either a fleeting appearance or an insignificant illusion! Nothing may make pretension to finality.

It means that we get only fragmentary views of the world and never see the world as a whole. It means that we get only an endless supersession of one doctrine by another. It means that the mind for ever displaces one set of ideas by another. It means that the fact itself depends on the standpoint from which we approach it. What is appropriate to one standpoint will not suit another. For we get at aspects, not at independent entities. The sight of one aspect excludes all the others. There is no finality in metaphysics also because it equally with science is afflicted by the stubborn and persistent malady of relativity. The attempt to attain an irrevocable system of explanation has proved futile. In short, the picture of the world which we possess or which science possesses is not the final one.

In this world of relativism where all views are both false and true, where what can be affirmed from one standpoint can also be denied from another, there seems to be no final meaning. Those Indian seekers who perceived the inevitability of this consequence became dissatisfied. They wanted to know whether it is possible to arrive at a view which would explain *all* the facts and not only some of them. So the cardinal question again forced itself upon them. They sought an answer, like Pontius Pilate, to their supreme query, "What is truth? Can we get at the last word of truth in its integrity?" By this they meant something that was not so imperfect, that was no less universally valid for all men as that the addition of one plus two results in three. Nobody in any part of the world or in any century has yet questioned this arithmetical result. Such an unvarying principle of truth was sought by them. This they called the *ultimate* truth. Finally they found a satisfactory answer and then the hidden teaching was formulated. They proved that it was all a matter of standpoint, of climbing sufficiently high until the summit of all possible peaks was reached. They urged that the failure to find any absolute characteristic in the materials of our knowledge of the universe need not frighten us into despair. It should stimulate us to listen to the voice of the hidden philosophy which explicitly says that a fresh approach to the problem should be sought for and may be found.

Euclid showed that parallel lines never meet; Einstein showed that they may. Yet both may be considered as right provided we remember that they differ according to the different standpoints taken. The inhabitant of another planet using a watch marked in exactly the same manner as our watches would apparently measure time in the same way, but actually the similarity would be fictitious. His day might be longer or shorter than ours, therefore his three o'clock might not be equivalent to ours. For the standards of spatial reference would be different and the time systems would necessarily differ too. The difference of standpoint will always be fatal to uniformity of observation; the appearance of what the earth-man sees cannot be separated from his own position in space. The shape of a thing, the position it occupies and the place in time and space which it possesses are after all appearances presented differently to different observers. This is the implication of Einstein's General Theory of Relativity.

The need of taking fresh standpoints to secure expanded outlooks is thus an essential and important lesson of relativity. The relativity principle does not put Newton in the wrong nor make it necessary to discard old measurements. It draws a line of limitation around every kind of result and within each such system of reference the old measurements and the Newtonian notions hold good. It shows that we must not expect them to be always applicable, because they are only relative to a particular standpoint.

One standpoint which is higher than another will reveal a wider horizon. Even the shallowest experience of life shows that many things are not what they seem at first sight, that the naïve immediate impressions of them prove to be insufficient when we move to a deeper enquiry into them. It is the first lesson of philosophy and the last lesson of experience. It is the difference between what actually is and what only *appears* to be, between what is substantial and what seems to be substantial; we meet this contradiction of experience everywhere. It is to be found in human society as well as in planetary processes. The course, size and distance of a starry body do not yield to the gaze, look at it as long as we will. We must put forth intellectual effort, take instruction from astronomy, and then only can we wrest its secret from the seen. If everything revealed its whole nature to first uncorrected impression, science would never be needed and philosophy would never have to fatigue itself by following on the heels of science.

The wide discrepancy between experience and the truth of experience compels us to press onward beyond the plausible fact to challenging reflection upon the fact.

To stick always to a single position and take things from that position only because it is troublesome to find a fresh one or because everybody else sticks to that position is ultimately unsafe and philosophically unwise. From what point of view are we seeking truth? On what point of vantage do we stand when gazing at what we deem truth? For all that will determine both what we see and how far what we see is true. The meaning of what we believe to be truth and the value of a judgment are entirely conditioned by the standpoint we take up. Thus the possibility of ascertaining more truth in the scientific sphere increases by the mere upward shifting of standpoint. Philosophy absorbs this lesson and then carries it still further, for it says: let us therefore rise to the highest possible, the ultimate standpoint, where there is no relativity, and make our final conclusions about the world only then. It points out that we cannot escape from the need of a double viewpoint, the first being inclusive of all possible and relative positions embraced by ordinary practical life and experimental science, the second being the remote, austere and unique one of purely universal reason *free from all relativity*. For the view which will be obtained from the latter will be absolutely independent of those personal human characteristics which render all results partial and relative. They may be most useful for immediate and practical purposes, but they cannot serve the more exacting quest of final truth.

A mind that tires easily will, at the sight of unaccustomed paths, be content with the first and most immediate standpoint, that of practical utility, taking things just as they are perceived by the senses, whereas one that is well imbued with the love of truth will exert itself to rise above first appearances or the homely surface of things and reach their explanation by taking up a critical and inquiring position. This is what the scientist does. But he stops there. Hence the plaint of hidden philosophy. It welcomes the forward march of the scientist. It is not, like religion, afraid of him. Only it would urge him to rest at nothing short of a position from which he can affirm the ultimate truth or uncontradictable judgment. Such a position can belong only to the rigorous activity of pure reason put on its widest stretch, and is not to be disclosed by physical observation or laboratory experiment.

The primitive standpoint is a necessity of day-to-day living. It may prove quite successful for practical as opposed to theoretical purposes and thus require no other sanction from the average man. It is generally based on the crude and naïve reports of the five senses; the fact of these reports is there and everybody must accept it. The simpleton is satisfied with the face-value of his fact and in his mental poverty refuses to go behind the actual experience, but both scientist and philosopher will accept it only tentatively and then proceed to question it for its meaning. Both perceive that it is essential to pass in thought beyond immediate experience into wider and deeper enquiry into the way in which the fact came into being. If popular thought were always right thought, instruction would not be required; if immediate impressions were sufficient to know the whole truth about anything, education would not be called in to correct them; and if men naturally perceived the meaning of the universe and of their own lives the work of philosophy would be quite superfluous. Men are, in fact, born in original and native error; they win through to sound knowledge only by laboriously rectifying their common and spontaneous judgments. Yet popular abhorrence of mental effort is usually content with the easier view, ridden with numerous fallacies though it be, and often suspicious of the philosopher's, although the latter's represents the long struggle and final victory of reason.

Thus we arrive at the conclusion that there will always be two possible ways of looking at the world. The first standpoint is multiple and may include innumerable degrees of what is believed to be real or true, but it is always involved in what is technically called in logic the fallacy of simplicity. It may be described as being primitive, inferior, relative, ordinary, simple, practical, common-sense, empirical, immediate, partial, finite, phenomenal, local, ignorant and obvious. The second viewpoint may be described as being absolute, ultimate, philosophic, unified, highest, noumenal, reflective, universal, true, full, unique, superior, final and hidden.

We have already seen how science offends the common-sense standpoint. Then how much more will the latter be offended by whatever takes up a stand which is higher even than that of science? This higher view is not only unquestionably necessary but happily possible. Philosophy alone provides it because it alone climbs to the very summit and refuses to limit itself to "compartmentalism", but surveys the whole of existence, *including the surveying mind itself*. Philosophy seeks to fill the lack created through the compartmentalism of practical life and scientific research by taking the utmost care that no aspect of mental and material existence—

THE REVELATION OF RELATIVITY 195

however insignificant it be regarded by others—shall be omitted from its wide purview and unique co-ordination.

Science can never complete its task alone. Its adventure is a grand one but it can come to no terminus. When it gets weary of this circle-travelling it shall seek for respite ; not by weakening into the soothing arms of mysticism but by rising into the arctic air of philosophy shall it find enduring peace. This vicious round of relativity has no outlet unless science has recourse to the help of the philosophic view. Two separate standpoints thus arise and bifurcate our view of nature. There can be only one ultimate truth and one final standpoint whose character will be both unalterable and invulnerable. The philosopher seeks to discover them and is satisfied with nothing less. The concept of the world which arises out of the utmost pure reflection is different from that which arises out of the first sensual impression. We must distinguish sharply between them. For the first is perfect whilst the second is premature. The first standpoint is that of the *universe* itself, the second is that of man : the first sees from the viewpoint of the whole universe and not merely from that of the knowledge of any particular man, hence it is absolute and true, whereas the second sees only anthropocentrically, hence always relatively.

The change-over from the lower to the higher standpoint taken by the hidden teaching can come only after one climbs up the scaffolding of long experience of life or after one struggles across the river of deep reflection about it. For it is the change from first love to final mating. It is often heralded when circumstances present hard problems which conflict with preconceived beliefs and perplex the unenslaved mind. This evokes the dark wraith of doubt, which in its turn calls for further and deeper investigation. But investigation soon causes pointed questions to arise. Knowledge resulting from adoption of the higher standpoint can alone proffer a satisfactory answer to these questions because it alone deals in ultimates, whereas all other standpoints offer answers which may serve for the moment, which are useful pragmatic working views for a time, but they too are bound to fail one later under the pressure of hard facts. History proves how governments, religions, theories and institutions break down in the end, despite their one-time invincibility. For there is no permanent settlement except in ultimate truth. It is far less important to travel from Canada to Cape Town than to travel from the primitive point of view to the philosophic.

Thus philosophy alone can become the sole apex at which all

lines of the pyramid of knowledge and action must meet. Its deliverances are adamantine, they may be ratified by time but not rectified by it.

The unique virtue and incomparable value of such an attitude displays itself in the daring claim which the hidden philosophy alone ventures to make, viz. that it arrives at completeness of results, uncontradictability of truth and the verified principle underlying all phases of experience and knowledge which, when attained, makes everything else understood. This claim must be tested, however, like all others, and the hidden philosophy will fearlessly and gladly submit to every imaginable test because having been always its own severest critic it is conscious of having reached a basis as solid as the Rock of Gibraltar. If everywhere that which passes for philosophy differs with the philosophers themselves nowhere can the genuine philosophy vary in essential principles by one iota from what it always has been and always must be.

Thus in our quest we must learn to apply the proper standpoint. Do we want the last word in truth? Then we must approach the world from the philosophic position. Do we want a practical working view? Then we may take the limited and lower view. But whatever we do we ought not to confuse our categories. For the penalty will be distortion of truth and inability to find a working rule. The philosophical viewpoint must be kept distinct and separate from the practical, otherwise we shall get a blurred and muddled outlook, says the hidden doctrine.

Moreover, it must not be thought that to take this higher view is to destroy the lower one. The antithesis between them belongs to the world of elementary thought and does not dislocate the springs of everyday action. They can be co-ordinated according to individual circumstances. The two viewpoints can be distinguished but cannot be separated, cannot be divorced. We may study one apart from the other, but in doing so we make a mere abstraction of both, whereas the real is the whole. They are not to be taken as rigid divisions but as necessary distinctions. Nobody can be negligent of the first without ceasing to be a human being, whilst nobody can be negligent of the second without condemning himself to remain outside the realm of truth. Nobody can dispense with the more primitive outlook because practical life has to be based on belief to a larger extent than on truth. We have to take our cook on trust, for instance, for there is no time to investigate or supervise every minor detail of the cooking every day. This means that we must be content never to know the truth about it, never to *prove* that everything is as it purports to be. Active life would be impossible if we had to wait and collect all the facts before every single deed or movement, so we are compelled to take much or most of it on appearance-value. Application of the higher standpoint to every petty concern of the day is neither desirable nor necessary. It would make every ordinary business a nuisance. It would be as foolish and as impossible as the attempt to apply the canons of common sense to the questions of pure philosophy. Thus it is enough that we keep perpetually present in *knowledge* the roundness of our earth and not demand that sight and touch should also tell us of it. It is enough that the philosopher remain a sensible human being, so long as he holds firmly to the *principles* that generalize the truth behind all the changing scenes of his daily diorama.

Such a method, however, as the practical one is alone too defective for philosophy, which must thoroughly test every inch of its forward progress. When man begins to think of what life means and what the world means he must leave the little compromises which make up popular existence and ascend to Himalayan mental altitudes. When he philosophizes let him be done with all such compromises, all easy concessions to the infirmities of our adolescent race, and let him be loyal to his mistress.

The movement of thought within both stages is inescapable. They are complementary. We have to co-ordinate them. But to confuse or to compromise the two standpoints is to mix up the issues of life and thought. From its unique standpoint philosophy seeks to provide the final and consistent explanation of everything that exists, yet it does not deny the value of the work accomplished by those who are confined to the ordinary standpoint alone nor the experience of those who can find truth only in what *they* see. But it shows up the purely relational character of such work, experience, judgment and knowledge as being quite inadequate to a comprehensive view of life which omits nothing from its survey.

Thus we can adjust the claims of practical life with the claims of philosophical truth and harmonize all knowledge. For experience, science is the starting-point of genuine philosophy. When it can summon up sufficient courage to make the leap, when the revelation of relativity forces it to confess it can never alone attain certitude, it will elevate itself to the mantled dignity of philosophy. It need not abandon the pursuit of practical achievements if it does this, for the two can and should be co-ordinated. And thus it must labour amid the turmoil of earthly strife while holding to the inner silence of unearthly being; it must reconcile the limitations that surround man on every side with the freedom that dwells deep within him; it must dissolve the false opposition between the practical and the philosophical and take them up into a higher unity. For whereas the first standpoint provides views of truth, the final provides truth itself! The latter rests on the twofold basis of reason and experience. It is impregnable because it carries both to an undreamed-of extent.

Those who graduate from the relativity of thought in the first view to the rigidity of certitude in the other undergo the supreme revolution of the human mind. The new position becomes crucial for their thought about the universe and for their attitude towards their fellow men. When such reflection is carried to its utmost degree, which demands as much patience as courage, the relativity of all their psychological knowledge will emerge. This principle, applied in its proper place at the very opening of the second volume which shall complete this work, will act like a surgical operation for cataract on a blind man. Then will it be possible to arrive at staggering results which are unique in the history of world-knowledge, and which reveal an unsuspected world of being wherein the loftiest hopes of the human race can find fulfilment as its grandest intuitions gain perfect realization.

Man's Expanding Space-Time Sense. It was pointed out in the opening pages of this book that recent inventions were compelling mankind to widen its space sense and expand its time sense. Some further important implications of this development may now be stated. Do we realize that man came to the new notion that the earth was round through expanding his space sense? When medieval navigators made longer journeys and finally circled the globe, when astronomers devised superior instruments and became aware of more distant stars, the belief that the earth was flat became ludicrous and untenable. Copernicus introduced the idea of relativity of direction to European thought. When the medieval flat-earth notion prevailed there was only one absolute and fixed world-view possible. When the rotating-earth notion triumphed, the discovery of Copernicus changed the direction of European thinking and set forces going which gradually revolutionized its culture. The hypothesis of relativity was born out of investigation in a spatial field of a vastness that was beyond precedent in such experiments. This enabled Einstein to find that rays of light which are apparently straight are actually curved and that a straight line, if drawn far enough, would turn out to be a curve! Straight lines seem straight only because we do not follow light for a course of millions of miles and during a sufficiently long period of time. Could we but do so we should find them curved. But such a discovery is subversive of all the axioms of Euclid, of all the geometry that had been based on those axioms, of all the old concepts of fixed material bodies arranged in space according to the old Euclidean laws. Euclid's geometry worked well provided it was applied only to limited portions of the universe. But when a vaster field was brought into consideration it became unsatisfactory and non-Euclidean systems such as Riemann's were found more adequate to the measurement of the world. Here again the expanding space sense has revolutionized even the character of mathematics. If it has demanded the giving up of limited notions it has offered more comprehensive and more generalized explanations of physical phenomena in their place.

The expansion of the time sense of mankind is equally important to thought and culture and has shown itself in various ways. Men do not get giddy nowadays at this striking change, as they would surely have done five hundred years ago. The gramophone brings to their ears a voice which spoke a decade ago, the radio enables them to hear immediately speech or song which would formerly have required several days or some weeks of journeying to hear. The world of time has contracted whereas the sense of time has enlarged.

This widening of the space sense which brought the discoveries of Copernicus and of Einstein in science has also brought other new truth in its train. It is affecting the practical policies of statesmen and the theoretical principles of economists. It is influencing the major departments of human life and human culture. And to the extent that this alteration is bringing men to realize the unity of existence, to that extent it conforms to the practical teaching of philosophy concerning social life and ethical conduct. Both science and philosophy here tend to meet and their paths become increasingly less divergent. Moreover, all these new truths about space and time are bringing a great growth in the thoughts of men and a great growth in their conception of the world. They are thus preparing the public mind for more favourable reception of the truths of the hidden Indian philosophy, towards which they tend strikingly and inescapably to lead. As people get used to thinking in this newer way it will be easier for them to appreciate the higher philosophic outlook.

Relativity has provided a new world-view as the background for all future thought about things. A thorough grasp of the meaning of relativity cannot but bring to birth a new outlook for thoughtful men and emancipate their minds from dead ideas, for hitherto the characteristic of the external world was its inevitableness, its mechanical status. We were constrained and compelled by our feelings to accept it as it seemed to be. We instinctively felt that it was not a case of what we wished to think about it but of what we must think about it. Hence everybody, even the scientists, had cherished the belief that whatever was seen to occupy a certain shape possessed a separate appearance and measurement which was objectively its own precisely as perceived. They had also believed that whenever an event happened its duration was likewise precisely something that inhered within itself, as Newton had said, and all the scientists who followed after him had said, everywhere absolutely unchangeable and uniform and consequently quite independent of human experience of them. The stellar universe which we humans believed to be "out there" in space and enduring through time was quite unaffected by our position, presence or absence and continued a uniform existence whose fundamental characteristics were the same for all observers in all ages. Space and time were once and for all "given".

With Einstein's advent these views are shown to be fallacious, imperfect and misleading. He demonstrates that the conventional standards of measurement, as made in space and time, are not at all absolute and irrevocable. They are entirely dependent on factors, such as the position of an observer, which in themselves are variable and relative. What we really know of the world is not stereotyped for everybody and everywhere but is entirely relative to a particular standpoint which we have taken up. By changing the standpoint we shall visualize the same world in a different way. But, be it noted, to turn space into a variable is to deprive it of its Euclidean character and to make a mental factor enter it.

Through the whole of last century science, as if it were an observer who had scrutinized the world, did not know that the data it had thus gained was more useful for getting things done than for getting at ultimate truth. It was like a man in a closed astronomical system unable to tell that the earth was moving because he had nothing else with which to compare it. But the mental sleep of the race was ending. History had marked the twentieth century as the century of sudden awakening. Science began to scrutinize its own position, itself, and thus become conscious of a missing element in its observation of other movements—its own movement!

Science had absorbed itself in the study of the external world but omitted to take into reckoning the student himself, the conditions under which he worked and the preconceptions with which he worked; yet all these were factors which entered into the observations themselves and consequently modified the results obtained. To think of the objects apart from the men who study them is to think of abstractions. It is like two ends of the same stick—you cannot have one without the other, do what you will. Somebody must be there to know the object; so far as human knowledge of them goes they exist as *known* things. To treat them otherwise is to abstract one end of the stick and pretend that the other is not there. Relativity plainly states that the observer cannot be separated from his observations, that space is not a wide void in which objects are hanging nor time a broad stream in which they are standing. The shapes we perceive, the measurements we make, depend on the position of the one who perceives and measures. Let him shift his position and new shapes and new measurements will present themselves to his gaze. Therefore empirical knowledge is perpetually exposed to revision. We can never arrive without philosophy at a determination of the character of the universe which shall be and shall remain absolute.

The inner meaning of relativity is that the world may be known differently in the experience of different human beings. The principle may be applied to the particular way in which an object appears to us from a particular position or it may be applied to the fact that the object itself is known also as an idea in relation to a knowing mind. An object is never independent of the conditions affecting a particular observer.

The universe has been deprived of unalterable entity. Relativity has converted it into a universe of individual or collective interpretation. Even if the observations of a million persons agree more or less with each other they still remain interpretations. The principle of relativity does not forfeit its truth because a million people grouped together in a town find no difference in their general observation of a particular object; it still applies to them, albeit collectively, because they have used the same general position or set up the same general standard of reference.

Apart from its practical value, which is not under consideration here, the worth of Einstein's work to the cultural world is that it gives a jolt to the smug scientific tradition which tried to make a fixed representation of the universe. It inaugurates a new era of comprehension for thoughtful minds. For the aspect of it that matters most proves conclusively that the *observed* universe, i.e. the *known* universe, as apart from the one supposed to be outside, depends partly at least for its appearance upon the observer himself. And anyone may enter into this comprehension, however, without turning mathematician and trying to master the technicalities of relativity, if only he will set out to study his own world more closely for what it *is* rather than what he feels it to be. He will then perforce see that the space and time sides of his human experience are not so objective as everyday thought holds them to be.

If nothing exists in isolation, independently of its relation to the one who perceives it, then, without actually stepping into the shoes, the body and mind of another man, i.e. without becoming the other man, it is an impossible feat to observe any object precisely as he himself observes it. Thus we stubbornly carry our world-view with us wherever we go. The observations which we make are really made within it, are inseparable from it. Our world of observed facts is also a world of judgments! We separate out by abstraction some special aspect and call that the thing itself. We isolate special appearances of the object, we make an abstraction from all its possible appearances and then proceed to assert that we have seen the object! The logic which proves that the object known can never be separated from the knowing subject as an independent entity, that the observer is part of every observation which he makes, and that the world is describable only in terms of relations is unanswerable.

When Einstein shows that there is no space and no time common to all groups of human beings, it is like showing that various spectacles are in use, each group's glasses being tinted differently and hence producing a different-coloured picture. Where do these changes of aspect really occur? The resultant pictures when traced to their ultimate abode are not "out there" in the object but in the observers themselves. If five men studying the same thing from five different positions find that it differs in size, mass, rate of movement and so on, who but themselves are responsible for the changes in the observed object? This is the only possible way of construing such relativity. Throw the observer out of your calculation and the whole system of relativity collapses. The observations are to a large extent at least dependent on the observer. The world of massive continents and majestic oceans appears to be set out in space, and yet when we reflect upon the matter the space-relations themselves are somehow inextricably mixed up with the observer who is looking at it. If the earth looks flat and is actually round, seems stationary but is continually rotating, where is the error to be sought for? Obviously in the observer himself, for his senses are at work in moulding and presenting the picture of the earth to him.

The plausible assumption which inheritance and habit have engraved upon our minds that we enter into *direct* connection with a world independent and apart from ourselves can no longer be justified. Relativity drags from us the rueful admission that there are always different ways of looking at the world, that there are no fundamental characteristics which all observers perceive, and that alteration of position or reference standard will alter the sense-picture of the world in the observers themselves.[1] And that sense-picture is the only one which they unquestioningly invest with reality, for they know no other.

We get our facts about the world ordinarily through the use of the five sense-organs, those complicated structures which began in the far past as simple sensitive patches of skin. The scientist has to work on measurements which he has read off an instrument or an apparatus with his own faculty of sight. To that extent he is entirely dependent on the services rendered him by his two eyes. The chemist alters weights in the scale pan of a laboratory balance and then reads the figures indicated by a pointer which moves over a figured scale. Actually his consciousness has noted certain visual sensations, certain experiences which have occurred to nervous mechanisms in his own body. Science is said to be based on measurement alone, but this is evidently an incomplete statement; the human observer must be reckoned as a part of the results too. Science cannot be separated from the scientists. Therefore the pattern which science has created is also a pattern of human experience. This has been granted by Einstein, for he included a mathematical idea of an observer in his conclusions. And the observer in turn depends on his senses for information.

"But what has all this analysis to do with me?" some will ask. "Is it not the special preserve of scientists and mathematicians?" The answer is—everything! For you, dear reader, are yourself an observer with the world which you see and the environment around you as your field of observation. Einstein's work is being used here only as an example, only to illustrate some most important tenets

---

[1] We may watch on a cinema screen a slow-motion picture of a horse leaping over a hurdle. Its legs move so tardily that the animal takes sixty seconds for a feat which was actually done in two. What has happened? The photographer has accelerated the turning of his camera handle so as to take hundreds of pictures per second, whereas the operator has projected them on the screen at such a retarded rate that the movements are slowed down to diminishing-point. It is not an illusion. The machine has acually expanded our measurement of time by altering the number of our sensations. It has simply and practically illustrated what the principle of relativity expresses in mathematical formulae.

of the hidden Indian teaching. He has shown that we know nothing definite about reality and he has shown by implication the need of the higher philosophic standpoint. Moreover, although his discovery referred to quantitative measurements in space and time it may be extended to many other fields of enquiry. Relativity is a principle which holds good almost everywhere, and its *philosophic* study is of consequence to you. It will serve as a useful stepping-stone to a unique level of reference, where the true character of the world and later the true meaning of *your* existence can be unveiled.

Relativity reigns in the mental world equally as in the physical. Belief colours or conditions perception. Predilection is selective and shuts out whole strata of facts from observation. Egoism is deceptive and often sees only what it likes to see. Assumption falsifies even that which it does see. Emotion overweights the trivial, deflects the mental and ignores the substantial. Imagination effortlessly manufactures the most improbable data.

Moreover, Einstein's work not only strips both time and space of their independent reality, but leads logically to another point which should not be overlooked. When he makes it clear that a man on the moon would have a different kind of time to a man on the earth the time-reference is shown to be somehow mixed up with the space-reference. Relativity shows that you cannot separate space from the observer, that you cannot separate time from the observer, and that both time and space form part of a single thing. The space-time continuum is one thing, not two : there is no space without time as its inseparable co-existent companion. The "when" and "where" are for ever in union.

All perceptions of time must involve reference to the external world and hence involve perceptions of space too. They are inseparables. The time at which an object occupies its three dimensions in space must be brought in to complete its measurement. All our knowledge of nature is the knowledge of things extended in space and occurring in time ; all our experience is the experience of objects occupying a particular spatial position and a particular time-order. It is not only that we see the surrounding world but we see it in a space-time relation.

Time and space mutually imply each other, are dependent on each other. For we see objects in space separately and therefore successively and therefore in the total dimension of space-time. Conversely, if we could not separate the earth from the sun in space we would have no means of measuring time, nor any revolutionary movement wherewith to mark it. Thus all our sensations are co-related in space-time. We spatialize by arbitrary withdrawal from the fourth-dimensional continuum where both space and time lie perpetually united. The space-time continuum is the foundation which underlies all our experience of the world.

We need not let ourselves be intimidated by the formidable sound of this word "continuum". It becomes explicable when we know that space and time are relative to the mind of the observer and that this continuum is somehow inextricably mixed with the mind itself. Space time is after all a mathematical idea, a conceptual picture, and hence a mental thing.

How comes it that we seem to find space and time as separate realities? It is because the mind has unconsciously picked and partitioned them out to some degree from itself and then arbitrarily imposed them as objective discoveries upon itself. Thus the structure of the world depends partly on the structure of the mind. We must not overlook that the mind is constantly interpreting the world for us, constantly at work behind every measured movement in time and every measured thing in space. The farthest point to which science has gone is that space-time is the ultimate matrix which moulds the objects and events that emerge into being: it is both their mysterious source and the fourth dimension of matter. When, however, we come to realize that space-time is itself inseparable from the mind we shall see what direction science will be forced by further investigation and discovery to follow. The longer it hesitates to take this step the larger will be the accumulation of proof that will confront it.

From the moment that Einstein announced his discoveries, physical science could no longer stand aloof as it had done in the past from the problem of the relation of mind to the world. For relativity undermined the entire objective nature of such science and involuntarily introduced a subjective factor. Nothing therefore, according to relativity, is completely self-existent. This interpreted world is partially, at least, dependent on the interpreting mind of the observer. The old notion that space and time were containers in which things were exhibited must go. The new notion that space and time are contained within the observer must come in. The corollary to be drawn from this is that mind and sensation are inescapable factors in the making, as apart from the perceiving, of the world we know, for that world is as inseparable from space as it is from time.

Truth as it exists in itself, unconditioned, is in Einstein's belief unattainable; truth as it exists in relation to the faculties of individual men is alone possible of attainment. The hidden teaching emphatically disagrees with this pessimism, pointing out that entity exempt from all relation can only be of a common mental nature and that it might be apprehended through a non-individual approach. Anyway, somehow and to some extent the principles which determine human knowledge exist within the human senses and the human mind and not definitely beyond them in the universe. Without the aid of mind we are unable to know anything at all. This proposition is irrefutable. Thus in the stage to which we have travelled the world hinges largely upon ourselves as observers of it. But what are we without our instruments of observation, without the five senses? Nothing! Everything is received through them. The earth on which we walk and the chair in which we sit enter into our awareness only because they are registered on the skin, the eyes and the ears. The world we *know* is a sense-world, whatever else lies beyond it or outside it. It will vary as our fivefold sensations themselves vary. What they tell us constitutes our world. And they can tell different things to men who are differently placed. This is the fundamental lesson of relativity. Relativity introduces an individual or group character into all observations. Unreflective people do not understand that part at least of what they take to be outside themselves exists rather as sense-impressions *within* themselves. What is believed to exist beyond these impressions is not *definitely* known.

We are following a suggestive and exploratory trail which has led us back through the things of time and space to man himself, partly to his mind and particularly to the sensations which he forms of the world without. This raises the physiological and psychological question of how we get sensations and what they really are. We habitually accept the deliverances of the senses as true and therefore do not pause to consider how far they are true. It is the next task to investigate their precise nature, as well as to ascertain *how much* of what we see is dependent on this mental factor.

CHAPTER IX

FROM THING TO THOUGHT

WE are now on the threshold of an ancient mystery. There is a stirring and stimulating aspect of the scientific discovery of relativity which has not been allotted its proper significance and its adequate value by the West, but which was known, understood and valued by the Indian thinkers of antiquity. And this mystery is the relation between the things of our experience, the senses and the mind. For we have come to see at this stage that every separate thing of which man is or can be aware of is apparently a product of two ingredients, the mental and the material, and not of the material alone. But in what proportions the two are mixed is a question which we have yet to answer. How much of a thing is supplied by the mind and how much is received from the external world is a riddle which has puzzled men from Kapila to Kant, more because its right answer is too unexpected and unsuspected to be acceptable than because its difficulty is too insuperable to be overcome.

We know that there is around us a world of common objects such as brick houses and leafy trees. But *what* we really know of this world depends on *how* we come to know it. Talkative ignorance can assert that we see it, that certain corresponding images register on our eyes and are somehow grasped by the mind. Sight, however, is not such a simple matter as it seems, for it will yield surprising revelations when subjected to analytic treatment. The average untutored mind with usual and unquestioned habit is satisfied that its awareness of the world, its personal experiences and environmental changes, are simple affairs, but the scientific mind knows how complex and elaborate they really are.

The forms which we see on every side do not explain themselves. If we want to know the truth about them we have to make rigorous enquiry. The world that is "given" to the mind is not given with its easy explanation accompanying it. We have to hunt and ferret the latter down with all the energy we can muster. Otherwise it will not be forthcoming and we shall remain in the kindergarten stage of thought.

Before we should credit or discredit the testimony of our senses we ought to *understand* properly how they come to offer such testimony. We need not deny that they will tell us of a world without, but we ought to ascertain what it is precisely that they are trying to tell us. Those who have the patience to take up these enquiries in an earnest spirit are taking important steps to awaken from the dream of ignorance which holds almost all mankind in its heavy folds; they will have begun to break up the universal illusion in the only way that it can be broken because they will have begun to interrogate it. They will be the forerunners of a rightly educated and nobly elevated populace.

We must start like modern science, lucidly and logically from the standpoint of the known, and only then may we work our way to the unknown. Therefore we must for the moment triply turn ourselves into physicist, physiologist and psychologist. We must examine our bodily apparatus, watch the way in which it behaves when sensing things and search our field of awareness. And if a few technical scientific terms will have to be introduced into this account they will be found simple and well-known to most readers; nevertheless their full explanation will also be given so that none may be unclear to anybody.

Physical and physiological enquiry should come first, for the body is better understood than the mind. Such study will reveal some peculiar facts about the working of our senses. All experience passes into awareness through the portals of the sense-instruments: eyes, ears, nose, tongue and skin. It is hardly necessary to point out that perception of and intercourse with the world would be impossible if we did not possess these five sensitive bodily instruments which keep us informed about the world of surrounding things, five channels of sense: sight, hearing, touch, smell and taste. A life without any of the senses is a tragically limited one. That is why we instinctively feel pity for the blind, the dumb and the deaf, who live in colourless, speechless or silent worlds.

The skin is crowded with the sensitive bulb-like terminals of numerous delicate nerves which lie beneath its surface. Through these terminals we get our senses of touch, of temperature and of pressure, which are simpler reports than those of the other sense-instruments. The tongue and part of the mouth are lined with hair-like nerve-endings which tell us about the taste, the sweetness and the sourness of things. The upper part of the nose contains a nervous membrane whereby we smell the fine gaseous particles of odours which enter the air. The flap-like ear we see is not the real instrument of hearing but a kind of shield for it. We really hear waves of sound through a drum-like membrane which lies inside the head at the end of an inch-long channel.

A sixth sense is the awareness of our own muscular movements, a seventh is the sense of keeping bodily balance, but it will suffice to restrict ourselves to grasping the essential principle which runs through all the senses.

Our senses tell us something about an object but never tell us more than a fraction of the facts concerning it. For they function within a well-defined and limited range of vibrations. Were they able to tell us everything, were the ears bereft of the capacity to cut out sounds with high frequencies or the nostrils fully sensitive to every odour, life would become intolerable, if not unlivable. This should be a serious warning to us not to be over-confident about the adequacy of sense-gathered knowledge. And it should be a plain hint that whatever we know from this source should not only be supplemented by the use of reasoned enquiry but also checked by it. Something of this was learnt in the last chapter in our study of the principle of relativity, a study which showed the imperative need for setting up a double standpoint, and something more will be learnt about it in the present chapter. Philosophy is therefore not recalcitrant in being discontented with our first view of the world as it immediately presents itself to the senses. It perceives mystery where the ordinary mind perceives none. It seeks in fact to unravel the mystery behind sensed appearance.

Of all the five senses, that which tells us of an external world is chiefly the sense of sight. We usually apprehend the existence of each individual thing through the instrumentality of vision. All the other senses are subordinate to it. Sight, therefore, is the most important of all our senses, and only after it comes hearing. And it is also the most useful of all the five, for we mostly think of the world in terms of visual images, whilst the larger number of the pictures which enter into memory and imagination are visual ones also. Moreover, the function of the eyes is far superior in scope to the function of any other sense. Thus they can perceive a large number of different things both far off and quite near within a few moments, whereas touch, for example, is restricted to those immediately at hand. Finally, sight is the subtlest and most like the mental of all our senses.

What happens when we gaze out at the host of surrounding

objects? What do we mean by announcing that we have "seen" something? Vision is by no means the simple process that it seems to be. It is a highly complicated process. First in the series to be noted is that it shares with the other senses the need of a physical stimulus which will arouse it into activity. Waves of sound will arouse the ear when they touch its drum and it is waves of light that beat upon the eye and arouse it into action. Light is its actual stimulus. The nerve-tissue of the eye is sensitive to light as nothing else.

Here is a fountain-pen. Rays of light must therefore take their point of departure in this object by being thrown back from its surface and then they must travel and stimulate those amazingly effective mechanisms which are Nature's optical instruments—the eyes.

Two balls of fibrous tissue are set inside deep recesses of the skull. There are three coats of nerve-fibre upon each eyeball and it is the innermost one that is so sensitive to light and therefore to colour. This coat is technically called the retina. It plays the same part that a sensitive film or a ground-glass view-finder plays in a photographic camera, for it registers images of outside objects. But whereas a camera film can be used only once and must then be discarded, the retina can be used countless times and still render good service. The light rays meet in it and affect numerous little rod-like and cone-like nerve-endings, whose activity starts the second link in the chain of connected processes stretching from the fountain-pen to our knowledge of its existence. Every other sense instrument, such as the ear and the skin, also contains the terminals of suitable nerves, and if it did not possess them it would be utterly useless.

This retinal structure possesses microscopic fineness and consequently permits detailed pictures to form upon its surface of a precision and clearness unequalled by the data furnished by any of the other senses. We must not forget that the presence of such a picture is nothing more than the mere influence of light upon the retina.

In order to see any external object at all it must have a background of colour, for it is by the contrast of one colour against another that we distinguish the shape and size of the object, but in order to be coloured it must be lighted, for colour is a product of the rays of light. It is only when we can make a comparison between two colours that we can even assert that an object is before us. We recognize the flaming glory of the flamingo because of the duller

FROM THING TO THOUGHT

tints of the place wherein it is set. We perceive the massive pyramid because its brownish stones rise out of yellow sands and because its ruddy apex is thrust into the limpid blue of an Egyptian sky. If only a single colour surrounded us or were before us no object could take shape at all for our eyes, because the perceived shape of a thing is the consequence of having a second colour or several more colours against which to contrast it.

It is these rays that are broken by the objects into the browns and greys and greens that popular superstition puts into the things it sees. The rind of an orange, for instance, reflects and breaks white light in such a way that it appears to us as golden yellow. It is a schoolboy's experiment to prove that white light can break and divide itself into several other colours, technically termed the colours of the spectrum, for he has but to set up a prism of glass near the window of a shaded room and lovely hues like violet, yellow, red, blue, etc., will then appear.

Thus we do not see things directly but rather the light which they reflect or emit. It is not the pen that actually impinges upon the eyes; it is the light rays alone which travel from the pen and impinge upon the eyes. The superstition which science explodes is that colours are part of the things themselves. They are not. They are the result of waves of white light broken up. The light is not in the things themselves. It is only reflected by them. Scientific experiment has effectively proved this, but a simple instance will well illustrate its truth. Sunset lessens the light inside a house and with it things change their hues and darken. Brown tables become black and green curtains become grey. For their colour is not really their own essential property.

It might be said with actual truth that the only world we ever see is a mysterious world of light, as was once mystically affirmed by ancient cults and as is now experimentally demonstrated by modern science. But philosophy cannot stop there. It must penetrate to the very root of things. It must ascertain whence even light itself derives its own existence.

From Eye to Mind. Let us return to our fountain-pen. The impression of having seen it starts with light entering the eye, which, in response to this stimulus, forms an image on the retina. Nature turns artist, as it were, and paints a picture in coloured light on a canvas of nervous stuff. But we are not conscious of it as existing there, a proof of this being that the picture which appears upon the retina is inverted just as it is on the negative film of a camera. If we knew this picture alone the pen would appear upside down also! It is clear, therefore, that the picture passes through some further process of change and even transformation before we become correctly aware of the pen.

All that has happened is a chemical and structural change in the upper layer of the retina. No awareness of the glistening colour, the long slender shape and the golden head of the pen has yet managed to penetrate our ignorance of it. For us there is still no pen. The news of its existence has not yet reached the mind and has to be brought a stage farther than the eyes, has to be brought indeed to some central spot in the body which can act as a clearing-house for all the sense-reports sent in from various points distributed throughout the body's length and breadth. Such a spot exists in the brain.

Nature has therefore made admirable provision to carry out this task. The entire body is really a nervous receiving apparatus which reacts variously to each physical stimulus received. Enormous numbers of white nerves thread their way from the surface of the body to the brain and constitute a comprehensive system of communication, a kind of nervous and cerebral telegraphic system, in fact.

A general process of interaction between the external objects and the internal brain exists through the working of the medium between them, the five bodily sense-instruments. Certain events occur in the instruments and, through vibrations which pass along connecting nerves, initiate nervous impulses which diffuse themselves over a particular part of the brain.

The pen, which makes an "impression" on the eye, as it is technically termed, has aroused an activity in the numerous rod-like and cone-like parts of the retina and through them in the nerves which run from their bases. This current of wave-like movement is transmitted by them to the main nerve which leads out of the eyeball, called the optic nerve, and the latter again in its turn passes its response along its own entire length to its birthplace at the back of the brain. Here a portion of the brain-surface called the cerebral cortex becomes acquainted with the vibrating activity which constitutes the message sent by the eye.

Let us consider an aspect of this last point. That which makes the image possible and throws its form upon the retina is the combination lens furnished by the cornea of the eye and the crystalline lens. The surface of this lens is convex, and had Nature increased its convexity we would always have seen the pen with exaggerated dimensions and distorted shape. Everything else in the universe would have taken on the same grotesque appearance, whether it be a glacial mountain range like Himalaya or a tiny insect like an ant. From birth to death we would have firmly believed that the objects and people surrounding us were really possessed of such appearance. The so-called distorting mirrors of fairs and exhibitions provide comical illustrations of the kind of queer faces and figures our fellow men would then have had.

Why is this possible? Because the brain is entirely dependent on the image furnished by the eyes. It can obviously never come into direct contact with any external thing.

Again, some people are born colour-blind. Until their attention is called by others to this peculiar defect in their eyes they may not even know that their vision is peculiar. They may assert of two differently coloured things placed before them that they see the same colour in each thing. They may blandly assure you that a pink rose possesses the same colour as a yellow marigold, merely because they are incapable of seeing. They are unable to distinguish between unripe green strawberries and ripe red ones, or between the green lamp on a railroad signal which indicates the safe passage and the red lamp which warns of danger. For this reason the companies require their engine-drivers to pass a strict examination in distinguishing colours. The lesson to be got from analysing this defect is that the wrong colour, not being a part of the lamp or the strawberry, must be a part of the image which falls on the retina, and that the brain is limited to the material found in the retinal representation, not to that which is available in the external thing itself. The essential point here is what we *do* see, not what we should see according to ordinary observation.

All that the eyes can offer, in the case of our fountain-pen, is contained in the sensitive portion of the retina and consists of a picture which is less than one inch in diameter, which is upside down and which has the two dimensions of height and width only. But the pen which is actually there is six inches long and not one inch, is upright and not upside down, and possesses the three dimensions of height, width and depth, so that it stands out in solid relief. Here are three pointed hints that the external pen present to our sight is not the perceived pen of which the mind becomes aware and that the popular belief that we see things-in-themselves is sheer illusion. For the image with which the brain deals is within our eyes, i.e. within *our* body, hence within ourselves! We cannot even get beyond it. This means that we see pictures, appearances, and that these are always relative to the observer—a lesson which we learnt in the previous chapter from other data, as well as from reflection upon Einstein's work. For everyday practical purposes we must assume that we perceive a thing exactly as it purports to be, but for philosophic enquiry we must penetrate beneath the surface of such an assumption.

The eyes' message of the pen's existence is the only account which the brain can hope to receive, for it is too remote from the pen. Yet, physically speaking, quite clearly it offers only an inverted miniature. Such an imperfect message does not square with the external pen and cannot be taken literally. It must be worked upon until the pen is accurately represented by what is seen, i.e. it must be *interpreted*. The message reached the brain therefore in the form of a physiological Morse code. To imagine that the visual image itself travels along the optic nerve is equivalent to imagining that actual words and not corresponding short or long electrical impulses travel along a telegraph wire. These impulses splutter out at their destination in the form of meaningless sounds until taken up and interpreted according to the Morse code by an operator, a human being whose *mind* translates them into significant alphabetical letters and words. Moreover, a telegram itself is nothing more than a series of black marks on a sheet of white paper. These marks have to be deciphered and converted into thoughts by the person who reads it. The mind must similarly set to work to decode the wave-like nervous impulses which the brain has received and translate them back into awareness of the corresponding impressions of their original physical stimulus, which in this case is a pen. It is extremely difficult to define the word *mind*, as most recent scientists and philosophers have confessed. The hidden teaching thoroughly understands the significance of what lies behind this little word, but that significance can only be fully revealed near the end of this course, not when we are less than half-way as now. However, for present purposes we may briefly, simply and tentatively define mind as being that which makes us think of anything and which makes us aware of anything.

Such interpretation must necessarily be a mental activity. It must transpire in the mind, for it demands the positive activity of intelligence rather than the passive receptivity of eye, nerve and brain. Intelligence implies consciousness of some kind, and as we are normally unaware of such a process we must conclude that it occurs beneath the threshold of ordinary consciousness and is wholly subconscious. We know only the results of this unseen work. They appear to us as an accurate vision of this beautiful writing instrument.

This is the instant when awareness has stepped into the process and determined the birth of an observation for us. This is the crucial point when we first begin to *know* that the pen is there. Until this moment we are unaware of its existence, despite the picture in the retina, despite the vibration that passes along the optic nerve and despite the brain's response.

A proof of this is found in the annals of surgical science. The skin of each finger is linked with the spinal cord by bundles of fibrous nerves. If the latter are severed close to the spine the fingers may be cut or smashed, but no pain will be felt in them. The messages from them can no longer reach the brain and unless they reach the brain they cannot be taken up into consciousness. When therefore we speak of having a feeling of pain in an injured foot we are uttering misleading words for the feeling ought to be referred to the point where it is actually experienced, i.e. subsequent to the movement of a vibration in the brain. We localize feelings of sweet or bitter taste on the tongue when they really occur after the brain has responded. But in both the cases the foot and the tongue can only receive the impressions of painful pressure and sweet fluidity respectively, whereas the impressions are not transformed into bits of conscious experience until *after* the nerves have vibrated them as far as the proper cerebral centres. To place these feelings *locally* at the nerve-endings is to fall into gross illusion, albeit perfectly pardonable illusion.

The important places assigned by Nature to the nerve-paths and brain-centres may now appear clearer. So long as the nerve-connection with the brain continues unimpaired so long does the sense-instrument continue to function. But a leper whose nerve-communication between hand and brain has been eaten away will have no sensation of touch. His leprous hand may be burnt or cut off yet he will feel no pain. Destroy the nerve, paralyse it or let a lesion appear in the appropriate brain centre and the sense-instrument fails to perform its work—sight goes or feeling in the fingers vanishes. Therefore our knowledge of an object cannot be got without nerve and brain. The eyes might be perfectly unharmed and show all their normal physical response to light and yet a man might see nothing more than a blind man could see if the cortical section of his brain were injured, diseased or cut or if the optic nerve were severed midway. No sight is possible without the vital co-operation of both brain and nerve with the eye—thus making a triple partnership.

The plain meaning of this is that knowledge of an object's existence does not arise in the bodily eye, ear, skin, tongue or nose which lie at the ends of the nerves but rather only *after* the message has reached the brain-centres which lie at the starting-points of the nerves. For only then does that mysterious element called consciousness reveal itself. We first come into cognition of a thing in sense-experience by noting the particular characteristics that distinguish it from other things, such as its special shape, particular size and degree of hardness, for instance; we can become conscious of it only through knowing these qualities of it.

Now we know that a thing called clock is before us because there is a tiny picture of the clock in the eyes, the sound of its rhythmic ticking in the ears and the feeling of its resistant touch in the fingers; all these impressions combine and corroborate each other. An orange is known to us because it looks round and yellow, tastes sweet and feels pulpy. These are its well-known characteristics. But how do we become aware of them? We can do so only by experiencing the immediate effects which the orange produces in our *mind* through the senses. Each *individual* effect, such as the pulpy feeling of the orange alone and not the whole orange itself, which arises in our consciousness is technically called a *sensation*.

Whatever is perceived by the senses or thought of in reflection becomes an object in the field of awareness. We may therefore attach the technical term of "object" to it. Every object possesses certain recognizable qualities which are presented to the mind as sensations. The latter are greatly varied: they tell us where the object is, how small or how large it is, what its shape is like, how sweet, sour or salty its taste is or how disagreeable its odour, how much weight or how much warmth it possesses, and whether it is lying still or actually moving.

When transmitted nervous impulses originating in the ears complete their journey and reach the brain they arouse sensations of sound. The latter will vary in pitch, strength and character. The pitch may be high or low, the strength loud or soft, and the character mere noise or musical tone, but each sound effect will be a *separate* sensation.

From impressions made on the skin at one end and the processes consequently occurring in it related processes are excited at the other end in the brain, wherefrom we receive sensations of touch which fall roughly into three classes: those of contact, of temperature and of surface pain. These appear as recognitions of distinct qualities such as warmth or cold, smoothness or roughness, heaviness or

FROM THING TO THOUGHT

lightness, pain, movement or pressure. The largest number of touch sensations are received through the skin of the hand because it is the most active of man's limbs. Hold this book in your hand and you will experience the sensations of pressure on its skin as well as the sensation of strain on its sinews. These two sensations taken together form the combined sensation of the book's weight. When you pick up a piece of iron your hand comes in contact with its surface and a sensation of hardness is then felt. And your fingers will tell you that the fountain-pen's barrel is round and smooth, which means that you are getting sensations of roundness and smoothness. When you hold it tightly in the palm both finger and pen begin to repel each other and further sensations come to you, those of resistance and hardness. The tighter you hold it, the stronger will these sensations become.

The lights and shades which play upon and around things provide us with sensations of coloured shapes. When we pick up the pen and look more closely into its beautiful appearance we experience sensations of purple, grey, gold and black. The science of physics knows that the different rates of vibration of one and the same light-ray are read by the eyes as different colours. The colour of a thing is therefore an optical interpretation. What we perceive as colour is not perceived separately from ourselves.

When we speak to a man and hear him reply, what is really happening? Sound, a vibration in the air, acts on both bodies, and certain movements then occur in the nerve-endings at the tympanums of the ears; whilst light forms certain retinal pictures in the eyes. These stimulations are propagated as commotions along the main nerves to the brain where corresponding sensations subsequently arise. If we touch the man's body we shall garner in the form of muscular sensations of pressure and relaxation the results of impressions made on the skin.

Where do the sensations of hardness and roughness, for instance, originate? Are they in the thing or in the observer of the thing? A little analysis will show that they are in the observer, superficially in his body but actually in his mind. Similarly the sensations of heaviness and roundness are not to be found in the material things themselves but in our sensations of them.

Where is the point when a man becomes conscious of having smelt the rose? Is it when the rose approaches the nostrils? Is it when the minute particles of perfume touch the inner membrane of the nostrils? Is it when the olfactory nerve registers the disturbance? Is it when the disturbance reaches the brain? No! He does not know and he cannot know what the rose smells like until his mind takes up the registration, until he *thinks* it into existence. Only at this point does the physiological intercourse which has taken place between the rose and himself assume meaning for him. The interpretation of the impressions of physical experience communicated by the nerves is followed by a reconstruction of the resultant sensations in mental experience. Each sensation is therefore, speaking in terms of physiology only, a purely mental response into which a material nerve stimulus has somehow translated itself. Each sensation is a mental affair; it is within consciousness, whereas sense-impressions are within the body.

It is easier to grasp this point by considering what happens when we cut a finger with a knife. A feeling of pain arises. That feeling is indubitably within ourselves and in nobody else; moreover, it is a state of our consciousness and not a state of the knife. It is, in short, a sensation of pain. Similarly, if we place our hand upon a book the act gives rise to a sense of resistance as the surface of the palm meets with resistance from the surface of the book. We then say that we feel the book, but this is not the case; what we actually feel is that part of our skin which the book touches and from the skin a message is sent to the spinal cord and thence to the brain until a sensation of resistance is born into our individual zone of awareness. Hence we do not feel the book but rather what is happening to our own self. All the other kinds of sensation—whether the smells, the tastes or the sounds of daily experience—are likewise states of our consciousness.

Where is the bitterness that we taste on eating an unripe fruit? Actually, like all tastes, it is a sensation derived from the tongue, for it is primarily an *awareness*, an item furnished by consciousness. It must be identified with our mind. Therefore as an experience it is in us, yet we unconsciously project it outside on the fruit. The fruit produces the sour taste in *us* but we wrongly say it is itself sour. A state of consciousness is thus erroneously ascribed to an external thing! Such an instance shows how faulty language misleads our thought. We learnt in earlier chapters to beware of words and to watch for the pitfalls and snares they prepare for our understanding of the world.

Do we know anything more of a clock than these sensations which tell us what it looks like and what it sounds like? If we pause to analyse the position and if we make our analysis correctly and deeply we are compelled to confess that it is these sense-reports *alone* which make up for us the actual clock that we know. Take away the brown, gold and black colours, the hard, round, cool and smooth feels, and the rhythmic ticking sound—how much of the clock will remain ? Without these there can be no clock at all in anyone's experience. Yet without exception these are all *sensations*, they are all events in the mind, ideas if we wish to call them so. What *we* see, what *we* hear and what *we* feel are the *first* things that we become aware of in relation to every object. The movements within sense, nerve, brain and mind are made with such lightning-like speed that we are unable to notice the process at all. The sensations are therefore not only the first things we know about the clock but actually the *last* things also. It is this incredible rapidity of mental action which creates what is nothing less than an illusion of having entered into direct contact with something outside when in fact we have only entered into our own sensations. Similarly the sight of somebody standing near is a composite result of various sensations, i.e. the sum of what the senses represent to our mind, but nothing more. Every separate thing that we see or experience possesses therefore an assemblage of qualities and characteristics and each quality impresses itself individually on the senses, thus yielding a separate sensation of colour, sound, taste and so on. When we cut deep down into the foundation of our knowledge of the world we find this primal fact of sensation is its support and origin. No such knowledge is at all possible unless sight, hearing, touch and other sensations or their revived memories are first present. For each is an item of human experience.

We may know many things but the only things we know for *certain* are the conditions of our consciousness, i.e. our sensations and nothing else. It is our five senses alone that tell us about the existence of this familiar world and provide us with information about it. It is impossible to get directly at the object as an independent existence. We get only at the sensed interpretation of it ; that is to say we get at a physiological condition in *ourselves*.

Every sensation is a private and individual matter because it is an activity originating in one's own self. It is not shared in common with others ; we cannot ordinarily see directly into the mind of another. Every man can normally only observe what is passing within his own consciousness. He experiences sensations which are separate and may even be somewhat different from those of another man viewing the same object. These personal impressions of light and sound and touch which tell us of the external object are what we know at first hand, what we are immediately aware of and what we are alone sure of experiencing.

The point which must be grasped—and it will need a concentrated subtlety of thought to grasp it—is that *we never know the panoramic external world in itself. We see that world only through the immovable spectacles of the sense-reports which we receive concerning it.* We cannot bring it under direct observation. What we directly observe is—our mental reaction to it, i.e. ourselves! *Without ever being conscious of this certain and simple truth we live day and night in no other world than that whose form is figured for us through what is termed sensation.* Unscientific and unphilosophic persons never suspect the existence of this truth. Let it not be forgotten that these statements are drawn from a long series of observations in the storehouse of modern science and that they are based on experiments made on living persons no less than on dissections performed on dead ones.

Let none become impatient with these pages for repeating scientific facts already known to the world. They are certainly known, but chiefly to the narrow circles of students of medicine and psychology. They are not generally known to the wider circles of layfolk. They are important to our purpose for two reasons. First, they amply confirm a crucial tenet of the hidden teaching which must be absorbed at this stage of our studies. Second, because we are appealing to facts, because we are interrogating Nature in the spirit of Francis Bacon, the founder of modern science. A modern presentation of the ancient Indian teaching must be based on science because the latter is the dominant trend of modern culture and because the new scientific discoveries are beginning to support and vindicate the old Indian discoveries. But whereas science is bewildered by the facts it has gathered and does not quite know what to make of them, the hidden philosophy has a perfect grasp of those facts, for it fully understands their place and significance. Whereas science must sooner or later become philosophical or continue in perpetual bewilderment, the hidden teaching has worked out every tenet in a form which is finished to the last syllable. It knows no uncertainty, no doubts, no bewilderment. It has ascertained truth and can lead willing votaries straight to truth. If therefore we take science in our stride here we shall not stop with science. We shall move fearlessly on and far outstrip it until we reach a verified knowledge compared with which the utterances of science are but broken stammerings before the universal mystery. Let readers be patient therefore, for we are keeping something quite *new* in reserve for them. Let them await the further final volume in which shall be presented for the first time in any modern form or any Western language the advanced and secret teachings of the oldest philosophy known to Asia, the home of this world's oldest culture.

The Birth of Conscious Experience. Any fact or event which is actually observed becomes entitled to the term *experience*. We ordinarily think of objects and happenings without ever realizing that we are thinking of sensations. Such realization can come only afterwards, when thoughtful analysis endeavours to understand the actual experiences. Ordinarily we are more concerned with an object than the mental content immediately referring to it or than the way in which we become aware of its existence. For this is the specialized business of the psychologist.

At the moment of looking at a pen we are quite unaware of the extraordinary complexity of this seemingly simple act. It might be believed that when we are conscious of *all* the sensations produced by the pen we perceive it. Uninstructed opinion usually, believes that recognizing the existence of a pen is a perfectly simple matter of passively receiving all the sensations it yields and nothing more. Scientific investigation reveals, however, that the operation is much more complicated than that.

A sensation is not further divisible by analysis, since it distinguishes a single basic quality of the object. But we are not normally aware of a single isolated sensation. That is to say we never see the golden colour of our fountain-pen nib apart from its shape as a nib. Colour, for instance, does not come into consciousness divorced from size and form. Nobody can examine one apart from another by the light of consciousness. Such a thing exists for us only in theoretical study and is the consequence of theoretical analysis. This is because what we are aware of is a variety of different experiences at one and the same moment, a rush of several sensations simultaneously. Thus the feeling that here is something that is hard to the touch arrives *simultaneously* with the feeling that here is something that is smooth-surfaced and with the visual recognitions that it is purple coloured and round shaped. All these separate qualities, if taken in isolation, would not tell us that the object is a pen. Just as a jumbled heap of bricks produces nothing more than a sense of chaotic confusion until they are built up to make a house, so the sensations have no rational value until they are brought into related and intelligible order. We must not only form sensations; we need to be able to distinguish one thing from another, we need to be able to discriminate the form of the pen from the form of a bottle, for instance.

We see a flower. We also touch it and smell its perfume. The sight, feel and smell of the flower are single sensations. The entire group of sensations must combine before they can constitute the flower for us. The simple stimulus of the coloured surface of a rose may result in a sensation of redness, but only the reaction of the mind, not only to this but to all the other sensations received—such as softness, fragrance and lightness—is what finally determines our understanding that here is a rose.

And what is true of the rose is true of all things experienced. To see anything is to think of it, to feel a piece of soft cloth or a log of hard wood is to *think* of it, and to hear any sound, whether it be the softest whisper or the roll of thunder, is likewise to *think* of it. All sense-experience is impossible without the association of an equivalent act of thought. Everything from infinitesimal microbe to infinite space is first an object of thought, an image or an idea.

Thus bare sensations remain meaningless until they are gathered up, not in series but simultaneously, and constructively put together to form a perceived thing by the mind which experiences them. A multitude of individual impressions may crowd in upon the eyes from a single pen, but not until the mental operations of associating and welding them are complete do they attain the stage of definite *recognition* as being the pen itself. Not until then do they divulge their meaning and their significance get appreciated. The identification of any object involves a creative process of implanting adequate meaning and giving significant association to the elementary sensations. This can arise only after all the salient sensations have been brought together in a single united experience. This is precisely what does happen and thus sensations are converted into the thoughts of things or events as we ordinarily *know* them. Mind arranges, synthesizes and constructs these single and simultaneous sensations into complete thoughts or images.[1] Each thought is contemporaneously compounded from two or more associated sensations. Each separate sensation is an element in the orderly building up of perception so that the perceived picture of the pen is really a group of such elements brought into the full light of consciousness. We have a sensation as the first subconscious reaction to a physical stimulus from outside things and we have a conscious thought as the first conscious reaction to the sum of sensations. The whole series appears, then, as a stimulus to the sense-instrument

---

[1] Such a thought is technically termed a *percept*, or more popularly, a *perception*. But as it is an actual construction within the zone of mind it is sometimes also called a *mental construct*, which is sometimes shortened to a *construct*.

by an outside object, then a sense-impression, next a nerve-transmission, fourth a brain-response, fifth a subconscious mind response (sensation), and finally a fully conscious response (mental picture, idea of event, image, thought). We ordinarily know only the sixth stage in this series because it is the finished and familiar conscious experience, whereas the fifth is only the raw material for such experience.

But we must not fall into the error of regarding such a perceptual thought as the mere adding together of new sensations: they certainly make its core, but it is necessarily supplemented by something more if every experience is to be adequately filled in. The mind must first interpret and then creatively form its own image of the pen not only out of the impressions gathered by the senses but also out of those associated with the memories of earlier experiences of seeing and handling pens. It must imagine and add something to the bare message received from the senses if it is successfully to re-interpret the inverted, undersized and two-dimensional retinal image. Hence three other mental contributions inevitably enter into each act of perception and mingle with the material supplied by sensations, thus elaborating the whole into a final thought of recognition. (1) Association with past similar experience, (2) anticipation of new experience, (3) personal interpretation peculiar to the experiencing individual. The most important of these elements is the first.

When we recognize the sensation of hardness in handling a piece of wood our memory automatically connects and classifies it with the store of previously experienced sensations of hardness. The remembered hardness fuses, as it were, with the new sensation of hardness. We graft familiar old impressions or unconsciously reproduce past experience on the new sensations. Thus old experience is revived and put with the new, appearing to us in the form of an actual perception. The hand may yield impressions of something hard and smooth, whilst the eye may yield impressions of something round and brown-coloured, but all these sensations are merely the material to which the mind must add an element drawn from the wealth of past experience which it possesses subconsciously and then synthetically construct the whole into the image of a table. This it does by welding all these sensations and at the same time interpreting them in the light of remembered experience. The memory of previous and associated sensations is brought in. In this way it arrives at the meaning of the thing as the round top of a table.

The mind draws upon the apparently vanished past, thus rising above time's limitation, and grasps at those experiences which are most likely to help it understand the present experience. The resurrected sensations influence the making of the new image.

Further proof of the contribution thrown by the past into the moulding of these mental images may be found in the relative swiftness with which an adult recognizes the size, distance and shape of a thing as compared with an infant. The little creature has to learn to distinguish between one vague thing and another vague thing until both slowly begin to acquire clearer outline through familiarity and clearer meaning through experience. The infant stretches out its hand to grasp the moon, thinking it is quite close, whereas the adult sees the moon as being quite remote from his own body. But the infant's eyes registered the impressions of the moon no less faithfully and accurately than the adult's, for their construction is not in any way different. The infant's failure to perceive its proper spatial relation to the moon is not to be blamed upon the eyes, but can only be accounted for by the feebler activity of its mind in constructing an image out of its visual sensations, due to the lack of sufficient former experience to draw upon. And a child who has only just learnt to read will peruse the printed page with slowness and difficulty, not infrequently mistaking one letter for another or even one word for another. The same child grown to maturity will read the same page with rapidity and accuracy. Yet the impressions and images registered by the retina are precisely similar in both cases. The eyes may be as perfect in the child as in the adult. Why then does this difference in result occur? The answer is that as the growing child reads printed books more and more frequently its mind remembers earlier images of letters and words and increasingly contributes these recollections to the operation of reading until finally each word is fully and correctly recognized, i.e. perceived for what it is. This is a plain proof of the complex and creative nature of every thought which refers to an experience.

Here is a simple way of grasping how powerfully the mind contributes to present experience by drawing on the past. Listen to the same person singing two different songs quickly, one of which is quite familiar and the other quite unknown. The words of the first song will be followed with ease, whereas those of the second will be followed with a little difficulty, so that it may be impossible to recognize some of them. The sounds will be heard but they will not be distinguished as recognizable words. On the other hand, memory has added something to the sensations of sound in the first case.

FROM THING TO THOUGHT

The impression produced on the ears is of the same quality in both. And yet the hearing is confused when the song is unknown but perfect when it is familiar and recollected. It is defective in one case and accurate in the other. A mental factor is therefore present in all cases of hearing and makes its due contribution to what is consciously heard rather than what is actually impressed on the ears by sound vibrations.

A strange illustration showing how the past exists as an ingredient in human perception is to be found in the case of those who have lost a leg or arm through violent accident or surgical amputation. Medical annals reveal that such persons have in several instances complained of feeling pain in the foot or fingers of a missing limb as if the latter were still connected with the body ! Thus the mind can even wreathe fictions into its experience under the powerful influence of memory. This indicates that the testimony of memory prepares the way for the entry of expectancy. Hence a further element which enters the making of an image along with the new and remembered sensations is anticipation of what the object is or ought to be. It is the final factor in shaping the thought. Not only do images of past experience enter into the train of mental activity, but so do personal emotions. Each mental construct is conditioned by our individual organization. This is well illustrated when certain optical illusions arise. We do not directly draw, therefore, entirely on new sense-impressions for all our awareness. Memory of the past supplies some of it in the form of revived mental images, whilst expectant imagination supplies others, but indirectly both of these are derived from earlier sense-impressions.

Thus deeply ingrained mental habits, strongly seated expectations and aroused associations also take their share in this work of moulding a mental picture or the thought of an event. The passage from bare sensation to full perception is not only the passage to a group of sensations simultaneously uniting in consciousness to form the experience, but is also the passage to mental interpretation and mutual adjustment of the simple sensations.

The idea is a completed product when we actually recognize it as belonging to a particular class, as when a red-and-gold-coloured, smooth-feeling, oblong-shaped, six-inch-long object is recognized as being one of the class called books. However, its formation of a percept must not be thought of as one of merely arithmetical addition. It is much more a process of *instantaneous* fusion. The sensations do not merely interlace, they fuse. All these operations which go to the making of experience are not performed by us so far as we are aware, nor are they directly accessible to our observation. They are performed automatically beneath the threshold of conscious mind. They are demonstrated by their effects. If we are unable to unravel these single and separate elements and expose them individually to our gaze it is precisely because a thought is nothing other than their final and permanent fusion into a unit. During the time of manufacture the thought forms itself automatically and beyond the control of the conscious will. We are not personally aware of this ceaseless activity of the mind in giving birth to the thoughts, images and ideas whose totality constitutes our world-experience, and therefore we are not aware of the fact that the pen as it appears to us is mind-made.

Thus the analysis of perception reveals that the form and size of any object which confronts us, no less than the feel and the colour of it, are qualities which ultimately exist for the *mind* alone. This is no less true of hard and heavy things like granite rocks, for they exist for us as fused groups of sensations. Only when we become *conscious* of the rocks can we regard them as being there. Only felt and seen rocks can exist for us at all. We know everything through the totality of the sensations, i.e. the awareness, it produces in us, through the colours, smells, tastes, feels and sounds which make up our physical experience and which are ultimately experiences of the mind. What we *see* is not the thing-in-itself but the thing-in-our mind. The thought is more intimate than the thing.

How is it that the formation of a thought takes place with such unbelievable swiftness ? We can only reply that originally it must have been a slow and conscious act which in the course of evolution through countless centuries was imperceptibly transformed by the individual and the race into an instantaneous and unconscious one. Familiar and frequently recurring experiences have rendered it easy for the mind to create its images practically instantaneously. The complex and complete act of seeing the object really occupies a number of successive steps, but they flash by with such unimaginable and incredible rapidity as practically to fuse into a single instantaneous operation. This rapid working is partly a result of the existing background of past sense-experience into which new sensations immediately merge, and partly a result of the mind's innate power.

These separate steps in the awareness of a thing do not disclose themselves to ordinary consciousness but only to scientific analysis. Hence they may appear to the uninitiated as a farrago of nonsense. They belong to a process which is entirely below the surface ; they

FROM THING TO THOUGHT

are subconscious to a partial or complete extent. They are described here in the way they would unfold themselves to us could we but view them individually. Perception is ordinarily such a tremendously rapid, perfectly smooth and automatic process that we do not pause to consider the great significance involved in its actual operation. Thus sight may be viewed from three distinct standpoints. The first is the physical stimulus and is a matter of the movement of light-rays from the object to the eye. The second is the physiological process and is a matter of projecting an image upon the retina. The third is the psychological construct and is a matter of first becoming aware that the object exists. Physics investigates the light, physiology investigates the eye and brain, psychology has to study the arisal of a conscious percept, whilst philosophy must not only co-ordinate the results of all three sciences but evaluate them and ascertain their true worth in a grander system of world-explanation.

Thus we may come to perceive that so long as we confine our examination to the top of the picture, so long any understanding of the way we enter into awareness of the familiar things and persons that surround us seems a simple affair, but the moment we try to view the lower part also and to gaze at the picture as a whole, then only do we begin to grasp how difficult and how complex an affair it really is. Thus too we may realize why the scientist to some extent and the philosopher to the fullest extent are not satisfied with superficial explanations of what they see and touch every day, as are common folk, but seek rather to plunge into deeper water. For in the case of the subject of this chapter we have been led step by step to the surprising discovery that however tangible be the every-day material things themselves, their existence is ultimately revealed to us only by our mental experience of them, i.e. our knowledge of these things shuts us up within the four walls of thoughts alone.

Put into plainer language, what we undoubtedly know are our ideas of what are usually said to be external objects, whereas what we erroneously believe we know are the objects themselves. The difference between the two is the difference between a cinematographic photograph of the inimitable and genial Charlie Chaplin on a white screen and the living Charlie Chaplin in the flesh. But there the analogy must end. To stretch it farther is to falsify it. For whereas a photograph is after all but a *copy* of something, a thought is not a copy at all; it is a mental *creation*. It is new because it represents a new birth into consciousness, a new arisal of idea. It is an evidence of the mind's wonderful power of constructing—and not merely exploring—what it perceives. And it is also an evidence of what was hinted in the opening lines of the present chapter—that the external world is entirely relative to the mind that perceives it, that the pregnant principle of relativity rules all our observations and all our experience. Here we carry this principle to a length which Einstein has not grasped and will therefore be unwilling to follow. Those who can understand this point have received an introduction to an infallible inoculation against the crude kind of materialism which prevailed last century among the proletarian camp-followers of science, and against the sanctimonious materialism which prevailed among the unintelligent upholders of religion.

The fountain-pen which began as a collection of sensed qualities has ended as a fragment of our mind. The last lesson of this chapter is that what we see is primarily seen as a thought, that what we touch is primarily touched as an image and that every human experience of the physical world is essentially a mentally produced experience. Our perceptions, which seem so physical, are prominently and paramountly mental events. All the coloured and odorous and felt things that we are acquainted with are ultimately experienced in the mind and nowhere else. In order to get in touch with the world of outside things we have to *think* them into existence; otherwise we remain totally unaware of them. The idea which the mind thus subconsciously brings to birth represents, rightly or wrongly, as much of the thing as we know and as much as we can ever know. For we cannot go beyond our thoughts. We cannot see what they do not picture forth for us. A pen itself may be six inches long, but if our mind were to play the trick of showing it to us as only one inch long we would continue in blissful ignorance to believe that the pen was only one inch long. Fortunately such tricks are rare, although they are certainly not non-existent, as the next chapter will clearly show. And if our mind did not know that the eyes were seeing a mountain and the hands were touching it we would not know that the mountain existed at all.

We need more truth. There is no other anodyne for our troubled age. It is admittedly hard to believe that we are aware of *thoughts* of external things only, when all these years we have fondly believed we were aware of the things themselves. Most men are inaccessible to this tenet. It sets them down beneath a sky which is strange, cold, unfamiliar. It will therefore be hard to divest ourselves of the familiar conventional outlook—that is to say, the materialistic outlook. But it can be done if only we are willing to give a little time and much inquiring independent thought to the task. We must

FROM THING TO THOUGHT

be pitiless and thresh out all error, all falsity and all illusion from our mentality. Our bondage to popular ignorance need not last for ever. It can grow weak and insignificant as our wrong thoughts grow weak and insignificant. Instructed and concentrated thinking can work miracles, for it can turn the water of error into the costly wine of truth.

CHAPTER X

THE SECRET OF SPACE AND TIME

WE must now enter the most difficult stage of our enquiry into the process whereby we perceive external objects—that is to say, of our enquiry into the nature of human experience of the external world. We must relentlessly pursue this enquiry despite its difficulties, for the world is ever confronting us and silently demanding adequate understanding of its nature.

It is impossible to think of the world, or of anything in the world, without thinking of it as existing in space and time. This, as has been shown, is because the mind itself plays a most important part in predetermining how we shall see the world, compelling us to *see* it in terms of separate and successive images. Therefore the Indian sages said that thinking *itself* cannot reach and observe the world's reality or essence. The scientists who have established the theories of relativity and quantum mechanics have now found themselves in the same plight. They have confessed that it is impossible to reach and observe the subtler phenomena of Nature without interfering with these same phenomena in the very process of observation. The moment scientific research entered the mysterious sub atomic world of electrons, neutrons and protons, it had to recognize that the observer himself played a role in determining the phenomena observed by him.

What is immediately seen as the outside thing is really the mental picture. Science has slowly begun to realize this. The older scientific theories of optical illusion, for instance, made it purely physical, attributing it to some physiological disturbance of the retina or to a defect in the muscles of the eye, whereas the later ones introduce a definite mental ingredient. Matter is no longer all that matters! The older theories thought illusion an unimportant abnormality, whereas the later ones find it is bound up with the process of perception from beginning to end.

To mistake the bodily structure for the immaterial consciousness itself and to fall into the old trap of regarding the brain of flesh as the mystery of mind, are natural and pardonable errors in unreflective and uninstructed persons, in those philosophically unsophisticated people who turn in disgust from the first mention of this mentalistic doctrine. That a thing which is touched, seen and tasted is as internal to the mind as it is external to the body, and that the body is in its own turn just as internal to the mind, irritates their common sense. Only the deepest reflection can show that the sensations derived from the human body itself are really as objective as sensations derived from fountain-pens, because they are capable of being observed by mind, the subject. Thus second thought refutes what first impression asserts.

However, it would be quite a mistake to suppose that this teaching asks us to believe that visible objects are not seen outside our own body, that because it describes these objects as mental perceptions they must therefore be placed somewhere inside our body and that the glazed window before which we are seated is no nearer than yonder twinkling star. To attempt to place a house within the bony skull of a man is the futile endeavour of those who have failed to understand this doctrine, which, it need hardly be said, is entirely exempt from any expression of such absurdity. No material object of such a size could possibly exist within the material head of a man. Such impossible and improbable beliefs belong to the annals of lunacy and not to the annals of the hidden philosophy of India. The latter does emphatically agree that we see objects like houses and trees outside our bodies and certainly not inside them, and that all such objects are most undoubtedly seen to be at a distance from us as well as from each other. What it does assert is that the perceptions of the objects being purely mental, and it being impossible to assign any special spatial location to the mind, it is consequently impossible to say that these objects are seen at a distance from the mind itself.

The notion of the body's existence as separate from mind, from awareness, is the fashionable fallacy entertained by the materialistic. To invest the body with the qualities which should be ascribed to the mind is strangely to misinterpret all experience. We have no right to treat our knowledge of all external objects as mental but that of our own body as material. Such a distinction is illogical and unjustifiable. If it be true to say that everything is known through the mind, it will be true not only of all external objects but also of our own body, with its head, hands, trunk, legs and feet. These also are necessarily known mentally. There are no grounds whatever for thinking that they come in a different class from that of external objects. We must, therefore, treat the body in exactly the same way in which we treat all other objects and regard our awareness of it solely as the awareness of thought.

Nor must we make the mistake of many novices in this study, and most critics who disdain it, of imagining that the human body is known through the body alone although the objects which are outside it are all mentally known. Our body with its five sense-instruments, the eye, ear, nose, tongue and skin, exists in precisely the same manner as a brick wall, so far as it exists as an idea of consciousness. We are aware of the sense-instruments themselves because of the sensations derived from them and not otherwise. For the reason that it consists of a certain shape, size, colour, etc., which are made known to us by the mind, the entire body—even the physical brain—is as much within the mind, and we are as much dependent upon the mind for awareness of its existence as we are for awareness of a brick wall.

The fact is that most men confuse their skin with their mind. They do not comprehend that the distance that extends from the surface of their body to the nearest thing is emphatically not the distance that extends from the latter to their mind. The cardinal error is to mistake extra-bodily existence for extra-mental existence. Mind unconsciously projects its perceptions into space and then views the things of its own making.

Let us sum up these statements by applying a little analytic treatment, a little corrosive criticism to this word "external". Nobody has ever seen an object outside the mind, but only outside the body. Putting aside the practical standpoint and speaking philosophically, it is wrong to talk of "external" objects, for even the body is known ultimately as a thought and is therefore mental: thus nothing at all is ever really external. To talk of an object being even outside the body is to talk of it being outside a thought, i.e. outside a mental thing, i.e. outside the mind—which is impossible. Those who use the word "external" ought to define whether they mean external to body or to mind. For if to body, then it has been shown that the body itself is internal to mind, so the objects themselves must also be internal to mind. And if to the mind, then the notion of inside and outside is wholly inapplicable. Hence we may not accurately say anything is external; we may only say it exists. The word contains its own contradiction. It belongs to an irrational and superstitious jargon.

From the first beginnings of consciousness each object is incessantly presented to the mind as being something apart and independent. We not only recognize a thing, but we recognize it as

THE SECRET OF SPACE AND TIME

having a particular shape and size and standing at a certain distance away from our own body and from other things. We recognize it to exist in space. We are seeing it spatially. We possess an inveterate conviction, for example, that the wall which we see is situated out there in space and we feel that we dare not desert this conviction without losing our sanity.

But we must begin to face a queer problem. If no sensation can extrude itself beyond the periphery of the body, because every sensation is supposed to be the internal result of the operation of a bodily sense-instrument, why do we perceive the finished thought as a form extended in space? All objects said to be external stand in spatial relation to each other, but how can our ideas of them, which are apparently all that we know, be considered as having positions in space? If it has been shown that our thoughts or observations of these objects really are our experiences of them, why is it that this self-same experience confutes our reasoning, for it reveals the objects as standing entirely separate from and outside bodies? How can an image which is said to be internal appear to us as an object which is external and which possesses spatial characteristics? How can colours which are scientifically provable as being optical interpretations, i.e. within the eyes, be able to assume the forms of independent outside things? The puzzle in short is how to account for the conversion of a purely mental experience into a seemingly separate and independent one, and for the projection of a purely internal experience into an external one.

To cast some light upon the answers to these questions we must make a lengthy scientific examination of certain aspects of the process of perceiving things through the senses. There exists a certain anomalous functioning of the senses which seems of trivial importance when considered from a practical point of view, but which actually offers unique material for an approach to profounder understanding of the places taken by the senses and the mind in observation of the world. Those peculiar errors of the senses which we call illusion and those mysterious derangements of the mind which we call hallucination provide interesting illustration of a principle whose weighty importance is usually overlooked by the unscientific or non-philosophical mind. To underrate their instructive value because of their practical pettiness would be a mistake.

The experience of illusion shares certain common elements with constant and habitual experience, although it appears to mock sardonically at it. The psychological act of perception is present in both although the causes differ. The process whereby we become *conscious* of an illusion cannot be different from the way in which we become conscious of any ordinary thing. As an act of awareness both are indeed the same, even though one is said to be erroneous and the other accurate.

Science has found that the study of what is abnormal sheds new light on what is normal. Disturbances in the psychic process and defects in the physiological mechanism sometimes reveal valuable clues to the working of both or confirm the results previously obtained by scientific examination and pure reflection. Therefore when the mechanism of sensation is disturbed, as in illusions, and the physical stimulus is misconstrued, we get a glimpse of how the mechanism itself operates. Careful and systematic dissection of these abnormal experiences supplies valuable pointers which will help to render the intricate processes of perception more intelligible and light up more revealingly the respective roles played by the observing mind, the observing senses and the observed object. Therefore it is because of its scientific worth in helping to explain sense-experience that the subject of illusion is here taken up.

The Greek intellectuals like Aristotle were troubled about the easy way men could be deceived by their senses, but the Indian sages like Gaudapada not only noted this fact but carried their investigation to the last possible stage. For they were troubled about the easy way men could be deceived by their *mind*. The full implications of the phenomena of illusions—which every philosophy worth the name is called upon to investigate—require for their grasp a refined subtlety of apprehension which is not often found among occidentals. The achievements of the Aryan[1] races in mental and physical spheres entitle them to superior status, but it is the Indo-Aryan branch which has proportionately produced the most men whose sharpness of concentration and subtlety of thought have combined with a singular subdual of the desires and egoisms which might weaken their undivided aim to pursue philosophy. Every aspect of illusion and hallucination has been thoroughly dealt with by the Indian sages, for they had a scientific bent of mind and would accept nothing until it had been investigated and verified. Unfortunately the sages disappeared, their knowledge was largely lost and Indian philosophy degenerated with the lapse of centuries into the empty babbling speculation which it became in other countries.

Illusions are connected with a strange factor in perception which ought long ago to have set enquiring Western minds on the correct

---

[1] This term is used only in its genuinely scientific sense.

track to psychological truth, for it was noticed and deeply pondered on by Indian sages thousand of years ago, but its significance has not received proper attention in the West. And this is that we observe only what we are paying attention to; that amid all the multitude of retinal experiences we unconsciously select those only in which we are interested. Thus we may be reading a book whilst seated in a room; or we may be in an office at work which is deeply fascinating or of high importance. A clock may twice strike the hour and yet we may not remember hearing its chimes simply because attention has been highly concentrated on the reading or the work. The impressions are actually made on the sense-instrument, the sound-waves succeed in striking the tympanums of healthy ears, but owing to the dissociation of attention they are not perceived by us although they are heard by other persons. We may be walking in the street and a passing friend may greet us. Yet if we are plunged in deep reflection we fail to see him and do not return his greeting. We see what we are looking for rather than what we are looking at. Consciousness grades down to dimness or even nothingness where we pay no attention to what we see whilst it compensatingly vividly lights up the object towards which thought has been surrendered in utter concentration.

When any piece of work is being attended to so completely as to occupy consciousness to the exclusion of all else, events may occur or objects may be present to the gaze and yet escape attention and pass unnoted. They remain outside the field of awareness although inside the field of sense-impression. That which dominates the mind dictates that which shall be perceived: this is one lesson to be learnt. When attention of the sensory faculties is preoccupied by the ideas of internal reverie the path to their external activity is blocked. This is practically illustrated by the case of yogis who are totally plunged in the state of trance or coma and then remain unaware or pain-free when cut with knives or buried beneath the ground. The mental factor of attention plays a powerful role in determining the content of what we perceive. The more the mind is directed to a bodily hurt, the more intense and intolerable does the pain become. On the other hand, the more the mind is occupied with some other event, the less troublesome will the hurt be felt. When thought flags or is totally withdrawn we may be blind to what is actually present before our eyes.

This extraordinary fact should alone have been a plain hint that the functioning of the mind both contributes to and withdraws something from the making of the world we witness. It should have been a warning that the mental factor cannot rightly be left out of any account of sense-experience. For if the mind does not co-operate with the senses there will be no conscious experience of any external object, however much the physical conditions may be fulfilled ; or if it co-operates imperfectly, then experience will becomes less clear and less intense in proportion. It is difficult to become aware of the degree of mental interference when our normal state gives no evidence of it. We can hope, however, to do so by watching for abnormal experiences and unusual events which cause rifts in the veil of perception as it were. It has already been pointed out that psychologically it is an error to separate illusions from the accepted facts of normal life. It is from the analytic study of such exceptional deviations from the ordinary course of Nature that we gain fresh knowledge of what such course really is. If an illusion is a false sensory impression it is still an impression no matter how it arises.

Let us consider first the class of illusions which belong to Nature. The most elementary consideration of this question brings a startling revelation. Take, for example, the simple chair upon which you are sitting. Here is a solid, hard and tangible object made of a natural material substance, which you call wood. That is the truth about this chair so far as you are concerned. Go, however, to the laboratory of a scientist. Let him take a piece of this wood of which your chair is constructed and submit it to his searching analytic examination. He will successively reduce it to molecules, atoms, electrons, protons and neutrons. He will tell you finally that the wood consists of nothing more solid than a series of electrical radiations or, in plain language, of electricity. Yet despite such expert instructions and scornful of what irrefutable reason tells you, your five senses will continue to report wood as being something most substantial, the very opposite of whatever you can imagine electrical energy to be.

Does this not mean that you are experiencing an amazing illusion, one that is stranger than any conjurer's feat ? Indeed, the entire planet itself offers us a curious example of great masses of solid, liquid and gaseous substances which are not really what they seem. For, if scientific investigation has not deceived itself, they are whirling winds of electrical energy, i.e. the lofty mountains, flowing rivers, rolling seas and green fields are not really constituted as we see them. Their existence is certainly undeniable, but their appearance as "lumps of matter" is fundamentally illusory.

The study of modern scientific geography reveals the extraordinary fact that millions of persons are really walking upon this globe with their heads suspended downwards and with their feet clinging to rather than resting on the earth. Such a statement, taken as it stands upon the printed sheet, is so astonishing that so-called common sense, when it is common uninstructed opinion, refuses to believe it, although the acceptance of the proved fact of the globular shape of our planet leaves us with no other alternative but to accept this further finding which is so contradictory to what our eyes tell us. What man would have known this fact if the scientists, through constant probing, had not ascertained it for him and thus discovered that the popular belief about the human bodily relation to the surface of the earth is purely illusory? This simple illustration may help us to grasp why those who insist on accepting the testimony of their immediate sense-impressions as alone being true are unfit for philosophy.

When the full moon rises, glowing redly, near the horizon it assumes the size of an enormous wagon-wheel. But see the same moon when it is overhead and it has shrunk to the relative size of a coin. Which appearance are you to take as the correct one? Your eyes are not to be blamed, for the retina records a perfectly accurate image in both cases. The difference occurs because you unconsciously measure the suddenly rising moon on the same scale by which you habitually measure the hills, trees, buildings or other objects which also occupy the horizon, whereas you ordinarily use quite another scale to measure those which are far overhead. Thus the sun setting behind a familiar full-branched tree will appear tremendously magnified because it fills the space occupied by the branches. You set up a false standard of perception through established habit and then judge the sun's or moon's size by it. But where does this error really occur? It is not in the object nor in your eyes. It can only occur in your mind, for it is a mistake of interpretation, i.e. a *mental activity*. The apparent enlargement of sun or moon is actually present in your idea.

Look at the landscape spread out before you in the morning. Your eyes may see nothing more in the background than a dull mist which fills the horizon. Photograph the mist with the help of a special plate sensitive to infra-red rays. The camera will then grasp what the unaided sight cannot, for it will faithfully register the image of a hitherto unseen range of mountains twenty miles away. Similarly a sensitive spectroscope and photographic plate will reveal the existence of stars in apparently empty space even where a powerful telescope fails to reveal them. The fact that such natural illusions do exist and are possible is itself a critique of our knowledge of the world and its validity. If the senses can deceive us in these cases is it not likely that they can deceive us in others which pass unnoticed? These instances should give us ground not so much for distrusting the senses—for they are not directly to blame for these errors—as for distrusting our interpretations of the reports of the senses.

Yes, the senses can delude us. An observer in a rapidly descending aeroplane actually sees the earth rushing upwards and a traveller in an express train actually sees telegraph poles moving past him. These are visual errors. But they help to illustrate how the process of vision really works. For they betray an element of judgment, i.e. of mental contribution, in what appears as the finished deliverance of the senses.

Why do the last hundred yards of a four-mile walk seem much longer than the first hundred yards when the impressions made on the senses of sight and touch are still the same as before, still as accurate? The answer is that the tired muscles have *suggested* a different series of exaggerated sensations, which produce the illusions of magnified movement and lengthened duration. The sensations, we must remember, are *mental*.

Enter a room which has been somewhat darkened and let the light of a small window fall on a green-coloured coat. Look at it through a piece of red glass. You may be startled to discover that it appears black. Then look at a red garment through blue glass and it also will seem to be black. Fit a green electric bulb and look at a blue coat with your naked eye. It too will appear black! Or fit a red bulb and gaze at a bunch of yellow primroses. The flowers will look strange, for they will look red. And it is a common experience to find that certain shades of cloth which look green in daylight change their colour to brown in artificial light. And santonin, a poisonous drug, if taken in a certain degree, causes many things to appear yellow. The plain implication of such optical illusions is that you must be prepared at least to mistrust not your senses but their working. For they are unable to work without the mind.

When you gaze at a patch of green-coloured cloth for some time and then turn to look at a different patch of grey-coloured cloth, the latter will assume a rose-red tint. The sense-impressions of grey colour cannot have changed. What is wrong is that the mind has misinterpreted them because present sensations are relative to previous ones and affected by them because in forming the images of experience the mind works on what it receives.

You see a magnificent rainbow arched from earth to heaven.

But the pilot of an aeroplane passing through it will see nothing at all—a clear instance of relativity!

The lovely colours which touch the sky at dawn and sunset are partly the consequence of drifting dust and hanging vapour scattered in the air. Yet you see neither dust nor vapour and superimpose the colourings upon the space they fill. When water-drops are large enough to break light up into the spectrum we perceive a beautiful rainbow. When they are assembled as massed clouds they are radiantly white when they reflect the sun's rays to your eyes, but are dismally grey or black when they are so placed as to be unable to do so. Amid all these alternations of colourful dress and bleak veiling the light certainly does not change its own nature; it remains one and the same, but only *appears* to be different to different observers at different times. Thus the vast canopy of heaven is frequently a gigantic illusion of colour, teaching the unheeding minds of men to be wary of what they see, to reflect upon the relativity of all things and to grasp the grand difference between *seeming* and *being*.

Look into a tumbler of clean water. Your eyes tell you that it is absolutely pure. Examine the same water under a microscope and you will find it to be swarming with countless animalculae. Lettuce may be thoroughly washed and appear temptingly clean, but here again the microscope finds it to be full of bacteria. In both cases the unaided senses not only fail to tell you the truth, but actually mislead you into illusion.

When a stick is partly immersed in a glass bowl filled with water it will appear to be bent out of position at the place where it touched the surface of the water, so that the lower part will seem to be lifted upward out of its straight course. Here the visual experience gives definitely inaccurate information about the shape of the stick, and will persist in doing so however perfect your eyes and however often the stick is seen.

Here is a wooden telegraph pole. When we apply a measuring-rod we find it to be forty feet high. If we walk some distance away from it and view it it appears somewhat smaller. And if we proceed considerably farther in the same direction and again look at it the height has been brought down to a mere few feet. Is the pole this little stick which is now visible? Is it the object which was so clearly and so convincingly forty feet long when measured? Here are three different heights which the pole *appears* to possess. Which one represents the real as apart from the apparent height? If we reply that the measured figure is alone correct, then we must explain why a measuring-rod should be more privileged than a man and why the mathematical concept, i.e. idea, "forty feet" should be entitled to take precedence of the other idea, "four feet", which arises when standing a considerable distance away. Nor is this all, for we shall also have to explain why the measuring-rod—which is merely a length of wood—should be assigned certitude of length when there is such uncertainty about the telegraph pole, which is also a length of wood. For it is evident that whether we are standing immediately close to the pole or to the rod or whether we are standing at a hundred yards distance from them, what we see in both cases is only the object as it appears to us.

This point has been covered in our scientific analysis of relativity in an earlier chapter. It raises serious and startling questions. Is the pole one thing and what we see of it another? Do we see things as they really are or only as they appear to us? If the latter, are we doomed to perceive appearances only, never their reality? The answers to these questions now begin to reveal themselves from our study of the perceptive process. For we have begun to learn that what we really see are the images formed by our own mind. Whether formed subconsciously or consciously they are still nothing more than mental images, thoughts. All appearances of poles or rods are but the revelations of our mind. We see our thoughts of things, not the things themselves. The question of what is the reality behind these appearances, what is the real object that gives rise to the thoughts about it, is too advanced to be dealt with here and will be taken up later.

What is true of sight may also be true of other senses. There are illusions of touch, for instance. Take three bowls of water—respectively cold, tepid, and as hot as is bearable. Put your left hand in the hot water and at the same time plunge your right hand in the cold water. Keep both hands immersed for two or three minutes. Then withdraw them quickly, shake off the drops and plunge both hands in the bowl containing lukewarm water. The water will feel cold to your left hand but warm to the right one! The sense of touch in each limb will contradict the other, for it will estimate different temperatures for the same water. That the same water is both hot and cold is not only a clear discrepancy between sense reports but also an astonishing illustration how present sensations *do* depend on previous ones and that what we actually feel *is* partly a projection by memory from past experience.

Let a spade remain outdoors throughout a frosty night. Pick it up next morning. The wooden handle will feel a little cold, but the metal part will feel intensely chill. Touch will therefore yield a striking difference in the temperature of both parts of the same spade. Test them with a thermometer, however, and they will be found to register an equal degree of cold! So much for the dangers of trusting the accuracy of *what we actually experience*!

The Illusions of Geometry. Let us next consider a totally different class of illusions, those which man has artificially created. There are interesting instances of geometrical illusions which are known to students of physics, physiology and psychology. *Figure* 1 shows four horizontal lines of apparently unequal length each bounded by short oblique lines that turn inward or outward. Which line do you estimate as the longest? Measure them with a marked ruler and they will all be found quite equal! The top line looks the shortest because the eye locates its end somewhere in the arrowhead and does not follow it to the tip. The other lines also seem unequal because you do not isolate them from the rest of the figures. The retinal images of all four lines must nevertheless be the same size. So if we see the lines as unequal, then the eyes are not to be blamed, but the judgment. This means that a mental factor is at work in what we see and that it is powerful enough to make us see what it chooses, even when, as here, it is itself at fault by making wrong presentation, i.e. by constructing a wrong image.

Figure 2 shows a circle which appears to be unsymmetrical and flattened in four places, i.e. at the corners of the square. Test it with a compass and it will be found perfect! *Figure* 3 shows two long lines crossing a number of shorter lines and giving the impression of being curved in the middle, where the intersections are closer and more numerous. Actually they are straight and parallel! Here are two lines which are perfectly parallel, yet by the mere insertion of a few cross-strokes most observers will find that they yield the impression of being convergent. This is an illusion of direction. *Figure* 4 apparently shows the outline of an elongated irregular four-sided figure intersected by many parallel lines. But if you accept it as such you will be mistaken, for it is really a perfect square! *Figure* 5 provides a conundrum. Which of the double lines on the right side of the oblong continues the sloping line on the left side? Most people think it is the upper line. Apply a straight-edged ruler and their error will be clearly shown.

Look steadily at *Figure* 6. Sometimes it will appear as a flat pattern, an acute-angled intersection of two lines, but sometimes it will recede from sight and appear as a solid object, a right-angled

Q

242 THE HIDDEN TEACHING BEYOND YOGA

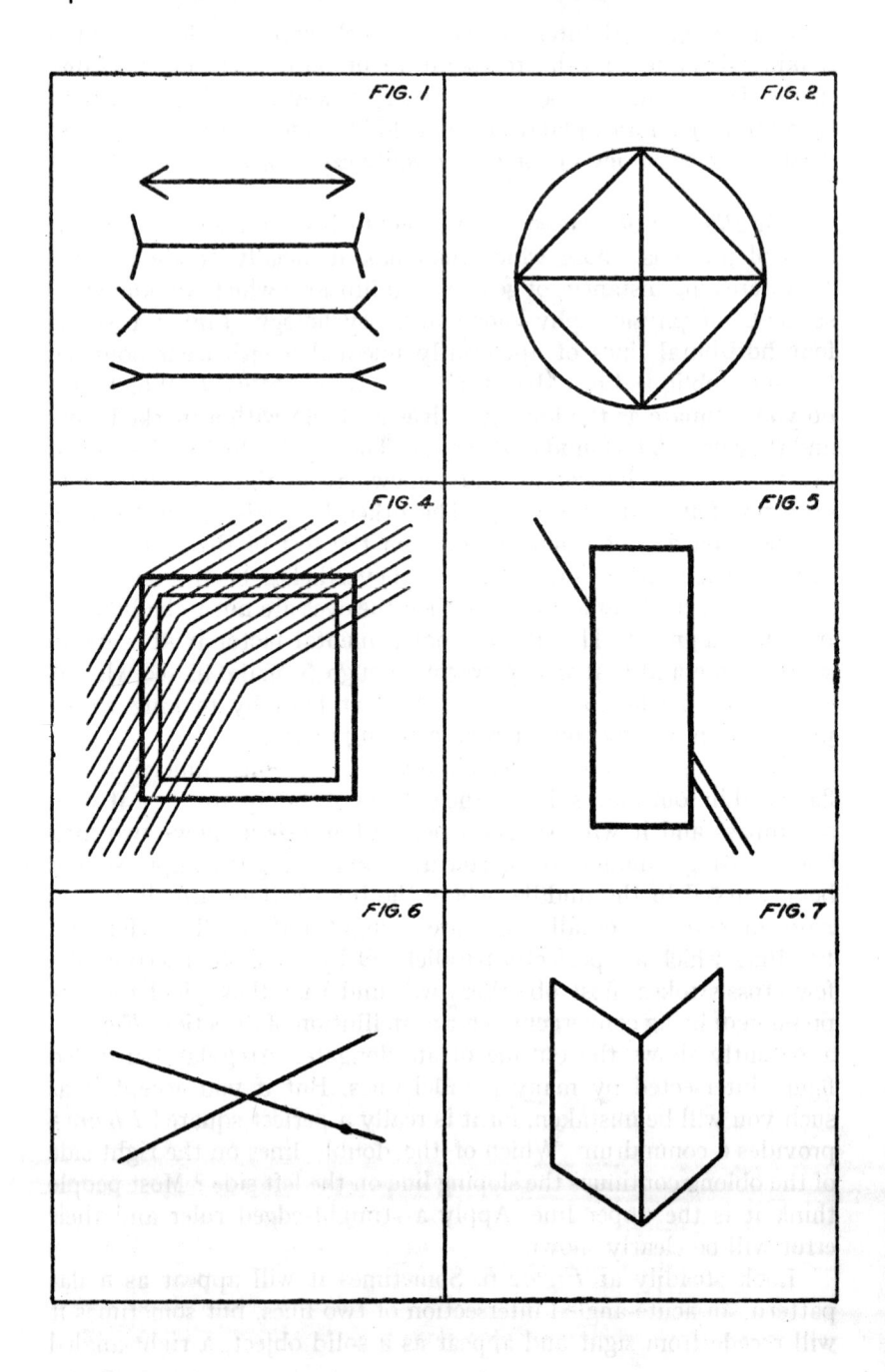

FIG. 1

FIG. 2

FIG. 4

FIG. 5

FIG. 6

FIG. 7

THE SECRET OF SPACE AND TIME

cross lying on the floor, at which you are looking obliquely from above. Close one eye and gaze for a time at *Figure* 7. Sometimes it will appear as a folded sheet of paper seen from outside and sometimes as if seen from inside with the fold farthest away!

The unshaded illustration in *Figure* 8 is more ambiguous and complicated than any of the others. A transparent cube confronts you. It will at first show one of its surfaces nearer the eye, but continued attention will suffice to reverse the experience and bring the other surface to the fore. The original surface will then appear to have retreated to the back and to be looked at through the body of the cube. This will convert the flat transparent cube into a solid opaque one. When steadily looked at the cube shifts alternately back and forth into different positions from moment to moment. The consequence is that different corners of the figure will be drawn forward in turn. It is important to note that the reversed interpretation will possess all the force of any ordinary everyday perception. You begin to see not what the artist has drawn in black ink on white paper but what your mind has imagined, i.e. constructed, out of its former experience of similar or related figures. The actual impressions made by these simple lines upon the sensitive retinas of your eyes are perfectly correct, as has been proved in cases where photographs of the retinal images have been taken by ingenious methods and reveal that no change has there occurred. Nevertheless, the figure of which you are aware is not merely a compound of these sensations but an entirely re-created one. That the mind itself can contribute largely to what it perceives is well shown by this experience. The illusory figure which is intermittently seen is the direct consequence of a subconscious *mental* labour upon the materials proffered by the artist's drawing, for the latter remains unchanged.

Figure 9 should be held with the book askew. The horizontal lines will hardly look parallel, but they are! And when the illustration in *Figure* 10 is brought in the field of view the oblique lines will meet exactly at the same point on the right vertical line, although the eyes will almost invariably mislead one into the belief that they will not meet there! The sense-impressions are valid ones, but the judgment which the mind unconsciously passes upon them is not. The impressions of the eyes are free from reproach, but the impressions of the mind are not.

Only a moment's glance is needed to tell you emphatically that the upper arc in *Figure* 11 continues the curve which begins and ends below the lower horizontal line. But take a pair of compasses and

244 THE HIDDEN TEACHING BEYOND YOGA

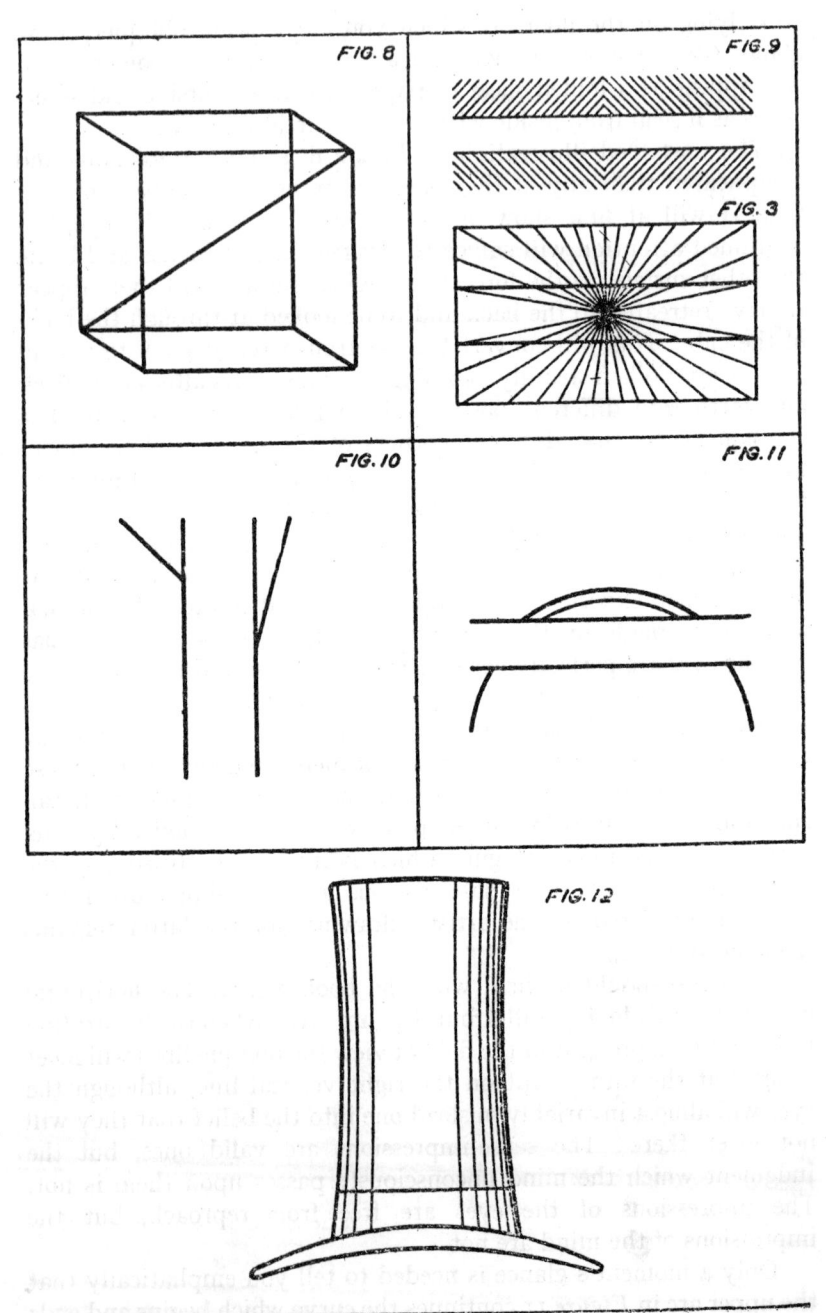

FIG. 8

FIG. 9

FIG. 3

FIG. 10

FIG. 11

FIG. 12

you will find how deceptive the simple faculty of sight can be. For it is the lower concentric arc which is the true continuation of the curve! *Figure 12* is an excellent illustration of an illusion which persists despite its conscious correction after being detected. No matter how often and how long you look at this picture, nor how familiar with it you become, you will hardly avoid seeing it possessed of the same illusory character which it possessed on the day when you first saw it. Here is a picture of a silk top hat whose height appears to be much greater than its width. It is scarcely credible, but measurement will reveal that both vertical and horizontal dimensions are equal! The instruments of vision are not at fault, for the retina records only what it receives. What is at fault is the judgment on the impressions received, i.e. the mind.

It would be a gross error to dismiss all these illusory effects as unimportant geometrical curiosities. They are psychological tutors. They possess profound significance because they provide special clues to elucidating aright the most advanced phases of the process of perception. They demonstrate that the mental interpretation becomes mixed with the physiological impression, and in the consequent confusion it is easy to perceive the projected mental image as superimposed upon the printed figure. We may see as fact what the mind perceives, not necessarily what the senses tell us. How difficult, then, to vindicate the validity of one class of things seen as against another! Thus these fallacies of vision throw light on normal vision itself. When we see a geometrical figure differently from the way it is actually drawn we are actually seeing a production that the mind has transferred from itself to the figure. This is the psychological law lying at the root of illusion.

It is necessary to note a further strange point about the mechanism of these illusions. Continued observation does not lead to better observation. Even when you deliberately continue to fix attention upon them, they are not eliminated. They remain and cannot be removed. They may be illusions but they are obstinate and picturesque illusions. You cannot by taking thought rid yourself of them. No matter how familiar you may become with the same simple diagram, different interpretations of its form fluctuate before your eyes although your reason tells you that it is fixed by printing ink to the white paper! What does this stubborn persistence imply? How are you to account for this strange fact? If it means anything at all it means that errors of sensation, i.e. the results of *processes which take place within the observer's own body and mind* may be projected from him so as to appear as physically *outside* things! For the illusory shapes which the drawings assume have no objective reality outside the mind that perceives them. *You must therefore be ready to accept if necessary the startling notion that your visual impressions of the "outsideness" of a thing may be an utterly erroneous interpretation of those impressions.* For the tricks of the senses are beginning to appear as triumphs of the mind.

Mental Projections. We now come to a third class of illusions which may seem simple yet which possesses serious implications. A machine called the vitascope was popular a score of years ago in amusement places. You put a coin in the slot and turned a crank-handle, when a brief but plausible moving picture was seen through a little window. The illusion of continuous movement was gained from a series of photographs mounted on cardboard which were brought into view one after another by the mechanical rotation of the handle. A further development of the same illusion is nowadays provided by the cinematograph. Here a series of individual static photographs are thrown upon a screen, but owing to the rapid succession in which they are shown they appear as actually moving pictures.

Where is the continuity of action which the beholder sees in such a picture? Is it in the picture itself? No, that cannot be, for it is only a lengthy series of "stills". Therefore it must really result from some process that occurs in the eyes and mind of the beholder himself.

If a burning torch is rapidly whirled in the dark in the form of a figure 8 an observer who is standing some distance away will actually see the illuminated figure as a steady, unbroken and complete shape. Thus at a particular fraction of a second when the torch may really be at the crossing-point midway in the figure the observer will nevertheless see it elsewhere forming the upper and lower curves of the figure. The explanation of science is that this happens because, as in the case of the cinema picture, the actual appearance of the figure depends on the persistence of the retinal image in the eye beyond the fraction of a moment when it actually caught the figure itself. Science has experimentally ascertained that a sense-impression may persist for a time even after the original stimulus has been withdrawn. The image which results is termed an "after-image". The response of the retinal nerve-centres outlasts the stimulus itself and thus continues an independent existence of its own.

It is necessary to gaze a little more gravely, to penetrate a little more deeply, into this case. The eye is like a camera and faithfully photographs whatever it sees. It is even superior to a camera, because the necessary adjustments of focus, etc., are usually made automatically. It can therefore only actually register, in the case of the figure 8, a series of individual images of *points* of light. The registrations succeed each other so swiftly that the brain cannot separately take them up quickly enough. Consequently it fuses the multitude of visual impressions into a single sensation and holds to the general image of a scintillating figure 8 which is consequently formed. It is the latter that then is taken up by the mind. *Thus the mind continues to see what is virtually its own creation.*

There are two stages to be noticed here. First, the varied positions of the torch-flame as it is swung round are presented to the senses and immediately registered for what they are. Second, the sense-impressions are transmitted by the optic nerve to the brain so rapidly that the latter is unable to cope with them individually. So it uncritically receives them as an apparently continuous figure 8. The latter is then mentally seen and accepted as assuredly real. Nothing but close investigation can eliminate the error and correct the false perception.

It is most important to understand that the figure is physically non-existent even when it appears to be seen. Where is it really seen? It can only be perceived by the mind as one of its own images, for it is connected with the observer himself, not with the torch. And it is still more important to understand that it is seen *outside* the observer's body although it is actually *inside* his mind. It appears as a "given" presentation to his bodily senses. Yet this illuminated figure is after all only an intellectual construction.

The observer is not conscious at the time of having mentally constructed the figure, nor is he even later conscious of what he has done. Furthermore, even when he has learnt that the figure is merely an optical illusion, nevertheless *he continues to see its illusory form.* Thus the deception remains despite the fact that it is now understood to be such. Such a feat sounds almost self-contradictory. It is, however, a contradiction of the conceivable, not of the inconceivable, like a round square, nor of the fantastic, like a goat with lion's head. It remains something which mocks at man's belief and violently disrupts his conventional idea that what he sees is actually and necessarily just as he sees it. And it hints strongly that what he elsewhere takes to be valid observation may possibly be nothing more than mere credulity.

Consider the case of a still more significant illusion belonging to the same family. How often, at a certain moment of the falling twilight, when the galaxy of stars have not yet appeared, does the lonely wayfarer in Oriental jungles mistake the brown stump of a tree by the pathside for a wild animal crouching to spring upon him?

> ... In the night, imagining some fear,
> How easy is a bush supposed a bear,

says the poet. And how often does a solitary leafless shrub by the roadside with a pair of bare short horizontal branches swaying in the wind as the same lonely traveller approaches it from a little distance away appear to be a menacing brigand waiting in ambush? The traveller will suddenly notice the figure in the dusk and start back in fear, hearing suspicious movements in the innocent rustling sounds, yet he is perceiving nothing more than a contrasted play of failing light and growing darkness acting as a background for the imaginary figure of a living man superimposed upon an inanimate shrub.

Insufficient or diverted attention, mental preoccupation or incorrect judgment, defective sight or dimness of light, may be said to explain why he sees a brigand and not a bush. This, however, does not explain the deeper significance of the illusion, which is why he should see externally an image which is existent either in the senses or in the mind. For it certainly cannot be said to rest in the object itself. Nor can it rest in the eyes alone, for they are, after all, only a natural photographic apparatus. They can record only what is physically present. It can therefore only be an imposition of imagination upon the object. It is here, when the interpreting faculty of the mind gets to work on the accurate data supplied by the senses, that the possibility of false interpretation enters and it is thus that illusions are created. Psychologically, it is impossible to distinguish a wrong image from a right one, because both are intimate personal experiences. Hence we may believe that we have observed something when, however, we have done nothing of the kind. Memories that burgeon out of the past or personal expectations of what should happen may incline us to *expect* to see the same thing again, even when it is not there. Under such mental preoccupation we tend to assume its presence. Thus the eyes are deceived because the idea is faulty.

If the illusion is produced by the man's own mind, then its substratum is not to be sought in the swaying bush but in himself. The brigand in the bush is ultimately peculiar to himself; it is a part of himself. When it is closely analysed the illusory thing ceases to be external and becomes internal to his mind. The mind has put itself into a frame of vivid expectancy and intense anticipation, which has moulded through morbid fear or cowardly timidity the very image that it perceives. The impressions of the bush which it has received may provide the slightest resemblance to a brigand, but that is enough for the mind to seize and work it up into an illusory percept which falsifies the act of seeing not because fear and suspicion fill the man's physical eyes but because they fill his mind. The misinterpretation of scene and sound is mental. The force of suggestion in the brigand illusion is so powerful as to superimpose a mental creation upon the physical thing registered by the sense-instrument. The image which should be the normal consequence of such registration is displaced by another which takes its place as the perceived object. Thus a fiction of the imagination displaces part of a physical fact : the form of the bush is merged in the form of the brigand.

These statements provoke an interrogation. What is the practical difference between a genuine brigand who is somewhere seen and this illusory brigand? In both cases the terrified traveller really believes he has seen a brigand. Yet in one case he has only seen a bush which does duty for a robber. His eyes can only have recorded the impressions of a bush, for a camera placed in the same spot and using the new kind of films which are ultra-sensitive to images even in darkness would have photographed a bush and nothing more. The eye, we know, is really constructed like a camera. The image of the brigand must therefore have existed somewhere else if it never existed in the eyes themselves. And the only other medium wherein it could have existed is the mind. The mind, therefore, must possess the amazing power to fabricate images which strikingly resemble ordinary percepts as well as the astonishing capacity to throw them seemingly outward into space.

Shall we raise our eyebrows in astonishment at these provocative paragraphs or shall we merely dismiss them with a tremendous sneer ? Shall we hesitate to admit that the mind possesses the power to put forth and retract images that are seen externally to the body ? For this would indicate that men unconsciously possess a kind of magical power. But is it not heresy to declare this ? Well, let us be bold and admit that we do not know what limits to set to the faculties of the mind: it is an ineluctable mystery, and stranger things have been recorded in the annals of abnormal psychology which stagger the unfamiliar and perpetually puzzle the researcher.

Or if this is not to our taste let us agree to call the possibility of objectifying a mental picture, not a mental power but a mental defect! That will not, however, remove the fact that it is universally shared, and therefore we must all be prepared to suspect the presentations of both sense and mind. This is the startling implication of the impregnable logic of these facts. For it opens up the strangest possibilities. If a single illusory object may thus be perceived, why should not a world-wide range of illusory objects also be perceivable within self?

We must try to assimilate these luminous discoveries to our world-outlook and to our view of man himself. We must become courageous iconoclasts and refuse to remain intellectual idolators. We need not fear to follow up such thoughts to their logical conclusions if we are to winnow out some wisdom from these studies. Is not the immutable stability of the earth but a deceptive show, a flagrant error of sensation, a visual and tactual experience which reason boldly denies, for it is easy to prove that the globe is in perpetual movement?

There are two kinds of illusions, those which deceive us about what we do physically see and those which deceive us into seeing something that is not founded on any physical stimulus at all. The second kind is called *hallucination* and is an error of thought alone, whereas the first is an error caused by imposing a mental image upon a physical object.

Sensations suggest the presence of an external object, but when sensations arise in the absence of such an object, then we have a case of hallucination. Hallucination of the higher senses, i.e. sight and hearing, are the most common. An hallucination might be termed an illusion that has no physically objective basis. Illusion approaches the degree of hallucination when there is physically nothing at all present to the bodily senses to justify it. If a man vividly sees something where there is nothing to justify what he has seen he is under an hallucination, whereas if there is some physical thing to afford a basis, however slight, for his perception, then he is under an illusion.

It is common to regard hallucinations as occurring only among the mentally deranged and the cerebrally diseased. This self-flattering error arises because it is in such circles that the most striking and the most distressing forms of hallucination exist. But aside from these pathological cases it is nevertheless true that everyday experience in politics, business and society shows that numerous individuals who are apparently normal and sane in every other respect fall under private hallucinations of their own at some time or other of their life.

The roots of false perception and illusory sensation lie precisely where the roots of right perception and normal sensation lie—in the mind. From the standpoint of psychology there is no antithesis between the hallucinations of madmen and the illusions of the sane. Both are so closely related at bottom that the one class passes by imperceptible degrees into the other. Hallucination is the strong conviction that something is present when it is not. The insane, the delirious and the feverish are attacked by wild beasts or hear strange voices which obviously exist only in the patients' own imaginations. The fact that hallucinations may arise out of such abnormal sources as disease, exhaustion and drugs does not diminish their value for helping to understand the normal processes of perception.

There was once a painter who after a first sitting could call up the face, form and dress of his sitters with such vivid accuracy that he would glance from time to time at the imagined sitter in order to compare him or her with the picture whilst he worked. In the end he became convinced that these imagined persons were as real as the flesh-and-blood ones. So a sapient civilization rewarded his remarkable development of the imaginative faculty with a long stretch in a madhouse. He was certainly suffering from hallucinations, but his case was full of instruction for the humble. For a mental process like this that ran off the usual track made it possible to approach the study of mental workings to a degree that would otherwise be impossible.

The significance of such an hallucination lies in its indication that the mind, without any extraneous aid, possesses a power to project convincing images which have no corresponding physical stimulus and which are then taken for perceptions. Such images also possess the capacity to recur or even to persist. The mistake in identity made by maniacs who fancy themselves to be Napoleon, etc., reveals the power of a dominant idea to create wrong sensory impressions. When the mind is dominated by a fixed preconception of this kind the likelihood of falling victim to illusion or hallucination is increased. We begin to see what we expect to see. The hallucination has a reality not less cogent than that of physically-based experience. Yet if we are willing to be patient and without prejudice whilst we make a deeper analysis than habit usually permits, examination will show that the same characteristics may be found in all other mental images, whether they be the reproductions of fancy or the products of dream. For fancied objects will be hard to the touch of a fancied finger, and dream landscapes will be coloured and lined to dream eyes. If, however, we set up the wrong standard and demand that fancied things should submit to physical tests we are mixing our planes of reference and confusing our standards of dimension. We must be fair. For the reply to such unfairness could be a demand that our physical things be tested by dream standards! The sense of externality in our view of the physical world seems inexpugnable. But close the eyes, shut the doors of all outer sense-organs in sleep, and lo !—in dream you will find a world as vividly external as your physical one. This betrays the mental character of the feeling of externality. The existence of abstract reverie and the experience of dream provide evidence of this power to project mental pictures into space and impregnate them with the force of reality. We must make it perfectly plain to ourselves that the processes of consciousness are so amazing that mental images may appear objectively to the body. Hypnotism proves this, dream illustrates it and the phenomena of illusions demonstrate it completely.

The difference in content between an hallucination and a dream is, from the psychological standpoint, non-existent. Consider for a moment how imagery that has no objective basis at all develops during dreams abnormal states like hypnosis and insanity into actual perceptions that are in no way different and in no way distinguishable from those seen in the case of physically-based ones. A hypnotized person may readily observe what the hypnotist suggests to him as being present, whilst on the other hand he may fail to observe an object confronting him if a contrary suggestion is given by the operator. If it be suggested that he is sniffing pepper he may begin to sneeze violently, even though no pepper is actually there. And mystics who concentrate excessively on a particular image during meditation find in time that it takes on the vivid immediacy and colourful actuality of a physically stimulated percept.

It is the revolutionary lesson of hallucination and of illusion that things and persons seen standing outside one's body and yet having only mental existence are seen as objectively as things and persons having a physical existence. We need this lesson badly, for we are all equipped by Nature and heredity with a bias which falsely believes that everything seen outside the body must therefore be outside the mind and that the products of pure consciousness are only to be experienced internally to the body, i.e. within the head. It would be well to give such an outworn doctrine a valedictory dismissal.

We have learnt that a group of images can appear within the field of consciousness and yet appear as though they were outside oneself. It has been sufficiently shown that the mind can certainly throw its pictures outside the body—the analysis of illusions alone has yielded this startling fact. Illusion shows that we can perceive what is not in our physically derived sensation of an object, whilst inattentive mind-wandering shows that we cannot perceive all that our physically derived sensations tell us about an object. Ordinarily the transformation of mere sense-impressions into full percepts is instantaneous, and therefore indistinguishable to self-observation. The entire physiological and psychological movement occurs with such kaleidoscopic quickness that nobody is able to detect the two stages. This is one of the important reasons why the study of errors of sense and hallucinations of mind is such a tremendous help in throwing light upon the manner in which sense and mind combine to construct our experience. For they open a gap, as it were, in this movement and enable us to observe something of what is really happening. It is an error to regard them as extraordinary perception. They are not. They are normal perception operating as it always operates by an act of mental creation.

Let us attempt to assess the valuable lessons which we may draw from illusions. The richest of all the broad veins of gold in this neglected mine of study are twofold. First is the striking proof thus offered that the whole of perceptual life can be a mental construct. For the apparently abnormal experience of illusion demonstrates how the acceptedly normal experience of everyday life is not something solely and passively received by the senses from an outside world but something which still more is formed, arranged and imprinted by the mind from its own inner store. It is itself the main source of its own experiences. Each perceived thing is indeed known only as a mental one. And this is true even of such hard and heavy things as the thousand-ton statue of Rameses II, which lies prostrate and broken on the desert's edge, as it is true of such soft and delicate things as the winter snow which lies thickly on the Himalayan passes. For the empire of mind extends over all that is seen, heard, touched, tasted or smelt.

The varying causes of illusory appearances may be trifling or important, may be flaws in the mechanism of perception or images brought up from the past, but this does not reduce the significance of the point. The arisal of the spectacle of such externally perceived objects is a mysterious and meaningful event. It must be understood. And it can only be understood when understood as a mental experience, a pictorial and creative effort of mind. The inner working of illusion, which is said to be abnormal, becomes a guide to the inner working of sense-awareness, which is admittedly normal.

We may now understand that illusions and hallucinations are ultimately mental in character merely because *all* sensations and *all* perceptions are mental in character. There is no difference in the ultimate origin of both, for although one *seems* subjective and the other *seems* objective they arise alike from the same source—mind.

The second noteworthy lesson from hallucinations and illusions is their bringing things into awareness that are *seen* to be extended in three dimensions of space, lit, shaded and coloured, and are nevertheless nothing but ideas, mental pictures. Where have we seen the illusion? It has been seen outside the body. Where *is* the illusion found to be when we thoroughly investigate it? Inside the mind. The conclusion can only be that ideas can be projected so as to appear outside the body and that *the common belief that ideas are only to be seen within one's head is a false belief*. So far as any illusion is an act of *perceiving* something, it stands on the same footing as the ordinary and authentic perception of everyday life. But if the former has now been shown to be a mental act, then we must conclude the latter to be mental likewise. The final conclusion is that the analysis of illusion verifies the primary character of the mind's contribution in the knowledge of external things and vindicates the doctrine that ideas can be objectified into space-relations with the body.

The Making of Space and Time. Our earlier enquiry into Relativity revealed that much of the fixity of space and time was fancied, for they were found to vary with different observers. Man thinks he is experiencing real space when he looks out at his external environment and sees one thing here and another thing there and so on. If that is so, why does he see the sun as the size of a silver coin? And why does he still perceive that the sun rises and sets daily when reason denies it and proves its denial? It is clear that he is not aware of the real dimensions of the sun in space, and therefore either cannot be experiencing space as it is or else is experiencing space as he unconsciously *thinks* it is. The paradox is that although he never meets with such an unchanging space in experience he is constantly subject to the belief that he does. It is a pure illusion but one which binds the mind more tightly than it ever knows.

The three-dimensional world which stands behind his reflected image in a glass mirror is purely illusory. He knows that it is illusion

THE SECRET OF SPACE AND TIME

and yet his knowledge cannot get rid of it, do what he will. Hence something may be immediately "given" in his experience and yet its existence may be only apparent and not real. Similarly the philosophic attitude which labels its percepts of external things as mental does not change them in the philosophic experience. They still remain as they are, i.e. external and extended in space, and remain so throughout a lifetime.

Let it be clear therefore without the possibility of misunderstanding that the hidden teaching does not deny in any way whatsoever that a world of objects is set out in space beyond our bodies. The fact itself is indisputable, the notion of it is universal, and none but a lunatic would set himself up to question it, but the *form* in which it is maintained is not. All these things—the objects, the spaces and the bodies—may still exist as they appear and yet be known only as phases of consciousness. If sight tells us that an object has distance in the field of vision, reason explains that the distance is a mental construction.

When we reflect that a stereoscope shows flat surfaced photographs in all the depth, solidity, relief and perspective of the natural scenes, we have to grant that it is not more miraculous for us to perceive the actual scenes themselves as projected at a distance from our bodies and outside them in space. For not only are two slightly different drawings or pictures made to appear as a single and complete one but their flatness totally disappears and what is portrayed upon them is made to appear in perfect relief, actual depth and natural solidity. Thus the stereoscope produces the illusion of a single picture when actually two separate and distinct pictures have been placed in the apparatus and are both being gazed at. We do not explain this strange fusion by explaining that the two lenses of the stereoscope, like the two eyes of the human head, being set in different positions, reveal different aspects of the same object and the two resultant pictures coalesce into one. This is certainly the beginning of the process but not the end. Such a case of plane illusion which appears to have depth when there is only length and breadth alone indicates that the mind co-operates in vision and is finally responsible for what is seen. For the work of uniting the two pictures is a constructive and creative one. Therefore it is done by the mind. The final integrated percept is fully mental. Its manufacture may be a subconscious one but it is certainly a mental one.

Mind puts forth its own constructions. All these analytic processes which make sensation possible and all these synthetic workings which present us with an external object are ultimately of the nature of mind itself. Perceptions have all the spatial qualities and all the spatial relations, all the solidity and all the resistance to touch, all the coloured surfaces and all the lines, angles or curves when they appear before the mind, that we believe the outside objects to have. Nevertheless it is unavoidable human habit to objectify and spatialize its images and solely attribute them to a non-mental, i.e. material, basis.

To understand the final phases of the perceptive process let it first be noted that we never directly see the real size of an object because only the image which it produces on the retina of the eye is reported to the brain. Look at a lofty telegraph pole, for instance, through a pair of spectacles whilst standing some distance away. Give part of your attention to the lens of the spectacles and part to the pole. You will then become aware of the fact that the pole stretches across half their diameter and no more—that is, less than three-quarters of an inch. This is the image on your lens. Let us suppose that the pole is about forty feet high. Do you see a forty-feet image? No, you actually see upon the spectacle lenses an image which is one six-hundredth smaller. Now remember that the pair of spectacles are simply like projected portions of the eyes but slightly larger than the eyes themselves. What appears to be seen as though it were in the lenses of the spectacles is very little larger in size than the image which appears on the retina of the eye. It is quite impossible for the optic nerve to report to the brain and hence to the mind any dimension larger than the dimensions of the retina itself. The mind never learns directly the size of the external pole but only the size of its greatly shrunken image. The up and down, right and left movements of the eyes produce muscular sensations of the pole's distance, position and direction. The image of the scene pictured on the retina is a spatial one, i.e. it has length and breadth. But no such spatial picture can itself be conveyed to the brain by the optic nerve, but only "the telegraphic code" vibration concerning it. Therefore the mind has somehow to imagine, construct and project such a picture as well as the space needed for its background. This it does and then an image arises. The space, the space-properties and the space-relations of the pole are therefore purely mental creations.

The flow of *sensation* is uninterrupted. We are continuously giving birth to numerous thoughts, for that is the essential meaning of human experience, and the mind must discriminate one from another. Every perception of an object must be different from every other if it is to be perceived at all. *The mind must determine a*

THE SECRET OF SPACE AND TIME

separate form for all its images. This it does by spatializing them, by spreading them out, by setting up each image in space dimensions of length, height and breadth. Consciousness could not operate otherwise in the form of perception unless it did this, for failure to do so would mean that no image could exist separately and therefore could not exist at all.

No object could ever be visible to us unless it appeared to be *outside* us in space. For in no other manner could it be formed into a distinct separate thing apart from the seer. If the object were in the inside of the eye it could not be seen at all. Therefore it must appear to be existent *beyond* the eye if the eye is to function like a photographic camera at all. Any object to be visible must be visible as separately individualized and independent of the eye which beholds it. We have already learnt, however, that all sense-function is performed only mediately by the sense-instruments and immediately by the mind. If therefore the mind is to possess the power to perceive any particular object it is compelled to form such perception by *externalizing* the object and thus extending it in space. Mind must set out all perceptions in space, i.e. localize them, and it must project them outside the body and thus finally perceive the entire result as an extended and external object. The space, however, is not really a property of the perceived object; it is a property of the mind itself and is bestowed by the mind upon the object.

A striking illustration of such working is provided by the cases of persons born totally blind and afterwards cured in later life through surgical operation. During the first period after the restoration of their sight they are unable to judge size, shape or distance without making the most ludicrous errors. Objects appear to be so close to the eye as almost to touch it. Neither externality nor distance takes on proper meaning, for although the eyes have been put in good order the ideas supplied by memory or association, which enter into the formation of ideas of space, are lacking. One blind man who was operated on and recovered his sight thought at first that all objects "touched his eyes". He could not judge the smallest distance, could not tell whether a wall was one inch or ten yards away from him and could not understand that things were outside each other.

Precisely the same necessities apply to the mind's need of setting up images in time. It is forced to put them into sequence, to make them succeed each other, in order to put them into existence at all. Everything crowded together in one point and one moment would be equivalent to nothing appearing. Hence the need of time, which mind accordingly makes for itself. Thought becomes possible only through the mind making it take its passage through time. Time is the very form of thought.

Why is it that despite the fact that we are all travelling through space at a speed of not less than one thousand miles an hour—a motion easily determinable by the earth's relation to other heavenly bodies—we feel no sensation of this enormous velocity at all? Why is it that the passenger in an aeroplane who shuts his eyes can hardly realize a sense of journeying and notices its movement only to the degree that it proceeds more slowly and not more quickly? The answer is that the world of time is entirely based on relativity, which is ultimately mental. Time is so elastic that it is a completely variable relation and its power over us is due to the peculiar way in which the mind naturally works, to the manner in which thought manufactures the arbitrary distinctions between slow and fast, present and future.

The distance, the size and the shape of a fountain-pen appear to be outside us. In the case of distance it will be found that sight is unable to determine by itself *without* the aid of judgment, i.e. without the aid of mind, the relative distances at which objects are placed from the eyes and from one another. The impression of the pen is mental, hence inside us, but we think of it as being outside us. We refer the perception of it outward to space, projecting its qualities to points or areas external to the body; we think of it as existing at a distance from us, although the sensation which constitutes the first conscious knowledge of it occurs within ourselves. Thus the appearance of its spatiality is mind-born.

When we say that the pen is outside us we are saying something about its position in relation to the eyes but nothing about its position in relation to the mind. We are reckoning its distance and direction by setting up the body as the spatial centre and confusing that with the mind. Ordinarily we locate the mind somewhat indefinitely in the head, but never dream that the picture of the pen which is presented to our eyes may actually be immaterial, i.e. mental. This is because we become aware of our own body and feel that we are spatially situated inside it. This feeling plays a central part in space-perceptions and arises chiefly because of passive sensations of touch originating in the surface of the body, together with sensations of pressure received through the muscles, and also through sensations of sight. We are not immediately aware that it is the mind which has brought into being this field of touch,

THE SECRET OF SPACE AND TIME

pressure and sight. The qualities are transferred externally to the body and thus given an objective existence.

It is said that a thing must be there in the external world because the eye tells us so, because the ear informs us so and because the touch so reveals it. But here a most important question must be asked. Where are these three senses? Where are eye, ear and skin? Are they not where the thing itself is because they interact with it? Do they not occupy the same world as the table that is seen and touched? This cannot be denied. But if that is so then they are part of the external world themselves. Therefore to argue that we know a thing is outside because our senses tell us so is to argue that it must be outside because our senses themselves are outside. But this brings us back to the starting-point. For if *everything* is outside, then the term "external" loses all meaning. There is then no "outside" at all. We may only say that the world is there and that the senses are there but we may not say that they are external to the mind.

From this we may deduce that the old notion that the body is a sort of perishable box containing a permanent soul inside is fit only for children. The newer notion that it is itself an idea within consciousness is more in consonance with modern science.

The situation of a thing and the period of time during which it is situated—these are the twin moulds in which must perforce be thrown our entire knowledge of all things. Thus space and time are the mind's very modes of arranging conscious experience. No other modes are possible if we are to become aware of anything—whether it be a vastly distant star or our own finger-tip. The mind, by making its images conform to the laws of space and time, *anticipates* the very form of all its possible experiences of the external world. The images are not produced by experience, but themselves produce our experience. This is the iconoclastic but clear truth.

When the true nature of perception is placed in a clear light it will be seen how doubly we may be deceived by the very senses which pretend to reveal the external world to us. For they may not only distort the thing they have to report, as in the case of illusions, but also deceive us into thinking that our direct experience of that thing in space and time is physical and not mental. It is now possible to understand why the revelation of Einstein mentioned in the previous chapter, although but a partial and limited one, was nevertheless on the right track. He found that space was a variable relation and showed why it must be so, but he never attempted to explain how it was so or how it came to exist for us.

Thus the clusters of sensations which constitute the things we view are automatically and inevitably moulded by the mind into space-time form. In short, so long as we continue to experience the world we must perforce experience it as an appearance in space and as an event in time. This is a predetermined condition of human existence and applies to everyone, and nobody, not even the philosopher, can escape from this condition. The very principle which accounts for our knowledge of the existence of this world accounts also for its space-time characteristics. They are but necessary factors in the formation of our sensations. *We are ourselves its source.* Our faith in the objective character of space and time relative to *mind* is, however, so strongly inborn and inherited that its validity passes unquestioned. Only a tremendously bold effort of enquiry can ever bring us to repudiate this belief. Cowardice is not caution. Truth wants no timid friends.

For practical purposes we believe, and we cannot but believe, that the printed book which lies so plainly before us is perceived outside ourselves but inside space. The very constitution of human awareness tells us so with an irresistible authority that cannot for a moment be denied. Any other assertion runs contrary to common sense. Yet we have previously proved that space is a constituent of the mind, that without its presence the mind would refuse to function. In short, space dwells within the mind. This leads us inexorably to the next conclusion. If the book exists in space, and if space exists within the mind, then the book can exist nowhere else except in the mind itself. That which we are perforce compelled by Nature to see as the printed page outside us, i.e. as the seeming not-self, is none other than a perception of the self itself, a refraction of its own light, a presentation of the mind to its own sight.

People think that the mind must dwell only within the confines of the skull. But if the mind is the secret manufactory of space, how can it be itself tied to spatial limits? How can it be limited to this or that point in space? How can it be placed only in each man's head? We shall look in vain for a plummet which shall fathom the mind's depth or a rod which shall measure its breadth and length.

There confronting us is a world of hard realities, a panoramic procession of solid objects and substantial things. He who comes, like Socrates, to persuade us to call into question their "outsideness", which seems so certain and so irrefutable, has no easy task. He is quite unwelcome, for even were his queer ideas to be true they are most distasteful. They appear to remove the very ground from beneath our feet. There are inherent properties in such ideas which

THE SECRET OF SPACE AND TIME

render them chemically repulsive to the crowd mentality, which flies from truth to take refuge in self-deception. Hence philosophy has kept them hidden in the past for the benefit of a truth-loving few. The fact that every surrounding thing is known only as an integral mental construction rather than as an outside material one, that it is seen as an image produced in the mind, will appear to be a miracle to untutored people and utterly beyond belief, just as popular uneducated thought naturally and inevitably assumes that the earth is flat and that the sun revolves around our planet. It holds firmly to such an opinion and deems the contrary statement that antipodean lands exist and that the earth circles the sun to be sheer madness. How then has it been possible to establish this startling astronomical truth among men? It has been possible only by supplying them with certain related facts, and then by persuading them to use their reasoning powers courageously upon those facts until deeper significance stood revealed. Precisely the same problem confronts us in the popular belief that every material thing exists outside, apart and separate from the mind. Philosophy refutes this naïve overwhelming belief and removes this misapprehension, but it can do so only if men will look at the facts it offers and then study them deeply and impartially with inexorable logic to the very end. Without such absolute rationality it could never hope to triumph over such a powerful and primeval instinct of the human race like materialism, which is not truth but rather a travesty of truth.

Our knowledge of the outer world and our perception of things in space and time are the forms taken by our mental processes. We need to absorb this hard truth here ascertained that what is inside the mind can be seen outside the body. The case for it is unanswered and unanswerable. Its position is unassailable. All counter-arguments, all contrary views, can be met and mastered. For it is not merely the odd notion of amiable cranks but as certain and as proven as any other verified fact in the armoury of *science*. Therefore this shall be the truth which shall take a new incarnation for tomorrow.

Those who fear to follow reason when it leads them into the strangest paradoxes are lost to truth. These doctrines may startle and frighten us, but if they be true then they must be accepted.

We look up at the skies above like prisoners with space-covered eyes and time-fettered hands yet know not that our deliverance is close at hand. Thought has imprisoned us: thought may release us.

Once we begin to understand this awe-arousing mystery of the tyranny of space and time we begin to understand why we should hearken to ancient voices like that of Jesus and what was meant by the marrowy phrase which he uttered to a worried and weeping world: "The Kingdom of Heaven is *within* you." The mysterious kingdom wherein man may get his best hopes fulfilled is not to be found in future time, as in a next world after death, nor in remote space, as in some region beyond the stars, but *here* within our own mind and *now* within our own thought.

Such a realization of the mind's innate power to contribute to the making of its own world will raise men—be they saints or cynics—to the level of self-poised sages, calm their agitated minds and soothe their suffering hearts.

CHAPTER XI

THE MAGIC OF THE MIND

WE must now consider the most crucial point in this elementary course on the hidden teaching. The concepts of modern science have got rid of the static things suspended in space and replaced them by fields of force. If it is difficult to credit that we are knowing thoughts of things when we believe we are experiencing independent external things, is it not equally difficult to credit the knowledge offered by science that a pen is made up of electrons which cannot even be imaginatively compared with the hard stuff out of which we experience the pen to be made? Nothing that we see or can possibly see even roughly resembles the electronic "stuff" to which science has reduced our familiar fountain-pen. And if science may thus undermine our realistic experience, why not philosophy? And if the electronic pen is the real pen, then we are seeing only an image, only a representation of it, when we see the material pen. Yet such a representative image must be in our mind, for it can be nowhere else. If the idea is but a mental copy of a material object which is outside mind and therefore a separate and distinct entity, why is it that the two of them cannot be brought simultaneously before awareness and compared with each other? If the external pen which is given to us in sense-experience were the cause of the thought of it we would never be able to verify its existence, for every attempt to observe external pens would only end in the observation of thoughts.

We cannot get at things first hand, cannot inspect them directly, do what we will. We can never get beyond the thoughts of them. Hence we cannot even verify their separate existence. We cannot exhibit the objects to our eyes because both eye and brain are themselves known mentally, i.e. they are ideas, and through them we can become conscious of mental things, of ideas alone.

When we try to test our mental constructs by turning to the things themselves, by comparing one with the other, all that we succeed in doing is to test one construct by another, i.e. compare one thought with another.

The perception of a thing and the thing itself are the two sides of a curve, the inside and the outside of it. Do what we will, we can never separate the one side from the other. The thing is on the outside and the perception is on the inside. But the curve is not two things, but one. The thing refuses to be taken apart from its perception. We cannot separate the perception from the thing, but we can distinguish them in speech and thought by making a mental abstraction of one or the other, although with wiser speech and profounder thought we shall find that even this feat is impossible.

Now we cannot see any object without *thinking* of it as being seen. If it is to exist for us at all it must exist as something that is perceived. Let us try to think of a pen, without thinking of personally seeing it, without permitting the operation of actually seeing it to mingle with the pen itself. We shall find that it is impossible to sever one from the other. We can think of the pen only through and by the thought of perceiving it. Do what we may, we shall be utterly unable to think of it otherwise. Nobody can separate in thought an external pen from his actual perception of it. What is the conclusion to be drawn from this? That the pen is not purely objective but both objective and subjective, both material and mental in one.

If it is objected that when the pen is in a dark room where nobody can see it its existence is not thereby cancelled, the reply is that we cannot talk or mention such an object without thinking about it and we can only think of it by constructing a mental image of it, and if we wish to do this then we are forced to imagine it as being seen, we are compelled to think sight along with the pen. It is only by thinking both together that we can come to the idea that it exists at all.

A further objection may be made that a thing may exist in some remote untrodden part of the globe where nobody has ever perceived it and where nobody is ever likely to perceive it. Here the reply is precisely the same as to the previous objection. Wherever the thing may be, it cannot be discussed as existent unless it is thought of, unless it is mentally pictured, and it cannot be so pictured unless we regard it as perceived either by ourselves or by some unconsciously assumed imaginary observer. Similarly, if it be objected that it is easy to imagine a scene like the North Pole, where no observer is likely to be present but where great masses of ice exist and are known to exist, despite the non-presence of anyone to see the ice, to walk upon it, to feel its coldness and to admire its white purity, the answer is that in thinking of the polar region and of the ice that fills it we have not kept out an observer but have actually, although unconsciously, brought him to the scene to note its details. We have imagined an observer but we are quite unaware of having done so. And in bringing such an imaginary observer to the Pole we have brought his mind there and made him think of the scene. The solid ice is known to be solid only because our unseen spectator feels its resistance beneath his feet.

We can think of an object only by thinking of the seeing of the object: it is not humanly possible to consider its existence in any other way. Therefore sight becomes an indivisible concomitant of existence. Nothing can possibly possess any being for us independent of our awareness of it. Both thing and thought must be understood in the united idea of a thing seen by somebody or by ourselves.

A similar analysis holds good of the other forms of sensation. Objects cannot be separated from the thought of their being felt by us for instance or by someone else; they exist only because they can be thought of as being hard, solid, heavy and so on to the touch. The same is precisely true of heard things. The sensation of hearing comes first and the sound itself is subsequent to that. Sounds exist only because we can *think* the hearing of them at the same time. We can think of them only as *heard* sounds.

Remove mind from our picture of the world and we remove space and time from it; we knock the bottom out of it. The world as idea exists for some mind or it cannot exist at all. For every object seen there must exist a seer. In other words, whatever is known is known by some mind. Nothing has ever been known and nothing can ever be known apart from a knower. This is incontrovertible. No object can exist alone and unknown. Those therefore—and they are in the vast majority—who believe and assert that a thing can possess a separate existence of its own are really talking nonsense. If they indignantly deny it, let them show a single object, let alone the whole world of objects, without also simultaneously showing it to be connected with a knower! They cannot do so, for they cannot separate anything from mind. The world is inextricably and inevitably bound up with mind. Thus the final conclusion is that, look where we will, in the universe everything is because it is thought of.

The reverse is equally true. We cannot think of perception without thinking also of perceiving some object, nor of the act of hearing without coupling some sound with it. There is no hearing without sound, no sense perception without its object. Therefore we find again that the two cannot be imagined save as one, that sight and the thing seen are two sides of a single coin, that touch and a thing touched are the subjective and objective halves of a unity.

When the scientific principle of relativity says that the observer is part of his observation, this means that the person who has experience of anything is part of his experience. We may carry this further and now say that it means that the thought is part of the thing thought of. If we ponder well upon this statement we shall see that the mental factor is inseparable from every object known. And if we ponder deeper we shall find that the two are really one.

We cannot hold existence and the perception of existence apart from each other and so we are forced to form the conclusion that the two are not two in reality but indissolubly one. The thing and the sensation of the thing live in fundamental and inseparable union. Thus there is nothing else but awareness. Ask yourself whether that statement will explain all your experience and you will find that it will do so quite adequately. Try, on the other hand, to discover whether the theory of the materialists will explain your experience of the world, the theory that there is nothing else but independently existent physical things, and you will find that it does not and cannot explain the existence of thoughts and feelings. For if you believe that you can put something material into a test-tube you cannot do the same with thought.

It must therefore be emphatically repeated that a percept is not a mere copy of something external. It is primal and not secondary. This should not be overlooked, because it is a key to correct understanding of "mentalism", which is the doctrine that all things are mental things.

We see that the notion of a pen existing independently of the mind to which it is present is a pure fiction. The percept of the pen is nothing less than the pen itself. That any other pen exists separately and materially is utterly beyond our range of possible knowledge and must therefore be ignored if we are to deal with scientifically ascertained facts rather than uncertain assumptions. The pen is a construct in consciousness. Its being is being known. There are not two pens, a material one and a mental copy of it. There is only one. The image which is immediately before consciousness is the pen itself. It is so vivid, so perfect and so convincingly stamped with the characteristic of objectivity that we do not stop with merely seeing it : we go on to infer that it is nothing less than the independent pen itself and refuse to believe otherwise. Yet the pen which is known by the senses is none other than the percept which is known by the mind.

But we must now face an objection: "Here am I with direct experience of a pen which lies outside me in space, separate from me, which I can pick up and grasp in my hand, finding it to be solid, weighty and hard. How then can you expect me to believe that it is merely an idea in my mind?"

To this the reply is that this doctrine must not be misunderstood to mean that it is asserted that the pen is not directly present to our vision. It most emphatically is present. Its very immediacy disarms us. We have got to grasp this truth that the perceived pen is not less rounded and weighty and coloured and useful than the supposedly-existent material pen, despite the fact that the former is a mental construct. In the previous two chapters we have seen that the mind is involved in all our experience of the world and we have found that sensation, so far from being a purely passive and receptive process, is creative and even projective. But we are so enamoured of the sensations of solidity which we receive from the things around us, and so deceived by the sensations of distance and position which we receive from their relations to each other and to our eyes, that we habitually underrate the tremendously suggestive and creative force of mind. We are almost totally ignorant of the proven and provable fact that mental images can assume size, shape, length, height, breadth, solidity, relief, perspective, weight, colour and other qualities that we usually associate with external objects. They can provide all these sensations with perfect vividness and with all the actuality of ordinary experience. And yet they remain nothing more than ideas!

Thus mental experiences *are* the visible things that we take to be outside us. The thing itself is admittedly existent, but the character of the thing is what we have now found out and we have found it to be quite other than it is commonly thought to be. Those who would declare there are two separate facts, the fact of perception and the fact of an external material object, have made a false analysis of sensation. The oneness of both idea and object is a discovery to which the subtle thinking of the ancients and the sharp observation of the moderns inescapably lead, but it emerges only after the hardest and most rigorous reflection.

Once this point is grasped, then one may say to himself: "I am aware of my awareness of this thing," and he will then perceive that he cannot strip the second awareness from the thing in itself; they constitute an indivisible entity. Those who want to divide the fact, the thing known, into a percept of it on one hand and its material substantiality on the other, who make perception a mental act and substantiality a non-mental thing, who posit mind against matter, fall into a grievous fallacy. What we know is an idea, what we perceive is not a discovery but a mental construction. Those who deny this put themselves in the predicament of explaining away the inexplicable.

Comes a further objection: "Do you mean to tell me," cavils the sceptic, "that the abstract objects of my imagination, the phantasmagoria of my dreams, the pictures of my reveries and the phantom creations of my fancy are as real, are as existent and are as substantial as the twenty-ton locomotive engine which draws yonder train of coaches? Do you mean to say that this engine is nothing more than a thought in my brain like these other fanciful thoughts? If that be so, why is it I cannot think such an engine into immediate existence, think as hard as I may, or think such a train into existence and step into the train and be driven away? The contrast between a supposed train and a real train is so strong as to make the suggestion that they are in any way similar quite absurd. There is the real train standing clearly and distinctly before me, I can confidently step into it, I can hear its powerful engine roar and puff, but I cannot see my imaginary train so solidly before me nor can I get anywhere in it except in self-delusion. Therefore I cannot accept your doctrine of mentalism. There is a trick in it somewhere, a snare or a pitfall. The perceived train is most useful to me, but the imaginary one is useless. It is utterly ridiculous for anyone to tell me that both stand on the same footing."

Let it first be noted that what the critic cannot do has been done by others, i.e. find in waking fancies a reality and a vividness that make them completely present to the mind's eye. Great poets have done this, artists of genius have done this, celebrated mystics have done this and separated lovers have done this. They have found amid the scenes of their imagined surroundings and among their imagined faces a perfect sense of actuality. They did not at the time disbelieve in the real presence of the objects and persons thought of. There are indeed two conditions of the human mind which have been experienced by most persons and in which we find extraordinary illustrations of the possibility of doing part of what our critic cannot do. And they are when we are plunged in profound reverie and when we are plunged in profound dream. In these states the contrasts between the perceived world and the imagined world—a contrast which is admittedly felt at normal times by ordinary people—is spontaneously suspended. We may enter trains during these rapt states and be driven away in them and not for one moment shall we feel that they are not real trains and that our journey is not a real journey. On the contrary, we possess at the time a complete belief in the reality, solidity and existence of our reverie-born and dream-born universe. Were we to live mostly in such conditions they would certainly be more real to us than would seem any temporary lapse into full waking life that might occur. Indeed, we would then attach reality to them and deny it to the waking world. It is therefore unjustifiable to assert that because material things are so vividly and distinctly seen, whereas mental images are comparatively dim and vague, therefore the former cannot belong to the same class as the latter, cannot also be mental themselves. For it is here not a question of the manner in which a perception originates but of whether it is or is not mental.

But our critic will object that this is a perverse and not a proper answer to his criticism. It is certainly not intended to be a full answer, for it is offered only as illustration and not as proof. If it vindicates nothing it hints at many of the mysterious possibilities whereby the mind can fabricate reality. It is intended to warn him not to dogmatize too quickly about what or what not the mind can do.

The *full* answer to our critic cannot be given here because it involves an explanation of the final secret of human personality, a revealment which falls into its natural place in the second and last volume of this work, which is yet to be written. And what the mystic apprehends with dreamlike vagueness about this secret the philosopher determines with amazing precision. Suffice it to say that our critic is right in making the latter part of his objection, for it is *not* contended by the hidden teaching that the *individual* mind, the ego, of any man can create his familiar world at its sweet will. Within this limit the criticism shall find some answer in the present and the following chapter.

The Riddle of Sensations. The further question will be asked by the critic, "What then is the real nature of the independent objects which cause these thoughts to be presented ? You tell us that what we *see* are only thoughts. Admitting this point, there is still a question which troubles us and which all this demonstration has completely if not cleverly avoided. Even if it be admitted that we know only the thoughts of things, there are still the things which seem to make the impressions on our sense-instruments and so bring these thoughts ultimately into existence. If what we perceive is only a thought felt to be external, what becomes of the object which gives rise to this thought ? Surely you would not ask us to identify the real thing with the mere thought of it ? Surely that which causes the mental image to arise is not the same as the image itself ? We may discredit the testimony of the senses but we are unable to discard it. Nor is this all. You have passed over in complete silence the process whereby a sensation is born out of the vibrations in the brain. How is such a thought created ? You have told us how the thing thought of is produced but not how a thought itself comes into being."

What is the independent object ? How does the brain communicate with the mind ? Certainly these two questions may now properly be asked, for they have not been explained so far. But can the existence of anything rightly come under consideration until what it is that is *known* to exist has been made clear ? Yet this in turn depends on *how* we come to know it. Therefore it will be easier to see clearly the answer to the first question when we have learnt the answer to the second one. We shall therefore begin with the latter.

Let us begin by noting that each sense-experience is a twofold fact, first the physiological impressions experienced by the body and second the consciousness of these impressions. This consciousness may be termed the *perception* of the object. The combination of these two factors, physical impression on eye, ear, etc., and conscious thought constitutes our perception of it. Hence when we smell a rose we co-ordinate a state of mind with a state of physical disturbance. But how can the latter resolve into the former ? How can mind take in what is non-mental ? A physical disturbance is the very antithesis of a mental one. Where is the medium, the connecting link, which can bridge the striking gap between both these opposites ?

Here is a doubt which may legitimately be raised, a question which demands a direct answer. How does mind make the miraculous leap from a physical to a non-physical immaterial entity like sensation ? How can mind testify to the existence of anything outside itself ? Nobody has ever been conscious of the mind taking this distinct step of attending to and interpreting the activity in the grey matter of the brain. To say that we are never aware of the process whereby a sensation is born and to say that the nerve-vibration is converted into unconscious thought is to take a leap in the dark and to land on entirely different territory. To make the process a subconscious one does not solve the difficulty, for it still remains a mental process. We come to a sudden full stop when we come to

THE MAGIC OF THE MIND

the molecular change in the brain. There the continuity ends. Consciousness makes an abrupt appearance at the other side of the chasm and we do not know how to unite two such totally different orders of existence together. How can physiology bring the two ends together?

The answer is that it does not bring them together. It leaves them precisely where they are. It bridges the chasm by using the word "somehow", by assuming that the ends are somehow united. It accepts the chasm and then assumes that it is not a chasm. When therefore the science of physiology says that the gap is somehow closed, although it is quite unable to say how it is closed, it is indulging in a play of speculative fancy, not in a discovery of ascertained and verified fact. The leap it makes is not natural but arbitrary. Thus we return to the troubling question: How is it possible to relate mind which is immaterial to the brain which is material?

Physiology confesses that the clearance of this gap between a wave-like movement in nerve-stuff and a conscious movement of thought is incomprehensible to it although it has tried to advance various hypotheses and guesses. None of these have been able to secure wide agreement. Nobody has ever adequately explained the facts of psychology by the phenomena of physiology. All such efforts have failed because they failed to understand the connection between mind and matter. Those who complacently assert that the crowning function of the nervous system is to "produce" thought beneath the bony rind of the skull assert a miracle more marvellous than any. Let them take up a measuring-rod and mark the distance between one idea and another, between one conscious thought and another. They cannot do it. For nobody knows where the mind begins or ends. Is it not foolish to imply that in nodding their visible heads men nod their invisible minds at the same time? For under no conceivable circumstances can the mind be seen to reside in the head. Yet materialists accept unthinkingly the vague belief which regards the mind in the same way as it regards material objects. Nobody can bring an immaterial presence like mind together with a material place like the head, for there is no point and no surface in mind to meet any point or surface in the head. Yet they still talk as though mind were definitely located at the brain terminals of the sensory nerves. For the sake of convenience in common talk we may —perhaps must—continue to speak of the mind as though it were in one's head, but for philosophic purposes it is reprehensible to do so.

Perception is a mental process, i.e. thought, and reason demands that the thought be referred to some subject to which it occurs, to some consciousness whereto the process happens. We must not therefore mistake the movements of material molecules in the fleshly brain for conscious thoughts. Those who cannot grasp the difference between both can never grasp the meaning of sensation—which is the most elementary fact of psychology. And the first steps in psychology are inescapable steps in philosophy. No microscope has ever discovered consciousness, and no opening of the skull has ever done it either. It is not observable. It must be treated for what it is—a separate and distinct *fact*. To treat the physical brain as identical with full consciousness is to deal in pure fancy. The attempt to explain perception away as being merely a matter of nervous functioning is nothing less than to beg the question.

When the physiologist follows a sensation through its entire course from surface of the body to centre of the brain, what has he really done? He has followed it in his own mind, he has performed an act of consciousness. It does not lose its mental character because he chooses to affix the name of "nerve-change" to its corresponding physical vibration. His difficulty is that he cannot actively take a percept apart and yet keep it in full consciousness. It can be divided only theoretically. It is an entity, and now beyond any possibility of practical analysis. The dissecting knife can expose the nervous substance of the brain to sight but it cannot expose a thought, an idea, a fancy or a memory-image. The chasm between both seems quite unbridgeable.

Here physiological science must frankly stop, bewildered and dumbfounded, for it is totally unable to explain satisfactorily this sudden and startling leap from unconsciousness to consciousness. Despite the best efforts of the best thinkers of modernity, physiology has failed to solve the following problem satisfactorily: What is the connection between the human mind within and the material universe without? What is the nature of the intercourse between thought and thing? Herbert Spencer, for example, who tried to interpret science to the nineteenth-century world, who wrote scornfully of the philosophical attempt to reduce knowledge of things to knowledge of thoughts, had to confess that "how the material affects the mental and how the mental effects the material are mysteries which it is impossible to fathom".

For the fact of consciousness is a primary one. And it is the most mysterious fact in all human existence. No movement of material molecules can directly explain it, as nothing non-conscious can adequately account for it. We do not know that molecules possess the power to reflect upon their own nature. Mental experience is and has ever been the supreme enigma set in the midst of a seemingly non-mental world. To confine consciousness to its events or to its contents, as is so often done, does not help to explain its own existence, but merely evades the issue. Science has succeeded admirably in telling us what mind does and how it behaves, but it has so far failed to tell us what it is. Mind is the recalcitrant entity which refuses to be disintegrated into anything else. Therefore we must keep on asking: How is it that a physiological process is converted into a mental one? For mind is both mysterious and unique—nobody seems to know what it is although everybody guesses. This we do know, however, that there is nothing else like it in the universe.

Physiology has well considered and has long considered this problem but has given it up as insoluble and inscrutable. The hiatus is utterly insurmountable. And such it must remain for ever unless and until we recognize two simple yet subtle points which help to solve this problem and with it the whole train of foolish questions that drag after it.

The physiologist has not noticed these two points for the simple reason that such recognition would take him beyond the limits of his special science. If he is to remain a physiologist and nothing more he must pay the heavy price of narrow specialism—expertness within those boundaries but ignorance outside them! If, however, he is willing to pursue his enquiry farther, then he must turn psychologist; there is no other direction to which he may turn for light. For the psychological standpoint is a beginning of the still higher philosophical standpoint.

These two points are: first, the ultimate order in which the details of our becoming aware of objects follow each other and fall into their proper places; second, what it is that the mind can really know. When the answers to these are both forthcoming, the answer to the great problem which stands at the end of the physiologist's road will reveal itself of its own accord.

The first point bids us find out at which precise and crucial moment we actually become conscious of the objects around us. We then remember that *according to physiology* during the whole passage of the impression from nerve-ending to brain-centre there is no moment that leaps into awareness of it; there is no fraction of a second of consciousness of the independent thing supposed to be outside and supposed to be reported. Only *after* it has reached its terminus, only as a subsequent act, does the striking contrast of the percept arise.

We think of an object, and then mind, curious to know how the thought has arisen, tries to get behind it, with the consequence that the sensory side of the science of physiology gradually comes into being. The physiologist then slowly ascertains bit by bit the whole sensory process until he gets back to the thought again. He reveals nothing about the perception as a moment when thought flashes into the mind when he reveals the way in which the object makes an impression on the sense-instrument or the way in which this impression is carried to the brain. For all these things imply the *primacy* of consciousness, whose presence is not explained by noting the things of which we are conscious, but is only described. The physiologist is like a man who can construct a violin and explain the laws of sound but who cannot produce or explain the music itself.

He does not realize that all his descriptions, which purport to account for the existence of his consciousness of an object, are descriptions of what occurs *after* the consciousness of it has already arisen. He does not perceive that his explanations of the action of nerve and brain processes which are the result of interaction between the body and an object are catalogues of occurrences which appear *subsequent* to consciousness of the object. Therefore his attempts to explain awareness explain everything but the percept itself, a fact which he unconsciously accepts when confessing that there is an *inexplicable* gap in the entire series of events.

Now pose yourself the question, "How do I *first* know that anything exists at all?" And you will have to reply that you know or become aware of anything primarily through the mind and only secondarily through the senses. *This is proved by the phenomenon of mind-wandering and distracted attention described in the early part of the previous chapter.* The brick wall that confronts you may remain outside the threshold of your consciousness so long as you persist in profound and attentive reflection upon a bygone experience or an immediate problem. This does not mean that the eyes have not performed their duties. On the contrary, the image of the wall will be found perfectly registered on the retina. Nor does it mean that the optic nerve has not performed its task of vibrating a message to the brain nor that the cortical centre in the brain has not received the message. All this has been done, the sense-impressions have been made and the excitations have arisen in the brain. Why then does the wall remain unseen? Because all these have been unattended to by the mind. Because they have not been taken up into consciousness. Because, to put it briefly, we can experience only what the mind experiences! When therefore you say that you have become aware

THE MAGIC OF THE MIND

of a wall before you, what you really mean is that you have become aware of the percept of a wall, i.e. of the idea of a wall as an object of consciousness.

Moreover, this same theorem was demonstrated in the examination of illusions and hallucinations likewise recorded in the previous chapter.

When we put on a pair of spectacles for the first time we become quite conscious of their presence on the face. But after a while the glazed circles before our eyes and the pressure on our nose fade off from our awareness and we finish by becoming completely oblivious of both presence and pressure of the spectacles. The nerve-endings in the skin, i.e. touch, tell us that they are there. The nerve-endings in the eyes, i.e. sight, likewise report their existence. Yet we habitually fail to notice these impressions. Perception of the spectacles disappears from the mind and their existence with it.

Why? Because the thought of the spectacles comes *first* and when we cease to think of them, being engrossed with other matters, the perception of the spectacles ceases also. Because the external aspect of the spectacles is only a projection of the internal idea. A thing cannot exist for us when there is no thought of it *first*—this is our experimental proof!

Every event and every object is an event which must first be perceived and an object which must first be recognized. But perception and recognition are states of consciousness, ideas. Their dependence is on mind. Can any man be competent to know what "solidity" is apart from first becoming aware of it? Can a thing come before the mind unperceived? Can it be known at all unless a knowing mind is apprehended along with it? Can there be any sort of cognition of something solid without the mental principle initially entering into it? We do not know and we cannot know any object apart from knowing the idea of it. The birth of awareness begins first.

We have to get firm hold of this fact: that we are not first aware of a pen or a pageant but only of our sensations of them. We must make this distinction as clear to our experience as it is self-evident to our reason after we have analytically enquired into the process of our knowledge of external things. We become aware of thoughts, images, representations of things, not the things themselves. We feel sensations, touch them, smell them and taste them. Those who deem this impossible know neither psychology as science nor philosophy as interpretation of science. We know that things exist only because we originally know them mentally. Mind is the final ground of them. The thought of the thing comes first and must come first if we are to know it at all. Therefore consciousness *must* arise before anything else, even before the whole sensory process operates.

To sum up: The analysis of perception which physiology offers us is the result of direct observation. But nobody has ever seen the external object *before* it has passed into perception. This is irrefutable, for the seeing of it presupposes the perception of it. Therefore the object is brought into the field of notice for the *first* time *with* the perception of it and not before. Thus the analytic series which physiology originally offered us turns out to be incorrect from the higher standpoint of psychology, which makes the birth of the thought the first item in this series, although quite correct from its own. Were physiology to rise to philosophy it would be forced to revise its own analysis and offer a less fallible one. For physiology has fallen into this error because it insists on regarding the body as that which is alone real and enduring in comparison with thought, which it regards as ephemeral and illusory. The physiologist's "gap" appears only whilst he begins the series in the wrong order. Let him reverse it and put his idea, which he has put last, at the beginning where it ought to be, and then the gap will vanish.

Consciousness is the inaugural fact of all our knowledge of the object without. Until it comes into operation we cannot even conceive that such an object exists. Yet after it comes into operation we do not even grant this simple primary condition! We perceive the object because we think it; we do not think the object because we perceive it. This truth is not one of those which man can make his own by merely glancing around: he can comprehend it only after hard thinking and relentless enquiry.

It was earlier mentioned that there were two points which would help to bridge the gap between brain and mind. The first has now been explained and the second will now be explained: what is it that the mind does really know?

There exist various theories of knowledge which are technically termed the double-aspect theory, interactionism, psycho-physical parallelism, the emergent theory, etc., but they all fail to meet different objections adequately. Above all, they have yet to perceive that the place occupied by mind is paramount, for nothing can be known unless mind is present as an entity in its own right. If anyone makes the assertion that mind can take direct hold of a material object or of a collection of material objects, and if *matter were something quite different from mind*, then he is making an assertion which inextricably falls into self-contradiction. For if mind and matter do interact, then there must be a link between them, and this link can only be that they are ultimately of the same nature. If matter were not the same as mind, then the process of knowing external objects could not take place, for knowledge is a mental activity ; ideas are its product, and all that we know as perception or as reflection are ideas.

Knowledge is an inner psychical process, and when we know a thing we are compelled by a law of relation to know it as a thought. The ultimate act of vision is a mental one. A multitude of images may fall on the retina of a dead man but he will see nothing. His mind is not active, and no relationship can be set up. Where do the sensations really fall ? Do they fall within the mind or without it ? Because they occur to the mind and because the mind cannot overstep itself we must admit that they fall within it. An object must fall within the unity of the same stuff as consciousness if it is to be recognized at all ; which means it must first be converted into mental stuff. Therefore an object or an experience must first be transformed into an idea before the mind can become aware of it.

The five senses seem to tell us of material things, but without the mind they would be struck dumb and remain for ever silent. Analysis of the process of knowing has already revealed that sight, hearing, etc., really and finally reside in the mind and nowhere else, and that what is actually brought into awareness is a mental thing. That is to say, the mind's immediate and direct knowledge is of things of its own nature, of the same character and not different from it as material things are supposed to be different.

Thought and feeling are the prerogatives of mind. That which is thought or felt is therefore mental, i.e. idea, whether it be a wooden table, a distant star or hot anger. Nothing is perceived without being thought, hence nothing that is seen is known as being other than idea.

What is the relation which exists between your perceptions and your mind ? Do they exist outside of your mind ? Reflection will show its impossibility. They are themselves of the very nature of mind ; that is, they are conscious, invisible and immaterial. They are, therefore, composed of the same stuff as that of which the mind itself is composed. The activity of the experiencing mind generates whatever it knows. Hence consciousness, as we ordinarily know it, is a continuum of ideas and images. It is the mind that makes it possible for us to see, hear and feel and it is seeing, hearing and feeling that make it possible for us to experience the object. Therefore no internal idea—no external object !

The common belief is that what is experienced in sensation is identical with the physical object. Actually we do know more of the nature of the object than what it is in terms of sensation, i.e. idea. The unreflecting attitude of a common-sense view of the world takes what is seen for a truism; it knows little of the process of perception whereby that world of what are said to be physical things becomes known. It does not know that the world is never directly apprehended and consequently never really gets within our experience. The mind actually takes hold of something related, some sensation, percept, image or picture which is essentially mental. It becomes aware of what is akin to it, which means that it may know ideas, but nothing else. It sees finally that which represents itself in consciousness rather than that which represents itself to the senses. The known is not less mental than the knowing element itself.

The mind thus fulfils a double office. It is both awareness and the idea of which it is aware. Its nature is such that it becomes directly conscious of nothing that extends beyond itself but only of the changes within itself, i.e. of thoughts. To make the mind the passive recipient of impressions from an alien world is to ignore the *fact* that mind knows only mental things, i.e. ideas. Whether an outward thing gives birth to sensation or not, it can still only be an idea in itself if it is to be apprehended.

A whole train of false interpretations and futile questions disappears when this truth is seen. Mind does not depend on any external thing for its awareness of that thing, because there is nothing that is external or internal to mind. The thing must be present to mind as an idea and can be immediately present in no other way. Thoughts, indeed, are all that it possesses, all that it experiences, whether they be thoughts of hearing something or seeing something.

It is not the five physical senses which finally feel the pleasure of a summer's garden walk or the pain of a winter's icy exposure, but the immaterial mind. It is not the visible fleshly eye which really reads the words imprinted upon this page, but the invisible mind. The truth of this fundamental fact of existence is as scientific as it is philosophic, and will become an accepted axiom of college textbooks before the troubled sands of this century have run out.

The Primacy of Thought. We must now gather up whatever insight into our external experience of things we have gained. When we first picked up our fountain-pen we started with the physical notion that but for the light-rays we could never have seen it. We went on to the anatomical notion that but for the eyes we could not have seen the light-rays. We proceeded to the physiological notions that but for the nerves the eyes would have seen nothing, and but for the brain the nerves would have experienced their vibrations in vain. Then we rose to the psychological notion that here, at this point, the mind began its constructive work and that but for the latter we should still have failed to see the pen. For we become aware of it finally as a thought, the instant of conscious perception being the instant of actual experience of the pen's existence. But we noted that there was no ascertainable connection at the point of transition from the physical brain to the non-physical sensations, so that the continuity of the whole process was broken. In searching for an explanation of this break we made the startling discovery that because the mental image of the pen was the first intimation we had of its existence, and because the only things perceptible to mind were such images, such thoughts, then it must have constructed the idea of the pen before it could have known that the pen existed.

We began by making mind, light, eye, nerve and brain partners in this game of getting experience of the pen. We have ended by finding not only that mind alone underwent the experience, but that it also produced the idea which constituted its experience! What does this mean ? It means that we have begun by knowing there is a pen, but in making an analysis of how we came to this knowledge, this thought, we return to our starting-point, the same thought. We have been travelling in a perfect circle. This implies that at no point of the circle have we touched the object other than as a thought. Stranger still, it further implies that we have been travelling within the realm of thoughts throughout. We have only succeeded in passing from one mental construct to another!

This last conclusion is strange, because it compels us to place within the mental circle not only the brain but the nerves, and not only the nerves but the eyes, and not only the eyes but the light. Then what of the actual pen itself ? Let us put that question aside for a brief while and concentrate on this astonishing state of affairs in which we have somehow got involved. For the sum of all these statements is that in moving from light-ray to physical brain we have merely moved from one thought, one percept, to another at every separate stage of the journey!

What takes place in the eyes, in the nerves, and in the brain we can learn only from what we can observe therein, i.e. from sensations formed into percepts and from what we can infer from such observations, i.e. from inferences. But both sensations and inferences are thoughts. Unless we have the intellectual courage to come to this conclusion we shall make the serious blunder of treating one group of sensations, i.e. the percept of the reflected light-image of the pen, as mental, but treating another group of sensations, i.e. the percept of our bodily sensory system, as non-mental. The two realms of observations are identical in so far as they are both objectively experienced and both physically seen. Both light-ray and fleshly body stand on precisely the same footing!

We must be consistent, therefore. What is valid for the lit and coloured image of the pen formed by the light-rays is equally valid for the lit and coloured images of the eyes themselves, of the nerves and of the brain! We know all these things because they are thinkable things, because they are known in the last analysis as ideas. Therefore we have no alternative but to make the whole system of eyes, nerves and brain a system of ideas.

Science has never been able to demonstrate how objective sense-impression and subjective idea can coalesce. This is because it has artificially divided that which forms an indivisible union. It has severed in theory what has never been severed in reality. The question involved in the problem of the physiologist's "gap" is unanswerable because it is unaskable. The broken continuity of explanation can only be maintained if he has the boldness to throw the whole nervous system, the entire body and the external object into unity with the sensation itself, i.e. to deprive them of their material character and convert them all into ideas. He must take up the view that their place in the sensory circuit is as mental as is the idea in which this circuit ends. Otherwise the process of knowing the varied things of this world becomes unaccountable and must ever remain an insoluble mystery.

Both the initial and the ultimate acts in sensation are thus seen to be acts of mind! All that occurs between them occurs within mind. Similarly the initial and ultimate substance dealt with is also mind : where then is room for a *material* structure of eyes, nerves and brain ? They must be mental constructs too, for neither nerve nor brain nor eye can sufficiently account for the formation of a perception if they are to be taken as non-mental things. Their very nature offers intrinsic obstacles to the building of a bridge between the conscious act of perception and the supposedly unconscious materials which are worked up into the act. Science has not succeeded in overcoming these obstacles and it is impossible to conceive that it can ever do so. Physiology can minutely describe these materials and the way they are arranged, but it cannot do more. For the final perception is a mental affair and hence beyond its boundary. The solution is to recognize that mind is present and active throughout.

The hidden teaching disturbs none of the scientific facts about sensation and perception already narrated; on the contrary, it allows for them. What it does is to complete them by casting a bridge across the enormous chasm left by them. It explains that the entire structure of eyes, nerves and brain falls inside mind and has never existed outside it, which means that we are dealing with ideas all the time when we believe we are dealing with non-mental material substances fashioned in the forms of eye, nerve and brain. The reason why we are not aware of this is that we circumscribe the mind within a small space inside the head and therefore have no option but to place the sensory and nervous structure outside mind. We forget that the entire body itself is but a complex of mental percepts. All the delicate physiological apparatus which manufactures impressions, all the marvellously responsive eyes, nose, ears, skin and tongue, all the network of complicated nerves and winding convolutions of the brain which belong to the physical body and which are taken to be solid material things, are themselves enclosed within the charmed circle of consciousness, are only mentally known : they must be in short nothing more and nothing less than mental constructs.

What!—it will be objected—are we to regard our awareness of a person standing before us as being merely the awareness of a group of ideas ? The reply is that both touch and sight and all the senses are mental, that beyond these sensations which tell us of head, trunk, legs and arms and which ultimately resolve themselves into conscious states, we know for certain of nothing. Our consciousness and its states exist with a surety which is irrefutable but the materiality of the other person's body exists only as an idea. The whole content of his being is identical for us with our conscious states. He is not and he cannot be extra-mental. He cannot be independent of our consciousness.

Once we abandon the futile attempt to regard sense impressions of the human body, whether of our own or of another's, as being material activities and take them for what they are—purely mental —the picture of our universe becomes clearer and the puzzles which beset the materialist view disappear altogether. Nothing else will perfectly answer our question and nothing less will profoundly satisfy our reason.

Thus our ultimate awareness of the existence of all these sensory nerves and sensory organs is itself an act of perception. If we have had to end with the mind, it may dawn on us that we unconsciously began with mind too. We have been travelling in a circle and never really got away from mind at any moment. The terms "brain", "nerve" and "sense-instrument" are indeed merely terms used by the mind to describe its own experiences. They are themselves perceived objects! The whole of man's physical body is nothing less than a percept, for we become aware of it because we see parts of it and feel its surface, etc., all of which are simply internal sensations.

Finally it may be suggested to those who find difficulty in grasping these admittedly difficult points that a helpful illustration is to consider the dream experience of dream bodies.

So long as men come to premature unreflected conclusions about this familiar act of experiencing an external thing, which recurs continuously throughout their waking lives, so long will they be unable to comprehend its vital and immense importance as one key to the right understanding of life's mystery.

Let it be emphasized that what is written in this chapter is not written from the practical standpoint of everyday living but from the subtler standpoint of what is ultimately true. Our criterion of truth is not to be what the lined palm of one's hand feels, which is satisfactory enough to the plain man, but what the reasoning and judging power of the mind ascertains, which is alone satisfactory to the philosopher. Nobody will ever be able to dislodge reason from this central fact of mentalism, do what he will.

What Are Things? It is now time to face one of our final problems. What becomes of the independent externally experienced thing which has somehow been left out of this reckoning whilst we were so preoccupied with ascertaining how we formed our idea of it? We seem to ourselves to have entered into close intercourse with those external objects but we now know that we never attain to more than intercourse with ideas. We seem to have immediate experience of the material things, but it is wholly impossible to prove their *immediate* presence in our experience. We can testify only to the experience of pictures in the mind and to the fact that the independently existing object has never really been revealed to our senses; we have only *thought* of it, just as we have thought of the senses themselves. We can make no truthful statement about it for the simple reason that our experience is completely cut off from it. We cannot place ourselves beside it.

Must we then bow our head humbly and admit that this mysterious thing in itself remains outside the other end of the eye-

THE MAGIC OF THE MIND

nerve-brain series, apparently an unknown and ever unknowable object?

We accept the existence of things because we perceive them. Let us look into the point. It is necessary to examine this act of perception more closely. We take it habitually for granted when we attend to sensations and perceptions that we are attending to material things and that we are receiving information about objects which exist quite separately from ourselves. The philosopher cannot afford to take anything for granted, however. He endeavours through the profoundest possible reflection to enter into an understanding of what is actually occurring, rejecting all assumptions and inferences in the process.

First of all, we must make it clear beyond doubt that the very *moment* of sensing the existence of a fountain-pen is an act of mind, consciousness, and no longer an act of nerve vibration or cerebral change; that it is not a physical process at all. The physiological account of sensation accounts for everything except for this first moment of awareness when the pen becomes known to us. It does not account for the birth of consciousness of the pen, for the mental act of knowing it as apart from the supposedly physical act of entering into relation with it. Moreover, the mere act of judging the impressions of objects is itself a mental activity which cannot be explained by any physical process. Thus instead of separating percept from object we ought to separate the awareness of perception from the percept itself, both being mental; and instead of separating the subjective from the objective we would do better to separate consciousness from the object of consciousness, i.e. idea.

When we examine this verbal symbol *idea* we find it to be an expression of an awareness which is immediate, innate, direct and obvious, whereas that of things is indirect, added and interpreted—in short, inferred.

It is because we see the mental image of a separate independent external material man that we automatically and unconsciously think that there is also a person to whom that image corresponds. Nevertheless, such is the relativity of thought that the very presence of an idea forces us to prejudge the issue and think that there is a material thing outside which has given birth to the idea. The percept of a man is alone directly known. Any other must be a mentally constructed one. The awareness of sensations is certain and indubitable. The knowledge of an external cause of those sensations to which they answer is entirely inferred and supposed.

We see, taste and feel external things as being absolutely

independent merely because we *start* with an inborn belief that they are absolutely independent. If A and B are in causal relation, then A always comes first. Cause precedes effect. Now what do we experience first of the external objects? Why, we become aware of the mental impression of them, and nothing else at any time! Hence, if the mental impression comes first, it must be the cause! To make the external object the cause of the internal sensation is equal to making sensation the cause of sensation, i.e. to beg the question and to attempt what is impossible and inconceivable.

We must emphasize what will appear only from acute analytic reflection—namely, that mental experience precedes physical experience and that the latter follows the former merely because it is a subsequent inference. The image is antecedent to the inference that the object exists. We unconsciously and almost instantaneously decide that the object is outside *after* we have perceived the image; it is a later act. But granting that the knowledge of the independently existent object comes second after the knowledge of the percept, how is it proved that it is only an inference? The answer is that everything that cannot be immediately known, everything that cannot be known as it is in itself, must necessarily be brought to our knowledge by the working of imagination. We must represent it to ourselves through the image-making faculty of mind. And to know what particular image to construct we have to pass through the corridor of subconscious reasoning until we come to a final conclusion, which could only be an inference even if it were a right inference, which it is not.

The thought is primary, whereas the thing is secondary. The idea is factual, whereas the object is inferential. *Before* the mind reveals the perception to itself there is no knowledge of any external object. Such an object appears *subsequently* on the scene; until then nothing can be said of it. It is this important distinction which forms the very foundation of mentalism. And this distinction is not the fanciful speculation of imaginative metaphysics; it is slowly beginning to be the factual finding of leaders like Eddington and Jeans, who are in the front ranks of modern science. The meaning of this distinction is that the object veritably depends for its existence on the idea of it, not the idea on the object. Nobody can prove that it possesses any independent existence. Mind is its basis and upholder. It is a mental derivative.

We may find enough courage to face the truth about these external objects. For we found in our study of illusions that the *capacity* of an illusion to deceive us disappeared after we took the trouble to enquire into it, even though the *existence* of the illusion remained. Similarly the external objects have now, after we have taken the trouble to inquire into them, turned out to be inferred, although they continue to remain in experience. Now an inference is an imagination, i.e. an idea. So our external object turns out to be an idea just as much as our actual experience of it is an idea. When analysed it also turns out to be a thought. What does this mean? As in illusion the mind creates an object of its own and then proceeds to assume its reality, so in the case of ordinary everyday experience the mind has created an external thing and then assumed its existence; and as in illusiòn the assumed thing was indubitably and repeatedly seen, so here too the inferred object is also plainly and persistently seen. That a percept is an item of consciousness is indubitable, that the object is outside it is merely an idea. The first is fact but the second is unproved and unprovable. An independent object is never seen separately but only inferred psychologically. We may pay it the utmost attention and give it our alertest awareness, but we will never detect it apart from the idea. For its very existence rests on inferences and involves assumptions. But truth does not deal in inferences. It must keep its feet on firm ground—fact verified and ascertained.

Whoever has been impatient at this venture into seeming abstractions has erred. For until he has formed a correct idea of how we come to know the external world of things which rest or move in space he cannot penetrate to its reality. Until he has analysed the content of world-consciousness he cannot understand how it has been built up. We habitually consider the wall that confronts us as standing quite aloof from our sensation of its existence. We hold unreflectingly to the view that we see the wall first and then make a representative image of its appearance in the mind. The wall falls into first place and the mental picture into second place in the order of our supposed awareness of it. We have already found how little this is correct. We shall now arrive at the right view and it will sap the foundations of our age-long human certitude about the nature of the world, the position of the body and the dimension of the mind.

How can we continue to take it for granted that although we cannot directly know the object, our idea of it is an image which duplicates it more or less satisfactorily, a kind of photograph made on the mind by the object? How can this belief continue to stand in face of all that we have discovered by our prying analysis? How can it be that the object is really there outside us and the perception of it is only a copy of it, albeit a mental one ? How can it be that our superficial apprehension of a material universe is correct, is just as it seems to be, and is in no need of analysis ? For all our facts show that we have unconsciously begun with the idea of the object and consciously ended with it, and that perception is a psychological act, and that the perception of a fountain-pen is not merely seeing the mental copy of a pen but literally seeing the pen itself, because it is identical with the mental percept and not merely related to it. The theory that although it is true that we know only our mental constructs, nevertheless these constructs are only copies, representations, of some unknown external material object, is utterly invalid. For the object is itself part of the construct and no justification exists for separating it from the totality of perception other than the justification of ancient and habitual prejudice. Those who believe in the "mental copy" theory, who put idea and object at different ends of the same pole, are joining together complete incompatibles.

Material things are not only just as much mental as their so-called "subjective" perceptions but are intrinsically the same. It would be a gross error to believe that a perception is a mere mental copy of a material object. The latter itself is as subjective as the former. Both the supposed material thing and the conscious registration of it are mental constructions and nothing else. The notion that the construct itself conforms to the material thing is pure supposition.

The idea of a wall is all that we know for certain because it is all that we really experience, the rest is but unconscious deduction and automatic erroneous judgment. For our entire attention is directed towards the externalized wall and not towards the awareness of what is actually taking place during its perception. Hence simple and superficial persons fall into easy error by taking this idea for an external thing. The idea, the mental copy which is supposed to have come into existence in consequence of the presence of the material wall is the first thing we really know, whereas the matter is the second thing. But it has not the advantage of being known, it is only inferred and remote and as an inference it is only a copy of the first idea, i.e. we have multiplied the construct itself. We can get along quite well without such multiplication. The lesson is that we must give preference and allow priority to the perception itself rather than to the object of perception, because we must mark out a strict boundary-line between what is actually perceived and what is merely inferred.

THE MAGIC OF THE MIND

But we are not yet done with our critic. He may very properly ask: "If there is nothing external, no independent thing at all, then the question will inevitably arise: 'Why do we get the idea of an object when there is apparently nothing to cause it?'" This and other criticisms and objections which can be made and are likely to be made against mentalism must regrettably be left for further consideration when the doctrine is more adequately explained and finally proved in the succeeding volume of this work. They are linked together with more advanced problems. For unless the nature of Mind, the mystery of sleep, the meaning of dream, the secret of the *I*, and the significance of creation are thoroughly understood, the conviction of mentalism's truth cannot be finally clinched nor can its own tremendous contribution be brought into relation with our common life. Philosophy in general has hitherto offered many questions but few final solutions, whereas the hidden teaching offers a complete key to the understanding of the ALL. Let it be noted that it touches on these tantalizing mysteries only to solve them, but that solution belongs to the more advanced tenets and can only be grasped after the difficult preparatory studies have been made, and may not be separated without causing bewilderment arising from the strange facts there to be revealed. Such is the regrettable position and there we must perforce leave it for the present.

Meanwhile, in reply to the questions, why does the independent object contribute to our sensation of sight, smell and touch, and why does it induce those sensations by its mere presence?—we may now say that because the percept manufactured out of such sensations is the object itself, the questions collapse as unaskable. Thing and thought are identical. Those who would distinguish between the thing as apart from our mind and the thing in relation to us attempt what is impossible, for they are as inseparable as the sun-ray and the sun. The thought *is* the thing, the percept is the object, rather than the reverse. Every object, together with the space and time relations that go with it, is an object perceived in consciousness and nowhere else, and therefore dependent on it. What we call a material object really is the percept of a material object built in our minds, and the outward projection of a percept really is the outward object itself. That which immediately and indisputably exists for us is the finished percept. We need not hesitate to apply this principle with the utmost boldness. Locomotive engines and reinforced concrete skyscrapers, broad lakes and lofty mountains are as much mental constructs as any other things that we see amid teeming cities or in placid landscapes.

It is hard at first but easy in the end to grasp this primary fact, that the supposed deliverances of sense-activities, i.e. sensations, are themselves the objects with which we are dealing in our intercourse with the world. When we ponder reflectively we shall find that thing and thought meet, that objective and subjective merge, that any distinction between them is arbitrary, for it is made by man and not by Nature. Thus subjective and objective elements merge into unity, into radical identity. It is impossible to think thing and construct asunder when we deeply consider what they really are. Reflection relentlessly demands that we blend them into one. It is an iron necessity of the laws of thought against which no shuffling convention can prevail.

What is the distinction between a thing as we see it and as it is in itself? For us there is none. The purposes of the practical activities of mankind quite entitle us to enquire no farther than the common view which does not take the thought for the thing. But this will not stand up to critical philosophical enquiry, which demands the whole truth and nothing less and which therefore finds that the thing is really the thought of the thing. Hence for philosophic purposes we are compelled to rub out the distinction between the thought and the thing. It might exist in Nature but it does not exist in knowledge. It is impossible to prove that it is a fact and it is equally impossible to prove that it is a fiction. For the thing-in-itself is beyond our reach as any thing other than as a thought.

The setting up of a material activity in opposition to a mental one rests on the false and perverted notion of a bifurcated world containing both outside things and internal thoughts. The superficial masses immediately make this discrimination, but were they to think deeply enough they could never maintain this absurd thesis. Uninstructed and unreflective persons believe that they have direct awareness of external objects, for they call the mental construct the material object. The best philosophical psychologists know better, for they know that the mental operations concerned are the *first* to enter the field of awareness, as they are also the last.

So long as we stubbornly persist in drawing a line between things and our perception of these things, so long shall we be unable to comprehend their real character. So long as we sever the one from the other, so long shall we find ourselves in this *cul de sac* which renders the problem wholly insoluble. Once we throw this primary error, this fundamental and fatal miscalculation, into the crucible of intent reflection, we may hope to find the true fact about our knowledge of the world but not before. The masses naturally think

THE MAGIC OF THE MIND

and feel that every external thing comes first and the mental image of it is merely a copy that arises subsequently. They are not to be blamed for this, for Nature hides her gold in the depths of earth and hides her truth in the depths of reflection. Habit forces us to establish this separation of thought from thing, but reflection equally forces us to repair this error. Those who will not take the trouble to pick their way through this tangled enquiry cannot hope to perceive the truth about the familiar things around them. That whether it be a pen or a pageant each of these things is mental, is a truth which stands in direct and primary opposition to their first and foremost impressions. Nothing but the severest scrutiny of himself and the subtlest thinking within himself could ever have given man the knowledge of this amazing truth.

When we carry this line of reasoning to its farthest end with thorough consistency we cannot fail to conclude that although it has converted objects into ideas it does not stop there, but converts ideas back again into objects!

CHAPTER XII

THE DOWNFALL OF MATERIALISM

LET us return to our locomotive engine. Even when you stretch your hand out and feel that it is standing there in space, separate and apart from you, still the whole event occurs within your consciousness and nowhere else. For space is as mental as time.

The locomotive engine is but a mental construction. Try to become aware of it without those characteristics which produce the sensations of its existence within your mind. You will find the feat impossible. Think away its colour, form, hardness, weight; think away all its properties, in fact, and what will remain? There will be nothing left, because it is through the sum of these properties that you are able to perceive the engine there at all.

"Admittedly," you may say; "the engine must disappear for me when there are no sensations of it; but have we not forgotten the substance of which it is made, the stuff to which these characteristics belong, the root of all these properties?"

Let us reflect if this be so. Can you see this substance? "Yes," you answer, "it is green." But that which you see as green is a colour, and it has already been shown that colours do not inhere in the things themselves. If your alleged substance is really there then it should possess no colour at all. Can you see a colourless substance in the engine? You will be forced to admit that you cannot, and that when you think of it without simultaneously thinking a colour you are compelled to imagine that some colour must subsist in it and that therefore colour is a part of matter. This, however, is an illusion on your part, because science has demonstrated that the colours of every object which we see, have seen, or are likely to see do not form a part of the object itself but come into being through the play of light-rays upon it. In other words, the colour is really an optical interpretation of the light itself and not of the object revealed by the light. The physiological analysis of sight proves that the production of colour is the work of the eyes, whilst the sensation of colour is the work of the mind. The feat of imagining a colourless matter is impossible; no matter how hard the mind may strive not

THE DOWNFALL OF MATERIALISM

to do so, it will have to assign some kind of colour to every seen substance, because the two must coincide together. Therefore it is impossible to separate colour entirely from any perceived object.

But this leads to a curious situation. For the colour cannot exist within us whilst the thing itself exists without us. They must both be together, and as we find that colour finally has a mental existence, so must the object's substance or "matter" also possess a mental existence. Both are built up out of mind and nothing else.

"But how is it that colours vary if they are interpretations? What is the cause of these changes?" This question brings up the complex problem of cause and effect. Immanuel Kant pointed out that this relation was a natural form of human thinking, that it is the mind which begins by believing that there is such a thing as cause and consequently seeks for it, and that there is a mysterious unapproachable substance-in-itself whose presence gives us the idea of material substance. What the hidden teaching has to say concerning such a substance will be explained here, but the more difficult problem of cause and effect must be reserved for the further volume.

"But," you will add, "even if I cannot see this substance, nevertheless I can feel it with my fingers." To this the reply is that what you feel are solidity and roundness, resistance and impenetrability. But these are qualities which reach you as muscular sensations and therefore belong to your mind. They are not apart from it. They are not the non-mental substance you allege them to be. It is impossible to separate the size and figure of an object from the colour and the feeling which it produces when touched. That is, we cannot put the former outside and the latter inside the mind. They both exist and from their nature can only exist together. We are able to identify a form by its feel and colour, and if we put the latter in one place and the mass or volume in another, then we are doing violence to the very act of perception and rendering it impossible. Therefore the final conclusion is that the entire object and not merely a part of it, the entire matter of which it is composed, can exist only mentally.

The earlier objection that if this doctrine of perception be true, then a large locomotive engine should not be either heavy or hard if it is composed solely of mental substance may again be mentioned as inadmissible. For we may now perceive how it has confused issues and failed to grasp the true nature of the doctrine. Nobody denies the hardness and the heaviness of the vehicle. We accept both because they come to us in the form of sensations. We actually feel that we can touch but cannot shift the locomotive engine and that it is hard and heavy. Yet the hardness, heaviness and resistance of which we become aware are known only by the mind and within the mind. This proves that the mind is entirely capable of experiencing every kind of sensation whether it be of hardness or softness, or whether it be of heaviness or lightness. Therefore it is erroneous to declare that what is mental cannot be experienced as such substantial and touchable sensations. Were that correct, then we could never have dreams!

At this point you may retire in annoyance, or if you remain it will be to persist stubbornly in asserting that there is and must be something more of the engine's stuff than mere sensations, that no delicate nervous registration like a sensation could possibly resemble a substantial thing like matter.

We are forced here to ask a direct question and demand a direct answer: "What is this 'matter' like?" Do what you will, rack your reason and torment your knowledge as you may, you will be unable to speak of it except in terms of sensation. You will be unable to assert in what single instance matter is different from sensation. Any view that you take of it will necessarily make it visible or touchable, smellable or hearable or tastable; that is to say, will make it reside in your sensations and hence in your mind. Let your awareness of the engine be bereft of all sensations and there will be no engine left for you to be aware of and no material stuff to remain as a residue. Why therefore should anyone believe in this mysterious matter? We may believe in sensations because we know they exist, but this alleged matter cannot be truly grasped either by hand or mind. Substantiality exists as a sensation of the mind, whereas substance by itself exists only in imagination. The critic's matter is simply an unnecessary addition to his sensations; it is fictitious and non-existent. When closely peered into it collapses as a mere figment of the human mind. True, pure mind is in itself as remote from sight, as alien to touch and as empty to human perception as matter. *But whereas we know its effects in thoughts, ideas and images, i.e. in consciousness, we never know any effects of matter at all.*

A dictionary tells us that matter is the substance of which a physical thing is made, and it is in this sense that the word is used here. But when we open its pages again we learn that substance is the essence or most important part of anything, and that physical means that which is of matter. The upshot of all these definitions is merely this: that all the things around us are essentially material, and that matter is matter! Looking into the dictionary has been a vain exertion. What we have really learnt is nothing more than, in Hamlet's phrase, "Words, words, words!" The application of semantic analysis is most important here. We are often led away by the customary use of innocent-looking words to believe that they represent facts, whereas they represent only mere sounds. For analysis shows that the word "matter" is a meaningless one. We are entitled to write an interrogation-mark all over it. We are entitled to pose the questions: Has anyone observed matter in itself, as apart from the objects in which it is supposed to clothe itself? Has it ever been accessible to the five senses of man? Has anyone ever observed it before the idea of it was formed? Thus to define matter adequately is to deny it.

The existence of matter or substance stripped of every quality which enables an object to exist for our senses is unthinkable. It is the totality of these qualities which constitutes the object; this we know, but the knowledge of matter itself is psychologically impossible. Apart from percepts, there is no trace of such a thing as material substance. We can pick up no object, whether it be a stick or a stone, which is not picked up in *conscious* experience, i.e. mentally.

Matter as an independent entity stands in direct antithesis to mind, unless we recognize that it is none other than mind. The notion of the latter's immateriality will for ever come into conflict with that of the former's *separate* substantiality. That which is present before consciousness is hardly entitled to be regarded as being more real than the consciousness itself. Matter is not different from mind, although thought to be so by those who have not enquired deeply into it. This is as true of engines as it is of the steel rails along which they run. The mental not only explains the existence of matter but also its own existence, whereas it is utterly impossible to explain the mental by the material unobjectionably. It may be disconcerting to be told that matter is only an idea, but no mind has ever been able to form a conception of this phantom in itself, but only as it is *thought* to be. It is the act of a child to accept the sense-reports as really being reports of a material world, but that of a thinker to question them. If matter is theoretically sundered from mind it becomes a spurious substance, a chimera, which we may seek but can never find. Such a thinker will therefore uncompromisingly repudiate its existence.

Several thousand years ago, solely by the keenest possible concentration of mind, the Indian sage perceived what the Western scientist has merely *begun* to perceive in our own time—that matter is not the independent substance that it seems. Those who took college courses in physics hardly more than a single generation ago learnt of matter which has since disappeared from scientific reckoning, but where it has disappeared what scientist clearly knows? For his mind battles with the incomprehensible unless and until he is willing to turn philosopher. The unpalatable dilemma in which science will soon find itself and from which it cannot escape is: How does it know that there is a material object corresponding to the idea of it if it has never once seen a material object, and if it can never have any experience of such an object?

For one of the greatest theoretical achievements of science in this century has been the dematerialization of matter! The conception of matter has undergone such a radical and rapid change that no scientist now dare dogmatize about its existence. The notion that matter is substance has been replaced by the notion that matter is wave-energy. Nevertheless, the latter, although far more plausible, is still as much of an inference as the former. Matter, accepted by the man in the street, converted into waves of force by the man in the laboratory, is returned into mind by the philosopher. What we know of it is only sensation, and the sensations of light, stone or iron are entirely mental in their origin.

We touch and grasp something firmly, we press and contract our muscles as we hold the solid thing in our hands, and thus seem to reassure ourselves of the existence of matter, but all that we have really done is to betray ignorance and show bias. Those who take matter to be real and, like impatient Dr. Johnson, stamp their feet impulsively on the ground to prove it, merely prove that they take their muscles as fit criterions of truth! Their triumph is grotesque and illusory. For the shape-showing muscular sensations of resistance and pressure are still sensations, and sensations in the end are events in their consciousness; that is to say, in themselves and not in matter. The muscular kind of sensation is ultimately as much mental as the visual kind.

Those who regard a perceptual world as a spectral one have not understood these explanations. For it *is* the solid and graspable world that we daily live in. The habitual assumption that some kind of mysterious substance called matter, of which all things are composed, exists outside this perceptual world deceives them. They do not comprehend that they have assumed its existence when they ought to have questioned it. There is not the slightest evidence that anything exists in this mind-fashioned universe which is not wholly mental. It should now be clear that when we are talking about "matter" we are talking about a delusive word and not about a thing graspable by the senses, about a vague abstraction and not a concrete object, about an illusion rather than a reality. For it can neither be pictured by imagination nor justified by reason.

Nevertheless our belief in matter—this vaguest of all vague abstractions—is almost incurably ingrained. This is because we habitually narrow the mind down to the confines of the head, wrongly believing it to be kindled inside the phosphorized cerebral mass instead of habitually expanding it to contain all things perceived. We believe that we see and touch matter and even move it merely because we do not grasp this fundamental point that mind is dimensionless and measureless. Thus mentalism is based on proven fact and not on mere inference as is materialism. The mentalist has the positive assurance that he is not affirming a supposition or a deduction as does the materialist, but rather an ascertained and irrefutable actuality. The materialist's demand that we accept as real something which he himself confesses we cannot know in itself, and that we shall take as independent and external something which is really given only internally as an object of consciousness and which can be fully intelligible to us only through the activity of consciousness, is absurd.

Materialism does not adequately explain the higher mental life. It does not throw full light on why we can form abstract ideas, why we have the capacity to conduct thought along a line of pure reasoning, the power to judge between truth and error, the creative imagination of the artist, the inventive faculty of the scientist, the ability to construct generalized ideas, the metaphysical thinking of the philosopher, and, above all, why we can reflect about our own consciousness as being an immaterial thing. Materialism never even touches the hem of the garment of consciousness.

Yet such is the intellectual degradation of mankind that it irritably denounces the truth of mentalism as illusory and impulsively upholds the error of materialism as truth! Materialism succeeds in solving its numerous minor problems only by shutting its eyes to its single major problem—itself. For nobody has ever seen matter, nobody has ever handled it and nobody has ever known where to detect its presence. Its existence is a bluff. Matter thus becomes a merely illegitimate entity in our explanation of the world, a fiction which works quite well for the purposes of practical life but becomes meaningless for the purposes of philosophical truth. When such an erroneous notion is seen for what it is it will simply vanish from one's understanding and be regarded no more. One will still be active in the world of things, but they will no longer be "lumps of matter". They will be ideas. They will no longer be in opposition to mind but integrated with it.

We have travelled far from the ordinary man's argument that matter is much too self-evident even to need discussion. For we have converted it into a significant appearance, pointing to mind as its hidden reality. Yet it is a most extraordinary anomaly of human reason that consciousness, mind, is popularly regarded as being much less real than matter, although adequate reflection reveals it as being entitled to a status of reality which is unique and primary.

Popular belief, never having enquired into the truth of its intuitive beliefs, is alarmed when it first hears of this terrifying tenet of mentalism which throws doubt on a thing it has hitherto held to be beyond discussion. For there can be no way of reconciling the common-sense view of the world with the philosophic fact of mentalism.

In our earlier study of illusions and hallucinations we traced their origin primarily to the natural bent of the mind to externalize its own images and to see them as separate entities. It is now of grave importance to remember that even when we know any illusions to be such, and when we have discovered and mentally corrected errors of sense, still we cannot free ourselves from perceiving them in precisely the same way in which we perceived them formerly. Their appearance continues to persist contrary to our knowledge. We may see through the deception by our power of reason, but that does not cause the deception itself to disappear. We may know by reflection and reason that the appearance which presents itself to consciousness is illusory and yet we may be quite unable to resist its power of continued existence and its spell of solid reality.

This is a positive demonstration of the complex character of our percepts and of the mysterious power of the mind to impose its own manufactures upon our senses without our personal awareness and beyond our power of control, just as it does during dream.

The possibility and prevalence of these illusions should constitute a warning to all mankind and start them reflecting whether they are not subject to illusion in other matters which they habitually take to be correctly perceived. It should also guard against overconfidence when indignantly denying the frank hint that the *materiality* of the whole world may after all be a still wider illusion. Moreover, the public feats of jugglers and the staged phenomena of conjurers which compel us to see what is quite contrary to fact prove that illusions may be collectively shared by a large number of people at the same time ; whilst they point to the important possibility of even the whole of mankind being susceptible to a general illusion. May it not be that the collective illusions of the world's externality and materiality have arisen in the minds of all people because all share psychological and physiological similarities ? When we discover how deep-seated hallucinations may sway the individual we are prepared for the further discovery that they may also sway and coerce the collective human race. And it is a fact that the forceful illusions of materiality and externality are indeed shared persistently by all men throughout the world. For this reason the ancient Indian sages compared ignorant mankind to a race asleep and dreaming, but compared the wise to those who were awake and fully conscious.

Belief in matter, in short, is belief in a gross but mesmeric illusion. This is the emphatic message of the hidden teaching to a materialistic age, a message that also yields a warning against the useless pursuit of mere phantoms. We destroy the power of a terrifying nightmare or unpleasant dream when we awaken and discover its unreality. Similarly we destroy the power of illusive matter—this idol with feet of clay whom myriads of blind worshippers have wrongly revered—over the mind when we awaken into Truth. Yet the stupendous difficulty of this revelatory task of philosophy may be grasped by comparing it with the task of convincing a dreamer *whilst he is still dreaming* that his environment of houses, persons and conversations is an imagined one. We who are in the waking state live also in an imagined world, but the statement sounds as incredible to us *whilst we are awake* as it would to the hypothetical dreamer.

The wise old Greeks said that philosophy was death. We may interpret these words as we wish. Many dying and most drowning men perceive their past as a swift-rushing vivid dream. So far as human life is mental life it is a series of ideas, i.e. of the same stuff as dreams. Philosophy seeks to make men realize that the entire texture of life is pure thought, but it wants them to see it here and now, not when they are dying. For if they can awaken to truth when it is most needed, i.e. when they are in the midst of work and living, suffering and pleasure, health and sickness, they will know how best to deal with those alternating vicissitudes from which none can escape.

Let it not be feared, however, that we shall then become mere dreamers ; on the contrary, after we shall have penetrated to the reality hidden behind and within both dream and waking we shall henceforth be done with dreams and learn to be truly and incessantly active not only for our own benefit but also for that of others. Whereas the ignorant live blindly, we shall live in the light, and whereas they cherish illusions, we shall cherish truth. We shall not flee from this dream of earthly life, for we cannot: it is not our individual finite mind that brought this dream into being and it is not our individual finite mind that can put an end to it. We shall accept it in all its comprehensiveness and not vainly seek to negate it. We shall firmly encourage action and not discourage it, but in the midst of our dream we shall be somewhat like a sleeping man who knows at the same time that he is asleep and dreaming. Thus we shall not suffer ourselves to be swept away by bitter nightmares or pleasurable reveries: always we shall seek peace in place of agitation.

From the Unreal to the Real. We have laboured to cross a difficult frontier, but at different points of our journey a certain problem has met us again and again. It must now be faced. For the question will necessarily arise that if externally experienced things are but thoughts, do they exist at all? Is each object unreal? If so, how is it that our daily experience flagrantly contradicts such startling possibilities?

None need be alarmed. We do not deny the existence of a single thing that forms part of our world-experience. But we must get our minds clear about this problem.

The experiments of Michelson and Morley which preceded the experiments of Einstein demonstrated that the velocity of light remained constant when all ordinary experience, common sense and scientific reason said that it ought to have risen to a much higher rate. Hence they were an astounding surprise. For this was not a mere piece of metaphysical speculation but a scientific piece of work performed with appropriate instruments. The experimental results contradicted what was expected and what ought to have happened. Science might have got rid of this awkward piece of data by conveniently explaining it away as an illusion of the senses. But to its credit it had the courage of accepting the "illusion" as a reality.

Is the brigand which the observer sees in the bush a real one or not? If not, what is it? That the brigand was seen means that he exists, even if he exists only as an illusion. This brings up an important difference—that between the meaning of *real* and the meaning of *exist*. We may here seek to profit again by the lesson learnt from the sixth chapter, where the need of analysing words for

THE DOWNFALL OF MATERIALISM

the factual rather than apparent meaning was strongly emphasized. It is necessary to consider the question and to discover what we mean by these terms, for relativity also raised the entire issue. Properly to do this we must first return to our earlier consideration of illusions.

Both the brigand and the bush share the common characteristic of being experienced, and only in this way do they certify to their existence. But the first is negated by closer investigation, whereas the second is confirmed by it. It is only when we find it impossible to reconcile the spurious knowledge of such an illusion with the content of normal experience that doubt begins to awaken within us and we are led to discover that it is illusory. So long as we remain content with the knowledge we have, we accept first impressions about things or people for what they seem to be, but when they come into direct conflict with other facts which emerge in the course of subsequent experience the question of their criterion of validity arises. Then the need of putting them to the test and where necessary correcting them is felt.

If an illusion is to be recognized as such, then the evidence of the senses is to be denied, whilst if the evidence of the senses is to be accepted, then we have two co-existent "realities" claiming to be one and the same thing. This absurd situation means that we are not to trust entirely to what our senses tell us about a thing's reality although we may trust them to tell us about a thing's existence. It means also that to call anything real is a dubious and dangerous procedure. What becomes of everyday experience of "matter", for instance, when it is contradicted by pure reason? Therefore to *appear* is one thing, whereas to *be* is another. We must learn to take care to distinguish between the two concepts. The puzzling contradictions of illusion vanish when we understand that different standpoints produce different perceptions, that from the standpoint of reflective reason we may possibly perceive a thing differently than from the standpoint of sense experience, and that it is a primitive attitude to take such experience as always possessed of decisive sanction. The existence of an illusion like the brigand seen in the bush cannot be denied. It would be absurd to reject anyone's experience of it; for to deny an illusion is to deny the content of experience and to negate what is given in consciousness. All that we may rightly do is to reject a particular interpretation of it; that is to say, to reject its reality. It *exists* but it is not *real*.

We have in fact to distinguish between the various kinds of existence, for we now see that something can exist and be real whilst another thing can exist and yet be unreal. Here again the need of penetrating behind the façade of a word becomes plain. In an earlier chapter it was shown that the term *fact* was open to unsuspected interpretations, and so here analysis of the two terms *exist* and *real* proves useful, although everybody who has never reflected about the matter wrongly assumes he already knows this meaning!

These words mislead most people because they think that whatever *appears* to them or whatever looks like reality must necessarily be real. Their error is to be satisfied that merely because they perceive things the latter are therefore real things. Perception is no proof of reality. For we may have wrong perception and imaginary perception even among the so-called·*real* perceptions! Men in delirium may see blue snakes and nobody dare deny that they are perceived. Such snakes must therefore be said to exist, for they do exist in the mind of the sufferers, to whom they are unquestionably real. Similarly nobody can deny that objective things exist, for they are perceived by the minds of men, who also regard them as unquestionably real, but in both these cases the philosopher is entitled to question not their existence but their reality.

Everybody can see and nobody can dispute that there is a brick wall confronting us, for instance. When it is said, however, that this wall can have only a mental existence, it is totally unjust, totally false and totally stupid to misrepresent this assertion as meaning that the wall has no existence whatever. And when we say that we are touching this wall we do not mean that we are touching the shadow of a real wall called an idea, but that the touch itself is an idea and that the various mental sensations of the wall is all of the wall we shall ever know, not that it is a copy of the real material wall, which appears to be somewhere beyond our body. It is preposterous and unintelligent to misconstrue the results of this analysis into a statement that a wall which is plainly beheld is but a shadow of the real wall and that the chair in which we now sit is but a mere copy of the real chair, which exists somewhere else in space. Both chair and wall do in point of fact exist quite as much for the mentalist philosopher as for the materialist, the difference being that the former by a profound and habitual reflection has pierced into the true nature of their existence. He has certainly never denied them away. And if such a philosopher thinks that the chair in which he sits and the pen with which he writes do not really exist, he will not go to the trouble of writing any book. And to those who would object that a mental reality is equivalent to no reality at all, he would reply that there is no other that we human beings know.

THE DOWNFALL OF MATERIALISM

The word "real" has a meaning only when it is distinguished from the word "unreal" in the same way that one colour can only be distinguished by its contrast with another. Therefore no adequate definition of reality can be found until the proper meaning of its contrary is also found. Now people often make the mistake of thinking that because a thing is unreal it should therefore be invisible. Illusions prove the contrary. The world will be visible both to the philosopher and to the ignorant man, but whereas the latter will deem it to be just as he sees it, the former will deem it physically unreal but mentally constructed.

Objects are seen physically and externally but cannot exist apart from the mind's construction of them. We are not asked to doubt the actual appearance of the things we see nor give up our belief in their existence: we are asked to ascertain the kind of their existence, whether it be illusory or real; and we are asked to distinguish the pretended reality of what is merely an idea from the genuine reality of what unchangingly is—a point into which we shall shortly inquire.

There is vital difference between the terms "unreal" and "non-existent". Let us not leap hastily past these words: we need to be most careful when we denounce anything as such. We may rightly speak of "a barren woman's son" as being non-existent. We may not however label the brigand seen in the bush as equally non-existent but only as unreal. For he acquires existence, although not reality, by the mere act of being perceived. The two categories are totally different in meaning from each other and ought not to be confused. Non-existent things must be carefully distinguished from existent ones when we class both as illusions. A unicorn and a round square belong to the first class because you cannot even think them or imagine them. They are hollow meaningless phrases, whereas a mirage seen in the desert belongs to the second because it is a discredited appearance. The former can never be observed under any conditions but the latter may be seen under certain conditions.

It is important that we take care therefore not to confuse absolute mental existence with absolute non-existence. Everything which we see and touch really does exist. There is and there cannot be the slightest doubt of that, but it may not exist in the way in which we believe. It may exist mentally whilst not existing physically.

It is now needful to enquire still more closely what we mean when we use this word "real". Are we able to form any picture in our mind to correspond with it? If we are, there is the bewildering situation that other people may and will form a different picture, giving it a different definition.

The notion which postulates the real as what can be weighed and measured, and which implies that all mental things are a kind of luminous haze floating above the "real" physical world and unable to affect it at all, is, as has been earlier shown in our study of matter, bad science and worse philosophy; we must protest against it. What then are the tests and characteristics of reality? To reply with most that experience of the external world of things is alone real, or to assert with a few that experience of the internal world of thoughts is alone real, is to ignore that such a view is based on the feeling of reality and to forget that we have a similar feeling during dream which both these views may denounce as unreal. Hence it is useless to judge by feeling. We must first find a definition that will hold always. Few people care to define so scrupulously; they want to judge by feeling or by temperament alone. The consequence is that they *imagine* reality, they study their own *idea* of it only, and thus lamentably fail to avoid deceiving themselves into accepting what merely pleases them, not what is true.

At one time science said that the reality behind the world was made of atoms, later it said that the real stuff was made of molecules, still later it said things were really electrons. Now it is beginning to stutter something else. Science now confesses that there is no guarantee that it has reached the *last* secret of the supposed world-stuff. Should it therefore not drop the word *real* from its vocabulary—and should we also not drop it—altogether? For both science and we are dealing only with what appears to us, with what is presented to us, but not with what is ultimately hidden beneath all these presentations of atoms, molecules, electrons and what not. Having burnt its fingers, however, science has learnt to keep itself fluid to its conception of reality. Therefore it has now learnt never to put forward a final statement about this elusive word. Thus the path of human knowledge is a progressive awakening from illusory things which *exist* but which are ultimately *unreal*.

The fact finally known for what it is is the reality, whereas the final knowledge of the thing is the truth. This is correct only from the standpoint of practical affairs and until we reach the Ultimate. Then there are no two things, but unity, and hence no distinction between truth and reality. European metaphysicians have evolved a plausible doctrine which multiplies the degrees of reality. They would have come nearer to truth had they said that there exist degrees of the *apprehension* of reality. In that unity which is the unchangeably real there can never be any gradation whatsoever. For, as the ancient Indian philosophers—not mystics—have rightly said: *that is real which can not only give us certainty about its existence in its own right beyond all possibility of doubt and independently of man's individual ideation but which can remain changeless amid the flux of an ever-changing world. Such a reality is, after the pursuit of ultimate truth, the foremost pursuit of philosophy, whether it be labelled "God", "Spirit", "Absolute" or otherwise.*

What has become of the millions of human beings who have died? What has become of the prehistoric palaces of unrecorded kings? What has become of those kings themselves? All have crumbled away into dust and vanished. But what has become of THAT which appeared in the forms of those men and buildings? Whoever took it to be matter did not even know he was dealing with mind. Our own enquiry into it must take us not only through the appearances of matter but also beyond the workings of mind. This is the enquiry into ultimate permanent reality; this is philosophy.

When it shall be our good fortune to come into the fuller understanding of such reality we shall find, as the old sages found, that this puzzling world does not stand in startling contradiction to it as we fear. For in a subtler sense which we do not grasp at present the one is no less real than the other. The world is not essentially an illusion. Ultimately it is as real as the world of this unnameable uniqueness that is the true God. Things therefore are not themselves illusory, but it is our apprehension of them, as furnished by the senses, which is illusory. Nobody need worry over the loss of matter. It is something which we have never possessed and consequently the loss is not a real one. The world which has been revealed by our thoughts is the only world we have known, although it is not the ultimate world that we shall know. Therefore the truth robs us of nothing. He who flees the world in ascetic disdain flees from reality; he should correct himself first and thus learn to understand aright what is that something which appears as the world. What it is, what that ultimate reality means to the life of man, is the second quest of philosophy after the quest of truth, because we soon find that both quests are involved in one another. And this is therefore the second reward which philosophy holds out to man, that he shall learn how to live consciously in reality rather than blindly in illusion.

The World as a Thought. We have been dealing with the cases of single objects and isolated things and found them to be ultimately ideas. But we have to remember that these fragmentary facts which are ideas appear continuously in our daily life. It is therefore now necessary to take them up into a unity, to connect them together into the world-process and thus relate them to the world in which we are living. We have discovered every inanimate thing and every living creature to be a mental construct. Now the whole world is only an assemblage of all things and all creatures in their totality. Have we then the courage to take the intellectual plunge, to be bold enough and march straight to the logical conclusion that the whole world is itself but an idea also?

The world is a world of relatives, a network of connected colours, sounds, spaces, times and their dependent things; all things exist in relation to other things, but relations themselves are ultimately ideas. The limitless panorama of the passing world is a mental one. Such is the tremendous thought with which we are faced that age-old solar systems rolling through space are as much mental constructs as the pen which we analysed down to the point of regarding it as a pure percept. The universe in all its immensity consists in the end of a construct of mind. This is the psychological picture of our external world; it is a gigantic mental construct and nothing more. For perceptual experience stretches its embrace over everything and nothing known to man can stand outside it.

Mentalism alone provides an adequate explanation. It expounds the manner in which mind creates its own space to contain all the objects which it equally constructs from itself. Space is as much an idea as the things that seem to stand in it. If, as relativity has begun to show, space-time is the continuum of the world of material objects, then whatever this mysterious fourth dimension may be it can only be something that is within mind and therefore ultimately mental itself. Thus although we begin by contemplating the universe as being *presented* to mind we end by contemplating it as *constructed* by mind.

That a world exists around and outside our bodies is a certainty and not a deception. That this world exists around and outside our mind is a deception and not a certainty. For there is no such thing as existence outside or inside the mind. Ideas may be outside or inside each other but all stand in non-spatial relation to mind. There is no such thing as an extra-mental world of objects. Yet men are everywhere convinced of its existence! The human body is a part of the world, the world is an idea and the body must be an idea with it. If the world stands outside body it does not stand outside mind, but must fall within it. If the world existed outside the mind that perceives it it could never be perceived at all, for the mind does not get beyond its own states, i.e. ideas.

THE DOWNFALL OF MATERIALISM

The part played by the five sense-instruments is therefore to provide the conditions whereby man participates in the perception of objects as external to the body. The senses are the means whereby he shares the ideas of a material world which subsist in the dimensionless mind. The function of the body would then be to provide the conditions for that event which is the arisal of finite individual egoistic consciousness; without these conditions ultimate mind remains as it is, the mysterious and unique fact of all existence.

In that first moment when consciousness breaks into ideated being the silence of mind has spoken. *Not that it needed voice nor that it needed listeners—but this is a mystery to be kept for a while in reserve.* The tick-tock of time and the impressive landscape of the universe exist only mentally. This world which weighs so heavily upon us is but Appearance, a shadow flung out of the Timeless. Thus we arrive at the final conclusion that, not because things are outside our bodies, nor because they are very far from our bodies, nor because of their immense size, nor because of their great number, nor because of the varied elements which compose them, can we deny the mental nature of those things. The notion of the world is, in the final analysis, fabricated by the mind. It is a transitory mental construction.

When we look out on a stretch of country scenery and observe a chain of hills far away with a small forest in the foreground we do not dream for an instant that we are looking on a reconstructed scene. The hills are so high and so substantial, the trees are so green and so leafy, that we take these for solid things not in any way comparable with the pictures the mind constructs during daydreaming. But the science of psychology teaches that the entire landscape is as mind-made as the images that pass through consciousness during reverie. Every time a percept appears in the mind it must necessarily be reconstructed anew and therefore no one thing can have continuous existence nor appear twice in the same experience. What does appear is an incessant reconstruction of what is believed to be the same thing, and this is the real secret of the mystery of *maya*, that celebrated but misunderstood Indian doctrine. In this way we learn the larger lesson of illusion, a lesson which is applicable not merely to our perception of solitary things but to our perception of the whole world.

> This vault of Héaven under which we move,
> Is like a magic lantern, this to prove:
> The Sun there—is the flame; the World—the lamp,
> And we the figures who revolving move.
> *Omar Khayyám.*

But the solid objective world is not destroyed by mentalism. It is left precisely where it is. Its five continents are not denied, its impressive grandeur not banished. Only, for the first time it begins to be understood instead of being misunderstood.

The whole of your past is now a thought. The whole of your future is likewise a thought. The present is unseizable and indeterminable, as was shown in an earlier chapter. Even if you could catch it the past would at once claim it and it would be converted into an idea. Therefore *all* your life—which includes all its background of a panoramic world—is but a thought! If no other proof were available this alone would suffice!

Until you see that the world is only an idea you are a materialist, no matter how pious, how religious, how "spiritual" you think you are. You take matter for what it is not. When you find that the material universe is just a mental experience, then alone do you become liberated from materialism.

But the presence of ideas postulates the fundamental presence of mind, of that which makes us aware of ideas. Hence the materialistic picture of the world accounts for everything except the world itself! For it leaves out our conscious awareness of the world, which awareness is the only world we know. Any other world is merely an inferred one. Just as you cannot take the centre out of a circle and still keep your circle, so you cannot take the mind out of the universe and still keep your matter. Both are indissolubly bound together. All materialistic theories are shipwrecked on this fatal fact. Whatever we examine in this world, mind is present at the very beginning, for the former exists only to consciousness. Moreover, mind is also the final entity. It cannot be kept out of any reckoning at any point.

We are nearing the end of the first lap of our quest. We have brought the world down to the position of a great and grand appearance, but still a show. Every spectacle implies the existence of a spectator. What is this mystery that hides beneath the world-show? It might be thought that the weak point in mentalism is its likelihood of leading to the position that the world is one's own personal mental creation, a position which would be demonstrably absurd. For it would imply that we could capriciously form new stars at will merely by imagining them or construct whole cities by the voluntary exercise of fancy. Moreover, the latter existed before we appeared in the world and will probably continue after *we* are gone, whereas our imagined stars and cities will vanish in a few moments. The Himalaya mountains are still there to someone else whether *we* think of them or not; their existence is at least relatively more permanent, whereas our personal thought of them is transient. They are beyond the control of our own mind to make or unmake them. How then can mentalism make the bold fantastic assertion that the majestic Himalayas are merely ideas, merely mental states of feeble humans who cannot even create a single cedar tree by thought, let alone the world's mightiest mountain range?

This criticism is quite just, but it embodies a complete misunderstanding. Whilst it must be rigidly maintained that every formed physical thing which exists must exist as a thought, we must not fall into the profound error which regards these thoughts as originating in the finite mind of a particular *individual*. They do not. They can not. For this will lead to the further notion that there is no thing, no person and no world other than one's individual self. Such is the erroneous conclusion which might be drawn from these statements. But such is not the finding of the hidden philosophy. The latter does not set up one's little limited self as alone real and all else as illusory. This error is technically termed "solipsism". Solipsism is sheer lunacy. Were it true this poor finite brain of ours would then become the creator and sustainer of the universe!

Every object is an idea; it is an idea present to man's mind; but it is not created by man's individual and independent mind. He merely participates in it. For when we enquire more deeply we shall find that his individual mind is ultimately part of a universal mind, and it is *there* that we must look for the origin of this idea. We dare not say that man himself *creates* the ideas of the material objects, but we can say that he *has* them. For an idea without a mind to which it belongs is inconceivable. The myriad manifestations of mind stand in striking contrast with the perfect and primary unity of the mind itself. The multitude of individual things that are really ideas must ultimately be ideas of an all-comprehensive mind. We must penetrate beneath the individual mind and lo! there is a universal mind as its hidden reality and as the origin of his ideas of material objects. Mentalism does not claim the world to be any individual's creation. It claims that the world is this mind's creation, not "my" mind's creation. It does not teach that the world is a product of one's individual mind, **of** one's personal self. Common experience is alone sufficient to invalidate such a tenet. It cannot possibly be held by any philosopher who has investigated the nature of mind and self, an investigation which will be made at the proper point in the second volume of this work, where the higher mysteries of mind will be unfolded.

At this point we may again take up the two loose ends of yoga and philosophy and tie them together. For when the mind is better understood, then the proper place of mysticism and the extraordinary practices of yoga will likewise be better understood. It is much easier for one who has pursued such practices to grasp the truth of mentalism. He has already *felt* the world's unreality, but those who have never practised find it difficult at first to credit mentalism. "How," they say, "can this solid tangible world be only an idea? Nonsense!" The hardness of matter deceives them, but it is more easy for the yogi to convert this hard matter into imagination and thus the whole world into a thought.

Yoga was partly devised as a means of preparing the mind to accept the teaching of mentalism. For when the mind has become subtle, detached and concentrated by the practice of a yoga system it can more readily grasp this difficult doctrine with conviction. The power which is developed by such practice to abstract attention from physical surroundings and focus it upon internal states or ideas proves its value as an accessory to philosophy by rendering the truth of mentalism less hard to accept. The mind that has never practised meditation or never engaged in the labours of artistic creation inevitably stumbles at the very threshold of this grand doctrine, whereas the flexibility and abstractiveness of the mind which has previously disciplined itself to the point of easily attending to its own thoughts with complete concentration and complete forgetfulness of its material environment assist it to walk across this threshold and perceive the heretofore hidden ideality of things.

The universality of mind and the implication of mentalism also make it possible for us of the West to *begin* to understand how strange faculties whose existence has long been known to hoary Asia may operate in perfect obedience to scientific laws; how telepathy, apparitions, thought-reading and thought-transference, mesmeric feats and all the marvel magic and miracle of primitive and medieval religious, mystical and yogic history may be factually based; and how the little-understood energy of "karma" may be as universally and ceaselessly present as the equally mysterious energy of electricity and be just as precise in its workings and effects.

We have reached the position that the world is an idea but we have reached it through acute analysis of experience and with minds sharpened by concentrated reflection on ascertainable and verifiable facts. The yogi who succeeds in his practices of meditation reaches the same position, but he has reached it by reverie or trance based on subtle feeling. But feeling is not a valid standard for others.

His conclusion is purely personal and therefore not of much value to them. When he is plunged in his meditation he has a vivid sense of the dreamlike character of the world, how like a great thought it really is. But he can go no farther. He cannot penetrate to the reality which so expresses itself. So he contents himself with the illusion of his own "spiritual" reality (by which he really means "mental") which the standpoint of regarding the world as a dream gives him. Henceforth he becomes temperamentally detached from the world, whose practical activities he comes to regard as a vain useless pursuit.[1]

Thus the highest effect of successful yoga, apart from intermittent tranquillity, is to make man see the world as he would see a dream object and to feel acutely that the everyday experiences of ordinary existence suffer from unreality. Hence the mystic's attachment for "escapism", his dislike of useful activity and fear of the practical world. But this is to stop half-way on the quest. It is certainly not the goal of philosophy. For the highest effect of philosophy is to make man *feel* the forms of this world to be dream-like but to *know* it as real in a higher sense, its essence being nothing less than reality itself.

Again, just as the mystic receives the illusion of penetrating reality, so he also receives the further illusion of giving up his ego. This happens during meditation, and therefore intermittently, or more enduringly in the outer world through the development of a martyr-complex or through the practice of *external* non-resistance to evil. The philosopher, on the other hand, first loses the sense of reality of ego through insight into its relation to the whole and then gives it up in the outer world through service to mankind. Hence the true sage is keen on constant action because he is keen on real service.

Yoga is a step, not a stop. When we are wiser we shall ascribe to it the significance of being a most important milestone on our road, but still a milestone. Its delight should not be permitted to deceive us. There is still much more of the road to be travelled. Those who are mystically inclined or religiously bent will inevitably weary of the foregoing pages and mutter impatiently at their semi-scientific

---

[1] A quarter-century ago, as a consequence of the full-time practice of meditation in virtual solitude, the present writer underwent in Europe the series of mystical exaltations in the deep-trance state referred to in the first chapter. Afterwards he returned to social existence, but found that all activities seemed empty and purposeless, all persons mere wraiths. Such was his unbalanced state resulting from mysticism unchecked by philosophy. The philosopher, on the other hand, does not lose his balance in the slightest way.

detail. This is because they do not understand that we are engaged upon a momentous journey and that if we are using science we shall not remain in science. They yearn for inward ecstasies of the soul or new revelations of Deity. Let them learn that we are on the move. If we have taken this deep plunge into mentalism it is because there is no other route that we could take if we are to carry out the allotted task of leading them *intellectually* to the true God, the real "Spirit", and to that satisfying realization of "soul" which can alone endure. The way to the promised land lies through the wilderness of seemingly arid facts ; but this need not cancel out the enjoyment of peace-filled meditations. For right reflection upon these facts will yield understanding, and this effort, when made with proper concentration, rapt absorption and repetition, is the yoga of philosophical discernment. We are not moving farther away from God, as the ignorant may wrongly think, but actually moving nearer. We need not give up the grandeurs of mystical ecstasy for dull and dry intellectualism, but may retain them, the while we discover a permanent satisfaction that will not come and go intermittently like these ecstasies.

Let not these criticisms be taken amiss. Let them not blind us to the true worth of yoga in its rightful place and within its lawful limits. There it can help much: And we may now see the deep and practical wisdom of the early Indian teachers who prescribed yoga to those whose intellectual power was not strong enough to grasp the truth of mentalism through reasoned insight, for thus these men were enabled to arrive at the same goal through feeling, not through knowledge. For the same reason these teachers also prescribed the study of illusions to ordinary people because the sciences of physics, physiology and psychology were then too primitive to afford the comprehensively detailed analysis which has been made for modern students in the foregoing pages. However, the yogi untrained in philosophy is always in danger of losing his conviction that the world is idea because being based on feeling he is subject to the law that feelings are always liable to change. On the other hand, the yoga-prepared philosopher can never lose the profound insight he has gained through the use of pure reason. It is something that has grown up within him and achieved maturity. He cannot "ungrow" it any more than a year-old infant can "ungrow" itself and get back into its mother's womb. Permanent certitude must come through making the truth of mentalism our own with a rigid certitude which needs no prop of fallible authority or fading emotion. Such certitude can arise when this truth is seen, not even as scientific theory but only as scientific fact.

Yet we must never forget that mentalism is only a step leading to ultimate truth. It is a hurdle which blocks the path of the truth-seeker. It must be climbed and crossed. In its own place this crossing is of vital importance. It is also a temporary ground which the questing mind must occupy whilst consolidating its first victory, the victory over matter. Once the consolidation is fully effected it must begin to move onwards again ; it must leave mentalism ! The ultimate reality cannot consist of thoughts, because these are fated to appear and vanish ; it must have a more enduring basis than such transiency. Nevertheless we may see in thoughts, to which we have reduced everything, intimations of the presence of this reality, and apart from which they are as illusory as matter. The further and final battle must lead to victory over the idea itself. Both materialism and mentalism are tentative viewpoints which must be taken up and then deserted when the ultimate viewpoint is reached. Then alone may we say : *"This is real."* Hence if we must close this study with the questions, "What is a thought ?" and "What is the mind ?" regretfully left unanswered, this is because those answers belong to the further and final stage of our journey, which not merely the necessities of space and the compulsions of time bid us reserve for a later volume, but other reasons which are more important still. Meanwhile it is essential to study well this basis of mentalism, because upon it shall later be reared a superstructure of stupendous but reasoned revelation.

The foolish who cling to what is personal when all the pangs of a suffering epoch teach the futility of doing so will be dismayed at the apparent blankness of these teachings and they may turn away with a shiver. But the intelligent, who have learnt much, thought deeply and suffered long, will be ready to accept it, blankness and all. For they will understand that in so doing they are accepting truth after lies, peace after pain, sight after blindness and reality after illusion. If later they pursue it to its farthest end and gain the fullest realization, thereafter they shall beat out the measure of their days in an interior harmony that shall be more holy and more blessed than any ritual of religion could ever be, more serene than any yogic experience is likely to be.

Thus far we may not have outpaced, except in certain slight hints, the foremost Western cultural thought. If those who have pursued technical courses in philosophy find some of these tenets familiar, their indulgence is craved and they are asked to remember that these pages are written primarily for anyone who cares for truth, whether he has some academic acquaintance with philosophy or none at all. Ramifications of this doctrine are already known to the West under the technical term of "idealism". Nevertheless it must be pointed out that this is a generic term covering contradictory tenets. Whoever studies in their totality the absolute idealism of Hegel, the subjective idealism of Berkeley, the objective idealism of Kant and the nihilistic idealism of Hume, for instance, will depart bewildered and confused. For it will be like studying religion, a word which may mean the gibberings of Central African Negroes around a grotesque wooden figure or the quiet still meditations of Quaker Christians. Nobody seems to know the truth about idealism or the falsity of it. There are idealists who accept God and idealists who reject God just as there are idealists who uphold the existence of matter and idealists who deny it. In any case beyond idealism all reflection shades down to twilight and then darkness, for even the proponents of idealism perceive nothing but mystery beyond it. Every step forward into that mystery that they venture to take causes them to lose their way in guesswork and speculation. Only the hidden Indian teaching has bravely and boldly explored and explored successfully the lands which stretch from idealism all the way to final truth.

Bishop Berkeley had the quaint notion that those whom he ignorantly termed idolators might be persuaded to relinquish their worship of the sun could they but learn that it is nothing more than their idea. It never dawned on his pious mind that the God whom he posited in a lengthy argument, which incidentally is full of fallacies, as having put the ideas of the sun and of all other external objects into the minds of men, was only an idea also. For this personal and providential God was an imagined one who who did not exist independently of Berkeley's thinking. But there is neither the time nor place to enter into academic argument here. This book is not a treatise on metaphysics ; it represents a formal and final testament of truth.

However, it may be advisable to explain to those who fear that the hidden teaching necessarily leads to atheism that the term "God" is not a term to our taste because it means all things to all men. But descending to an unphilosophic level it may be affirmed that we shall find God at the end of this quest, but it shall be God as He really is. It shall be neither the glorified man of religion nor the attenuated gas of metaphysics. Yet it shall still be the God whom men rightly but remotely revere in oriental temples and occidental churches, in sunsplashed mosques and grey brick chapels, but whom they tread underfoot and try to torture with their ignorant hatreds and intolerant persecutions of other men. We shall find the God whose caricatured image scornful rationalists or bitter atheists rightly reject and against whose cruelty they justly rebel, but whom they wrongly deny, for He is none other than their own ultimate self. We shall find the God whom lean ascetics seek but do not find in gloomy caves and starved bodies and upon whom satiated sensualists shut the door in night clubs and jazz halls, yet who paradoxically dwells in both cave and club unseen, unnoticed and unknown. We shall find that God whom meditating mystics and trance-wrapped yogis prematurely grope for within their hearts : God's aura of peaceful light is all they touch, for the flame would shrivel their ecstasy-seeking ego in an instant of time ; but once they have obeyed the angel whose sword shall sooner or later drive them back to the world they would forsake, and learnt what this thing is that surrounds them, search into the self will soon yield its final secret for them, as ancient Indian sages have pointed out. All these men who have vainly yet unconsciously tried to displace reality and who have set up for worship a God of their own imagination, a mere idol of their own making, philosophy will lead to the true God, whom they shall henceforth worship in full awareness of what they are doing. Finally, we shall find that elusive world-essence now unknown to scientists and which they think to be some kind of energy.

We may now begin to grasp why the ultimate path was always taught in secret. The books and texts were kept in the possession of the teacher, to be revealed and expounded only when candidates had travelled through the other paths. It would have been unwise to teach the general public. Men cannot bear to learn the truth about the real nature of this world, and so they flee from its first glimpses towards the immediate comfort of illusory existence. For the notion that there is a material world confronting them and existing outside them is instantaneous, immediate and irresistible. It is not something which they arrive at by any laborious process of logical reasoning from something else : it is a self-evident overpowering intuitive perception which seems undeniable and which apparently does not depend on any worked-out case which is liable to be overthrown. Only a continuous series of clever questions spread over a long-drawn course of personal instruction could ever show the ordinary unreflective man that his materialistic realism is foundationless and that the philosopher's thought-out mentalism is based on solid rock-like fact,

The great fear that descends on anyone when he learns that matter and space and time do not exist apart from man himself is unjustified. For this non-existence does not deprive him of the *sensations* of matter and space and time. Is it not enough to see an apparently objective world extended in space and to watch its events extend in time and to feel its solidity ? Mentalism does not rob him of these sensations which he experiences ; it merely explains them. What difference does it really make to give up his illusions about them ? Why should he demand anything more than truth itself ? For philosophy must stick to facts ; sensation is a fact, but matter, time and space are proven suppositions. Here philosophy is far more rigorous than science. There is no tangible difference in his practical life and only a rectification of wrong notions in his mental life. Chocolate will taste just as sweet and just as delicious when he knows it to be a cluster of sensations as when he erroneously believed it to be a material substance, whilst the engines of his car will purr away as noisily as before. He will lose none of the things he cherishes, none even of the joys of life, only he will understand them correctly. For the streets, the houses and the people around present precisely the same aspect to the sage as they do to the ignorant man. The former, however, is enlightened by reflection and thus knows that these varied forms are all mental ; he knows too that mind is the stuff of all these productions, whereas the latter is quite blinded by unreflection to this truth. Mentalism staggers the simple-minded with its apparent profundity and complexity, yet once well enquired into and therefore well understood nothing could seem more simple or more apparent.

Thus the ancient Indian sages wrote down a teaching which foreshadowed some findings of the best modern Western scientists. The same science which gave us the bleak hopelessness of mortality and materialism last century will give us the bright hopefulness of mentalism in this one. Truth will be established on a basis of proven demonstration ; it will need nothing mystical to support it. The time is riper for the world to come to this age-old truth, but it must come to it in terms of twentieth-century scientific concepts. This doctrine has remained insulated from the world long enough. Nor will it suffice merely to translate its teaching into Western tongues ; it must also be constructively interpreted.

We live in an age of revolution. Kings, Governments and Constitutions have been hurled from their pedestals and familiar scientific concepts have been hurled out of laboratory windows. But the greatest revolution of all in the world of twentieth-century knowledge is that which the front rank of scientific investigators

THE DOWNFALL OF MATERIALISM

is effecting before our eyes. This fundamental turnover in the outlook of edueated men will consist of nothing less than bringing the whole world into the circle of thought and thus converting matter into idea. Just as the study of radio-active substance opened a new horizon for science when its old lines of research seemed to be at an end, so this study of the relation between the world and man, between matter and mind, will before long end in the discovery that the entire panorama of the world from telescope-seen star to microscope-seen cell which confronts our eyes is in reality a mental construction. It will destroy materialism root and branch, and will throw wide open the gates which lead to the infinite reality whose knowledge is *Truth*.

EPILOGUE

THE PHILOSOPHIC LIFE

THAT this teaching has been forgotten, neglected and misunderstood for so many centuries in sleepy monasteries or remote mountain-caves is not its own fault. It is the fault of men. Those who could understand its immensely practical bearing, its vital immediacy, were necessarily few in number. Such understanding could be got only by arduous intellectual efforts beyond the capacity of most men. But generally we get what we pay for. The one teaching which could guide mankind to the right solution of difficult problems is to be valued accordingly. It is a costly genuine diamond, not a cheap bit of glass.

We live in a practical world. Men may theorize as they like, but they have to act, to work and to deal with other men. Therefore the question must come up, will this teaching make any difference to the way in which people live on earth?

For it is a widespread belief that philosophy is aristocratically cut off from the pressing concerns of everyday existence, that the philosopher—if not a fool or even a lunatic!—is a hopelessly impractical man occupied merely with manufactured problems and that the pursuit of truth is a pastime for those who have no burden of practical responsibilities, or for library-crawling bookworms or for armchair dreamers who wish to escape action. It is widely believed that the philosopher makes an unnatural dichotomy of attitude between the inner life of thought and the outer life of action.

This may be true of that merely metaphysical speculation or theological web-spinning which passes itself off for philosophy, but it is not true of genuine philosophy, such as some of the best ancient Greek citizens followed, whilst utterly untrue of the hidden Indian philosophy. If so-called philosophy has lost touch with life this is because it has lost itself in a maze of long technical words or made such a fetish of clever logical subtleties which delight nobody but dialecticians that it has forgotten its foundation—the facts of human experience. Perhaps in no other study are men so carried away by sounding words and polysyllabic names which disguise

EPILOGUE : THE PHILOSOPHIC LIFE

error and crystallize fallacy, and in no other study has such a forbidding terminology arisen with so little necessity. A philosopher who cannot say what he has to say with a minimum of long, difficult and unfamiliar words, but must get himself involved into using a maximum, is not only likely to get himself involved in hidden untruths but is sure to keep not a few sincere aspirants outside the portals of philosophy itself.

If such philosophy has vanished from everyday ken into a verbal vacuum or fallen from high regard into contempt, then the so-called philosophers themselves are to blame. They write their thoughts down in a technical jargon which hides meaning and harms clearness, and which builds forbidding bulwarks of unintelligibility around the grandest truths. They construct systems of reflection about the world and about life which do not take into account the primary facts of the world and life. They ignore the tremendous asset of science and find themselves left to play with their own fancies. They start their reflections with the arbitrary fancies of other philosophers instead of starting with the verified facts of the world that confronts them. In this they are curiously like unto mystics. They imitate each other and get caught in the literary history of philosophy instead of actively creating fresh philosophy.

What is the business of philosophy? What definite end has it in view? What is the proper vocation of a philosopher? What are the practical lessons of philosophy? The briefest answer to all these questions is: genuine philosophy shows men how to live! If it could not do that, if it could not serve practical ends, it would not be worth having. It does not toil through the profoundest strata of thought merely to become alienated from the suffering world. It does not end in abstraction, but in action. The fruits of philosophy can be gathered only on this hard earth, not in some remote metaphysical empyrean. It embraces an individual and social labour which must visibly contribute to the welfare of our race and make itself felt in living history, or else it is not true philosophy. It must justify its existence by what it can do, not only by what it can imagine. It must show men not only what they really are but also what course of life should be the object of their behaviour.

The fact is that philosophy does make a revolutionary difference when applied to human existence, expressed in human deeds and inlaid in human intercourse. It is the deep-held desire of those who are the living custodians of the hidden teaching in our tormented age that the artificial divorce which exists between philosophy and practical life should come to an end. It is their heartfelt wish to bring men to realize that philosophy is intimately linked with life and is useful as a guide, an inspirer and a judge. It will be one of the missions of the subsequent volume to challenge the validity of the common criticism that philosophers can deal with concerns that are too remote from everyday life to be of use to anyone. It will there be shown that the very contrary is the correct case so far as the hidden teaching is concerned, *for its final teachings affect every moment of a man's earthly existence.*

For philosophy is not a pale fiction fit for dreamers only, it is primarily for men living in the world of action. It is interested in the full circle of existence, not merely in a segment. The moment we begin to reflect upon life, the moment we begin to consider the lessons of experience, the moment we search for meaning or explanation of the world in which we find ourselves, that moment we become a temporary philosopher. Where the specialist philosopher goes farther than us is when he demands that *all* experience be taken as the material for reflection, that the experience of all existence be meditated upon. But the critic will ask how can that be when history has not written its last word, experience is continually increasing and life never comes to an end? The answer is that just as a circle may be indefinitely enlarged without ceasing to be a circle, so experience may be continually expanded without the *truth* of experience ceasing to be the truth. And that truth is the philosopher's final target. This is why he must work methodically, why he must first establish the true meaning of universal experience and then seek to translate this meaning in terms of concrete activities. His visible actions must first be justified by his invisible reflections.

The world has no use for a doctrine which treats the common life of men as something alien and apart. The world is right. The philosopher does not know any point in this wide universe where truth should be kicked out. Hence he finds its principles are everywhere applicable and everywhere present and that whoever neglects them does so at his own peril. Philosophy is what is workable; it is put in practice, or it is only half philosophy. It believes in inspired action and illumined service. Its worth is not known to dilettanti who play with academic theories for a day and then forget them. It can be carried into action: it can be made of worth to the toilers, the sufferers and the executives of society: it shows everybody how he ought to live amid the particular circumstances in which he finds himself. For every deed of the genuine philosopher is the direct

EPILOGUE: THE PHILOSOPHIC LIFE

descendant of those ideas of truth for which he has struggled so arduously. He learns the right rules of the game of life and sets out to obey them.

Therefore philosophy is equally for the man doomed to hang from the ghastly gallows as for the man who dooms him from the grand judicial bench. It reveals a truth whose application to daily living arrests fear, removes doubt, supplies inspiration and kindles mental strength. Be we workers with hoe and plough, or surgeons with scalpel and lancet, or directors with glass-topped desks, we all meet with critical moments when we need the sure guidance, the firm pointing finger which philosophy alone can offer. For it alone is concerned with the rigid truth of a situation rather than with emotional distortions of it or egoistic veilings of it. Therefore the value of philosophy is the value of its practical contribution to day-to-day living. The connection between the office, the factory, the farm, the theatre and the home with philosophy is direct and plain. Philosophy is the guide of all life. Its final worth is to tell us how to live, and how to meet and master our difficulties and temptations.

The study of the hidden teaching demands that one pass through a severe intellectual discipline which may extend over some years, according to the reasoning capacity of the student. It certainly cannot be got in a hurry. Once this knowledge is won, however, it proves its practical worth by standing every test. The wisdom it confers, the ethic it upholds, the strength it gives, the tranquillity it sheds and the intellectual capacity it develops—all combine to make the student who completes his course, who passes from nescience to knowledge, a better man. If he turns to politics he will render superior service, and not inferior. If he takes up manufacturing his products will be honest and meritorious. The man trained in the labours and pains of philosophical reflection will tackle each practical problem as it arises with clear insight, and only he—other things being equal—will be the most likely to give correct judgment upon a matter.

All our ideas are dumb until we try to put them into practice. They then gain voice and people our message. The philosophic life is not a mere fragment to be lived out in a dusty library; it is a continuous experience whether it be lived in a home, a business, a senate chamber or a farm. And a man will be a better citizen because he is a philosopher just as he will be a better philosopher because he is a citizen. If his studies separate him *outwardly* from the general life of his community, then whatever else they may be they are certainly not philosophic studies. For the philosopher has got to put the content of continuous disinterested action into the fine or clever phrases that he writes or utters, or he will merely be a half-philosopher. Only when the tenets of philosophy have entered his blood-stream can he become a real philosopher.

Truth is a dynamic, not a narcotic.

The philosopher will always be found a rational, sensible, practical and balanced man in his everyday dealings. He well understands that the two wings of a bird must move to keep it in balanced flight, and that the two sides of man—thought and action—must operate to keep him in balanced existence. But his balance is wider than that. Amid the restless hustle of modern society he keeps inwardly calm and undisturbed. And his peace is so hard-forged as to endure when he passes out of the quiet philosophical sanctus into the busy street.

The philosophic discipline trains the mind and through the mind all the acts of a man. Thoughts that are constantly and intensely held tend sooner or later to speak in deeds. It is because men have not realized the power of concentrated thinking to help or hurt others that they have brought forth the hideous age in which we are born. Without joining those who harm a good cause by poor logic and worse philosophy when they deny the power of external surroundings, we may yet say that the general and habitual line of thinking tends ultimately and largely to reproduce itself in the features of one's environment. The mind has both attractive and repulsive properties. It attracts other minds and material conditions of a like nature; it repels those of jarring kind. This activity constantly goes on in man's subconscious self; he need not always be aware of it to make it effective. This silent influence never ceases operating. Only when we see it strikingly made evident in the lives of good or evil geniuses do we dimly realize what potency lies hid in controlled and concentrated thought.

It is the invisible inner man of thought and feeling who dictates man's daily actions and reactions, who faces him when he is alone and who lives a secret existence which imperils or protects his whole external existence. The thoughts which most often occupy his mind and the moods which most frequently fill his heart are his invisible rulers and, in comparison with the physical body, constitute his more important self. The younger races of the West look first to the outward stature of a man when they wish to measure him, whereas the older people of Asia knew thousands of years ago that his greatest power for weal or woe lay hidden in his mind. The ancient

EPILOGUE: THE PHILOSOPHIC LIFE

sages who sat with crossed legs and benignant faces in the Himalayan forests taught their reverent pupils this vital truth. Thus this teaching amply justifies itself on the most utilitarian grounds.

On Conduct and Art. Everything or everyone is in relation to something or someone else. Nothing or nobody stands alone. The life of every creature is interwoven with the lives of others: its fancied separateness of vaunted independence is a delusion. Humanity especially is interrelated. Therefore the philosopher is not merely a philosopher; he is also a member of society. He cannot escape being so, cannot completely disentangle himself. Even if he retreat to a cave he will need another to attend him or a dog to accompany him or a cow to give him milk, and lo! there is a society of two already. How he conducts himself in this society will depend on ethical principles which will remain precisely the same even if it were a society of two millions and not merely of two. Does philosophy, then, contribute anything to ethics, anything to values, anything to point out the right path of duty?

The answer is that philosophy is the only thing in the world which makes such contributions to the fullest extent needed by human existence. Once we come into consciousness of this great truth all the most important questions that trouble mankind take on a totally new appearance. Then, and then only, can satisfactory solutions of ancient and perplexing problems be got at. The very atmosphere in which these answers have to be worked out will be wholly changed. We shall be compelled, whether we like it or not, to force the old queries into new shapes, because the standard of reference will now be far other than it hitherto was. Here the student of philosophy finds the actual value of his studies and gets his reward in the awakened insight which shows him how to act rightly, wisely and well. The philosopher could never be a failure in life, however much he might fail in fortune.

Philosophy is meant not only to interpret the world, but also to better it, for it pursues ideas through to their practical conclusion. Social or personal idealism must be related to an attainable goal, otherwise it will be harmful. Philosophy provides drifting men with a compass. Hence it is as much for those who are conscious of the absence of any principle of ethical guidance in their lives as for those who seek pure knowledge. They will find philosophy of the greatest help in reaching right decisions at the demands of practical life. What, in the whole range of human culture, could be more useful than this?

There is no minute of the day when we are not engaged in doing something or thinking something and this process goes on all through our waking life; it is an endless and incessant activity. The problem whether what we are doing or what we are thinking is right or wrong, best or worst, that is to say the problem of ethics, is one of the most fundamental and most important we can raise.

There are two questions which face every man every day. They are: What is the right way for me to act? And what is the right thing for me to seek? Several other problems are involved in and hinge on this single problem of what constitutes the duty of man; some of them are: (*a*) What is my highest duty as against my immediate duty, the intrinsic as against the instrumental? (*b*) What is the justification for accepting the notion that there is such a thing as duty and that it is not the creation of human fancy? (*c*) What is the standard of measurement which permits me to grade duties on any scale?

All these, however, are philosophical problems. This indicates that pure philosophy does have the most practical bearing on life. And whatever a man sets up as right or wrong is the conscious or unconscious reflection of his conscious or unconscious philosophy of life. His general view of the universe, that is to say his conscious or unconscious philosophic view, supplies him with a standard to mark out or to test either duty or desire. When it applies itself to conduct, philosophy is less concerned with laying down particular rules than with laying down foundational principles. It cares less for little legal clauses and more for large ways of living.

Human conduct is ordinarily governed by desire. All desires, emotions, passions, energies, longings, sympathies and antipathies begin to regulate themselves when we understand them better, when we understand ourselves better and when we understand the world better. The value of this study in restoring emotional balance may be expressed in such physical terms as these. It normalizes blood-pressure and beneficially regulates glandular secretions. Still more, it harmoniously integrates the neurophysiological functions. It disciplines passions, overcomes bad habits and eliminates nervous fears. It tranquillizes the heart, puts reason into the head and purpose into life. It is of special value to kings, rulers, presidents, ministers of state and governmental chiefs, and to a lesser extent to professional men such as physicians, lawyers, educators and business executives. The benefits received affect both the personal and professional sides of life.

It is a misapprehension, however, to imagine that the philosopher must be an acolyte of asceticism, a votary of life-negation, utterly remote from human interests and human enjoyments. There is no room in true philosophy for the incurable antinomies of the ascetic-hedonistic conflict. The narrow ascetic denies life and views the world as a treacherous trap. But the philosopher finds it a useful school wherein he learns much and lives understandingly. Experience does not merely offer him theoretical food for thought but also practical training for wisdom.

Nevertheless Cupid and cupidity need to be well-reined. Every sensible man who wants to fortify his life is indeed something of an ascetic. The power that self-restraint give his mental, ethical and physical character helps him in every way. And when such a man betakes himself to the quest of truth he will need even more of this inner strength. The flabby weakling who yields to every impulse does not know the delight of being independent, the satisfaction of being in bondage to nothing. But such sane restraint is never to be confused with the unhealthy and unnatural total rejection of everything human. We are here to live and not to run away from life. We must find a way of existence that is reasonable and balanced, not fanatical and remote. Anything overdone is a mistake; a good overdone generates a fresh evil, a virtue overdone creates a new vice.

The philosopher is not afraid of any facet of life. He makes the contradictory the complementary! That is why he does not need to run away from the world like the ascetic. Whatever running away he deems necessary is done secretly inside his heart and is not publicly advertised by donning the coloured robe of the monk. No amount of world-desertion will lead to wisdom in his view because he knows that he was put into the world to learn its lessons. Nevertheless he is at one with the monk in wishing to be free from enslavement to desires and in seeking dominion over his own emotions. Beyond this he cannot travel with the fanatical ascetic. His chief effort being directed towards the control of thought and disciplining of the intellect, its success will reward him with the ability to pass through comfort and discomfort with sufficient detachment to keep his mind unruffled and provide him with the power to work amid the intense hustle of any environment without any loss of inner calmness.

Ascetic life is a good and necessary beginning, but when it congeals into rigidity, frigidity and a profession it is an imperfect end. The wise man is not afraid to endorse the generous and excellent lines of Terence: "I am a man; nothing pertaining to humanity is alien to me." He will move untempted amid the fretting tide of a city's crowds, where he is needed, whilst the fearful hide in caves; he will keep his serenity amid labour or leisure, for his ascetic abandonment is hidden deep within the mind. He will not need to crush out human affection in order to crush out human egoism. He will not need to ignore the treasures of art or fail to respond to the charms of Nature in order to maintain emotional equipoise.

But the problems of action and conduct do not exhaust man's concern with society and the world. He seeks also to beautify both. Thus art is born. Philosophy has also to find a place for it, and to consider its contribution to the whole. Art indeed is fuel for the philosophic enterprise. Why is it that man feels drawn to music, painting, architecture, poetry, drama and the other arts? What is this beauty which lures man on through his lesser loves? Is the culture of artistic sensitivity a stage on his quest? Those who imagine that philosophy isolates man from all that is warm and beautiful in life are mistaken. The fragrance of white jasmine gives him pleasure as much as it does to others, the ravishing beauty of the sun dying in a great ball of fire does not leave him unaffected, and the tender voice of a violin is not meaningless to him. He is different from other men in this, that he keeps always moored to the higher viewpoint which places these experiences where they belong and does not permit them to overwhelm him utterly.

The work of the genuine artist is primarily an imaginative one. He is entitled to call himself a creative artist to the extent that he can carry out an original work in his first available medium—*imagination*. If he can work only in his second medium, that is to say merely copy photographically in paint, wood, stone, word or sound what others have thus created, we call him a talented artist, but not a creative one. Indeed, competent critics have gone so far as to separate both classes, refusing to dignify the unimaginative with the title of artist and calling him but a workman. There are usually authentic indications in the works of genius to show the profundity of its imaginative power.

Yet the imagination itself is nothing else in the end than a tissue of mental pictures, i.e. of *thoughts*. Mozart, who was a genius even as a child, described the process of his experience of musical composition in a brief but illuminative sentence: "All the finding and making only goes on in me as in a very vivid dream." In this self-created world the artist must make himself at home so completely and so absorbedly that he will resent the coming of meal-times as a disturbance and the coming of friends as an intrusion. This is why Balzac locked himself in a room literally night and day. When he wrote those wonderful novels he was as much in a state of semi-trance as any Indian yogi. That Balzac well understood the mystical character of his art is attested by his own utterance : "Today the writer has replaced the priest ... he consoles, condemns, prophesies. His voice does not resound in the nave of a cathedral, it spreads thunderously from one end of the world to the other." For the production of genuine art is nothing less than the practise of genuine yoga. The artist is on a perfect level with the mystic, only he seeks memorable beauty where the latter seeks memorable peace.

Inspiration simply means that the artist is so carried away by a series of *ideas* that for the time being their reality dominates him completely. For him thought has temporarily become what is felt to be the Real. In this respect the artist is a veritable mystic. Both come to acquire a fervent faith in the reality of their mental constructions. Both arrive unconsciously at the truth of mentalism through the same avenue—intense concentrated self-absorption in a single dominating idea or a single series of thoughts. Both are in the end conscious, semi-conscious or unconscious believers in mentalism. The painter Whistler saw great beauty on the mist-covered river Thames shrouding its dirty barges and rat-ridden wharves and raucous steam-tugs ; this really means that the beauty he saw was contained within his own mind. The artist who would attain to the front rank of creative genius must be a mentalist. He must be a believer in this subtle and refined doctrine which is fit only for subtle and refined temperaments. Were he otherwise he would be false to his own experience and blind to its implicit meaning.

We hear often of the enthralling ecstasy wherein he creates his work and of the moody melancholy which succeeds it later. He walks on air for a while but then treads the earth with leaden feet, regretting that he did not know how to hold his high mood, how to retain it. Let us not envy him. For he pays heavily for his ecstasies ; he pays for them in the coin of gloomy moods and black depressions.

There are two explanations, two causes to account for this fact to be found in all the biographies of genius : the first is that during creative work he forgets himself, loses his *I* utterly, because it is only by perfect concentration that he can accomplish perfect work. If he cannot forget his ego, then he cannot concentrate perfectly, hence cannot become a perfect artist. Or else he unites in feeling with his prospective audience, i.e. merges his individuality in *others*, and thus loses his ego for another cause. The second is that the brief pleasure he derives from those precious minutes when he is absorbed in his imagination is the same that his audience will later derive when beholding or experiencing the finished product of his work. But if this second fact means anything at all it means that at the precise moment of inspired production by the artist or of engrossed reception by the audience, both are or should be utterly immersed in the world of imaginations. At this sacred time they find thought to be all-important and as real as they had heretofore regarded the material world of their own belief. Moreover, in the artist's yearning to find perfect expression of his ideas in paint or on paper he is unconsciously seeking to break down the fancied barriers between thought and thing, between mind and matter. He is, in short, striving to construct a second idea which shall be a perfect copy of his first one.

We may now understand why the artist suffers when his creative mood passes away. For it is then that, psychologically, he lapses back into the ordinary egoistic state and the ordinary unconcentrated state. The contrast is as striking as that between black and white and affects his emotions accordingly. These are some elementary lessons which philosophy teaches in regard to art.

The Doctrine of Karma. Because of its neglect of the primal fact of mind being the ground that supports all else in human life, the scientific culture of the last century found itself in the position of an ethically-dangerous materialism which made man into a mechanically-manipulated biped. Although the front-rank scientists themselves are now emerging from this materialistic phase, the onslaughts of their predecessors have seriously damaged the fabric of religious authority and greatly weakened the strength of religious influence. The popularization of science in the West has made the masses less amenable to the checks and disciplines offered by religion. Moreover, the aftermath of all wars has often been a decay of religious faith and an indifference to codes of morality.

We are therefore approaching a period when the chief social justification of religion—its power to restrain the conduct of the masses within certain limits—will be definitely impaired. The example of Russia's violent rejection of organized religion following war and revolution is a phenomenon to be calmly and dispassionately considered. It is not to be enthusiastically admired by the irresponsible and unbalanced, nor to be violently denounced by the reactionary and unteachable. For we face a period when the decay of moral sanctions, the loosening of social ties, the lowering of individual standards and the general inclination to unsettle and disturb society combine to constitute an ethically dangerous

EPILOGUE: THE PHILOSOPHIC LIFE

situation. Those who care for human welfare should understand that to apply antiquated sanctions which have lost much of their force will not meet this situation satisfactorily. Religion will be unable to avoid the straight issue and will do better for humanity and for itself if it faces the problem with courage and common sense. Its contribution is always needed, but it ought to be a right one.

Every institutional orthodox religion can save itself from the crisis whose preliminary rumbles herald its approach, and even effectively expand its influence, if, first, it will have the courage to cast bad custom behind if need be and find a better life for man, and if, second, it will live up to its ethical highest and not down to its ethical lowest; and if, third, it will abandon the mental slavery of childish dogma and become intellectually progressive. It should add new beliefs, or alter and adapt its system wherever needed. It must progress parallel with the intellect of man, be on the move with our moving age, and not remain an inflexibly obstinate creed. Some of the more sensible ecclesiastics have already yielded their old crude ideas in surrender to advancing knowledge, but many more are merely parcels of timid conventional superstitions, neatly tied together and adorned with hat, suit and shoes. The Very Reverend Inge has not hesitated to advocate bold rational changes in Christian doctrine, while in Africa and Asia, Muhammedan, Hindu and Buddhist divines have done the same to a lesser extent. But until the highest dignitaries boldly promulgate more refined and rational conceptions, a more tenable faith, until they value living ethics above dying history, present trends will injure their obsolete dogmas and, what is worse, injure the moral supports of their devotees.

The illusions of their flocks may be excused, but the ignorance or obstinacy of the clerics themselves is unpardonable. The world is in pregnancy with new thoughts. The labour pains of commencing childbirth affect it and the cries that come from it are to be expected. The whole universe is subject to the law of change; all history is but a tale of continuous adaptation to environment; and when the leaders of a religion submit to this law voluntarily their reward will be great in every way. Those who submit at the proper time will be practising wisdom; those who resist at the wrong time will be practising foolishness. In an age of advancing education such as ours religion must voluntarily clear its labyrinth of traditional rubbish and reorganize itself on a more intellectual basis. Mystery and tradition have made the organized religions powerful institutions; science and the spirit of enquiry are unmaking them. Therefore the last word of counsel from every well-wisher who is not dead to the time-spirit nor blind to the world crisis is that religion must grow up with the growing mind of man. The position of an unprogressive religious institution which rigidly rules its adherents, binds them for ever to believe in a kindergarten creed, and discourages interest in contemporary knowledge is not different from that of a schoolmaster who, whilst welcoming new pupils to his class, prevents the old ones from passing up to the next higher class and would for ever detain them under him in the same class. It ought never to forget its higher purpose, which is to fit the more advanced among its flock for the next higher degree. It will then cease to resent the individualism of mystics but rather delight in their progress. In this way it will best help others and most help itself. Finally there is plenty of hope for religion for the reason that it *is* needed, if only it will arouse new energies and bravely reconstruct itself.

But even if this unlikely event occurs the ethically-dangerous post-war situation will not be fully solved thereby. Many people will still be irrevocably lost to religion, however much it adapt itself. For when ignorant men think that religion is a delusion they often leap to the false conclusion that morality is a myth. History shows that it has proved disastrous in times of great social change to identify ethics with any special religious creed. When the creed goes the ethics entangled with it goes too.

Whoever cares for the well-being of the race cannot look unconcerned upon this dark prospect. What is to be done? The remedy lies in remembering that those who have caught the modern attitude are not going to yield to ethical exhortations unless these are scientifically based. But is such a basis obtainable? Is a rational ethics available for them which will uplift and not degrade them and which will supply a sensible motive for well-doing? The answer is that a most reasonable doctrine has long existed in Asia. Unfortunately it has not kept its pristine purity, but degenerative time has mixed much irrelevant superstition with it, whilst imaginative man has tangled much religious dogma with what is the fundamentally sane and scientific basis of a sound ethical code. The Indian name of this venerable doctrine is *karma*.

The essence of this doctrine is, first, psychological *reaction*, i.e. that habitual thoughts form themselves into tendencies and thus affect our own character; this in turn expresses itself sooner or later in deeds; these, again, not only affect other persons, but also, by a mysterious principle of reaction, ourselves. The working out of this principle implies, second, physical *rebirth*, i.e. the persistence of

EPILOGUE: THE PHILOSOPHIC LIFE 329

thought in the sphere of the Unconscious Mind, as well as sooner or later the reappearance of more or less the same "character" or personality upon this earth. Karma creates the need for readjustments and inevitably leads to rebirth, to an outlet for the dynamic factors which have been set in motion. The consequence of this principle is personal *retribution*, i.e. that acts whereby we injure others are inevitably reflected back to ourselves and thus injure us, whereas acts whereby we benefit others eventually benefit us too.

This doctrine, like that of mentalism, was discovered by the astute Indian sages through the revealing power of intense concentration of mind, used to sharpen an intelligence devoted to the perplexing problems of the inequality in character and circumstance of human beings. In this manner they came to discern a certain rhythm at work beneath the incessant flux of man's fortunes.

There is no such thing as a natural law in the sense of an arbitrary or authoritative commandment issued by some supreme being. Man makes a law of Nature in his thought in order to describe how a particular part of Nature behaves. Karma is a perfectly scientific law. It dovetails smoothly into three great scientific discoveries whose verification and proclamation during the nineteenth century stirred thoughtful men with the tremendous possibilities thus opened up as well as into two others which have not been so sensational. The first two were: (*a*) the evolution of animal and human forms, (*b*) the conservation or indestructibility of energy. The former brought together all the myriad kinds of species in Nature into some kind of scheme of progressive improvement, giving at least a cold justification for the agonizing immolation of the individual upon the altar of its class, whilst the latter brought together the different manifestations of heat, work and chemical power into a simple unified system. Although more modern views have largely modified the original explanation of the method of these processes, and although the "how" of both still remains much of a mystery, nevertheless their basic principles remain untouched. The evolutionary character of Nature's larger changes and the persistence of force still fit better to the known facts of the general universal movement than any other hypotheses.

A third scientific teaching which requires mention is that of heredity. The patterns of the fleshly body are inherited ones.

If we go farther back in time we shall find a fourth significant scientific teaching. Newton's third law of motion reveals that for every action there is a reaction, which is equal and opposite.

But we are not yet done. For there is a fifth discovery of science

—which cannot be overlooked—that all life is ultimately unitary. The universe constitutes a single entity. All the sciences touch each other at some point and none can stand alone. The unity of the universe is the fundamental law of its being.

When we bring all these scientific principles into harmony with karma we find how they analogically support it. The law of evolution reveals that life is a continuation of all that has gone before. We are but links in a long series. We begin as primal molecule and end as complex man. We press towards an unseen goal because we feel the need of completion. We have already travelled a long journey from the planetary mud up to our present-day self. But we shall have to travel still farther. For the end of this journey will be the sublime discovery that man is no mere cypher in a statistical census, no mere glorified ape of the jungle, but an unconscious partaker of a blessed and benign Reality.

The principle of conservation of energy expresses the fact that no energy can be destroyed in the process of its transformations. In the same way human thoughts and deeds are nothing else than energies which are not destroyed but which reappear in the form of their effects upon others and upon ourselves. They are seeds which sprout eventually into time-and-space manifestation.

Science admits in the doctrine of heredity that every body has had some kind of existence before birth. Similarly, the mind must have had some kind of existence before birth. The mental characteristics are transmitted ones and can have been derived from a former earthly existence alone.

Newton's law of equal return reappears in the world of ethics, where the same sequence holds true. Whatever we do unto others is returned to us in some way and at some time. Life pays us back in our own coin. Our misdeeds find us out one day. The good deeds we do foreshadow the good fortune we shall eventually reap. We get what we give.

The unitary character of the whole universe must also include man's life. Any violation of this law of his own being must, by reaction, sooner or later bring its own punishment in the shape of suffering or discord. Any fulfilment of it must equally bring harmony and happiness. Moreover, this same individual unity indicates that rebirth is inevitable because of the continuity of the world process, because each appearance of life must emerge out of what has somewhere gone before, because the present cannot be sundered from the past.

Thus human life becomes, broadly speaking, an education of

EPILOGUE: THE PHILOSOPHIC LIFE

mind, character and capacity. This education develops over long periods of time in a series of related physical re-embodiments, each of which provides appropriate lessons through the experiences and reflections therein generated. All living is learning. All incarnation is education. To take a new body is to take a new seat in life's school. The growth of mind is the true biography of man. All history becomes allegory. Just as a child's understanding of the three R's—reading, writing and 'rithmetic—constitutes its elementary education in school, so an adult's understanding of these three R's of Reaction, Rebirth and Retribution constitutes his elementary education in the larger school of life. Mentally, the struggles of existence tend first to unfold and then to sharpen reason; ethically, the notion that whatever seeds we sow we shall reap an appropriate harvest becomes slowly borne in upon us; technically, ability rises from untrained mediocrity and gradually gets concentrated along special lines until it achieves its culmination in facile unlaboured genius.

The law of karma is the only one which will reasonably account for those blights on existence which must otherwise be accepted as the awful products of mere chance or as the unjust fiats of an arbitrary Deity. Without karma we must give up these problems in despair as being pieces in a perfectly insoluble puzzle. The babe helplessly born blind, the child brought up in a squalid filthy slum, the fame-hungry young man who struggles in vain to find a fit outlet for unrecognized ability, the middle-aged woman whose whole life has been wrecked by an unfortunate marriage, the elderly family breadwinner who falls fatally under an automobile—these are the tragedies which make life seem either a hideous game of sheer luck or the unfortunate plaything of a cruel God. Karma, however, puts a more rational face upon these enigmas by turning them into the outcome of wrong acts done previously, either in the same existence or in an earlier fleshly embodiment. Thus it responds to a profound need of the human heart for more adequate justice in life.

An imperfect notion of this tenet is that which places the effect of present thoughts and deeds only in future births and remote incarnation. We must impress firmly upon our minds that the consequences of our actions may have to be reaped at any moment here in this birth; that the wrong or right behaviour of one incarnation may determine the misery or happiness of the same incarnation: and that there is no necessity to wait for lives yet to come before we can feel the benefits of virtue or pay for the pains caused to others. Karma covers *both* the present and future births.

Its reactions can come into operation on the very same day that an act is performed or the same year or the same birth without waiting for a future embodiment. The relation between an evil deed and its inevitable retributory consequences is a sure one, but the time when it manifests itself is obscure and must necessarily vary with each individual.

Nevertheless this doctrine does not imply that all our sufferings without exceptions are merited. For humanity is so interlinked that we cannot always escape the effects of the evil acts performed by others with whom we are thrown in contact even though the misfortune thereby wrought is not our due. But in that case we may rest assured that the compensatory working of karma will eventually bring into play some good fortune which would not otherwise have been ours.

Karma therefore does not doom us to complete fatalism. It is only a *part* of life. The element of freedom is likewise present. There is no absolute freedom in life, but then there is no absolute fatalism either. Karma makes us personally responsible for our thoughts and deeds. We cannot shift the blame for wrongdoing on to the shoulders of another, whether he be man or God.

We take up our old tendencies with each new birth in this frail tenement of flesh, renew great loves and grand friendships, face afresh the problem of old enmities, suffer or enjoy our proper deserts and drink from the cup of life's experience until we are satiated. But satiety forces reflection, and this in turn brings wisdom. When we have moved up and down the ladder from ragged beggar to bejewelled king we learn at last how to handle the contrasting situations of human existence correctly. When we have been tempted, tantalized and disillusioned, when we have burnt our fingers because of wrongdoing or been benefited by well-doing, we understand finally the best way to conduct ourselves in all dealings with others. We are all the products of our unseen past experience and our unremembered past thinking, i.e. of time, and are not to be blamed for being what we are: we cannot help that, but we are to blame for not trying to be better. Time is thus the supreme teacher. No mortal can give us the lessons it places before our eyes. It brings all the wealth of varied experience, it assuages errors into wisdom, pain into peace, disappointment into discipline and hatred into goodwill. Time will turn better pages for us than those in books, and speak more sagely than the lips of men. It teaches us to learn from our weaknesses, not to weep over them.

It is an error to put karma on a moral plane only. It also operates

EPILOGUE: THE PHILOSOPHIC LIFE

on the intellectual plane. Thus a good man's feebler intelligence pitted against an evil man's superior intelligence may bring the former loss and even suffering for a time, even though he is morally better. For he has to learn to build a balanced personality, and not merely a lop-sided one. Moreover, pious persons who suffer from an excess of sentimentality do not understand that charity only becomes a virtue when it is done at the right time to the right person, and that it is nothing less than a vice when it is misplaced or mistimed. Karma provides us with the assurance that no efforts are wasted. Whether in this birth or in a later we shall enjoy their just consequences. Where heredity fails to explain why a clever son should be born to foolish parents, karma steps in and smooths the problem. We inherit physical characteristics from our parents but mental characteristics from our previous personality on earth. This explains why there are children who are old for their age and adults who are children for their age. It puts order and justice where formerly chaos and cruelty alone reigned.

Those who reject karma reject what is patent all around them. Their own lives are unalterably predetermined to a certain extent, do what they will. The good or bad family into which they were born, the wealth or poverty they have inherited, the white or black skin they possess—all these are matters in which they have been powerless to choose and wherein they have been but the unconsulted recipients of the awards of karma. To a limited extent, therefore, but no more, karma forges a steel ring around every man.

Others who raise the ancient bogey that where there is no remembrance of past lives there can be no benefit from present pleasure or pain arising out of them overlook two points. The first is the very constitution of the mind itself, which presents the double faces of the Unconscious and the conscious to our gaze. The merest initiation into psychology is an initiation into this undoubted fact. How much of present experience has already disappeared into the storehouse of the Unconscious? The second point is that they cannot have the memory of one previous embodiment without having the memories of all the thousands which preceded it. But who could endure such an opening of the bound volumes of human experience for even a single day? Who could take in all that cinematograph-film of a myriad bestial horrors and a myriad primitive joys that are now no longer joys? The upshot of such an experience would be a complete lapse into madness. Rather should we be thankful to Nature for this gift of forgetfulness as we should be thankful to her for the gift of sleep. For if we had not received it we should be totally unable to concentrate upon the present life at all.

Karma properly understood never kills initiative but positively promotes it. What we do now will actively contribute to the making of our future, no matter what we have done in the forgotten or remembered past. Therefore there is always some degree of hope for everyone. We are simultaneously the hapless creatures of our past and the hopeful creators of our future. What men do not comprehend about fate is that although certain events of life are more or less predetermined by karma at birth, still they can sometimes be changed to some extent by changing character. For character is the seed, the root, of all fate. If we have to endure certain limitations imposed by destiny we have also got certain freedom to work within those limitations. It is the art of right living to reconcile both factors and adjust them sensibly.

Here it may be well to observe that the Indian teaching adds that the last thoughts of a dying man will conjoin with his general and subconscious tendencies to determine the characteristics which will take a foothold in his next embodiment. It would be well therefore if this were better known and more widely utilized. For thus we may more readily meet again those we love, thus we may mentally picture and obtain a particular field of desired service and thus the disciple ties himself more closely to his teacher.

There are times to fight fate and times to endure it. When the latter periods come it is wise to apply the Chinese technique of handling a cycle of misfortune as expounded in their ancient classic texts. This is based on the principle of adapting oneself to the cycle by conforming patiently and voluntarily to its restrictions and anticipating them in self-restraint. Just watch a juggler catch falling eggs on porcelain plates without breaking egg or plate! How does he do it? When the moment of meeting between egg and plate occurs he gives a slight downward movement to the latter. The speed of this movement coincides with the speed of the fall of the egg and thus reduces the shock of contact. Or observe the technique of expert boxers. When one launches a hard blow at the other the latter will sometimes make a backward motion as though apparently yielding to the blow. Were he to move forward to meet the attack the force of impact would naturally be greater just as the combined velocities of two trains approaching each other is greater than that of any single train. The boxer who yields by slightly retreating lessens the force of the blow which he receives. In the same way we should meet the blows of karma by flexibly adapting

EPILOGUE: THE PHILOSOPHIC LIFE

ourselves to the inevitable, by not attempting new enterprises during a dark cycle, for instance.

Here again we can call in the confirmation of science. Quantum theory and uncertainty principle have shed startling new light on physics. The old views of science were favourable to faith in the notion of karma; the new views are favourable to faith in the notion of freewill. The old views were based on a world-structure which was clasped in the iron clutches of physical law. Determinism and necessitarianism were inevitable outlooks in such a universe. The new science has passed beyond this cold-blooded rigidity and has penetrated into the strange spontaneity of sub-atomic life. Its discovery completes the circle. The truth is that the universe has freedom at its heart but fate at its circumference, and that man consequently is a creature of *both* influences.

The practical lesson is: change the prevailing tenor of your thoughts and you will help to change, in time, the prevailing condition of your affairs. Correct your mental and ethical errors and the correction will ultimately tend to become apparent in better character and improved environment. To a considerable extent man builds and changes his environment, constructs the history of his life and shapes his own circumstances by the simple power of mind, for destiny is *ultimately* self-earned and mind-made. Karma shows how this can be so, and the doctrine of mentalism shows why this must be so.

Lastly we must learn through yoga-practice and philosophic reflection the art of being unruffled. For troubles must come, but as they come so will they go. The same power that brought them will also take them away. Fortune is a turning wheel. Meanwhile the mind should remain firmly anchored where it belongs—in truth, not in illusion.

Although karma is really a scientific law it was appropriated by the Asiatic religions as well as by the pagan faiths of primitive Europe. But for an apparent accident of history it might also have been an item among the tenets of modern Christianity, for it lived in Christian faith for five hundred years after Jesus. Then a group of men, the Council of Constantinople, banished it from the Christian teaching, not because it offended the ethics of Jesus (what could be nobler than its perfect harmony with the Master's own statement: Whatsoever ye sow, that shall ye also reap?), nor because it offended the integrity of Christianity (where is there a clearer advocacy of it than in the writings of the great Christian Patriarch Origen?), but because it offended their own petty personal prejudices. Thus a little band of foolish men sitting near the shores of the Sea of Marmora so late as five hundred and fifty years after the appearance of Jesus have been permitted to banish a Christian tenet which did not suit their own cast of temperament. Thus they have robbed the West of a religious belief which, in the turn of history's wheel, must now be restored to the modern world for the scientific truth that it really is.

It is the duty of those who rule nations, guide thought, influence education and lead religion to make this restoration.[1] Truth demands it in any case, but the safety and survival of Western civilization imperiously demand it still more. When men learn that they cannot escape the consequences of what they are and what they do they will be more careful in conduct and more cautious in thinking. When they comprehend that hatred is a sharp boomerang which not only hurts the hated but also the hater, they will hesitate twice and thrice before yielding to this worst of all human sins. When they understand that their life in this universe is intended to be an evolutionary process of gradual growth in understanding they will begin to assess their physical, moral and mental values aright. A sound ethical life will follow naturally as a function of such understanding. The West has great and quick need for the acceptance of karma and rebirth because they make men and nations ethically self-responsible as no irrational or incoherent dogma can make them. Modern scientific knowledge can easily fit these doctrines into its framework of reference, provided they are properly presented, because they alone explain neatly how the simple-minded Hottentot evolves into the subtle-minded Hegel.

We live in a shrieking tower of Babel. Nearly everyone has something to say, says it at the top of his voice, and yet for all this shouting few succeed in saying anything that is worth while, for few tell us why we are here on earth at all. Hence the urgency of popularizing the karma doctrine.

The Welfare of the World. We have so far treated karma from the scientific and practical standpoint. What the hidden philosophy has to say about it puts an entirely different aspect on the matter, but that is a reserved subject too. We have indeed forgotten the philosopher for the moment to remember the more urgent needs of

---

[1] The Right Reverend Sigurgeir Sigurdsson, Bishop of Iceland and a personal friend of the author, has courageously made this experiment. The result has been remarkably successful among the younger generation, who have responded energetically.

EPILOGUE: THE PHILOSOPHIC LIFE

the unphilosophic masses who have been touched by the questioning ferment of our time. It may be said, however, that as our studies in mentalism have revealed that the primal substance of this world is thought and that matter is nothing other than mind, so we must concede to mind in actuality and universality a permanence with which we normally refuse to endow it. And we must further concede that because man's whole life and activity are purely mental his thoughts may vanish into the depths of the Unconscious and yet not be lost. For mind is incessantly generating its constructions anew, unhindered by limitations of time and space because the latter are also its own constructions. Hence the individual streams of ideas may reappear again or react on each other across long lapses of time and great acres of space. Thus the doctrine of karma can find a mentalistic justification.

The philosopher, however, finds a still higher basis than karma for lofty and unselfish personal and social ethics when he finds truth and reality. To understand this we must anticipate advanced studies and consider for a moment that the ecstatic peace which comes to the artist during his creative moments is not dissimilar from that which comes to the mystic. It has been pointed out that this is mostly due to their temporary release from the ego. The *I* carries a great burden, be it one of ulcerous worries or gay pleasures. Few know that forgetting oneself is the key to a larger happiness. In philosophy, after all the facts have been ascertained and verified, this ideal is set up as one of its rational conclusions; it is then also found that there is a secret thread running from man to man, from creature to creature, and that the hidden constitution of the world is so unified that whoever believes he can assure his own happiness and welfare regardless of what happens to others is for ever fated to be bitterly disillusioned. So long as the chasm which separates the *I* and the *you* remains as wide and as deep as it is, so long will *I* and *you* be foredoomed to suffer. Moreover, one of the philosophical implications of the principle of relativity is that no single thing in the whole universe stands isolated from anything else, no single thing exists in its own right. A web of interrelatedness stretches right across the world. Even the interdependence of modern society —with its economic, political and social reactions from one corner of the world to another—is alone enough to hint at this. There is hardly a half-educated man in any country of the globe who is not more familiar with international affairs than was the average educated man prior to 1914. Such is the growing awareness of this interdependence.

Philosophy preaches self-control and advocates service of humanity not because these might be good for the other man alone or good for the philosopher alone, but because it is good for *both*! Its view of man is a view of society as a whole. Hence it teaches and proves that no individual man can attain other than illusory happiness so long as his fellows are unhappy. The old notion that a philosopher is impervious to current events must go. He *is* interested in them because he is interested in the welfare of his fellow men. But he will not permit them to swamp his judgment or menace his peace, for amid all else he holds to philosophic calm and impartial reason.

Whoever finds the high privilege of this wisdom conferred upon him will automatically find that it comes like a double-edged sword—the new privilege upon one side but a new responsibility upon the other; for the lofty knowledge which he has attained enjoins upon him that he shall henceforth practise the highest of all ethics. In discovering the final unity of all things and creatures, in being born again, as Jesus put it, in realizing that the Overself[1] of which he is now aware is likewise the Overself of all other living beings, he has no alternative but to perceive that the welfare of the world is equivalent to his own welfare. The service of the ALL will henceforth replace in his heart the service of the individual ego. His acts must not only satisfy his own self but also be beneficial to others: they must always try to perform this twofold function. It is for this reason that a real sage is not a hibernating hermit.

Such a sage makes the discovery that the Golden Rule of doing unto others what we would have them do unto ourselves is uncommon sense made common. No religion has ever taught a higher ethic than this and no experience can ever suggest a more sensible one. No other maxim for the conduct of life than this simple maxim of Jesus and Krishna, Confucius and Buddha, will help a man more to travel smoothly and unhindered along the stone-scattered highways of existence. It is a rule which works wonders and which can be universally applied to all men in all stations of life and at all times. It is as good with brown-skinned Orientals as with white-skinned Occidentals, as satisfactory with ragged outcasts as with well-fed millionaires, and its value is out of all proportion to its simplicity. For we are all children of the one Infinite Life, members of the same vast human family. Let us therefore do the considerate, the generous,

---

[1] This invented term is here introduced and will be frequently used later because it has already become familiar to readers of the author's other works. It is intended to signify the ultimate reality of both man and the universe.

EPILOGUE: THE PHILOSOPHIC LIFE

and the compassionate deed whenever possible in preference to the mean, the selfish and the cruel one, if we would have karma deal kindly with us.

If it be asked why should a man trouble to learn or define truth if he is already practising goodwill to all beings, the reply is: because, first, he will not *know* that it is truth and may therefore change his mind tomorrow, and so give up his goodwill. It will be based on feelings, which are admittedly volatile. And, second, human affairs are notoriously complex, and right and wrong are often curiously intermingled. And, third, philosophy offers the only warrant for an ethical and selfless life which is based wholly on reason and yet does not lead to selfishness or wickedness.

When the Buddha, therefore, inculcated compassion it was not on the basis of mere sentiment but on that of profound knowledge. The man who left loving wife and marble palace in quest of intangibles like peace and truth was no sentimentalist.

It would be a profound error, however, to suppose as is usually supposed that because Buddha also taught the doctrine of non-violence (which Gandhi has made famous in modern times) he meant this for the practice of all men. He meant it only for monks and those ascetics who had renounced the worldly life with its responsibilities. Like all true sages the Buddha recognized that there was no universal code of morality and that there were gradations in duty, stages in ethics. Hence when General Simha came to question him about this very point, torn by doubt whether he should give up his profession of soldiering or continue in it, the Buddha replied: "He who deserves punishment must be punished. Whosoever must be punished for the crimes he has committed suffers his injury not through the ill-will of the judge but on account of his evildoing. The Buddha does not teach that those who go to war in a righteous cause after having exhausted all means to preserve the peace are blameworthy. He must be blamed who is the cause of the war. The Buddha teaches a complete surrender of self but he does not teach a surrender of anything to those powers that are evil."

These words are quoted only because they express exactly the viewpoint of the hidden teaching upon the same question. It is not denied that the correct attitude for monk or mystic is to take no life under any circumstances, but rather to suffer his own, martyr-like, to be taken away instead; and to cause no hurt to any other person even in punishment. Gandhi, therefore, with his doctrine of non-violence, represents Indian mysticism at its best; but it would be a gross mistake to take him as a representative of the far higher

Indian philosophy. The latter does not teach an ethic of emotional exultation but an ethic of reasoned service. It is strong where the other is sentimental.

The famous injunction of Jesus to resist not evil must also be interpreted in the same light. It is to be followed literally and externally by mystics and renunciants but intelligently and internally by the wise. For although the latter have come to know their ultimate oneness with the crook and criminal, this need not prevent them from protecting themselves or others against crookedness and criminality or from punishing wrongdoers for their malpractices, provided, as Buddha further pointed out, this is done without hatred. For then, observed the great Asiatic teacher, "the criminal should learn to consider that this punishment is the fruit of his own act, and as soon as he can honestly arrive at such understanding the punishment will purify his soul and he may no longer lament his fate but actually rejoice in it".

A mysticism which makes a man into a passive spectator of aggressive injustice or violent murder or an asceticism which makes him condone evil done in his presence on the plea that he has renounced the world and its ways does not represent the real wisdom of India. It is the duty of a philosopher not to refuse help when suffering victims cry out against attack, but to bestow it, using force if necessary. A doctrine that preaches lethargic inertia or flabby nonviolence in the face of acts of flagrant violation of justice and goodwill is completely unacceptable to philosophy. Such misunderstanding of the old sages and such weakness of heart and mind have never helped India but merely degraded her. The mystic who is afraid of administering punishment because he is afraid of causing suffering is guided by emotion. The philosopher who is not afraid to do so when necessary knows that suffering is the greatest teacher of man; for what man will not learn by reason he must learn by pain. He who will not think must suffer. What he might learn in a few minutes through reflection will be whipped into him during a few years through pain. Many a blow falls on the head of a man just to get a single idea into it. He must learn by personal anguish what he has refused to learn by personal reflection. He must understand by bitter pain what he would not understand by the persuasions of philosophy. For the mystic wishes to be undisturbed and to disturb none, whereas the philosopher wishes to be altruistic and to serve all.

Nevertheless the philosopher helps humanity in his own way, not in theirs. For they know only what they desire, he what they

EPILOGUE: THE PHILOSOPHIC LIFE

need. He helps wisely, which means that he is not a sentimentalist. Heart and head must justify each other. Finally he prefers to go quietly to the fountain-head and help the few through whom he can help the many. Thus he economizes time, resources and energy and in the end achieves immeasurably more service than if he gave his whole time to individuals.

In our frankest moments we discover that we have never been altruistic, but we have sought a subtle or obvious self-satisfaction in all our deeds. Unselfishness is unnatural. We all look at life through *I*-glasses! "Why therefore should I do good to others?" is a natural and proper question to ask. Philosophy answers by saying: "Because secretly and ultimately all mankind forms one great family. Because the full consciousness of this fact is the grand goal of human evolution. Because life is far holier than pious people realize. Because that unknown reality which men in their remoteness call God, which we may better call the Overself, is both our own secret self and the world's secret self. He who has realized this unitary consciousness has simultaneously realized that it is the duty of the strong to assist the weak, of the advanced to help the backward, of the saintly to guide the sinful, of the wealthy to lighten the burden of the destitute, and of the wise to enlighten the ignorant." And because ignorance is the root of all other troubles, therefore the Buddha pointed out that, "explaining and spreading the truth is above all charities".

Most of us have to work at something whether we like it or not and whether we are philosophers or not. Philosophy does not alter that, but it can alter the ultimate ends for which we are working. We can work to earn a mere livelihood or we can work to make a memorable life. For most people life consists of some pleasures but more burdens. Yet they think and act as though it consisted of some burdens but more pleasures. We must make men reflect upon the values they wish to obtain from life. Do they want to earn a livelihood? Do they want to enjoy themselves? Do they want the truth about the world's meaning and life's end? Yet they may have all these, for none are contradictory, provided always they learn to keep a sense of proportion, a proper equilibrium. Tremendous are the possibilities of an existence governed by the philosophic rule of a balanced life, actuated by the selfless desire to better one's corner of the world, dynamized by the pointed power of concentrated thought and guided by the full light of this new-old East-West wisdom. Men with far less equipment have amazed the modern world with their achievements for good or evil; are there a few courageous enough to gamble their personal lives with destiny that they may enrich their age and bless others, wise enough to give up this long littleness of the egoistic life whose ultimate end is but the cold grave? Can truth find a few friends to serve and support her with a wholly dedicated life? Who can put self strongly behind him and stretch out his hands far enough to grasp this great paradox?

A Philosophic View of the World Crisis. If the call for men who are actuated by the will to help not only themselves but also mankind is for ever sounding silently in the ears of those who understand the meaning of life, it is today sounding a hundred times more strongly. For in no previous epoch of world history has such misery and such ignorance been so widespread. The need of world enlightenment is immensely greater today than in the centuries of Jesus and Buddha—those grand figures who walk through history in auroral splendour. For consider our own time. The modern epoch was the most delightful and withal the most miserable of any. It was sired by Mammon, mothered by the misunderstanding of life's end and cradled in a comfortable automobile. It began with the cloud-high expectations and rosy promises of applied and inventive science, but has set low with disappointment and disillusion. It sinks in a dismal decrepitude of ideals.

We went forward so breathlessly that we deluded ourselves with the sensation of rapid and all-round progress. Now that delusion has been exploded. A day of relentless reckoning has come to the world. For our progress was a one-sided affair. It was mainly technological, not teleological. When men crystallize their habits of thought, ways of living and general outlook along materialistic lines they become unconscious of their ethical danger and of their waste of the precious opportunity of incarnation. Only a tremendous outside impact could shock them back into awareness of the futility and failure of such a life. Such an impact has been provided by the world crisis, with the two wars and the national nightmares which have been its spotlights.

Karma is for ever at work in the history of all nations and of all individuals. It does not merely operate among individuals alone: it can also be collective and operate among groups, such as families, tribes and whole peoples. But this fate is self-created. It is not imposed upon them arbitrarily by any outward power. The fortunes or misfortunes of a country are not wholly due to the capacity or foolishness of those who govern it. They are partly the reflection of the capacity or foolishness of the people themselves. We must

EPILOGUE : THE PHILOSOPHIC LIFE

always keep in mind that either in the past or the present both the people and the rulers of the country helped to create, often unconsciously, the causes and conditions which reach their climax with open sufferings. Until a transformation in their way of thinking occurs they will have to face intermittent recurrence of conflicts, with the consequent sufferings.

Nevertheless it is an inescapable duty of administrators, who are set by self or circumstance in a position to lead, control and influence people, to fit themselves for it. So long as their own mind is confused and bewildered and they are unable to put themselves in the position of posterity and gaze at our age through the telescope of time, so long is it impossible for them to guide or govern others aright. The mastery of philosophy, the study of its liberating thoughts, will help them to drive correctly instead of drifting wrongly.

These are hard words, but bursting bombs and grinding calamities have begun to burst the illusions of men and to grind to dust the lies under which they lived. The world crisis provokes the gloom of disillusionment and brings the stirrings of dissatisfaction to a head. It is worth remembering that philosophy appeared in Greece at a time when, as Socrates said, there seemed nothing to be done except crouch behind the wall until the storm passes by.

It is wrong thinking that has ruined and wrecked Europe. It is right thinking that can redeem it. The present state of Europe is but an expression of what concentrated and unbridled emotion—whether for good or evil—can achieve.

The racial antipathies and economic antagonisms, the nationalistic hatreds and militaristic horrors of our woeful planet bear terrible witness to the fact that we have forgotten the high business for which we are here on earth—the business of making our personal lives disclose something of *that* which is their fundamental reality, the business of breaking the ancient illusion that the ego is our only self and the body our only existence. We might well become sad at the thought of thoughtless mankind, attending to every concern except this first and fundamental one, if we did not know that suffering was itself a tutor. The world has trod its *Via Dolorosa* and learnt bitter truths from the breaking down of what it has built with deluded mind. A great war telescopes several decades into one, bringing about forced changes in men and their minds, in society and its systems. Calamity creates wisdom and forces people into the wiser path they ought to have travelled willingly. Thus their painful sufferings and disappointed strivings breed wisdom. War strips them of their smug complacency, stabs their frailties and comes as a grim corrective. The great wars which give us personal gloom give us also mental awakenings. The compensation of chaos and war are the new ideas they generate. The revolutions in historical events usually play the part of a prelude to the revelations in men's minds. It is a mistake to regard adversity as being always an adversary. It may sometimes be a friend in disguise.

It is true that the study of the theory of philosophy does not flourish during crises, nevertheless the practice of it does. For then its students can show the benefits of their attainment and understanding, then they can display how unflurried and unperturbed they are amid all trials and how sure and decisive when called to posts of responsibility and judgment ; then their thought can rest in the quiet inner citadel whilst their body acts energetically and fearlessly amid the grave terrific stresses outside.

We become unnerved at the outbreak of war and begin to see that life is largely transient, afflicted by disappointments and pain-laden. Ordinarily people do not observe this instability of existence, do not see that everything is either altering or vanishing continuously. But the contemporary period—with its characteristics of high speed and sudden surprise so well exemplified in its history moving overnight—has begun to make this evident. Such suffering is educative and brings thoughts into our head which would not otherwise have arisen. The instability of sensual existence and the successiveness of personal life are sharply brought home to us and thus our narrow egoistic outlook is diminished, i.e. purified through the arisal of a yearning to find something more stable, unchanging and lasting. This yearning can only be satisfied in the quest of a reality other than merely material existence. When we become conscious of our weakness we begin to search for a fresh source of inner strength. When we realize that we are unable to order life right we commence to take up the quest of its meaning. When we discover that we have been deceived by appearances we are ready to learn something about reality.

This war teaches us in the severest possible manner the transiency of all things ; let us therefore ask ourselves what this means. Where is the fine house which has been shattered to pieces, the beloved child slain, the modest fortune lost ? What are they today ? Only memories which seem like vivid dreams. But what are memories ? Mental constructions, i.e. thoughts ! What will these things be in the future ? Thoughts ! If therefore we have the courage to complete the logical circle, then we are forced to conclude that something which is purely mental both in the past and the future must have

EPILOGUE: THE PHILOSOPHIC LIFE

been purely mental in that which rests upon both—the present. Thus mentalism is being silently taught by the vicissitudes of life to ordinary unphilosophic folk.

We can keep calmer and saner amid the terrors of our time if we keep to the truth of mentalism, if we regard these terrors as experiences whose stuff is ultimately as mental as the stuff of dreams. And just as men who have bad dreams and fearful nightmares suffer most when they are deluded into clinging to the reality of their experiences, but will suffer least if they could know that they are dreaming and let go their delusion, so we too may modify our physical sufferings by remaining awake to the truth that they are all ideas which come and are felt indeed but will also vanish as they came.

The philosopher, more than any other, can show a path to other men at a time when they are bewildered and when the whole world is at cross-roads.

There is always a way of liberation.

It is the way of repentance and return.

Nothing seems simpler, yet nothing seems so hard. But another way there is not. And the way of unloosed suffering is still harder to tread.

However, it is not untrue that the night is darkest before dawn. We have been living through an unforgettable period. Here is history in the making, with all its terrific drama and all its tragic interest. For our age is transitional. Its very uniqueness prepares the way for a unique renaissance. The ravages of the war will need to be repaired. We must learn to meet bad times with better thoughts. We must struggle for a new era characterized by heartfelt universality. It is for us to spell the riddle of the future with letters drawn from the alphabet of the present. It is for us to evaluate the movements disclosed by history and follow its iron logic. It is for us to draw wise lessons out of the vanished centuries for our own ethical guidance and material profit.

First and foremost of these lessons is that we are living at the end of a cycle when karma is closing all the national accounts, clearing up mass arrears. We stand and watch the disappearance of an era. The circle is being completed. The monuments of the old world are toppling. This transition must necessarily be one of confused outlooks, convulsive ferment and contending ideals, or rebellious emotions and fanatic feelings!

Second and easiest of these lessons is that a stupendous process of swift change is going on before our eyes, such as no people has ever before witnessed. The practical import of this is that although society should certainly be stable it should also be flexible. A fossil is also stable but it is not flexible. The lesson of countries like China is that when the law of change is ignored, suffering comes. The dualism between these two forces, stability and change, will always persist, but the art of reconciling them must always be practised. In times like the present a deliberate emphasis must be placed on the aspect of change.

This does not imply that sudden and violent revolutionary changes are advocated. Revolution for its own brutal sake is the principle of unbalanced emotions and distorted minds. A mystical belief in the coming of a millennium lurks behind every fervid and furious revolution, yet has never been historically realized. Whoever uses wrong methods thereby ruins right aims. Whoever abuses freedom asks for restraint. For he cuts short the period of human adolescence in trying to make too much haste and thus infects society with a fearful psychological disease—hatred!

On the other hand, whoever fails to recognize the time-spirit —which is one of iconoclastic renovation proceeding at an accelerated pace—and foolishly resists it, will resist it at his peril.

There are various ways of bringing about social improvement. There is the way of suddenly beating your neighbour on the head, which is the way of revolution. . . . There is the alternative of persuading him to bring a more rational and less self-centred mode of thought to bear upon social problems, which is the way of reason. Both unreflective revolutionary and prudent reasoner may be motivated by the same concept of a better world. But the two trends are antagonistic and must inevitably clash. It is perfectly possible for men everywhere to have a finer and fairer existence. The attitude of constructive service and unselfish co-operation will meet all needs. But if it is absent, if men's desires conflict with fate's designs, there will then arise the misery of unnecessary strife. It therefore behoves all men to adapt themselves to these irresistible changes or suffer for their stupidity. The stubborn reiteration of loyalties that pertain to a disappearing past is meaningless. It is for those in authority to realize that iconoclastic forces are at work abrogating old dispensations, that new ideas are fermenting and that a new, noble and generous outlook is required of them. Let us not bemoan the passing of that which has outserved its time. The roaring imperious tide of the twentieth century cannot be restrained. It must be given its way, but it need not be permitted to destroy what is worthwhile in our inheritance. The commingling of keen thought

EPILOGUE : THE PHILOSOPHIC LIFE

with courageous action will bring tremendous possibilities. Let us envisage the integration of the highest ideals of Orient and Occident, of the union of their two streams of discovery—one coming from the farthest antiquity and the other from the freshest science.

Meanwhile we must keep our sanity. If we abandon all the cultural heritage of religion, mysticism, philosophy, ethics, ideals and intuitions which has come down to us from our forefathers we are making a terrible mistake. For we abandon the most priceless elements of human existence. Let us simplify and purify this heritage if we wish. Let us sift sound doctrine from superstitious belief. But let us not forget that existence ultimately turns to ash and dust when it holds none of the inner serenity of a good life and inner support of a true one which are needed more than ever by our bewildered epoch.

Can we not see in the awful position of the world woe's victims a forced asceticism, an involuntary and undesired renunciation, a compulsory giving up of every desired thing, person, attachment ? Can we not see in the sudden impoverishment of once-wealthy seats of empire like London and Paris a constrained self-mortification and a coerced putting on of sackcloth and ashes ? Can we not see that if millions have been beggared, if all this means anything at all in a larger sense, it means that humanity is being passed against its own will through a purifying process on a scale previously unknown in history ? Can we not also see that the financial avalanche which swept away the life-savings of millions of Americans in 1929 is of the same piece ? Are we not all being taught that the earth is but a camping ground and not an eternal home ? Is it not plain that what the sage learns through profound reflection and voluntary self-denial the peasant and the townsman are being made to learn through the bitterest misfortunes and the direct losses ; that nothing is to become the focus of our *whole* being save the aspiration towards truth, life-meaning, reality—the kingdom of heaven in Jesus' words —which are all within us ? The sage has sought and found his basic happiness in the Mind, which is his inalienable possession and of which no catastrophe can rob him. Everywhere we perceive that mankind is being blindly driven to seek in the same direction because all else has begun to fail it. This does not mean that wealth is to be ascetically spurned, property to be thrown away and money mentioned only with hypocritical horror. Such an attitude is right for the monk but not for the man of wisdom. What it does mean is that we may accumulate wealth if we wish to, possess property and estimate the usefulness of money, love and family and friends, but the moment we permit these things to absorb our whole mind and take up our whole time so that we have neither mind nor time to give to the quest of understanding what we are here for, then they become a disguised curse and a source of latent suffering.

Not that we need war to shrive our spirits and purge our hearts; life with its changing panorama of thought and deed, its endless personal struggles, is always assisting us likewise. But often war is the visible climax of graded periods of the cosmic struggle between the selfless and selfish tendencies in man's outlook, between whatever works towards unity and whatever works towards disintegration. Meanwhile humanity will rise to higher and higher conceptions of what constitutes evil, dropping its narrower outlooks and ancient brutalities with deepening shame. The horrors of bloody war will disappear and soldiers will throw aside their steel helmets when the beast in man is tamed, but the conflict of minds will replace it. Struggle must continue while the world lasts, but it will gradually be refined, modified, dignified and purged of its physical brutality. We must therefore admit with Socrates: "Evil, O Glaucon, will not vanish from the earth. How should it, if it is the name of the imperfection through whose defeat the perfect types acquire their value?" and with Buddha: "Struggle there must be, for all life is a struggle of some kind." But Buddha also pointed out that the conflict in life is not really between good and evil but between knowledge and ignorance. We must remember that the sages refuse to recognize evil as a positive independent existence but place it in the limited view of the man who believes in it. Our task is to learn wisdom from *all* experience, from pain as from pleasure, from cruelty as from kindness, and to express in the arena of everyday life just what we have learnt. In this way everything that happens gives us a better foothold for future living.

Fourth and last of the lessons we may draw is that intelligence, adequately sharpened, courageously accepted and selflessly applied, is always the dominant factor in the end. Those who worship force rather than brains as the highest social power should take a lesson from the calm perspective of history. If force were the greatest thing known the gigantic dinosaur would be king of this world, and the prehistoric monsters would have inherited the earth long ago. Yet how many herds of these animals have gone with the years and left no heirs? They have died out and disappeared. Why? Because there is something greater than mere force. That something is Thought. Man—puny animal that he was in comparison with these giants—conquered them all. He did it not by force, but by brains. There is

EPILOGUE: THE PHILOSOPHIC LIFE

no limit to what he shall be able to do when he shall have fully harnessed this wondrous power of thought, so little understood though it be. Science is only a stage in this growth. There are those who have become afraid of it because they have become afraid of what scientific war has done to man. But science is only a sword. With it you may pierce through your problems or pierce through your throat. Whatever you do the responsibility lies with yourself, not with the sword. Intelligence blossoms as the flower of well-reasoned thought and it matures gradually into the fruit of spontaneous insight. That which begins in the primitive savage as a glimmer of purely local inquisitiveness ends in the evolved man as a passion for consummate understanding of all existence. The innumerable lives on earth which intervene between both are but lessons in the school of intelligence. When intelligence is only partial, immature and incomplete it teaches man cunning, selfishness and materialism. When full, mature and perfect it teaches him wisdom, selflessness and truth.

Thus we return to the central thought that the world's greatest need is not the discovery of a new scientific marvel or a new momentary pleasure but the discovery of a new understanding of life. It is not enough to seek things which complicate existence; it must also be comprehended. We must make up our minds whether we wish to learn this truth through the pain which succeeds folly or through the peace which succeeds philosophy. We who have wandered this queer planet and kept its lessons at heart know inwardly that neither the peaceful, primitive settings of Nature in the colourful Orient nor the noisy, metropolitan complexities of man in the colourless Occident constitute our true home. We know that the latter lies in a remote place to which no rolling steamer, no puffing engine, no creaking bullock-cart could ever bear us. For it lies in the infinitude of the unpathed Overself.

The restoration of philosophy to its honoured place in the world of living men rather than dead ones has yet to come. After all, the world's search is not for men who must die but for truths which will live. Philosophy will gather a few votaries because it is our belief that it can be made intelligible to any intelligent man, even if he has never previously studied it, although it cannot be made intelligible to any highly egoistic man because, being nothing but a human bundle of prejudices, he cannot care for truth. The ego is a needle through whose eye the camel of truth cannot contrive to squeeze its way. And truth is the proper target of all genuine philosophy. Egoism and illusion are all that philosophy deprives us of, but in return it assuredly proffers much. The poet will see the radiance of the sunset but ignore the atmospheric conditions that cause it. The scientist will see the atmospheric conditions and ignore the radiance. The philosopher will see both atmospheric change and vivid radiance and something more which neither poet nor scientist knows, for he will know how to live amid the deceptive flux of the evanescent in the fixed serenity of the REAL.

The philosopher is he who has come to the understanding of *himself*, whilst his philosophy is his ordinary experience of the world come to the understanding of *itself*. The fact that we close this modern restatement of an ancient doctrine leaving loose ends of thought and discovery, that we have loosened the knot of the world-problem but have not untied it, should not mislead its readers into impatient judgment upon its contents. For there are no loose ends in the hidden philosophy. Everything is perfectly tied, and he who can master it will possess a finished attitude of mind. Meanwhile the groundwork for the teachings of the final volume of this work with which we shall humbly endeavour to ascend intellectually the highest peaks of human thought has now been prepared. The basis upon which the superstructure of ultimate truth may be reared has now been laid down. Correct comprehension of those higher tenets, which are reserved with regret, will cast a powerful searchlight upon mankind's most perplexing riddles such as, what is this mystery of Mind, what is the meaning of Death, what is God, what is Man, why has Nature given us Dream and Sleep and so on.

Let us not lose ourselves in despair because the world seems so bad. It is slowly coming of age amid apparent retrogression and periodic lapses. Its marred childhood draws to an inevitable end before our eyes; its agonies are but the throes of adolescent change. Those of us who have glimpsed both man and life beneath the surface can remain steady and affirm, with American Emerson, that "the age of the quadruped is to go out. The age of the brain and of the heart come in." If we have been witnessing the woes of an epoch struggling in its death-grapple, we are also about to witness the arisal of a new era where a humane life for human beings may be more possible.

We may honestly nourish the conviction that, amid all the constant alternations of ethical stagnation and awakening during mankind's long and painful journey from ignorance to truth, goodwill must prevail in the end— not merely because we want to console ourselves, but because the fundamental principle of life is *unity*.

EPILOGUE: THE PHILOSOPHIC LIFE 351

For seven thousand years at least according to the modern historian's reckoning, but for double that period according to ours, the Sphinx has squatted before the Egyptian desert, propounding its riddle to the unheeding ears of mankind in a silence as profound as that of Christ's when he stood in the court before Pilate with the shadow of a ghastly cross over him.

"What is truth?" asked the Roman Governor, thus echoing man's most perennial question. Did Christ know? Yet he did not answer. His lips did not move. But his eyes fixed themselves on those of Pilate's throughout that awed silence.

What he could not reveal by lip and tongue—for it transcends both—none else can reveal. But the road that leads to such sublime realization may be mapped out for the ardent seeker. Unto this difficult endeavour an eager pen and white waiting pages have been humbly dedicated.

This quality of the timelessness of truth thrust itself powerfully into the present writer's meditations one evening in a land of steaming jungles and dense forests, where forgotten Indian sages had carried their culture long ago. He sat amid the vast deserted ruins of ancient Angkor, in Cambodian Indo-China, and watched the night lay siege to day and then waited for the stars to rise outside its largest temple, so large that the enclosing wall was nearly two and a half miles in perimeter. Here and there the great building was ominously cracked; mutilated statues of Ramayana's gods strewed the ground; lichen and creeper laced themselves around the panels of carved goddesses; thorns flourished thickly around him as advance-guards of the invading jungle; lizards crawled blasphemously over the calm faces of fallen Buddhas; bats coated the holy shrines with their nauseous excrement; the bright constellations of heaven gazed down on a scene of solemn desolation; gone were the proud glories of the Khmer people, but the sacred truths taught by their sages still remained though their lips were dumb and their bodies annihilated by time. Was it not wonderful that the immemorial wisdom of these men, who flourished and taught when Europe lay benighted in the dark ages, could be known and studied today, and would be known and studied yet again when another two millenniums had once more passed over this planet?

Out of the burial-urn of the Past this same wisdom has been extricated. But because it has here been moulded in an ultra-modern form to suit both our time and need, its authenticity or truth may not be plainly recognizable to its present-day Indian inheritors. Yet there is not a single important tenet here which cannot be found phrased in the old Sanskrit writings. We are only the inheritors and not the discoverers of this ever-ancient but ever-new lore. Therefore the writer bends in homage before the Himalayan intelligence of those sages who, since untraceable antiquity, have kept Truth alive.

THE END

INDEX

INDEX

INDEX

A

Acharya, Sankara, 121
Action, 75, 319, 322-324
Ammonius, 86, 162
Angkor, 351
Animals, 80
Appearance, 192, 202, 236-246, 253, 256, 305
Art, 59, 268, 324-326
Asceticism, 60, 303, 313, 323
Ashtavakra Sampita, 36
Atmarama Swami, 42
Attention, 62, 73, 107, 108, 234, 235, 273, 274
Aurobindo Ghose, 27
Authoritarianism, 150, 152-155

B

Bacon, 10, 100, 145, 166, 220
Balzac, 324, 325
Beauty, 59, 324
Berkeley, 312
"Bhagavad Gita", 35, 42, 88
Bible, 64, 153
Body, 208, 231, 232, 257, 280, 281, 305
Boehme, 159, 160
Brabourne, Lord, 30,
Brahmins, 83, 86
Brain, 230, 270, 271, 274
Brunton's defence, 44-51
Buchman, Dr., 157
Buckle, 153
Buddha, 47, 66, 85, 86, 134, 339, 348
Bunsen, 153

C

Calmness, 61, 106-111, 335, 345
Change, 326, 327, 345, 346
Charlatans, 56, 83
Chinese technique, 334

Colour, 210-213, 217, 221, 226, 290, 291
Concentration, 106-111, 229
Consciousness, 221-227, 232-235, 274, 276, 277
Constructs, 225, 263
Copernicus, 198
Council of Constantinople, 335
Council of Nicea, 65
Credulity, 154

D

Detachment, 103-106
Determination, 100, 101,
Doubt, 55, 77, 155, 156
Dream, 252, 297, 298, 324, 345
Dying Man, 297

E

Ecstasy, 19, 61, 159, 161, 164, 325
Eddington, 21, 31, 179
Education, 8, 9
Ego, 116-119, 325
Einstein, 11, 49, 178-186, 198-206, 214, 228
Emerson, 27, 92, 159, 350
Emotion, 111-113, 204
Epicurius, 66
Ethics, 330, 336-338
Euclid, 183, 192, 199
Evil, 339, 348
Evolution, 10, 226, 329, 336
Existence, 177, 298-301
Experience, 149, 197, 221-229, 241, 348
Externality, 232-259

F

Fact, 114, 138-142
Fate, 48
Feeling, 111-114, 162

355

INDEX

Fichte, 93
Fox, George, 157
France, Anatole, 77
Freewill, 27, 332–335

G

Gandhi, 38, 167, 168, 339
Germany, 77
God, 11, 32, 54, 136, 137, 148, 151, 152, 310, 312, 313

H

Haldane, Lord 136
Hallaj, 64
Hallucination, 233–236, 251–253, 296
Hegel, 21, 312
Heisenberg, 11, 172
Heredity, 252, 329, 330, 333
Hidden teaching, 13, 39, 155, 193, 195, 196, 199, 206, 220, 269, 281, 313, 314, 316, 319, 351
Hui Ko, 160
Hume, 146, 312

I

"I" 7, 14–19, 117, 118, 156, 325, 337
Idea, 225, 306–308
Ignorance, 119, 150, 156, 229
Illusions, 156, 233–246, 250–254, 296–303, 349
India, 15, 24, 77, 78, 82–91, 327
Inge, Dean, 66,
Insight, 96, 164
Intellect, 17, 142
Intuition, 157, 158, 173, 174
Inventions, 9, 198

J

Janaka, the King-sage, 88
Jeans, 11, 31
Jesus, 65, 66, 118, 134, 335, 340

K

Kant, 82, 149, 207, 291, 312
Karma, 308, 326–336, 345

Kitchener, 30
Knowledge, 8, 41, 149–151, 163, 189, 190, 194, 195, 204, 277

L

Laughter, 106
Leisure, 12, 74
Light, 179, 180
"Lightning-flash", 175
Logic, 17, 157–159, 173, 202
Lotze, 189

M

Macaulay, 53
MacMurray, Prof., 120
Maharajah of Mysore, 34, 35, 37, 38
Maharishee, 15, 16, 18, 24–26, 49
Man, 13, 71, 72, 348
Mandukya, Secret Doctrine, 37
Matter, 185, 186, 276, 277, 292–295, 297, 303
Maya, 305
Meaning, 7, 18, 136–138, 143–147
Meditation, 16, 19, 20, 27, 57, 58, 62, 110, 161
Memory, 223–225
Mental abstraction, 60, 108
Mental constructs, 225, 227, 247–253, 255, 305
Mentalism, 263 266–269, 295, 304–308, 314
Metaphysics, 77, 78, 109, 191, 302, 303
Mind, 103, 207, 214–224, 232, 254, 263–289, 320, 347
Mind-splitting, 169
Monks, 19
Mozart, 324
Muhammed, 34, 64
Mysticism and Mystics, 12, 16, 20, 23, 57, 63, 64, 109, 110, 160–164

N

Nations, 9
Nerves, 212, 215–217
New Testament, 65, 87
Newton's Law, 192, 329, 330
Nicea, Council of, 65
Nietzsche, 59
Non-violence, 339

INDEX

O

Omar Khayyám, 77, 305
Origen, 335
Overself, 338, 341

P

Pain, 218
Pantajali, 42
Perception, 181, 182, 204, 222, 226-228, 231, 256-262
Percepts, 222, 256-266, 305
Philosophy, 69-91, 133, 141, 144, 146, 147, 152, 193-198, 316-319
Physics, 185, 227
Physiology, 271-276, 280
Planck, 11, 31, 172
Plotinus, 162
Plutarch, 75
Prayer, 58, 59
Psycho-analysis, 95, 96
Psychology, 97, 168, 333
Pythagoras, 86, 90, 183

R

Rajarishee, 38
Ramakrishna, 163
Reality, 51, 300-304, 309, 311
Reason, 111-116, 164-176
Rebirth, 328-333
Relativity, 49, 170, 177-186, 198
Religion, 8, 52, 64-66, 150-152, 327, 338
Reverie, 108
Röntgen, 11
Russell, Bertrand, 119

S

Sages, 11, 86, 88, 169, 171, 174-176, 183, 230, 234, 293, 351, 352
Sanskrit, 84
Science, 10, 11, 166, 167, 179, 192, 195, 200, 203, 230, 234, 246, 280, 294, 302, 349
Self, 20
Self-improvement, 100, 101
Sensations, 206, 216-226, 231, 250, 269
Senses, 203, 206-220, 231, 237-241, 277
Shankara, The Sage, 37, 86-88
Sight, 207, 209-217

Simha, General, 339
Sleep, 170, 171
Socrates, 91, 124, 260, 348
Solidity, 275
Space, 180-185, 187, 202, 204
Spencer, Herbert, 77, 272
Sphinx, 50, 351
Spiritual, 137, 138
Standpoints, 189-198
Substance, 291-294
Swedenborg, 159, 160

T

Things, 282-289
Thinking, 109, 110, 121, 174
Time, 10, 186-189, 258, 332
Times, The, 38
Trance, 24, 27, 61
Transport, 8
Truth, 7, 30-32, 49, 50, 69, 98-100, 143, 145, 164, 165, 189-191, 205, 228, 229, 260, 314, 315, 351

U

Ultimate, 42, 47, 49, 303, 311
Unconscious Mind, 322, 333, 337
Unity, 70, 304, 348, 350
Universe, 21, 177, 195, 201

V

Vasishta, The Sage, 72
Vivekananda, 163

W

Wang Yang Ming, 160
War, 7, 12, 167, 344-348
Whistler, 325
Women, 75, 104, 116
World as Thought, 303-306
World Crisis, 7, 12, 326-328, 345-348
Words, 120-148, 183, 293

Y

Yoga and Yogis, 22, 23, 25, 30, 36, 37, 39-44, 308-310
Youth, 116

Z

Zen (Japanese Mysticism), 28, 29